About the editors

Martin Reynolds, a lecturer in systems at The Open University, is course team chair for the OU postgraduate course Environmental Responsibility and, since 2002, chair for Environmental Ethics. He started work at The Open University in 2000 and has been writing for postgraduate courses on environmental ethics, environmental decision-making and institutional development. He has researched and published widely, including his book *Operational Research and Environmental Management* (co-authored with Gerald Midgley), and contributed many book chapters, journal papers and policy briefings.

Chris Blackmore, a senior lecturer in Systems and Environment at The Open University, is a founding course team member for the OU postgraduate course Environmental Ethics. She is currently a member of the management team for the OU-wide Ethics Centre and also the founding course team chair of the postgraduate course Environmental Decision Making and still one of its co-chairs and a course author. Her main research area, in which she has various publications, is in learning systems and communities of practice for environmental decision-making, including issues of ethics, social learning, global citizenship, sustainability and responsibility.

Mark J. Smith, Politics and International Studies and the Center for Citizenship, Identities and Governance at The Open University, researches environmental responsibility, transnational corporations, civic engagement and the role of ethics in politics and the environment. He is author or editor of numerous books, including *Environment and Citizenship, Responsible Politics, Ecologism, Social Science in Question, Thinking through the Environment* and *Rethinking State Theory and Culture*, as well as many chapters and articles. Formerly at Sussex University, his visiting professorships include the University of Oslo and Norwegian Business School and he has been a researcher in universities in the US and South Africa.

About this book

This book has been motivated by a recognition that complex questions of environmental responsibility are increasingly asked of institutions and individuals in situations of change and uncertainty. The book addresses such questions, recognizing that *both* a sense of care for our environment *and* appropriate forms of accountability are needed. It combines traditions of environmental ethics, systems thinking, social learning, and social and political thought as well as empirical research on environment and citizenship for helping to navigate through the interrelated dimensions of environmental responsibility confronting citizens, consumers, communities and corporations in the twenty-first century.

This book provides a component of the Open University course TD866 *Environmental Responsibility: Ethics, Policy and Action*, an optional course in a number of postgraduate programmes, including among others Environmental Decision Making (EDM) and Global Development Management (GDM).

Details of this and other Open University courses can be obtained from the Student Registration and Enquiry Service, PO Box 197, The Open University, Milton Keynes, MK7 6BJ, United Kingdom; tel. +44 (0)870 333 4340; email: general-enquiries@open.ac.uk.

Alternatively, you may visit the Open University website at www.openuniversity.co.uk, where you can learn more about the wide range of courses and packs offered at all levels by The Open University.

The Environmental Responsibility Reader

Martin Reynolds, Chris Blackmore
and Mark J. Smith | editors

The Open
University

Zed Books

LONDON | NEW YORK

FSC

Mixed Sources

Product group from well-managed
forests and other controlled sources

Cert no. SGS-COC-2953
www.fsc.org
© 1996 Forest Stewardship Council

The Environmental Responsibility Reader was first published in 2009 by
Zed Books Ltd, 7 Cynthia Street, London N1 9JF, UK and Room 400,
175 Fifth Avenue, New York, NY 10010, USA in association with The Open
University, Walton Hall, Milton Keynes, MK7 6AA, Buckinghamshire, UK

www.zedbooks.co.uk
www.open.ac.uk

Copyright © 2009, compilation, original and editorial material,
The Open University

All reasonable efforts have been made by the publishers to contact
the copyright holders of the photographs and work reproduced in this
volume.

Set in OurType Arnhem and Futura Bold by Ewan Smith, London
Index: ed.emery@thefreeuniversity.net
Cover designed by Rogue Four Design
Printed and bound in Great Britain by CPI Antony Rowe, Chippenham
and Eastbourne

Distributed in the USA exclusively by Palgrave Macmillan, a division of
St Martin's Press, LLC, 175 Fifth Avenue, New York, NY 10010, USA.

A catalogue record for this book is available from the British Library
Library of Congress Cataloging in Publication Data available

ISBN 978 1 84813 318 1 hb
ISBN 978 1 84813 317 4 pb

Contents

Acknowledgements

The book was produced with the help of the
Open University TD866 course team, including
Carolyn Baxter, Anna Edgeley-Smith and Marie
Lacy. Grateful acknowledgement is made to all
sources (see page 348) for permission to reproduce material in this book, and particular thanks
go to all contributing authors of the readings.

The Open University is incorporated by
Royal Charter (RC 000391), an exempt charity in
England and Wales and a charity registered in
Scotland (SC 038302).

Introduction to environmental responsibility

MARTIN REYNOLDS

> If you don't raise your voice, then your environmentalism means nothing; it's mere tokenism or opportunism [...] We have a special responsibility to the ecosystem of this planet. In making sure that other species survive we will be ensuring the survival of our own. (Wangari Maathai, 2004 Nobel Peace Prize winner)
>
> Responsibility is a cultural concept [...] how are we to regulate our responsiveness so as to preserve the stability of the manifold systems on which we depend, and how are we to make a collective world in which we individually can live? (Sir Geoffrey Vickers, 1979)

Alarm bells regarding the effects of our decisions and actions on the environment have been ringing loud and long. Why we need to take responsibility for these effects, and who takes responsibility for what and how, are issues that are as hard to pin down now as they were in the days of Sir Geoffrey Vickers, though the world has changed a lot since those times. While complex interrelationships among factors affecting change appear to be increasingly acknowledged, there is a wide range of perspectives to take into account. Wangari Maathai is a Kenyan environmentalist and winner of the 2004 Nobel Peace Prize for her contribution to sustainable development, democracy and peace. She was commended for taking a holistic approach that embraces democracy and human rights, in particular women's rights. The relationship between environmental responsibility and economic, social and political stability and justice was again acknowledged in December 2007, when the Nobel Peace Prize was awarded jointly to the Intergovernmental Panel on Climate Change (IPCC) and the former vice-president of America, Al Gore, for the documentary film *An Inconvenient Truth*. The award citation credited both parties 'for their efforts to build up and disseminate greater knowledge about man-made climate change, and to lay the foundations for the measures that are needed to counteract such change'.

While the extent of human-induced climate change may remain debatable, its increasing influence is not. In 2007 the United Nations' emergency relief coordinator was reported in a UK-based newspaper as saying: 'A record number of floods, droughts and storms around the world this year amount to a climate change "mega disaster"' (*Guardian*, 5 October 2007, p. 20). He further noted a pattern of increase in climatic disturbances which could not be divorced from global warming through greenhouse gas emissions. The report suggested that in South Asia alone more than sixty million people were made homeless. Later in the same year concern was increasingly surfacing about a global food crisis. Amid fears of socio-ecological collapse, it is necessary to understand in more detail why these events are occurring and what can be done, by whom, to improve this situation. Exploring where responsibility lies, who needs to take responsibility and what type of action is required is an important part of developing this understanding.

Locating where responsibility lies can in itself invoke a range of responses. Feeling overwhelmed, despairing or remote is not uncommon if trying to engage with such crises, particularly when it is not clear what might help. The causes of a food crisis, for example, are multiple and interconnected. Clearly, severe weather-induced events such as drought and flooding constitute one set of factors. The demise of insect pollinating agents through disease and pollution may exacerbate the biophysical situation. Other factors include the increase in oil prices affecting food production and distribution costs, a reduced supply of cereal crops as US and European farmers in particular have been encouraged to switch production from cereal to biofuel agriculture, and growing demand arising from increased economic prosperity in countries such as China and India. The dangers of ecological deterioration are clearly linked with the actual and potential effects of political destabilization.

Climate change, food and energy supply, waste disposal, loss of biodiversity, species extinction, access to clean water, airport expansions, land degradation, pollution, etc. are now recurring issues on the agenda of global as well as many national and local agencies of governance. Given the interdependencies between these agenda items, it is of little wonder that those who might take responsibility experience a state of helplessness or dissociation which can sometimes translate into apathy. To add to this state of murkiness, while there appears to be no shortage of advice on what is 'good' for the environment and 'best practice' associated with environmental responsibility, the advice is distributed over many disciplines and professional traditions, sometimes presented in inaccessible language and, moreover, often conflicting. So how might this collection of readings help? Who should be interested in an anthology about environmental responsibility? And why?

Our intention is that it will help provide insights into (i) what we can and need to take responsibility for; (ii) who might do it and how;

and (iii) why we should focus on environmental responsibility. We offer a working definition of environmental responsibility as involving two complementary actions summed up in terms of (a) *caring for* an environment comprising the natural world of life and life support in which humans are an integral part, and (b) ensuring guidance and *accountability* for any harm or wrong done to the environment. The two actions have soft and hard connotations respectively but, like the traditional Chinese philosophical notions of *yin* and *yang*, are best considered as integral actions. They also imply a particular relational understanding of 'environment' associated with decision-making; an understanding captured in the following description: 'the relationship between people and their environment has many dimensions – physical, biological, social, psychological, emotional, economic, even temporal – in terms of how we are currently affected by past decisions and how our decisions will affect us and other generations in the future' (Open University 2006).

Insights from complexity sciences – and particularly the science of climate change – since the late twentieth century have shown that any human activity can have very many consequences – foreseen and unforeseen, intended and unintended, beneficial and catastrophic. The phenomenon more generally is known as the 'butterfly effect'. The argument from complexity science being that a butterfly's wings flapping in one continent might create tiny changes in atmospheric currents that may trigger other chains of events that lead to large-scale phenomena, such as the creation (or prevention) of a cross-continent tornado. Some forty-five years before Gore and the IPCC picked up their awards, the systemic effects of human activity on our environment were signalled in one of the earliest popular expressions of environmental responsibility: *Silent Spring* by Rachel Carson (1962). Carson's book generated controversy over the use of chemical pesticides and fertilizers in agriculture and its effects on wildlife. At the time, *Silent Spring* was rejected as being too alarmist. But time moves on. Since 2006 concern has been mounting about the demise of honeybee colonies through what is called colony collapse disorder (CCD). One-third of all human food comes from insect-pollinated plants. Honeybees provide over 80 per cent of the cross-pollination involved in agricultural practice. The precise causes of CCD are not known, though we do know that honeybees are a domesticated species, reared for human purpose, and hence quite genetically homogenous and thereby not as resistant to diseases or other external changes to the environment as other insect species. There is also post-mortem evidence of pesticide effects on honeybees. Whatever the causes, clearly the 'butterfly effect' of human activity has contemporary resonance. In addressing what constitutes

3

environmental responsibility, then, we suggest the need for focusing on interrelationships and interdependencies of ecological and social factors, and that such attention is required in terms of both nurturing care for an environment and ensuring guidance and accountability for any harm or wrong done to the environment.

Our second question asks who should be interested in an anthology of environmental responsibility. Questions of environmental responsibility are very much entwined with the emergence of economic globalization. It is common to lay responsibility or 'blame' for environmental stress at the feet of the institutional pillars of economic globalization that grew in prominence in the 1990s – the International Monetary Fund, the World Bank and the World Trade Organization. Many individuals and groups have taken a more proactive anti-globalization stance that couples criticism of institutions and associated models of economic globalization with ideas on alternative models enabling citizen responsibility. For example, Walden Bello – a Philippines-born academic and activist – advocates a reversal in the way values are prioritized: 'instead of the economy driving society, the market must be [...] "re-embedded" in society and governed by the overarching values of community, solidarity, justice and equity' (*New Internationalist* 400, 2007, p. 11). Bello goes on to call for an alternative, deglobalized model of development. Such calls are not just directed to those in positions of power, but suggest that we all have some responsibility in sustaining or transforming models of development that affect the environment.

The third question invites us to step back a little. It asks more generally why bother with environmental responsibility. Reading 4 in this anthology attempts an answer in terms of a need to counter debilitating attitudes of despair, apathy and cynicism often used to justify business as usual. Using the example of the long-standing and controversial Narmada Dam project in India, three recurring and interdependent questions of environmental responsibility are explored: (i) what are the issues? (ii) how might these issues be attended to and by whom? (iii) why are some issues privileged more than others, and some ways of dealing with them prioritized over others? The reading uses these questions as a platform to introduce the relevance of three dimensions of ethics – normative, philosophical and political – and some associated basic concepts used in environmental ethics. The challenge is to mobilize these conceptual tools along with others to support environmental responsibility.

The same three questions provide the core storyline for this anthology. This compilation is structured to relate particular questions of environmental responsibility to relevant ethical viewpoints, policy design and

4

action. The readings in Part One provide an overview of and some background to ethical theories. Readings 1 to 3 focus on the 'what' questions regarding issues of environmental responsibility – the need for changing values and perspectives regarding, and a sense of obligation towards, the environment. These readings focus on the less formal 'caring for' dimension of environmental responsibility. Reading 4 provides a bridge from less formal towards more formalized questions of environmental responsibility. Readings 5 to 7 focus on the more formal dimension. Each of these readings offers an environmental perspective on 'doing what's good' (a consequentialist ethic), 'doing what's right' (through a deontological ethic) and 'being virtuous' (through a virtue-based ethic). All the readings in Part One also touch upon 'why' questions. Readings 1 to 4 suggest reasons why some issues are privileged over others, and readings 5 to 7 suggest reasons why some ways of dealing with issues are prioritized over others.

Parts Two, Three and Four provide readings that focus respectively on questions of what, who and why, but at a different level of engagement. Part Two focuses first on what matters. What do we profess responsibility for? The readings here explore the notion of engaging with 'nature' using the metaphor of conversation. What are the differences between conversation and debate in terms of framework devices used for constructing nature? Moreover, what are the implications of different framing devices for both aspects of responsibility: (a) caring for and (b) ensuring guidance and accountability? Attention here will be on contemporary initiatives to build on broad-based consequentialist traditions underpinning systems thinking, and environmental pragmatism. The shift is from constructing nature as 'resources' for economic development towards a more mutually dynamic process enabling socio-ecological well-being.

Part Three focuses more on the human world in relation to the environment. Who has responsibility for what and how? The readings examine individual and collective responsibility and the relationship between them; also, different kinds of responsibilities operating at different levels and in different contexts. Attention here will be on (deontological) rights- and contracts-based traditions because of their relevance to the environmental actions and interactions of humans. The early chapters in this part consider autonomy and responsibility and how individual responsibilities and actions accumulate, often in ways that do not address environmental problems as much as they might. Ideas for alternative ways forward are included. Ethical questions of obligations and contracts are then addressed from different perspectives – considering future people and shared commons such as public land, air and water. The role of corporations and how they relate to other stakeholders in terms of social and environmental responsibility is then debated. Governance and policy issues emerge in the later readings of this part, including why governance can be a struggle in situations of uncertainty and complexity and biophysical constraints. Several readings focus on multilevel, multi-stakeholder social learning as a complementary way of enabling environmental responsibility to be taken, alongside other mechanisms such as legislation.

The readings in Part Four focus on appropriate political, social and institutional space for reflecting and deliberating on which matters of environmental responsibility are given privilege and who has responsibility and how. What space is required to continually ask questions of purpose (why?) in environmental decision-making? How can we frame multiple, often contesting, values and enable development of individual and collective virtues? How might ethics, policy and action be constrained by as well as be providers of space for enacting environmental responsibility? Attention here will be on central virtues of ecological justice in relation to other virtues (hope, love, wisdom, forgiveness, compassion, courage, obligation, etc.). The readings explore initiatives relating to the politics of new types of citizenship where the framing of ecological citizenship might enable appropriate dialogue between public and private, local and global, future and present, acting and thinking, and rights and responsibilities.

Each of the parts to this collection includes an introductory section giving a brief overview of the edited readings. Each chapter is further introduced by an editorial comment providing some relevant contextual information. A short concluding section in each part reviews the main practical implications for practising environmental responsibility in terms of policy design and action. As with any anthology of this kind, the collection of readings provides a partial representation of a rich and developing landscape of literature. While the sections and individual readings can be dipped into at random, it is hoped that the storyline that brings this collection together enables more purposeful sense-making and engagement with questions of environmental responsibility.

Reference

Open University (2006) *T863 Environmental Decision Making: A Systems Approach*, Course Book 1, Milton Keynes: Open University.

ONE | Ethical and cultural traditions

Introduction to part one

MARTIN REYNOLDS, CHRIS BLACKMORE
AND MARK J. SMITH

Caring for an environment in which people see themselves as integral parts, and ensuring guidance and accountability for any harm or wrong done to that environment – as described in the Introduction – have probably been prevalent societal features since the beginning of human cultural evolution. Raising questions regarding the negative impacts of human activity on the natural world, however, and the evident widespread lack of care for the environment and accountability for these impacts in the context of human economic development, is a relatively recent phenomenon. Modern expressions of environmental responsibility can be dated back to a set of mid-twentieth-century writings that spawned the growth of what has been called the environmental movement. In this part we consider several of those writings.

In the first chapter, two readings by Rachel Carson from the seminal 1960s book *Silent Spring* provide a helpful and widely acclaimed point of departure for considering issues of environmental responsibility. Although Carson's primary focus is on the polluting effects of the pesticide DDT, her narrative speaks to a much wider concern regarding the many and complicated unintended consequences of human activity. *Silent Spring* is often regarded as having been a wake-up call for environmentalists.

The motivating sense of care that drives concern for issues of accountability is one shared by another celebrated text, *A Sand County Almanac*, by Aldo Leopold (1949). In exploring the close relationship between himself and the land in which he lives, Leopold effectively argues the need for an ethic – or set of moral guidelines – specifically related to the environment (referred to in the reading as 'land'). Unlike the many philosophers writing in his wake, Leopold himself does not formulate an ethic in the tradition of philosophical ethics but rather on the basis of a sense of valuing and having obligations to nature.

In the next reading, Luke Martell gives a broad and considered overview of problems associated with translating an intuitive caring sense of obligation and value to the natural world. He argues that the characteristic of sentience – the power to experience a sense of well-being or suffering – is an overriding basis on which to attribute intrinsic value and to extend obligations. The shift is towards formulating a more precise ethic relevant to environmental issues.

Following this, Martin Reynolds describes three dimensions of environmental ethics. The first dimension, normative ethics, relates to the kinds of concern regarding values and obligations raised by Carson, Leopold and Martell. The second and third dimensions relate to philosophical and political dimensions respectively. The philosophical dimension provides a more considered theoretical shaping of normative ideas, as exemplified by three main traditions.

The three philosophical traditions identified by Reynolds are the subject material for the final three chapters in this part. First, Daniel Holbrook explores the relevance of the consequentialist tradition to supporting the intrinsic (as against the instrumental) value of nature, and biocentric equality – a viewpoint that questions the privileged status of humans. Next, Robert Elliot explains the relevance of the deontological tradition to environmental concerns. In contrast to the consequentialist primary concern for value, the focus here is on agency and the bearing of rights. What opportunities are there for affording rights and/or autonomy to non-human nature? Finally, James Connelly describes a resurgent interest in the tradition of virtue ethics in relation to environmental ethics in general and ecological citizenship in particular. Virtues are understood as behavioural practice; a state of agency ('sufficient virtue') rather than a state of being ('perfect virtue'). Character traits provide the means for continually deliberating and acting towards a 'sustainable common environmental good'. Connelly suggests that as citizens start to understand the reasons for being responsible and develop ecological virtues, they cultivate their own character as well as making a positive contribution to other citizens and even the collective good.

1 | Silent spring

RACHEL CARSON

In the following two readings from the seminal environmental
book *Silent Spring*, Rachel Carson highlights the unanticipated
consequences of human actions that were also originally based on
good intentions. The human action in question is the use of DDT
and other pesticides to tackle such problems as Dutch elm disease
and agricultural pests that reduced agricultural productivity.
The first extract is the opening passage from *Silent Spring* and
uses a powerful storytelling device to convey the scope and the
urgency of the problem. The second presents the emerging
scientific evidence for the effects of pesticides on the complex
food chains of other species and highlights what was being lost
in the environment. Carson's book is often considered one of the
first environmental interventions of contemporary environmental
movements and was influential in inspiring many environmental
activists from the 1960s onwards. Her compassionately scientific
account provoked a severe reaction from agricultural and forestry
interests, scientists and the chemicals industry, but led eventually
to stricter environmental regulations on pesticide use. The key
message is that human beings have an environmental responsibility to understand the *unacknowledged conditions* of the environment and to be mindful of the *unanticipated consequences* of what
we do (an early expression of the precautionary approach).

Reading 1a: A fable for tomorrow

There was once a town in the heart of America where all life seemed
to live in harmony with its surroundings. The town lay in the midst of a
checker board of prosperous farms, with fields of grain and hillsides of
orchards where, in spring, white clouds of bloom drifted above the green
fields. In autumn, oak and maple and birch set up a blaze of colour that
flamed and flickered across a backdrop of pines. Then foxes barked in
the hills and deer silently crossed the fields, half hidden in the mists of
the autumn mornings.

Along the roads, laurel, viburnum and alder, great ferns and wildflowers delighted the traveller's eye through much of the year. Even in

winter the roadsides were places of beauty, where countless birds came to feed on the berries and on the seed heads of the dried weeds rising above the snow. The countryside was, in fact, famous for the abundance and variety of its bird life, and when the flood of migrants was pouring through in spring and autumn people travelled from great distances to observe them. Others came to fish the streams, which flowed clear and cold out of the hills and contained shady pools where trout lay. So it had been from the days many years ago when the first settlers raised their houses, sank their wells, and built their barns.

Then a strange blight crept over the area and everything began to change. Some evil spell had settled on the community: mysterious maladies swept the flocks of chickens; the cattle and sheep sickened and died. Everywhere was a shadow of death. The farmers spoke of much illness among their families. In the town the doctors had become more and more puzzled by new kinds of sickness appearing among their patients. There had been several sudden and unexplained deaths, not only among adults but even among children, who would be stricken suddenly while at play and die within a few hours.

There was a strange stillness. The birds, for example – where had they gone? Many people spoke of them, puzzled and disturbed. The feeding stations in the backyards were deserted. The few birds seen anywhere were moribund; they trembled violently and could not fly. It was a spring without voices. On the mornings that had once throbbed with the dawn chorus of robins, catbirds, doves, jays, wrens, and scores of other bird voices there was now no sound; only silence lay over the fields and woods and marsh.

On the farms the hens brooded, but no chicks hatched. The farmers complained that they were unable to raise any pigs – the litters were small and the young survived only a few days. The apple trees were coming into bloom but no bees droned among the blossoms, so there was no pollination and there would be no fruit.

The roadsides, once so attractive, were now lined with browned and withered vegetation as though swept by fire. These, too, were silent, deserted by all living things. Even the streams were now lifeless. Anglers no longer visited them, for all the fish had died.

In the gutters, under the eaves and between the shingles of the roofs, a white granular powder still showed a few patches; some weeks before it had fallen like snow upon the roofs and the lawns, the fields and streams.

No witchcraft, no enemy action had silenced the rebirth of new life in this stricken world. The people had done it themselves.

This town does not actually exist, but it might easily have a thousand counterparts in America or elsewhere in the world. I know of no community that has experienced all the misfortunes I describe. Yet *every* one of these disasters has actually happened somewhere, and many real communities have already suffered a substantial number of them. A grim spectre has crept upon us almost unnoticed, and this imagined tragedy may easily become a stark reality we all shall know.

What has already silenced the voices of spring in countless towns in America? This book is an attempt to explain.

Reading 1b: And no birds sing

Over increasingly large areas of the United States, spring now comes unheralded by the return of the birds, and the early mornings are strangely silent where once they were filled with the beauty of bird song. This sudden silencing of the song of birds, this obliteration of the colour and beauty and interest they lend to our world have come about swiftly, insidiously, and unnoticed by those whose communities are as yet unaffected.

From the town of Hinsdale, Illinois, a housewife wrote in despair to one of the world's leading ornithologists, Robert Cushman Murphy, Curator Emeritus of Birds at the American Museum of Natural History.

Here in our village the elm trees have been sprayed for several years [she wrote in 1958]. When we moved here six years ago, there was a wealth of bird life; I put up a feeder and had a steady stream of cardinals, chickadees, downies and nuthatches all winter, and the cardinals and chickadees brought their young ones in the summer.

After several years of DDT spray, the town is almost devoid of robins and starlings; chickadees have not been on my shelf for two years, and this year the cardinals are gone too; the nesting population in the neighbourhood seems to consist of one dove pair and perhaps one catbird family.

It is hard to explain to the children that the birds have been killed off, when they have learned in school that a Federal law protects the birds from killing or capture. 'Will they ever come back?' they ask, and I do not have the answer. The elms are still dying, and so are the birds. *Is* anything being done? *Can* anything be done? Can *I* do anything?

A year after the federal government had launched a massive spraying programme against the fire ant, an Alabama woman wrote:

Our place has been a veritable bird sanctuary for over half a century. Last

July we all remarked, 'There are more birds than ever.' Then, suddenly, in the second week of August, they all disappeared. I was accustomed to rising early to care for my favourite mare that had a young filly. There was not a sound of the song of a bird. It was eerie, terrifying. What was man doing to our perfect and beautiful world? Finally, five months later a blue jay appeared and a wren.

The autumn months to which she referred brought other sombre reports from the deep South, where in Mississippi, Louisiana, and Alabama the *Field Notes* published quarterly by the National Audubon Society and the United States Fish and Wildlife Service noted the striking phenomenon of 'blank spots weirdly empty of virtually *all* bird life'. The *Field Notes* are a compilation of the reports of seasoned observers who have spent many years afield in their particular areas and have unparalleled knowledge of the normal bird life of the region. One such observer reported that in driving about southern Mississippi that autumn she saw 'no land birds at all for long distances'. Another in Baton Rouge reported that the contents of her feeders had lain untouched 'for weeks on end', while fruiting shrubs in her yard, that ordinarily would be stripped clean by that time, still were laden with berries. Still another reported that his picture window, 'which often used to frame a scene splashed with the reel of forty or fifty cardinals and crowded with other species, seldom permitted a view of as many as a bird or two at a time'. Professor Maurice Brooks of the University of West Virginia, an authority on the birds of the Appalachian region, reported that the West Virginia bird population had undergone 'an incredible reduction'.

One story might serve as the tragic symbol of the fate of the birds – a fate that has already overtaken some species, and that threatens all. It is the story of the robin, the bird known to everyone. To millions of Americans, the season's first robin means that the grip of winter is broken. Its coming is an event reported in newspapers and told eagerly at the breakfast table. And as the number of migrants grows and the first mists of green appear in the woodlands, thousands of people listen for the first dawn chorus of the robins throbbing in the early morning light. But now all is changed, and not even the return of the birds may be taken for granted.

The survival of the robin, and indeed of many other species as well, seems fatefully linked with the American elm, a tree that is part of the history of thousands of towns from the Atlantic to the Rockies, gracing their streets and their village squares and college campuses with majestic archways of green. Now the elms are stricken with a disease that afflicts them throughout their range, a disease so serious that many experts believe all efforts to save the elms will in the end be futile. It would be tragic to lose the elms, but it would be doubly tragic if, in vain efforts to save them, we plunge vast segments of our bird populations into the night of extinction. Yet this is precisely what is threatened.

The so-called Dutch elm disease entered the United States from Europe about 1930 in elm burl logs imported for the veneer industry. It is a fungus disease; the organism invades the water-conducting vessels of the tree, spreads by spores carried in the flow of sap, and by its poisonous secretions as well as by mechanical clogging causes the branches to wilt and the tree to die. The disease is spread from diseased to healthy trees by elm bark beetles. The galleries which the insects have tunnelled out under the bark of dead trees become contaminated with spores of the invading fungus, and the spores adhere to the insect body and are carried wherever the beetle flies. Efforts to control the fungus disease of the elms have been directed largely towards control of the carrier insect. In community after community, especially throughout the strongholds of the American elm, the Midwest and New England, intensive spraying has become a routine procedure.

What this spraying could mean to bird life, and especially to the robin, was first made clear by the work of two ornithologists at Michigan State University, Professor George Wallace and one of his graduate students, John Mehner. When Mr Mehner began work for the doctorate in 1954, he chose a research project that had to do with robin populations. This was quite by chance, for at that time no one suspected that the robins were in danger. But even as he undertook the work, events occurred that were to change its character and indeed to deprive him of his material.

Spraying for Dutch elm disease began in a small way on the university campus in 1954. The following year the city of East Lansing (where the university is located) joined in, spraying on the campus was expanded, and, with local programmes for gypsy moth and mosquito control also under way, the rain of chemicals increased to a downpour.

During 1954, the year of the first light spraying, all seemed well. The following spring the migrating robins began to return to the campus as usual. Like the bluebells in Tomlinson's haunting essay 'The Lost Wood', they were 'expecting no evil' as they reoccupied their familiar territories. But soon it became evident that something was wrong. Dead and dying robins began to appear on the campus. Few birds were seen in their normal foraging activities or assembling in their usual roosts. Few nests were built; few young appeared. The pattern was repeated with monotonous regularity in succeeding springs. The sprayed area had

15

become a lethal trap in which each wave of migrating robins would be eliminated in about a week. Then new arrivals would come in, only to add to the numbers of doomed birds seen on the campus in the agonized tremors that precede death.

'The campus is serving as a graveyard for most of the robins that attempt to take up residence in the spring,' said Dr Wallace. But why? At first he suspected some disease of the nervous system, but soon it became evident that

> in spite of the assurances of the insecticide people that their sprays were 'harmless to birds' the robins were really dying of insecticidal poisoning; they exhibited the well-known symptoms of loss of balance, followed by tremors, convulsions, and death. (Wallace 1959)

Several facts suggested that the robins were being poisoned, not so much by direct contact with the insecticides as indirectly, by eating earthworms. Campus earthworms had been fed inadvertently to crayfish in a research project and all the crayfish had promptly died. A snake kept in a laboratory cage had gone into violent tremors after being fed such worms. And earthworms are the principal food of robins in the spring.

A key piece in the jigsaw puzzle of the doomed robins was soon to be supplied by Dr Ray Barker of the Illinois Natural History Survey at Urbana. Dr Barker's work, published in 1958, traced the intricate cycle of events by which the robins' fate is linked to the elm trees by way of the earthworms. The trees are sprayed in the spring (usually at the rate of 2 to 6 pounds of DDT per 50-foot tree, which may be the equivalent of as much as 23 *pounds per acre* where elms are numerous) and often again in July, at about half this concentration. Powerful sprayers direct a stream of poison to all parts of the tallest trees, killing directly not only the target organism, the bark beetle, but other insects, including pollinating species and predatory spiders and beetles. The poison forms a tenacious film over the leaves and bark. Rains do not wash it away. In the autumn the leaves fall to the ground, accumulate in sodden layers, and begin the slow process of becoming one with the soil. In this they are aided by the toil of the earthworms, who feed in the leaf litter, for elm leaves are among their favourite foods. In feeding on the leaves the worms always swallow the insecticide, accumulating and concentrating it in their bodies. Dr Barker found deposits of DDT throughout the digestive tracts of the worms, their blood vessels, nerves, and body wall. Undoubtedly some of the earthworms themselves succumb, but others survive to become 'biological magnifiers' of the poison. In the spring the robins return to provide another link in the cycle. As few as eleven large earthworms can transfer a lethal dose of DDT to a robin. And eleven worms form a small part of a day's rations to a bird that eats ten to twelve earthworms in as many minutes.

Not all robins receive a lethal dose, but another consequence may lead to the extinction of their kind as surely as fatal poisoning. The shadow of sterility lies over all the bird studies and indeed lengthens to include all living things within its potential range. There are now only two or three dozen robins to be found each spring on the entire 185-acre campus of Michigan State University, compared with a conservatively estimated 370 adults in this area before spraying. In 1954 every robin nest under observation by Mehner produced young. Towards the end of June, 1957, when at least 370 young birds (the normal replacement of the adult population) would have been foraging over the campus in the years before spraying began, Mehner could find *only one young robin*. A year later Dr Wallace was to report:

> At no time during the spring or summer [of 1958] did I see a fledgling robin anywhere on the main campus, and so far I have failed to find anyone else who has seen one there. (Wallace 1959)

Part of this failure to produce young is due, of course, to the fact that one or more of a pair of robins dies before the nesting cycle is completed. But Wallace has significant records which point to something more sinister – the actual destruction of the birds' capacity to reproduce. He has, for example,

> records of robins and other birds building nests but laying no eggs, and others laying eggs and incubating them but not hatching them. We have one record of a robin that sat on its eggs faithfully for twenty-one days and they did not hatch. The normal incubation period is thirteen days ... Our analyses are showing high concentrations of DDT in the testes and ovaries of breeding birds [he told a congressional committee in 1960]. Ten males had amounts ranging from 30 to 109 parts per million in the testes, and two females had 151 and 211 parts per million respectively in the egg follicles in their ovaries. (Wallace 1960)

Soon studies in other areas began to develop findings equally dismal. Professor Joseph Hickey and his students at the University of Wisconsin, after careful comparative studies of sprayed and unsprayed areas, reported the robin mortality to be at least 86 to 88 per cent. The Cranbrook Institute of Science at Bloomfield Hills, Michigan, in an effort to assess the extent of bird loss caused by the spraying of the elms, asked in 1956 that all birds thought to be victims of DDT poisoning be

17

turned in to the institute for examination. The request had a response beyond all expectations. Within a few weeks the deep-freeze facilities of the institute were taxed to capacity, so that other specimens had to be refused. By 1959 a thousand poisoned birds from this single community had been turned in or reported. Although the robin was the chief victim (one woman calling the institute reported twelve robins lying dead on her lawn as she spoke), sixty-three different species were included among the specimens examined at the institute.

The robins, then, are only one part of the chain of devastation linked to the spraying of the elms, even as the elm programme is only one of the multitudinous spray programmes that cover our land with poisons. Heavy mortality has occurred among about ninety species of birds, including those most familiar to suburbanites and amateur naturalists. The populations of nesting birds in general have declined as much as 90 per cent in some of the sprayed towns. As we shall see, all the various types of birds are affected – ground feeders, tree-top feeders, bark feeders, predators.

It is only reasonable to suppose that all birds and mammals heavily dependent on earthworms or other soil organisms for food are threatened by the robins' fate. Some forty-five species of birds include earthworms in their diet. Among them is the woodcock, a species that winters in southern areas recently heavily sprayed with heptachlor. Two significant discoveries have now been made about the woodcock. Production of young birds on the New Brunswick breeding grounds is definitely reduced, and adult birds that have been analysed contain large residues of DDT and heptachlor.

Already there are disturbing records of heavy mortality among more than twenty other species of ground-feeding birds whose food – worms, ants, grubs, or other soil organisms – has been poisoned. These include three of the thrushes whose songs are among the most exquisite of bird voices, the olive-backed, the wood, and the hermit. And the sparrows that flit through the shrubby understory of the woodlands and forage with rustling sounds amid the fallen leaves – the song sparrow and the whitethroat – these, too, have been found among the victims of the elm sprays.

Mammals, also, may easily be involved in the cycle, directly or indirectly. Earthworms are important among the various foods of the raccoon, and are eaten in the spring and autumn by opossums. Such subterranean tunnellers as shrews and moles capture them in some numbers, and then perhaps pass on the poison to predators such as screech owls and barn owls. Several dying screech owls were picked up in Wisconsin following heavy rains in spring, perhaps poisoned by feeding on earthworms. Hawks and owls have been found in convulsions – great horned owls, screech

18

owls, red-shouldered hawks, sparrowhawks, marsh hawks. These may be cases of secondary poisoning, caused by eating birds or mice that have accumulated insecticides in their livers or other organs.

Nor is it only the creatures that forage on the ground or those who prey on them that are endangered by the foliar spraying of the elms. All of the tree-top feeders, the birds that glean their insect food from the leaves, have disappeared from heavily sprayed areas, among them those woodland sprites the kinglets, both ruby-crowned and golden-crowned, the tiny gnatcatchers, and many of the warblers, whose migrating hordes flow through the trees in spring in a multi-coloured tide of life. In 1956, a late spring delayed spraying so that it coincided with the arrival of an exceptionally heavy wave of warbler migration. Nearly all species of warblers present in the area were represented in the heavy kill that followed. In Whitefish Bay, Wisconsin, at least a thousand myrtle warblers could be seen in migration during former years; in 1958, after the spraying of the elms, observers could find only two. So, with additions from other communities, the list grows, and the warblers killed by the spray include those that most charm and fascinate all who are aware of them: the black-and-white, the yellow, the magnolia, and the Cape May; the ovenbird, whose call throbs in the May-time woods; the Blackburnian, whose wings are touched with flame; the chestnut-sided, the Canadian, and the black-throated green. These tree-top feeders are affected either directly by eating poisoned insects or indirectly by a shortage of food.

The loss of food has also struck hard at the swallows that cruise the skies, straining out the aerial insects as herring strain the plankton of the sea. A Wisconsin naturalist reported:

> Swallows have been hard hit. Everyone complains of how few they have compared to four or five years ago. Our sky overhead was full of them only four years ago. Now we seldom see any ... This could be both lack of insects because of spray, or poisoned insects.

Of other birds this same observer wrote:

> Another striking loss is the phoebe. Flycatchers are scarce everywhere but the early hardy common phoebe is no more. I've seen one this spring and only one last spring. Other birders in Wisconsin make the same complaint. I have had five or six pair of cardinals in the past, none now. Wrens, robins, catbirds and screech owls have nested each year in our garden. There are none now. Summer mornings are without bird song. Only pest birds, pigeons, starlings and English sparrows remain. It is tragic and I can't bear it. (Coordination of Pesticides Programs 1960)

The dormant sprays applied to the elms in the autumn, sending the poison into every little crevice in the bark, are probably responsible for the severe reduction observed in the number of chickadees, nuthatches, titmice, woodpeckers, and brown creepers. During the winter of 1957–8, Dr Wallace saw no chickadees or nuthatches at his home feeding station for the first time in many years. Three nuthatches he found later provided a sorry little step-by-step lesson in cause and effect: one was feeding on an elm, another was found dying of typical DDT symptoms, the third was dead. The dying nuthatch was later found to have 226 parts per million of DDT in its tissues (Wallace 1959). [...]

Various scientific studies have established the critical role of birds in insect control in various situations. Thus, woodpeckers are the primary control of the Engelmann spruce beetle, reducing its populations from 45 to 98 per cent, and are important in the control of the codling moth in apple orchards. Chickadees and other winter-resident birds can protect orchards against the cankerworm.

But what happens in nature is not allowed to happen in the modern, chemical-drenched world, where spraying destroys not only the insects but their principal enemy, the birds. When later there is a resurgence of the insect population, as almost always happens, the birds are not there to keep their numbers in check. As the Curator of Birds at the Milwaukee Public Museum, Owen J. Gromme, wrote to the Milwaukee *Journal*:

> The greatest enemy of insect life is other predatory insects, birds, and some small mammals, but DDT kills indiscriminately, including nature's own safeguards or policemen ... In the name of progress are we to become victims of our own diabolical means of insect control to provide temporary comfort, only to lose out to destroying insects later on? By what means will we control new pests, which will attack remaining tree species after the elms are gone, when nature's safeguards (the birds) have been wiped out by poison?

[...] In each of these situations, one turns away to ponder the question: Who has made the decision that sets in motion these chains of poisonings, this ever-widening wave of death that spreads out, like ripples when a pebble is dropped into a still pond? Who has placed in one pan of the scales the leaves that might have been eaten by the beetles and in the other the pitiful heaps of many-hued feathers, the lifeless remains of the birds that fell before the unselective bludgeon of insecticidal poisons? Who has decided – who has the *right* to decide – for the countless legions of people who were not consulted that the supreme value is a world without insects, even though it be also a sterile world ungraced by the curving wing of a bird in flight? The decision is that of the authoritarian temporarily entrusted with power; he has made it during a moment of inattention by millions to whom beauty and the ordered world of nature still have a meaning that is deep and imperative.

References

Audubon Field Notes, 'Fall Migration – Aug. 16 to Nov. 30, 1958', Vol. 13 (1959), No. 1, pp. 1–68.

Barker, Roy J., 'Notes on Some Ecological Effects of DDT sprayed on Elms', *Jour. Wildlife Management*, Vol. 22 (1958), No. 3, pp. 269–74.

'Coordination of Pesticides Programs', *Hearings*, H. R. 11502, 86th Congress, Com. on Merchant Marine and Fisheries, May 1960, pp. 10, 12.

Dexter, R. W., 'Earthworms in the Winter Diet of the Opossum and the Racoon', *Jour. Mammal.*, Vol. 32 (1951), p. 464.

Hickey, Joseph J. 'Some Effects of Insecticides on Terrestrial Birdlife', *Report* of Subcom. on Relation of Chemicals to Forestry and Wildlife, State of Wisconsin, January 1961, pp. 2–43.

Hickey, Joseph J. and Hunt, L. Barrie, 'Songbird Mortality Following Annual Programs to Control Dutch Elm Disease', *Atlantic Naturalist*, Vol. 15 (1960a), No. 2, pp. 87–92.

Hickey, Joseph J. and Hunt, L. Barrie, 'Initial Songbird Mortality Following a Dutch Elm Disease Control Program', *Jour. Wildlife Management*, Vol. 24 (1960b), No. 3, pp. 259–65.

Knight, F. B., 'The Effects of Woodpeckers on Populations of the Engelmann Spruce Beetle', *Jour. Econ. Entomol.*, Vol. 51 (1958), pp. 603–7.

MacLellan, C. R., 'Woodpecker Control of the Codling Moth in Nova Scotia Orchards', *Atlantic Naturalist*, Vol. 16 (1961), No. 1, pp. 17–25.

Mehner, John F. and Wallace, George J., 'Robin Populations and Insecticide', *Atlantic Naturalist*, Vol. 14 (1959), No. 1, pp. 4–10.

Swingle, R. U., *et al.*, 'Dutch Elm Disease', *Yearbook of Agric.*, U.S. Dept of Agric., 1949, pp. 451–2.

Wallace, George J., 'Insecticides and Birds', *Audubon Mag.*, January–February 1959.

Wallace, George J., 'Another Year of Robin Losses on a University Campus', *Audubon Mag.*, March–April 1960.

Wallace, George J., *et al.*, *Bird Mortality in the Dutch Elm Disease Program in Michigan*, Cranbrook Inst. of Science Bulletin 41 (1961).

Walton, W. R., *Earthworms as Pests and Otherwise*, U.S. Dept of Agric. Farmers' Bulletin No. 1569 (1928).

Wright, Bruce S., 'Woodcock Reproduction in DDT Sprayed Areas of New Brunswick', *Jour. Wildlife Management*, Vol. 24 (1960), No. 4, pp. 419–20.

2 | The land ethic

ALDO LEOPOLD

Aldo Leopold's 'The land ethic' is an edited extract from his book
A Sand County Almanac – a collection of essays describing the
land around his home in Wisconsin, USA, published a year after
his death in 1948. It provides the first formalized expression of
an environmental ethic, and is the most celebrated and widely
cited work in the tradition of environmental ethics. As a forester,
ecologist and conservationist, Leopold does not use the vocabulary of traditional philosophical ethics. But his simple description
of what is required for environmental responsibility resonates as
much now in philosophy and politics as it did when his work was
first published.

§ There is as yet no ethic dealing with man's relation to land and to the
animals and plants which grow upon it. Land, like Odysseus' slave-girls,
is still property. The land-relation is still strictly economic, entailing
privileges but not obligations.

The extension of ethics to this third element in human environment
is, if I read the evidence correctly, an evolutionary possibility and an
ecological necessity. It is the third step in a sequence. The first two
have already been taken. Individual thinkers since the days of Ezekiel
and Isaiah have asserted that the despoliation of land is not only inex-
pedient but wrong. Society, however, has not yet affirmed their belief.
I regard the present conservation movement as the embryo of such an
affirmation.

An ethic may be regarded as a mode of guidance for meeting ecological
situations so new or intricate, or involving such deferred reactions, that
the path of social expediency is not discernible to the average individual.
Animal instincts are modes of guidance for the individual in meeting
such situations. Ethics are possibly a kind of community instinct in-
the-making.

The community concept

All ethics so far evolved rest upon a single premise: that the individual
is a member of a community of interdependent parts. His instincts

prompt him to compete for his place in that community, but his ethics prompt him also to co-operate (perhaps in order that there may be a place to compete for).

The land ethic simply enlarges the boundaries of the community to include soils, waters, plants, and animals, or collectively: the land.

This sounds simple: do we not already sing our love for and obligation to the land of the free and the home of the brave? Yes, but just what and whom do we love? Certainly not the soil, which we are sending helter-skelter downriver. Certainly not the waters, which we assume have no function except to turn turbines, float barges, and carry off sewage. Certainly not the plants, of which we exterminate whole communities without batting an eye. Certainly not the animals, of which we have already extirpated many of the largest and most beautiful species. A land ethic of course cannot prevent the alteration, management, and use of these 'resources,' but it does affirm their right to continued existence, and, at least in spots, their continued existence in a natural state.

In short, a land ethic changes the role of *Homo sapiens* from conqueror of the land-community to plain member and citizen of it. It implies respect for his fellow-members, and also respect for the community as such.

In human history, we have learned (I hope) that the conqueror role is eventually self-defeating. Why? Because it is implicit in such a role that the conqueror knows, *ex cathedra*, just what makes the community clock tick, and just what and who is valuable, and what and who is worthless, in community life. It always turns out that he knows neither, and this is why his conquests eventually defeat themselves. [...]

Substitutes for a land ethic

When the logic of history hungers for bread and we hand out a stone, we are at pains to explain how much the stone resembles bread. I now describe some of the stones which serve in lieu of a land ethic.

One basic weakness in a conservation system based wholly on economic motives is that most members of the land community have no economic value. Wildflowers and songbirds are examples. Of the 22,000 higher plants and animals native to Wisconsin, it is doubtful whether more than 5 percent can be sold, fed, eaten, or otherwise put to economic use. Yet these creatures are members of the biotic community, and if (as I believe) its stability depends on its integrity, they are entitled to continuance.

When one of these non-economic categories is threatened, and if we happen to love it, we invent subterfuges to give it economic importance. At the beginning of the century songbirds were supposed to be disappearing. Ornithologists jumped to the rescue with some distinctly shaky evidence to the effect that insects would eat us up if birds failed to control them. The evidence had to be economic in order to be valid.

It is painful to read these circumlocutions today. We have no land ethic yet, but we have at least drawn nearer the point of admitting that birds should continue as a matter of biotic right, regardless of the presence or absence of economic advantage to us.

A parallel situation exists in respect of predatory mammals, raptorial birds, and fish-eating birds. Time was when biologists somewhat over-worked the evidence that these creatures preserve the health of game by killing weaklings, or that they control rodents for the farmer, or that they prey only on 'worthless' species. Here again, the evidence had to be economic in order to be valid. It is only in recent years that we hear the more honest argument that predators are members of the community, and that no special interest has the right to exterminate them for the sake of a benefit, real or fancied, to itself. Unfortunately this enlightened view is still in the talk stage. In the field the extermination of predators goes merrily on: witness the impending erasure of the timber wolf by fiat of Congress, the Conservation Bureaus, and many state legislatures.

Some species of trees have been 'read out of the party' by economics-minded foresters because they grow too slowly, or have too low a sale value to pay as timber crops: white cedar, tamarack, cypress, beech, and hemlock are examples. In Europe, where forestry is ecologically more advanced, the non-commercial tree species are recognized as members of the native forest community, to be preserved as such, within reason. Moreover some (like beech) have been found to have a valuable function in building up soil fertility. The interdependence of the forest and its constituent tree species, ground flora, and fauna is taken for granted.

Lack of economic value is sometimes a character not only of species or groups, but of entire biotic communities: marshes, bogs, dunes, and 'deserts' are examples. Our formula in such cases is to relegate their conservation to government as refuges, monuments, or parks. The difficulty is that these communities are usually interspersed with more valuable private lands; the government cannot possibly own or control such scattered parcels. The net effect is that we have relegated some of them to ultimate extinction over large areas. If the private owner were ecologically minded, he would be proud to be the custodian of a reasonable proportion of such areas, which add diversity and beauty to his farm and to his community.

In some instances, the assumed lack of profit in these 'waste' areas has proved to be wrong, but only after most of them had been done away with. The present scramble to reflood muskrat marshes is a case in point. [...]

The outlook

It is inconceivable to me that an ethical relation to land can exist without love, respect, and admiration for land, and a high regard for its value. By value, I of course mean something far broader than mere economic value; I mean value in the philosophical sense.

Perhaps the most serious obstacle impeding the evolution of a land ethic is the fact that our educational and economic system is headed away from, rather than toward, an intense consciousness of land. Your true modern is separated from the land by many middlemen, and by innumerable physical gadgets. He has no vital relation to it; to him it is the space between cities on which crops grow. Turn him loose for a day on the land, and if the spot does not happen to be a golf links or a 'scenic' area, he is bored stiff. If crops could be raised by hydroponics instead of farming, it would suit him very well. Synthetic substitutes for wood, leather, wool, and other natural land products suit him better than the originals. In short, land is something he has 'outgrown.'

Almost equally serious as an obstacle to a land ethic is the attitude of the farmer for whom the land is still an adversary, or a taskmaster that

25

keeps him in slavery. Theoretically, the mechanization of farming ought to cut the farmer's chains, but whether it really does is debatable.

One of the requisites for an ecological comprehension of land is an understanding of ecology, and this is by no means co-extensive with 'education'; in fact, much higher education seems deliberately to avoid ecological concepts. An understanding of ecology does not necessarily originate in courses bearing ecological labels; it is quite as likely to be labeled geography, botany, agronomy, history, or economics. This is as it should be, but whatever the label, ecological training is scarce.

The case for a land ethic would appear hopeless but for the minority which is in obvious revolt against these 'modern' trends.

The 'key-log' which must be moved to release the evolutionary process for an ethic is simply this: quit thinking about decent land-use as solely an economic problem. Examine each question in terms of what is ethically and esthetically right, as well as what is economically expedient. A thing is right when it tends to preserve the integrity, stability, and beauty of the biotic community. It is wrong when it tends otherwise.

It of course goes without saying that economic feasibility limits the tether of what can or cannot be done for land. It always has and it always will. The fallacy the economic determinists have tied around our collective neck, and which we now need to cast off, is the belief that economics determines *all* land-use. This is simply not true. An innumerable host of actions and attitudes, comprising perhaps the bulk of all land relations, is determined by the land-user's tastes and predilections, rather than by his purse. The bulk of all land relations hinges on investments of time, forethought, skill, and faith rather than on investments of cash. As a land-user thinketh, so is he.

I have purposely presented the land ethic as a product of social evolution because nothing so important as an ethic is ever 'written.' Only the most superficial student of history supposes that Moses 'wrote' the Decalogue; it evolved in the minds of a thinking community, and Moses wrote a tentative summary of it for a 'seminar.' I say tentative because evolution never stops.

The evolution of a land ethic is an intellectual as well as emotional process. Conservation is paved with good intentions which prove to be futile, or even dangerous, because they are devoid of critical understanding either of the land, or of economic land-use. I think it is a truism that as the ethical frontier advances from the individual to the community, its intellectual content increases.

The mechanism of operation is the same for any ethic: social approbation for right actions; social disapproval for wrong actions.

By and large, our present problem is one of attitudes and implements. We are remodeling the Alhambra with a steam-shovel, and we are proud of our yardage. We shall hardly relinquish the shovel, which after all has many good points, but we are in need of gentler and more objective criteria for its successful use.

3 | On values and obligations to the environment

LUKE MARTELL

Luke Martell argues that we need to think quite clearly about valuing, and having obligations towards, our non-human environment. He does this from the perspective of a sociologist interested in the political and sociological dimensions of environmentalism. Rather than trusting our intuitions over the intrinsic values attached to non-human nature, he suggests that the capacity to experience well-being and suffering (sentience) is essential for attributing intrinsic value. In arguing his case, Martell also provides insightful notes and references to some of the important players in environmental ethics.

§ Ecologists argue that what is distinctive about environmental ethics is that it extends rights and obligations beyond humans to other entities in the wider environment: animals and other living and non-living non-sentient beings. Anthropocentric arguments justify protection of parts of the environment – resources, animals, wilderness, bio-diversity and such like – for the practical or aesthetic value they have for humans. Many environmentalists argue that such parts of the environment should command obligations in themselves. They should be protected regardless of, and in cases where they do not have, value for humans.[1]

Coming to conclusions on where value resides or obligations are due has implications for which parts of the environment we protect. It may mean, for instance, protecting parts of the environment which have little value for humans but have value in themselves. Intrinsic value in nature broadens our policy responsibilities.

I wish to discuss here arguments for extending obligations to non-humans, why we should do so and to what range of entities. Some environmentalists want to include animals. Others want to include living non-sentient entities like plants or even non-living things like rocks and stones. I will be making three sets of distinctions between (1) different sorts of value; (2) different bases for attributing value and moral standing; and (3) different sorts of being to which value should be attached.

The first distinction is between intrinsic and extrinsic value. Intrinsic value is in something itself regardless of its value for other things. Humans could be said to have a value in themselves in their capacity to experience pleasure or flourish or in their nature as conscious intelligent beings. Humans have a value in such properties regardless of their use or value for other things. A spanner has extrinsic value. It has a value which derives from its objective properties but it is not intrinsic in the spanner itself but in the use it has for humans by virtue of its functions. Its value comes from its objective properties but is a value for something else.

Another distinction is between the differing bases on which non-humans have value or moral standing. These are listed under 2 in Table 4. Finally, there are different entities in the world, as under 3 in Table 4. I wish to discuss to which of these entities in 3 the reasons in 2 suggest value and concern should be extended and whether this value is intrinsic or extrinsic as distinguished in 1.

Using the distinction between the two different sorts of value, let me proceed to category 2: different arguments for attributing value and being concerned for, or holding obligations to, things. Which arguments are favoured determines which entities are attributed value or moral standing.

1 *Sentience*. I will start with sentience – having the power to experience a sense of wellbeing or suffering.[2] We should extend obligations to entities in the world that have such a capacity. It is wrong to cause suffering to a being or curtail its ability to experience wellbeing. Using sentience as a basis for extending obligations incorporates animals alongside humans as a group to whom these are due. Animals, like humans, have the capacity to feel pain and pleasure and so on sentient criteria should also command obligations. At present we keep many animals in conditions that cause pain, distress or discomfort or we curtail their ability to lead a pleasurable life by killing them for sport or food. As such, animals are often not given the moral respect sentient arguments say they are due.[3]

Other living beings like plants or non-living things like rocks and stones do not, as far as we know, have the capacity to experience pleasure or pain. On sentient criteria, therefore, they do not have value in themselves and cannot command moral concern or obligations.

They do have a value but that value is for beings who can experience wellbeing or suffering from the existence or flourishing of plants or stones. They should be preserved for their value to such beings. But they cannot have a value or command obligations in abstraction from sentient experience which comes only in their relation to other sentient groups.

For many of us, our emotional feelings and intuitions are that there *is* an intrinsic value in the being, life or development of plants or rocks.

TABLE 4 Value in and obligations to the non-human environment

1 Sorts of value
a) intrinsic
b) extrinsic

2 Bases for attributing value or moral standing
a) sentience
b) capacity to flourish and develop
c) preservation of diversity
d) preservation of species and systems
e) membership of community

3 Entities to which value or moral standing attached
a) humans
b) non-human sentient living beings, i.e. animals
c) non-human non-sentient living beings, e.g. plants
d) non-human non-sentient non-living beings, e.g. rocks

But, as I argue below, we should not trust our intuitions. It is hard to see a value in just being, living or growing. Value is in the experience of these. Plants and rocks do not have the capacity to experience being or growing or gain wellbeing from them. But experience or wellbeing, which *are* of intrinsic value, can be felt by sentient beings – humans and animals – and it is in them that intrinsic value lies.

2 *Flourishing*. The debate with sentience is based not so much on a rejection of sentient arguments (although this sometimes features as I will discuss below) as on the argument that they are not enough. It is argued that sentience is part but not all of what gives a being value and a claim to rights and obligations. There are beings who do not have sentience, plants for example, but have a claim to rights and obligations because of other capacities they have which can pin down such claims – the capacity to grow, develop and flourish, for example. We should respect the rights of, and hold obligations to, anything which can flourish and develop and should restrain from actions which interfere with such capacities.[4]

A problem here is that arguments for the capacity for flourishing as a criterion on which obligations are due distinguish too sharply between it and sentience. What makes it of value is the joy of flourishing, not just flourishing by itself. Where it brings suffering it is not of value and we may not want to give rights and obligations to entities if their growth has ill effects. Think of locusts or plants that strangle other plants. We should judge flourishing according to the experiences it is wrapped up in. It is they which are of value.

The value in non-sentient flourishing beings is not intrinsic, as it is in its implications for things other than flourishing itself. Values and obligations of an extrinsic sort can be extended to non-sentient flourishing beings. They have a value but in the wellbeing which derives from their capacities rather than in those capacities themselves. They evoke wellbeing not in themselves because they are non-sentient but in other sentient beings. This is why their value is extrinsic (for other things). Intrinsic value is located in sentient rather than non-sentient beings because it is sentience which is of value in itself. Intrinsic value is not divorced from flourishing because sentient experience is wrapped up in it. But it is experience which is the locus of value and not flourishing independently of the experience it is associated with.

✢ We should, in sum, be responsive to the capacities of flourishing beings to flourish. But obligations go to sentient beings because it is the sentient experience involved in their own or others' flourishing which is of value. Flourishing itself cannot be a basis for commanding respect and obligations. First, it does not by itself have the weight commanding of respect that it has when wrapped up with sentient experience. Second, it could involve flourishing with ill effects to which we would not want to give value, respect or obligations.

3 *Diversity*. So far I have considered two characteristics of entities which might make them of value and deserving of respect or obligations: sentience and the capacity to flourish. I have argued for the former. Let me now turn to three other arguments in environmental ethics for giving value, obligations or respect to entities in the world. The arguments I want to consider now do not, on the face of it, turn so much on the characteristics of individual beings as on structures or principles which are seen to be of value: diversity; species or systems; and community obligations.

Diversity can be seen as a value in itself. It is of positive value and it is because it is good that we should value and extend respect, rights and obligations to diverse things in the world.[5] We should respect the place of all things in the world not so much for the sake of those things but because diversity is desirable. Plurality rather than the entities of which there are plural instances is what should make us want to respect them. In ecology diversity has a special ring to it because diversity and interdependence are said to be functional for the smooth running of ecosystems.[6]

There are a number of problems here. The first is on the functions of diversity for the system. If it is this that is desirable then it is the system, rather than diversity which is of intrinsic value and which we should want to protect. Diversity only has extrinsic value and we would not want to respect it where it fails to fulfil its systemic functions. It is not diversity itself which is of intrinsic value. The argument made for it here is better covered under the valuing of systems which I will discuss below. We should not extend rights on the basis of a respect for diversity if it is the system which is of value and not diversity, which could potentially be of disservice.

On the other hand, if it is a concern for the individuals in the system which makes the functions of diversity for the system valuable then the environmental ethic is concerned about individuals rather than diversity. The value of individuals is covered by the discussions above on sentience and flourishing or by properties of value such as consciousness, intelligence, control or autonomy which individuals have.

Functions apart, one of the things which makes diversity of value is the fulfilment that living in a diverse world brings to beings with the sensory capacities to experience it. It is that diversity has such consequences rather than just the existence of diversity in abstraction that is behind our convictions when we say the world is better for being pluralistic. It is not diversity which is of value but the benefits it brings. What is of value is the experience facilitated by it. Gaining this experience is based on having a capacity for sensory experience: sentience. In itself it is difficult to see why diversity – just having lots of kinds of things – is good on its own. What is good about diversity is in its connection with the experience it contributes to and it is of value where it does so positively but may be a principle which we do not wish to respect or value where it does so negatively.

4 *Species and systems.* In much environmental thinking value is put on the preservation of collective entities like species or ecosystems. These are said to have an intrinsic value in themselves. The death of the last member of a species is worse than the death of a member of a not endangered species. A species is seen to have a value in itself over and above the value of its individual members.[7]

One of the arguments on species comes from the case for diversity just discussed. We should preserve species because if one is lost there is a loss of a type of thing and a loss, therefore, to the diversity of things in the world. However, I have already explained why I think arguments on diversity are weak in abstraction from arguments for individual wellbeing. They are strengthened by being linked to wellbeing but then become based on the value of wellbeing rather than diversity.

In my view, it is difficult to see how arguments on species can work independently and without resort to other arguments on which they ultimately rest. They do not stand on the intrinsic value of having species alone but come down to arguments on the sentient wellbeing of members of the species or of other individuals who suffer as a result of the loss of a species. Loss of a species can be a loss because it involves losing its individual members. It is a loss of individuals rather than the collective entity they make up. Or it is a loss because a particular type of thing is no longer around. This does not make sense as a loss unless it is linked to a lessening of wellbeing of members of the world as a result. In abstraction from a diminution of wellbeing the loss of diversity of species remains statistical. It is difficult to see why there should be just more and more categories of things except if linked to the life of members of the species or the wellbeing of individuals from other species who benefit from the richness of life in a world of natural diversity or from the special value of a species.

The loss of species is bad. But it is so because of the loss of individual members or a diminution of the wellbeing of members of other species, rather than just the loss of a category itself in abstraction from such other considerations. Species have a value but it is not intrinsic. It is a value for members of the species or other beings in the world who benefit from its existence. Individuals of a species or the individuals of others may have a case on which to call for moral consideration from us. But abstract categories of species cannot make good claims for rights or value in themselves.

Another argument in which value is put on collective entities in the environment is on preserving ecosystems.[8] Leopold (1968: 224) argues that 'a thing is right when it tends to preserve the integrity, stability and beauty of the biotic community'. This suggests that value resides in the biotic community and that actions should be judged according to their contribution to the good of the community. The whole itself has an intrinsic value and characteristics worthy of respect and accommodation.

According to this view, our respecting and valuing of nature should be for it as a whole entity rather than, or as well as, for its parts because nature has an identity and functions as a whole. This can go further to a strong fetishizing naturalism. Nature knows best and we should not interfere with it as a system because this goes against what is natural and best for the survival of life. Nature is a whole, we should respect the 'natural' and we should practise non-interference with regard to it.[9]

In my view, there are a number of problems in the arguments tangled up in this 'holist' perspective. First, there is a question mark hanging over the scientific validity of what is claimed. Brennan (1988), by no means an opponent of a more relational and environmental ethics, argues that there is not a factual or scientific basis for the holism that greens aspire to. Greens tend to argue that we should respect ecosystems because we are bound up in them and because it is according to holist systemic principles that nature works. However, on Brennan's analysis it is not clear that ecosystems do actually function according to principles of holism and interdependence. The fact of holism should be analysed rather than assumed ...

Second, there is a problem with the view that we should respect the 'natural'.[10] It is not clear what it is about being natural that means we should respect it. To say we should respect something because it is natural is not enough. This fetishizes 'nature'. It needs to be said what it is about being natural that makes it worthy of respect.

Third, the very dichotomy between the natural and social needs to be challenged. What is it about humans that makes our behaviour not natural and in need of being accommodated to what is? It could be said that humans are just as natural as anything else. We have natural capacities and live within and in relation to nature. What reason is there to define our actions and capacities, development of social organization and technology and our purposive transformation of our surroundings as not natural or not taking place as part of nature? If humans *are* natural then accommodating to nature does not involve changing our patterns of behaviour to fit in with other principles. (On such issues see Dickens 1992.)

Fourth, what nature is is open to question. What goes on in nature is contradictory and often downright undesirable. Nature exhibits both toleration and killing, diversity and extinction, equality and exploitation. There is no apparent general design, guide, intention or rationale in this to show what is the preferred way of nature. It is not clear that there is something which is nature – distinctive or coherent characteristics which are identifiable and can be followed and given respect and value.

There is a fifth problem on interference and non-interference.[11] To defer to nature, not interfere with it and act in accordance with its principles can be a recipe for not doing what seems the best thing in the light of ethical consideration and the perceived best consequences. Further, it can inhibit actions which might seem to be the best for nature itself. Human interference may have played a large part in contributing to environmental problems but it is part of the solution as well. Yet interference in nature to protect it – building dams to protect natural habitats or killing members of species (e.g. locusts or strangling plants) to protect others, for example – is ruled out by deference to nature.

We may need greater restraint but on the basis that it is good for the environment rather than because it is 'natural' and not to the exclusion of intervention in 'natural' processes to protect the environment.

Sixth and last, there is a problem with value residing in systems. To say that a system has intrinsic value means that the value is in the system rather than the individuals who make it up. I would argue that there cannot be intrinsic value in an ecosystem. A system's value and claim to respect rest in the value it has for its individual members. This is not to say that value is purely a perception of individuals and not in the objective properties of the system itself. The value may be a result of properties of the system irrespective of whether individuals recognize it or not. My point is that it is a value *for* individuals who make up the system and not of the system itself. The system has no value in itself divorced from the wellbeing of the individuals it contributes to.

Giving value to systems has dangerous implications. It means we can value systems over individuals and individuals can be sacrificed for the sake of an impersonal structure. Making the ecosystem of intrinsic value creates a conflict between its interests and the interests of the individuals who make it up. Yet it is the latter who matter and the former which should serve them. If the system gains value in itself over and above individuals this can be very dangerous for them.

It ought to be mentioned that I am not arguing for epistemological, ontological or methodological individualisms. It is not my claim that individuals are the source of knowledge or value, or the basic building blocks in natural or social life or the unit on which explanatory analysis should focus. On epistemology, for example, my argument is that value is in objective properties of the environment and not just in the eye of the beholder. But it is a value *for* individuals if not one just dreamt up by them. I am arguing for an ethical individualism and within this for a particular variant of it. My argument in ethical individualism is not for individual liberty (although autonomy is an important *part* of the good of individuals) or for atomistic or egoistic individualism. A scheme within which the wellbeing of individuals is the end may be collectivist or one in which rules restrict the uninhibited pursuit of self-interests. The wellbeing of individuals is the end with which my ethical individualism here is concerned.

5 *Community.* Value, rights or obligations may be extended to non-human entities on the basis that they are part of the same community as humans. This is connected to the argument on systems and holism because it suggests that as members of the same whole different entities have obligations to one another. Humans have rights and obligations to

non-human entities because they are part of the interdependent whole to which we all belong. Different entities have mutual obligations which come from interdependence, participation and membership in the same community.[12]

I am not going to dwell on whether entities in the environment *are* interdependent or members of the same community (see Brennan 1988). In my view, the argument on community falls down earlier than this – on the idea that ethics should be based on shared community in the first place. Why should we have obligations to someone because they are members of the same community? And why should we not have obligations to someone because they are not? I have already argued, regarding future generations, that we should have obligations to people and other beings who are strangers and not members of our community and with whom we are not in a position of interdependence.

We have obligations to the present-day third world poor because they are needy and we can help them. Even were we not responsible for their circumstances or not dependent on them (neither of which is the case) we would still have obligations to them for these reasons. It would be irresponsible for us not to help suffering beings when we can, regardless of the status of any other connections we may or may not have with them. The same goes for future generations. Because we can both adversely and positively affect their circumstances, we are obliged to at least not do the former. This should be incumbent upon us whether or not we are in a relation of mutual dependency or shared community with them.

Shared community and mutual dependence as the basis for obligations depend on ideas of contract and self-interest. We are said to owe obligations to others because of the mutual contract involved in joining a society with them or because we depend on one another. We agree to hold obligations to others because we wish to take part in the community with them, depend on them or want them to do likewise for us. We have obligations to members of our own community rather than to non-community justifications that claimants from outside it could make for our attentions.

My argument, however, is that there are beings in the world who have the capacity to experience wellbeing and suffering. If we have it in our power to help them without sacrificing our own prospects we have an obligation to do so, as long as they are not needy because of injustices or lack of effort on their part. Obligations extend beyond boundaries of community and such boundaries as the basis of obligations can prevent us from fulfilling obligations to those outside our community to whom we owe them. Community is not only too exclusive in this way but also too inclusive. It incorporates among those to whom we owe obligations people who can make claims on us on the grounds of shared membership of the same community but who have no claims on grounds of needs or wellbeing.

Notes

1 For influential classic statements by deep ecologists on intrinsic value in nature see Naess (1973) and Leopold (1968). Also see the discussion of value in the environment in Goodin (1992: ch. 2).

2 Griffin (1986) discusses issues such as these using the term 'wellbeing'. I will return in more depth to sentience and the literature on this issue later in the chapter.

3 For recent discussions of animal rights see Tester (1991), Benton (1993) and Garner (1993). For influential 'classic' statements see Bentham (1960), Salt (1980), Singer (1976), Clark (1977), Regan (1988) and Midgeley (1983). Also the collections edited by Singer (1985), Regan and Singer (1976) and Miller and Williams (1983). Different theorists argue for obligations to animals on different grounds and by no means all do so on the sentient grounds that Singer (1976), for example, and I favour.

4 Clark (1977) argues on flourishing in relation to animals. See also Attfield (1983: 151–4) and Taylor (1986).

5 See Naess (1973), Dobson (1990: 121–2), Sale (1984), Norton (1987) and Attfield (1983: 149–50) on the intrinsic value of diversity.

6 Brennan (1988) suspects deep ecological appeals to scientific claims about diversity in nature do not hold up – see pp. 43–4, 119, 122–3. Further, he argues that if diversity is an ecological reality this is not a sufficient basis for it to be of value – see

pp. 152 and 164 [in Martell, L. (1994) *Ecology and Society*, Cambridge: Polity Press].

7 Naess (1984) and Norton (1986 and 1987) propose that species have an intrinsic value. See also Eckersley (1992: 46–7) and Feinberg (1980: 171–3, 204–5). Attfield (1983: 150–51, 155–6) is a critic of the idea.

8 On wholes or systems as having a value in themselves see Goodpaster (1978), Rodman (1977) and Callicott (1980). A scientific basis for ethical claims on holism is often made; see Lovelock (1979), Capra (1985) and Callicott (1985). See the discussion in Attfield (1983: 156–60, 179–82). Brennan (1988) argues that the scientific basis claimed by ethical holists and their ethical claims themselves are faulty. In this chapter I reject ethical holism. In chapter 6 [of source work] I reject ontological or explanatory holism which fetishizes the natural.

9 The idea that the system as a whole provides conditions optimal for life comes through strongly in the influential 'Gaia' thesis advanced by Lovelock (1979). For an accessible introduction to 'Gaia' see Dobson (1990: 42–7) and Dobson (1991: 264–8). Again, I discuss in this chapter why I think holist Gaia-type ideas are ethically dangerous. In chapter 6 [of source work] I explain why I think they are flawed as explanations of society–nature relations.

10 See Dobson (1990: 24–8), Sale (1984 and 1985), Bookchin (1982).

11 For an argument for non-

interference see Regan's (1981) 'preservation principle' rejected, rightly in my view, by Brennan (1988: 198).

12 On community and obligations in environmental ethics see Leopold (1968: 203), Callicott (1979), Attfield (1983: 157–8).

References

Attfield, Robin 1983: *The Ethics of Environmental Concern*. Oxford: Blackwell.

Bentham, Jeremy 1960: *An Introduction to the Principles of Morals and Legislation*. Oxford: Blackwell.

Benton, Ted 1993: *Natural Relations: Ecology, Animal Rights and Social Justice*. London: Verso.

Bookchin, Murray 1982: *The Ecology of Freedom*. Palo Alto: Cheshire Books.

Brennan, Andrew 1988: *Thinking about Nature*. London: Routledge.

Callicott, J. Baird 1979: 'Elements of an Environmental Ethic: Moral Considerability and the Biotic Community'. *Environmental Ethics*, 1, 71–81.

Callicott, J. Baird 1980: 'Animal Liberation: A Triangular Affair'. *Environmental Ethics*, 2, 311–38.

Callicott, J. Baird 1985: 'Intrinsic Value, Quantum Theory and Environmental Ethics'. *Environmental Ethics*, 7, 257–75.

Capra, Fritjof 1985: *The Turning Point: Science, Society and the Rising Culture*. London: Flamingo.

Clark, Stephen R. L. 1977: *The Moral Status of Animals*. Oxford: Clarendon Press.

Dickens, Peter 1992: *Society and Nature: Towards a Green Social Theory*. Hemel Hempstead: Harvester Wheatsheaf.

Dobson, Andrew 1990: *Green Political Thought*. London: Andre Deutsch.

Dobson, Andrew (ed.) 1991: *The Green Reader*. London: Andre Deutsch.

Eckersley, Robyn 1992: *Environmentalism and Political Theory*. London: U.C.L. Press.

Feinberg, J. 1980: *Rights, Justice and the Bounds of Liberty*. Princeton: Princeton University Press.

Garner, Robert 1993: *Animals, Politics and Morality*. Manchester: Manchester University Press.

Goodin, Robert E. 1992: *Green Political Theory*. Cambridge: Polity Press.

Goodpaster, Kenneth 1978: 'On Being Morally Considerable'. *Journal of Philosophy*, 75, 308–25.

Griffin, J. 1986: *Well-Being: Its Meaning, Measurement and Moral Importance*. Oxford: Oxford University Press.

Leopold, Aldo 1968: *A Sand County Almanac*. Oxford: Oxford University Press.

Lovelock, James 1979: *Gaia: A New Look at Life on Earth*. Oxford: Oxford University Press.

Midgeley, Mary 1983: *Animals and Why They Matter*. Harmondsworth: Penguin.

Miller, H. B. and Williams, W. (eds) 1983: *Ethics and Animals*. Clifton, N.J.: Humana Press.

Naess, Arne 1973: 'The Shallow and the Deep, Long-Range Ecology Movement: A Summary'. *Inquiry*, 16, 95–100.

Naess, Arne 1984: 'Intuition, Intrinsic Value and Deep Ecology'. *The Ecologist*, 14, 5–6.

Norton, Bryan G. (ed.) 1986: *The Preservation of Species: The Value of Biological Diversity*. Princeton: Princeton University Press.

Norton, Bryan G. 1987: *Why Preserve Natural Variety?* Princeton: Princeton University Press.

Regan, Tom 1981: 'The Nature and

Possibility of an Environmental Ethic'. *Environmental Ethics*, 3, 16–31.

Regan, Tom 1988: *The Case for Animal Rights*. London: Routledge.

Regan, Tom and Singer, Peter (eds) 1976: *Animal Rights and Human Obligations*. Englewood Cliffs, N.J.: Prentice-Hall.

Rodman, John 1977: 'The Liberation of Nature'. *Inquiry*, 20, 83–145.

Sale, Kirkpatrick 1984: 'Bio-regionalism – a New Way to Treat the Land'. *The Ecologist*, 14, 167–73.

Sale, Kirkpatrick 1985: *Dwellers in the Land: The Bioregional Vision*. San Francisco: Sierra Club Books.

Salt, Henry S. 1980: *Animal Rights Considered in Relation to Social Progress*. London: Centaur.

Singer, Peter 1976: *Animal Liberation*. London: Cape.

Singer, Peter (ed.) 1985: *In Defence of Animals*. Oxford: Blackwell.

Taylor, P. 1986: *Respect for Nature: A Theory of Environmental Ethics*. Princeton: Princeton University Press.

Tester, Keith 1991: *Animals and Society: The Humanity of Animal Rights*. London: Routledge.

Luke Martell

4 | Environmental ethics

MARTIN REYNOLDS

> Martin Reynolds highlights three dimensions of environmental ethics – normative, philosophical and political – in the context of a long-standing controversial development initiative for dam constructions in the Narmada river valley in India. In discussing these dimensions, he promotes the importance of environmental ethics in fostering responsible development intervention. A version of this reading can be found in *Environment, Development and Sustainability in the 21st Century: Perspectives and Cases from Around the World*, Gordon Wilson, Pam Furniss and Richard Kimbowa (eds) (2009), published by The Open University and Oxford University Press, for which the reading was originally commissioned.

Introduction

> More than any other time in history, mankind faces a crossroads. One path leads to despair and utter hopelessness. The other, to total extinction. Let us pray we have the wisdom to choose correctly. – Woody Allen, American humorist, quoted in Westley et al. (2006: 90)

Humour often provides respite in a perceived world of intractable dilemmas. Local issues such as access to clean water or availability of food can be driven by, as well as contribute to, global issues such as climate change and the global economy. Take for example the issues around constructing large-scale dams. The Narmada Dam Project in India is one of the longest-standing development and environmental controversies of its kind (see Figure 1). Box 1 summarises the history and some key issues. These issues are complex and they also generate some questions of responsibility.

The conflicts are formidable. Large-scale dam construction like other big socio-economic developments such as air-travel expansion have been subject to criticism, both through extensive consultant reporting and strong activism and protest. But often there is a sense of inevitability about such projects. Decisions appear to be made through some inescapable march of so-called progress. So perhaps Woody Allen is right to be cynical. But cynicism belies a wealth of opportunities for seeing and doing things differently.

An ethical outlook on such issues can help to realise such opportunities. For example, looking behind Woody Allen's acerbic observation, some basic ethical questions might be asked to reveal areas of responsibility that need to be and can be managed more constructively.

1 What are the particular issues that need attention? Does global warming deserve more attention than longer-standing issues of abject poverty in the world? Or should we just despair at the magnitude and complexity of issues confronting us?
2 How might these issues be attended to and by whom? Is it just 'them' out there or is it also you/me/'us'? Or should we just resort to fatalism, nurturing a general sense of apathy and blame?
3 Why are some issues privileged more than others, and some ways of dealing with them prioritised over others? What opportunities are there for challenging mainstream ways of dealing with harmfulness and wrongdoing? Or should we just remain cynical of human nature and the prospects to realise alternative ways of doing things?

Despair, apathy and cynicism are all too prevalent in modern society. Moreover they are human attributes sometimes encouraged by those with an interest in keeping things as they are – contributing to vicious cycles of business-as-usual and the type of eco-social collapse invoked by cynics. In what follows I'll use each of the three sets of questions above in turn to explain how ideas from environmental ethics can help guide more purposeful engagement with environment and development dilemmas. The Narmada Dam Project is used to ground the discussion.

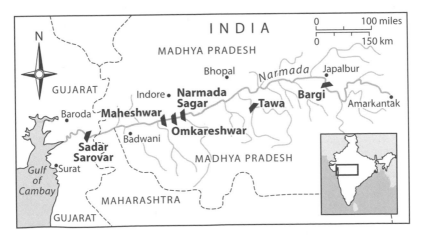

FIGURE 1 Map of Narmada valley and proposed dams (*source*: International Rivers Network www.irn.org/programs/narmada/map.html)

41

Box 1 Narmada Dam Project

The Narmada Dam Project in India involves the construction of 30 large, 135 medium and 3000 small dams to exploit the waters of the river Narmada and its tributaries for better irrigated agricultural practice to produce more food, and the generation of hydroelectric power. The idea was first conceived in the 1940s by India's first prime minister, Jawaharlal Nehru, but it was not until 1979 that the project took form. Of the 30 large dams, Sardar Sarovar is the largest and most controversial. In 1979, the Sardar Sarovar Project was proposed and attracted initial support from international financial institutions including the World Bank. But after much controversy and protest, particularly since the late 1980s, many financial institutions withdrew support. Protest was led by Narmada Bachao Andolan (NBA), a national coalition movement including people affected by the project, environmental and human rights activists, scientists and academics.

The construction of Sardar Sarovar dam itself was stopped in the mid-1990s. However, in October 2000, the Indian Supreme Court gave a go-ahead again for the construction of the dam. Other dams associated with the wider Narmada project have likewise been developing, come under criticism and have been the subject of protest.

Four general issues can be summarised in relation to the Narmada Project:

- Water access and quality (e.g. water-borne diseases from stagnant reservoir waters)
- Urban and rural economic development (e.g. displaced populations from rural areas)
- Change in agricultural practices (e.g. shift towards large-scale irrigated farming)
- Ecological impacts (e.g. loss of biodiversity in previously rich hydrological systems)

Source: Friends of River Narmada (2008)

Despair? Issues and values: normative ethics

Ethics concern contrasting questions of 'is' with questions of 'ought'. This is sometimes referred to as *normative* ethics. The 'is' comprises a descriptive world of *issues* that are experienced by different stakeholders.

The 'ought' comprises a normative world of *values* – often multiple and conflicting – which are used by stakeholders to make judgements on the realities they experience. Many issues relating to environment and development are experienced as complex questions requiring continual attention to value judgements on what ought to be.

So what role do value judgements play? Arguments for and against the Narmada Project can be considered as expressions of *value* judgements: arguments 'for' construction based on judgements on what ought to be the outcome, and arguments 'against' based on judgements regarding what ought not to be the outcome (Box 2).

One of the key problems arising from any controversial issue is sorting out judgements of 'fact' from value judgements. Scientific information on levels of domestic water supply, power generation, agricultural production, estimated numbers of poor and underprivileged communities being dispossessed of their livelihood, and ecological impacts, are vital. However, professed levels of impact, both positive and negative, are often contested even amongst scientists. 'Fact' and value are inextricably linked. So being aware of accompanying value judgements is also very important. Ethics makes values explicit. Box 3 provides an understanding of different types of value and different perspectives.

Arguments in support of the Narmada Dam Project can be said to have an anthropocentric perspective with a dominant, instrumental value judgement on water as a resource. Few would deny this as an important value judgement, particularly in a context of poor access to clean water. From a more ecocentric perspective, claims are made of providing flood protection for ecosystems, and offering compensation to support sanctuaries for endangered species.

Anthropocentric arguments can also be made against the project. The displacement of communities, loss of livelihood, and diminished access to water amongst vulnerable groups are particularly significant. The possible loss of biodiversity through deforestation and increased salinisation will have aesthetic disadvantages which can also be factored in from an anthropocentric perspective. Many of the arguments against such projects, however, derive from a more ecocentric perspective, bringing attention to wider and longer-term ecological impacts.

But values and perspectives are not fixed entities. They vary and develop according to the context and time in which they are applied. This is evident with the Narmada case study. As time has moved on, protest around Narmada has become symbolic of a global concern for how we engage with nature and the long-term consequences. Environmental ethics helps to explain such changes in terms of different types of value judgements

Box 2 Narmada Dam Project: value judgements

Outcomes judged to be good/ right/valuable (arguments for construction)	Outcomes judged to be bad/wrong/ worthless (arguments against construction)

1 Water access and quality

Supply water to 30m people including drinking water facilities	Increase prospect of insect-borne diseases
Irrigate crops to feed another 20m people covering 17,920 km² of land	Inundate areas causing salinisation of land alongside canals through build-up of salts

2 Urban and rural economic development

Provide hydroelectric power Improve access to electricity in remote villages	Dispossess large numbers of poor and underprivileged communities of their land as a source of livelihood
Develop facilities for sophisticated communication systems in the project areas	Provide inadequate compensation and rehabilitation for resettled people as with previous experiences in India
Increase employment both in construction and post-construction maintenance	Over-estimate power generated and under-estimate likely long-term dependence on private trans-national companies
	Prompt excessive profiteering amongst private contractors and possible corruption in dispensing large budgets

3 Agricultural practice and technological development

Modernise agricultural practices using irrigated farming	Lose skills in more sustainable farming practices
Provide irrigation infrastructure for biofuel agricultural production (and other genetically modified crops)	Undermine expert confidence (even the World Bank withdrew from the Narmada Project!)
Develop fisheries industry	Give false promises regarding maintenance of dams given seemingly disorganised State infrastructure
	Disrupt downstream fisheries

4 Ecological impacts

Protect against advancement of desert and provision of flood protection to riverine reaches	Diminish biodiversity through mono-culture irrigated farming Devastate existing riverine ecosystem
Establish wildlife sanctuaries protecting rare species (e.g., Sloth Bear, Wild Ass, Kutch Bustard)	Submerge current forest farmland Ignore possible long-term impacts (e.g. large reservoirs could cause earthquakes)

Box 3 Values and perspectives on environment and development

Values are an assessment or measure of the worth of something. Two types of value can be distinguished in environmental ethics.

1 Instrumental is the value that something has as a means to an end. So money might be good *only* because it leads to other good things (purchase of 'goods'). Putting monetary value on environmental 'goods', or considering nature in terms of natural 'resources', and ecosystem 'services', are typical expressions of instrumental value in relation to nature.

2 Intrinsic is the value that a thing has 'in itself', or 'for its own sake', or 'in its own right'. Money for example is not intrinsically good (unless you are a collector of historic or different currencies) whereas most other goods might arguably be considered as having some intrinsic value. Environmentalism as a social movement in the mid-twentieth century grew from an appreciation of intrinsic value for nature.

A third type of value can be associated with the valuer as against the valued. Here, value is linked with obligations and the boundaries of the *moral community* – who or what is worthy of respect (past, present, future generations? other animals? all living organisms? ecosystems? biosphere? universe? multiverse?)

3 Personal (or individual) is the internally held value of the valuer usually attached to character traits such as having 'integrity'. Behind any value is a valuer with particular perspectives on the world guided by personal values. Two perspectives on the environment based on personal values can be distinguished – anthropocentric and ecocentric.

Anthropocentric perspective places humans in a privileged position over nature. An extreme position of anthropocentrism – egocentrism – privileges *individual* humans. Other extremes assume that the destiny of humanity is to conquer and master the forces of nature. Such a perspective assumes that nature is only valuable in so far as humans have a use for it, in terms of human needs (i.e. instrumental valuation).

Ecocentric perspective regards human beings as simply one part of a moral community consisting of all living things as well as non-living natural objects (rivers, mountains etc.). Humans no longer occupy a privileged position on top of the moral community.

and perspectives. Environmental ethics therefore help to make sense of arguments for and against a project, and to respond effectively to such arguments using the appropriate language of value and perspective. In short, rather than despair at the complexity of issues arising, environmental ethics provides a handle – a vocabulary around value judgements – for appreciating and dealing with issues more constructively.

So with a means of surfacing value judgements, what guidance might be given towards using those judgements for responsible action?

Apathy? How to do ethics and be ethical: philosophical ethics

Whilst *normative* ethics helps in revealing the interplay of value judgements, more specific questions on what to do can draw on traditions of moral philosophy. *Philosophical* ethics is about searching for answers to questions about:

i) *doing what's good (or harmful),* and ii) *doing what's right (or wrong)* The first question invites consideration of the *consequence* of a decision and appropriate ways of measuring the consequences. The second invites consideration to the *intention* behind any decision and any particular obligations behind such intention. Table 1 provides some ideas about the kinds of benefit/harm and rights/wrongs that might be looked at in association with each of the four main issues arising from the Narmada Dam Project. (It should be noted that, as with any philosophical abstraction, the categorisation into 'good' or 'right' is a slightly artificial one and there is not always a clear distinction between them.)

The responses to each question – what's good and what's right – in relation to any issue can be contested. For example, on the issue of agricultural practice some might suggest that a more appropriate 'good' from an anthropocentric perspective would be to improve intensity of production. Further contestation may arise in privileging one type of question over another. Should a focus on 'rights' and obligations be advanced in spite of the effects of action, or vice versa? An obligation to respect nature may for example be inappropriate in circumstances where the effect is to further human impoverishment. Similarly, a focus on maximising human welfare may infringe on the rights of other life-forms to flourish. Reference to value judgements and associated perspectives (Box 2) can help make sense of these conflicts.

Environmental ethics also addresses character attributes around 'being' ethical or environmentally responsible. This invokes a third tradition in philosophical ethics drawing upon Western (e.g. Ancient Greek) and Eastern (e.g. Buddhism and Taoism) philosophy:

TABLE 1 Philosophical ethics: what to do?

Issues around Narmada Dam Project	Doing what's good (not harmful) Measures of success	Doing what's right (not wrong) Intentions and obligations
Water access and quality	Improve quality of water and access to clean water (avoid disease and drought)	Provide universal access to clean water (not reinforcing or developing skewed access)
Urban and rural economic development	Improve quality of life for citizens (avoid poverty and use of only economic indices)	Provide opportunity for all humans to flourish (not constraining humans from flourishing)
Agricultural practice and technological development	Improve range of productive capacities for farming (avoid loss of ecologically sustainable farming skills)	Provide expertise to support appropriate practice (not contriving a simplistic solution)
Ecological impacts	Improve quality of the natural environment (avoid ecological deterioration)	Provide protection against ecological destruction (not ignoring wider obligations to nature)

TABLE 2 Philosophical ethics: how to be?

Issues around Narmada Dam Project	Virtue	Vice
Water access and quality	Justice	Injustice
Urban and rural economic development	Moderation	Greed
Agricultural practice and technology progress	Humility	Arrogance
Ecological impacts	Compassion	Recklessness

iii) *being virtuous (or non-virtuous)* Table 2 summarises some virtues and non-virtuous ('vice') character attributes that might be associated with each of the Narmada issues.

Identifying human character attributes can help to ground instinctive feelings about responsibilities and make more relevant discussion about consequences of 'good' action and the obligations implied by 'right' action. As well as mediating discussion between Western and Eastern traditions, it also helps with appreciating the many helpful ideas of human–nature relationships amongst existing indigenous tribal communities.

The risk of philosophical ethics though is in confining it to academic discourse – a sure way of generating cynicism! So another task is to keep ethics alive and integral to all deliberations around planning and politics.

Cynicism? Ethics and politics

Ethics is, by its very nature, contested terrain. Disparate value judgements and perspectives, contested ideas on what is 'good' and what is 'right', and indeed contested virtues (should justice have privilege over compassion? is compassion an appropriate environmental virtue?), all clearly need appropriate space for deliberation. When reviewing the list of four issues associated with Narmada you may personally feel aggrieved at the priority given to an anthropocentric perspective on the issues ('ecological impacts' being the last and only issue that privileges nature). What opportunities exist for countering value judgements and the development of alternative viewpoints? In other words, what political space exists to openly challenge assumptions underpinning development initiatives? Political space, meaning opportunities for non-threatening discussion and debate in both formal and informal settings, represents the interface between ethics and politics. An engagement with environmental ethics demands political space to avoid being seen as the cosy arena of armchair philosophy prompted by cynics. Box 4 illustrates examples of how such space has been nurtured in India.

Box 4 Ethics and opening political space in Narmada

Narmada Bachao Andolan (NBA): their non-violent campaigns, including hunger strikes, a 36-day march, mass demonstrations, and use of the media, prompted institutions as powerful as the World Bank to withdraw support from the Project in the early 1990s.

Friends of River Narmada (FRN): an international coalition of individuals and organisations (primarily of Indian descent) supporting NBA in terms of providing a repository of information, on-going research, public education and outreach, promotion and publicity.

Navdanya movement: participatory research initiative set up in 1991 to counter corporate control over farming practices. Though not directly related to Narmada dams, Navdanya nurtures practices other than monocrop industrial agriculture promoted as part of large-scale dam projects.

Conventionally political space is dominated by men. Women activists such as NBA spokesperson Medha Patkar, and Vandana Shiva, founder of Navdanya, belong to a tradition of 'ecofeminism' reflecting an important gender imperative for creating new political space.

Sources: Friends of River Narmada (2008); Navdanya (2008)

It would be foolish to pretend that groups with more radicalised anthropocentric and ecocentric perspectives have 'won' the battle in Narmada against conventionally dominant economic interests. But it would also be misleading to underestimate the political space nurtured through the engagement of environmental ethics with social and political theory, policy advisers, and activist groupings.

Summary

Environmental ethics can provide support towards seemingly intractable questions of environmental responsibility that otherwise can lead to despair, apathy and cynicism. An understanding of normative values and perspectives – normative ethics – can help surmount a sense of despair. Practice in thinking about doing what's good, doing what's right, and being responsible – philosophical ethics – can help to overcome apathy.

Martin Reynolds

FIGURE 2 Massive rally in Khandwa, MP on June 4, 2007
by Omkareshwar and Indira Sagar dam-affected people

And cynicism needs to be continually checked through creating space for
engaging more passionately with normative and philosophical ethics.
Vandana Shiva provides a helpful riposte to cynicism:

> The big transformations always seem to move in the direction of destruc-
> tion. But if you look at the small actions, the hundreds of people saying 'I
> will speak against human rights violations, I will be part of the voice'; at
> the thousands of farmers who work with us who have created an alterna-
> tive agriculture in spite of the dominant policy; that's where change is
> happening, and that change will continue to grow. (Vandana Shiva in
> Davis 2008: 29)

Shiva surfaces three important virtues: hope in countering the despair
of real world violations; purposefulness in countering an understandable

apathy of a farming community subjected to industrialised agricultural policy; and trust in countering the cynicism that change to business-as-usual is unattainable due to 'human nature'. Environmental ethics alone is not 'the' answer, but it can provide precious support in guiding and keeping alive the right questions.

References

Davis, R. (2008). 'Making Waves: Interview with Vandana Shiva'. *New Internationalist* (410) p. 29.

Friends of River Narmada (2008) www.narmada.org/introduction.html. Accessed 25 April 2008.

Navdanya (2008) www.navdanya.org/about/index.htm. Accessed 4 August 2008.

Westley, F., Zimmerman, B., and Patton, M. Q. (2006). *Getting to Maybe*: Random House Canada.

Martin Reynolds

5 | The consequentialist side of environmental ethics

DANIEL HOLBROOK

This is the first of three readings outlining philosophical traditions – consequentialist, deontological and virtue-based ethics. Doing what's good constitutes a *consequentialist ethic*, which considers good and bad (harmful) as being drivers of 'doing what's right'. The most famous philosophical expression of a consequentialist ethic is utilitarianism, associated principally with original writings on the philosophy by Jeremy Bentham (1748–1832) and John Stuart Mill (1806–73). *Utilitarianism* focuses on maximizing the happiness of the greatest number and is sometimes discredited by environmentalists as being too human-centred and dismissive of nature as having only instrumental value. This extract from a paper by Daniel Holbrook signals utilitarianism as just one expression of a consequentialist ethic. The author wrote this at a time when many environmentalists were keen to produce an alternative unique ethic that broke from the tradition of standard philosophical ethics. Holbrook in contrast describes the value of a traditional consequentialist ethic within the more contemporary radical tradition of 'deep ecology'. Deep ecology was initiated in the 1970s through the works of the Norwegian philosopher Arne Naess and pursued by others, such as Devall and Sessions, referred to in the extract. The consequentialist tradition is considered an important complementary constituent of an environmental ethic. Holbrook suggests that an appropriate biocentric ethic such as Leopold's 'land ethic' (Reading 2) can prompt the development of a more dutiful (deontological) and virtuous relationship with nature in terms of 'self-realization', the implication being that environmental responsibility is not just about consequences but thinking about actual consequences certainly requires some prime attention.

1. Self-realisation

In *Deep Ecology*, Devall and Sessions identify two main principles that underlie their position:

1 *Self-realisation:* Persons will grow and mature through a new and

deeper understanding of their place in the natural world; and

2 *Biocentric Equality:* A denial of the privileged status of human life. This principle leads to a justification for the preservation and restoration of the natural world.[1]

Self-realisation, as understood in *Deep Ecology*, begins with finding one's 'sense of place' within a particular bioregion. Most humans are unaware of the complex system of water, air, animals, plants, and soil that lies beyond their cities, suburbs, and farms. They identify with their neighborhood, workplace, and schools; to them, this is home. But if you fly in a hundred-mile circle over most communities, there are vast tracts of 'unimproved' forests, hills, and valleys. Having a 'sense of place' is a feeling of being equal and united to all the other entities (both living and non-living) of one's natural surroundings in a way similar to the sense of community we have with those persons with whom we live, work, and play.

How does one achieve this unity with nature? John Muir's travels in the Sierra Nevada coupled with his conservation efforts provide a prime example. First, one needs to identify a bioregion; this is a fairly vague concept. The natural world is not a sum of distinct bioregions. Roughly, one bioregion is separated from another by geographic barriers and climatic differences such that there is a significant difference in their ecological characteristics. A bioregion might be defined by the range of a particular animal group including the surrounding area that affects its sources of food and water. Humans are not actually confined to any particular bioregion, since we may travel to any land surface in the world. Because our air and water pollution carry all over the world, the planet could be thought of as a single bioregion. [...]

2. Biocentric equality

Biocentric equality is based on the denial of anthropocentrism – the thesis that all value must be ultimately grounded in value for humans. It seems that a universe without human-like beings is a world without the concepts of good and bad, right and wrong. The 'law of the jungle' makes no provision for ethics. Predation of the weak and helpless by the strong, even the occasional acts of cannibalism of parents destroying their young, are not wrong in a pure state of nature. Callicott writes 'there is no value without a valuer,' and humans and human-like beings are the only valuers in the abstract sense of evaluation in relation to ethics.[2] But, as Callicott also observes, from that we are the only valuers, it does not follow that humans are solely the locus of all value.[3]

Biocentric equality might mean several different positions. One might begin, like Taylor, and identify each living thing as an individual and then argue that each has equal value.[4] The holistic position of Leopold's land ethic begins with the ecosystem. Individuals have value only in a secondary sense based on their participation in the system. We are then equal to the rivers, trees, and birds, in that our value also depends on our relation to the system. Again, to quote Callicott, the land ethic is 'holistic with a vengeance.'[5] [...]

3. The relation between self-realisation and biocentric equality

These two concepts – self-realisation and environmental preservation based on biocentric equality – are causally related, for if humans seek self-realisation through the interaction and identification with their adopted bioregions, there will be a tendency to defend the area against pollution and unwise development. When self-realisation is based on one's identification with a bioregion, attacks on the health and integrity of the bioregion are tantamount to attacks upon oneself. Thus, actions to protect the bioregion are like self-preservation, not only indirectly in the sense of the bioregion being a resource, but directly as if one's own being is assailed. If I have adopted the North Fork of the Clearwater as my bioregion, if my 'sense of place' is based in its watershed, then the dam at its mouth is drowning me in its backwaters, constipating my means of renewal by the fresh spring waters.

But self-realisation and environmental preservation are logically distinct; one can be conceived independently of the other. It is possible to attain self-realisation without actually preserving pristine ecological systems and vice-versa. On the one hand, human civilisation may die (archaeology shows the fragility of civilisations), and a world without humans precludes the possibility of self-realisation, but as a result the environment might prosper. Another possibility is that a few greedy humans will gain control of the majority of the planet's resources and then keep them in a pristine state for their own selfish reasons. These are, I admit, unlikely scenarios, but they do prove the independence of these two concepts. The one can theoretically exist without the other. [...]

4. The consequentialist side of environmental ethics

If self-realisation and environmental preservation are logically distinct concepts then their theoretical foundations may differ. This is the heart of my thesis. Self-realisation is mostly a matter of developing an attitude. Rather than viewing nature merely as a resource with value only in relation to providing satisfaction for humans, environmentalists such as Leopold, Devall, and Taylor recommend that we develop the attitude of appreciating the intrinsic value of wildlife, trees, and waterfalls. The value in developing an attitude may exist apart from the effects expected to follow from it. It need not be understood in a consequentialist framework. On the other hand, problems in the second side of environmental ethics – the preservation and restoration of the environment – are most reasonably cast in a consequentialist theoretical framework.

Consequentialism is the view that actions are right or wrong solely on account of their effects.[6, 7, 8] It is contrasted by views in which actions are found to be right or wrong entirely by reference to motivation. Kant's view – a right action is one motivated through a sense of duty based on the categorical imperative – is the prime example of the nonconsequentialist position. Cases in which badly motivated actions produce good effects and cases in which well motivated actions produce bad effects illustrate the essential difference between consequentialist and nonconsequentialist positions. According to consequentialism, actions with evil motivation that accidentally produce great benefits are the right actions to perform. Good motivation generally produces good results, so a consequentialist may hold compassion, honesty, and duty in high regard, but only insofar as they are seen as productive of benefits.

There are different versions of consequentialism according to what it is about an action's effects that counts for its being right or wrong, and whether actions are evaluated individually or collectively. Utilitarianism is a version of consequentialism in which only the effects of actions in respect to the pleasure, happiness, and/or preferences of sentient beings are relevant to actions being right or wrong. Although utilitarians usually limit the moral community to humans, Jeremy Bentham suggested that it include all animals capable of pleasure and pain; a position not fully developed until almost two hundred years later, by Peter Singer.[9] Usually, utilitarians evaluate the actions of each person individually, but in the case of public policy decisions, the theory might be applied to assess the actions of a society taken collectively.[10, 11]

There is also a distinction between actual and expected consequentialism. According to the former, actions are right or wrong solely on account of their actual effects. With the latter, actions are right or wrong according to the effects that most reasonably can be expected to follow from them. Actual consequentialism seems counter-intuitive when malicious or irresponsible actions accidentally produce good results. To unravel this dilemma, one needs to keep separate consequentialism as a theory of right action and consequentialism in relation to decision procedure.

An actual consequentialist tries to achieve the best effects, but judges actions, ultimately, on their actual effects.

Utilitarianism in the twentieth century has come to be associated with the cost–benefit analysis method employed by economists. Only humans participate directly in the economic system. The cost–benefit analysis version of utilitarianism is a combination of consequentialism, anthropocentrism, and a theory that what is good is equivalent to maximising the economic welfare of humans.[12] The shortcomings of the cost–benefit analysis version of utilitarianism do not necessarily extend to the consequentialist assumptions of the theory. I argue that Leopold's land ethic is based on consequentialism and a modified version of the maximisation concept of goods.

An analysis of environmental issues shows that only the actual effects of our actions are ethically relevant. This is the consequentialist side of environmental ethics. In other areas, we accept accidents and unforeseen outcomes as excusable, if one was being careful and trying for the best. For example, my car goes out of control on an icy road and I ruin your new BMW. My insurance will buy you another. An examination of our dealings with one another shows that motivation is an important factor. But being motivated in a way that was reasonably expected to preserve the environment will not excuse our actions, if the end result is failure. Well, this is not true of isolated actions of little consequence; for example, your straying from a nature trail to follow a path that is eroding the hillside. There are ways of remedying minor transgressions. But there is a point at which ecological systems are damaged beyond repair. When it comes to the large-scale effects of human civilisation, there are no remedies.

If we fall short of preserving the environment, all other than the actual effects of our actions, no matter how noble our intentions or reasonable our aims, will be insignificant. Environmental disaster precludes every other right and good. Imagine that one hemisphere becomes environmentally conservative and the other destructive. The efforts of the conservative half will have been in vain, if the actions of the destructive half destroy the global environment. Human-to-human, we might applaud the efforts of preservationists who fail, but in respect to environmental issues, motives are unimportant. Trivially, environmental preservation will be realised only if it actually comes about. It is an end to which all efforts will be measured according to their impact on its realisation. Dramatic changes in attitude which don't actually achieve widespread, concrete results are of little value here.

One would rather see highly positive results coming from actions motivated by the wrong reasons than less positive results coming from actions motivated by the right reasons. For example, a Central American forest might have gone unscathed through the nineteenth century because its capitalistic owners were purposefully cutting back production in order to drive up prices. Later, after a revolution in the twentieth century, the forest is nationalised and the new leaders want to cut it to buy military hardware, but due to a lack of organisation and machinery, the forest again escapes destruction. In both cases, there was the desire to cut the forest, but the relation of these motivations to the fact that the forest is still standing is irrelevant. From the standpoint of environmental preservation, all that matters are the actual effects, in this case that the forest remains uncut.

Problems inherent to consequentialism generally also apply to environmental ethics issues. Since we can never completely predict the effects of our actions, we can never know with certainty that we have done the right thing. Given the complexity of the environment, this seems reasonable. We can, at best, only be fairly certain that the reduction of greenhouse gases will contribute to the overall health and integrity of the planet. If well-conceived and motivated efforts fail to rectify the problem then they would have been less than the right course of action.

Consequentialism sometimes provides a justification for actions that seem to be horrible. Its application might prescribe that basic human rights be compromised for the sake of the health of the planet. Again, this seems reasonable, since some degree of environmental integrity is a precondition for the enjoyment of these rights. Consequentialism has been seen as contrary to personal integrity; it prescribes actions through a method external to one's own internally-held values.[13] Again, we must realise that a minimally healthy environment is a precondition for the existence of personal integrity, unless we are willing to face a dying planet before we are willing to compromise personal integrity, which is ridiculous.

A version of consequentialism, of interest to environmentalists, is the view that actions are right or wrong insofar as their effects contribute to or deter from the integrity of an ecosystem. The land ethic is consequentialist, it evaluates actions and policies in respect to their effects on the overall integrity of ecosystems. Although Aldo Leopold was not explicitly a consequentialist, there are passages that support consequentialism as being central to his position. For example, when writing of a botched soil conservation program and the proposed remedy of 'more education,' he replies: 'The *net result* (my emphasis) is that we have more education and less soil.'[14] Leopold is opposed to versions of consequentialism that try to reduce the value of nature to economic self-interest of humans; but this is not to be confused with consequentialism in general. He was concerned about developing an ecological awareness, but the fundamental principle of the land ethic is 'A thing is right when it tends to preserve the integrity, stability, and beauty of the biotic community. It is wrong when it does otherwise.'[15] Clearly, that an action or a thing 'tends to preserve' is a causal property, not a type of motivation or consciousness from which the action originates. Therefore, the land ethic is consequentialist.

Callicott asks 'Is the land ethic prudential or deontological? In other words, Is the land ethic a matter of enlightened (collective, human) self-interest or does it genuinely admit non-human natural entities and nature as a whole to true moral standing?' But the question, as he defines it, is not a choice between prudential (suggesting utilitarian) and deontological (the anti-consequentialist position that a right action is one motivated by a proper sense of duty). The choice, as he poses it, is more between an anthropocentric or extended moral community. Clearly, the land ethic is a rejection of anthropocentrism. But a rejection of anthropocentrism does not imply a rejection of consequentialism. Anthropocentrism is a theory of value. Consequentialism is a theory of the factors relevant to an action being right or wrong. Therefore, Callicott has not proven, as he claims, 'that the land ethic is deontological (or duty oriented) rather than prudential.'[16] The land ethic, aside from its implications in regard to self-realisation, is a thoroughly consequentialistic (and, therefore, not a deontological) theory.

Actual consequentialism as a theoretical basis for issues in the preservation and restoration of the environment gives us one piece of the environmental ethics theory puzzle. Some might find it a perplexing conclusion, since the main thrust of recent work in environmental ethics theory has been extending to non-humans rights and interests traditionally reserved for humans. The *key* is seeing that environmental ethics confronts *two* logically separate questions – self-realisation and the preservation and restoration of the environment. The latter question most reasonably is cast in a consequentialist framework.

Notes

1 Devall and Sessions, 1985, pp. 66–9.

2 Callicott, 1987.

3 Ibid.

4 Taylor, 1981.

5 Callicott, 1987, pp. 186–214.

6 Scheffler, 1988.

7 Donagan, 1977.

8 Holbrook, 1988.

9 Singer, 1986.

10 Donagan, 1977.

11 Holbrook, 1988.

12 Singer, 1986.

13 Goodin, 1990.

14 Leopold, 1949, p. 209.
15 Ibid., pp. 224–5.
16 Callicott, 1987, p. 212.

References

Callicott, J. Baird 1980 'Animal Liberation: A Triangular Affair', *Environmental Ethics* 2(4): 311–38.

Callicott, J. Baird 1987 *Companion to A Sand County Almanac.* Madison, Wisconsin: University of Wisconsin Press.

Devall, Bill and Sessions, George 1985 *Deep Ecology.* Layton, Utah: Peregrine Smith.

Donagan, Alan 1977 *The Theory of Morality.* Chicago, Illinois: University of Chicago Press.

Goodin, Robert E. 1990 'Government House Utilitarianism', in Lincoln Allison (ed.) *The Utilitarian Response*, pp. 140–60. London: Sage Publications.

Holbrook, Daniel 1988 *Qualitative Utilitarianism.* Lanham, Maryland: University Press of America.

Leopold, Aldo 1949 *A Sand County Almanac.* Oxford: Oxford University Press.

Riley, Jonathan 1990 'Utilitarian Ethics and Democratic Government', in Lincoln Allison (ed.) *The Utilitarian Response*, pp. 161–92. London: Sage Publications.

Sartre, Jean-Paul 1956 *Being and Nothingness*, Hazel Barnes (trans.). New York: Philosophical Library.

Scheffler, Samuel (ed.) 1988 *Consequentialism and Its Critics.* Oxford: Oxford University Press.

Singer, Peter 1986 'Animal Liberation', in Donald Van DeVeer and Christine Pierce (eds) *People, Penguins, and Plastic Trees*, pp. 24–32. Belmont, California: Wadsworth.

Taylor, Paul W. 1981 'The Ethics of Respect for Nature', *Environmental Ethics* 3: 197–218.

Williams, Bernard 1973 'A Critique of Utilitarianism', in *Utilitarianism: For and Against*, pp. 75–150. Cambridge: Cambridge University Press.

6 | Deontological environmental ethics

ROBERT ELLIOT

This extract comes from a chapter on normative ethics in a book on environmental philosophy. Robert Elliot discussed human-centred, non-human-centred and consequentialist environmental ethics before this section and virtue-based environmental ethics afterwards. Deontological ethical theories tend to focus on 'doing what's right' and on moral duties, principles, rules and rights, largely independent of consequences. Historically the ideas of Immanuel Kant (1724–1804) about morality as a matter of duty have been central to deontological theories. Contract theories following the ideas of Thomas Hobbes (1588–1679) and John Locke (1632–1704) are also considered deontological because they suggest that we, as members of a community, support an agreement that creates moral rules, rights and duties and accept certain restrictions on the free pursuit of our individual interests. Contemporary examples of the use of deontology in environmental contexts include Garret Hardin's 'The tragedy of the commons' (Reading 18) and work on animal rights such as that of Tom Regan.

This reading does not cover all aspects of deontology but it does distinguish deontology from consequentialism, and it discusses rights theories as deontological, Kantianism and some of the practical implications of using deontology.

§ [...] Deontological ethics are often characterized as ethics of principle rather than ethics focused on promoting intrinsic value. Unlike consequentialist theories, they offer principles of obligation or duty that do not reduce to functions over value, allowing the judgment that actions are obligatory for reasons in addition to the value of their consequences. Deontological theories claim that certain kinds of action are obligatory, permissible, impermissible, and so on, in virtue of specific, non-consequential properties of that action. They do not, however, necessarily exclude such axiological or value assessments, and complete deontological assessments may require some prior axiological assessments.

Thus it might be claimed that, since some natural object has intrinsic value, it is obligatory not to destroy it. The property of being destructive of a thing with intrinsic value would, according to this ethic, be a wrong-making property; the relevant maxim or principle being 'do not destroy things which have intrinsic value.' While this maxim has about it the flavor of a consequentialist principle, the normative assessment is not carried out by calculating the loss of intrinsic value associated with the destruction of the object and figuring it into some principle of obligation, such as [... with ...] variants of consequentialism [...] – that is, a function over value. Instead, the wrongness of the act can be established without having to look beyond the fact that it involves destroying something of intrinsic value. There is, then, no suggestion that one need look to the consequences of such acts or that one ought to act in accordance with some function of the intrinsic value of the consequences of the act and that of its alternatives. There is, moreover, no suggestion that it is permissible to destroy something of lesser value in order to protect or create something of greater value, which is one reason some environmentalists have felt less unease about deontology than consequentialism. The difference is akin to the difference between a principle that enjoins us to minimize pain, which is consequentialist, and a principle that forbids us to cause pain, which is not consequentialist. Indeed it may be impermissible to act in ways that maximize, improve, or even maintain intrinsic value – for instance, in situations where the only means of doing one of these things involves the destruction of something of intrinsic value contrary to the prohibition on destroying such. There is, then, a deontological structure that would sustain a distinctively environmental normative ethic, the scope of which extends beyond human interests and concerns. Thus destroying or degrading the natural environment could be wrong because, among other things, it is an act of destroying things which possess natural intrinsic value. But the wrongness does not result from the reduction of value as such: the wrongness results from an independent non-consequentialist principle.

There are other ways of fitting a distinctively environmental ethic into a deontological structure. Theories of rights, for example, are often presented as deontological theories because they imply the proscription and prescription of acts independently of the consequences of those acts. Thus, someone's right to life might be said to result in an absolute proscription on taking that person's life, except perhaps in self-defense or in a judicial context, irrespective of the consequences. The fact that value is increased as a consequence is not, it is often claimed, an acceptable justification for violating the right. Much environmental ethics might be cast in terms of rights. Most obviously it makes sense to invoke the rights of non-human animals in objecting to the destruction of natural habitat. But some have wanted to extend the concept of rights beyond the set of sentient creatures, suggesting that, in addition, plants have rights, that species have rights, or that ecosystems have rights. This proliferation of rights generates problems. In the first place there is the issue of whether the extension of rights in these ways is conceptually sound (Feinberg 1974). Does it, for example, make sense to attribute rights to entities that do not even have desires, that are not even conscious? And do we even want to suggest that non-living natural items, such as rocks or glaciers or rivers, could have rights?

Equally important is the practical problem of how to process and adjudicate the barrage of rights claims that would be generated by such profligate deontological ethics. The problem would be ameliorated if we could be sure that the rights in question would not conflict, but that is not at all clear even where we are focusing only on the rights of humans. In the context of extended rights theories, conflicting rights seem inevitable, with attendant problems of weighing up, balancing, and adjudicating countless apparently competing rights claims. Furthermore, the problem seems more acute for a deontological theory than a consequentialist theory because the former eschews trade-offs based on consequences. How exactly do we respect the rights of every organism? Is there a hierarchy of rights? Is there a hierarchy of rights-bearing individuals, such that, for example, the rights of humans have priority over the rights of sentient non-humans which have priority over the rights of other living things? The answer, even in theory, is not clear and the ethic that suggests the principle might therefore be thought vacuous. The prospect of vacuousness is brought out if we consider the claim, often associated with the Norwegian philosopher Arne Naess's (1986) deep ecology view, that every living thing has an equal right to flourish. Life on earth is such, though, that particular organisms can flourish only if others do not. Taking the right literally seems to leave no room for action.

Some are tempted to say that the problem just sketched is the general one that affects ethical extensionism as the method for generating an environmental ethic, namely that things go awry when we focus on individual entities at too fine-grained a level. Such theorists might suggest that we should be focusing on macro-entities such as whole ecosystems or the biosphere as the pertinent rights bearers. This move might stem the proliferation of rights but it still leaves the problem of how to make sense of the claim that entities that lack consciousness or desires could have rights. Of course there is no parallel problem in the suggestion that they have intrinsic value, and so no problem in a deontological theory that prohibits the destruction of what has intrinsic value. It is odd, however, to suggest that they have rights in the sense that humans and sentient non-humans have rights. For one thing, unless an entity is conscious there seems no content to the suggestion that from its point of view things are going well or badly. And the point of rights theories seems to be to create a set of entitlements on the part of individuals that allow things to go well from an individual's point of view.

In any case, there would still be a residual ranking problem in working out the respective priorities of the rights of sentient creatures, ecosystems, and the biosphere. A simple solution would be to give absolute priority to biospheric rights. This solution would be unpalatable to many because it would demote human rights to little more than an afterthought, making human interests subservient to those of the biosphere. Perhaps, though, this is an idea that we could get used to if we are convinced of the intense ethical significance of the natural environment. While there are limits to the capacity of a deontological theory based on rights to support the moral sentiments expressed by many environmentalists, such a theory can accommodate many. Certainly, acts of environmental destruction and degradation will be wrong for human-centered and animal-centered reasons that a deontologist would likely find compelling. For example, such damage would wrongfully injure and kill non-humans and wrongfully impose costs and burdens on humans, including future humans. The attendant ethical concerns can be powerfully and coherently expressed in the language of rights.

There is a deontological theory, Kantianism, deriving from the views of the eighteenth-century German philosopher Immanuel Kant [...], that is similar in structure to the rights-based theories and which deserves some comment. The central tenet of Kantianism is that each person is an end in herself or himself, having a capacity for rational autonomy and therefore requiring respect as a person. The idea of respect for persons indeed might be thought to be the basis of theories of rights that, among other things, articulate and elaborate the idea of respect for persons. At first sight, Kantianism, emphasizing as it does respect for persons, might not seem to provide an amenable structure for anything much more than a human-centered environmental ethic. At least one prominent theorist, the American philosopher Paul Taylor, has, however, elaborated a normative environmental ethic with a Kantian flavor. Taylor (1986) asks us to see all living things as autonomous, in that, at the very least, they have biologically based goals that are definitive of the kinds of organism they are and that define for them what counts as flourishing. He suggests that just as Kantianism enjoins us to

63

respect the rational autonomy of persons, so too a naturalized Kantian-ism enjoins us to respect the natural autonomy of all living things. The force of Taylor's position derives from whatever success he might have in convincing us that there is a useful analogy between rational autonomy and natural autonomy, and, of course, our views about the significance of rational autonomy. And Taylor, by the way, does not seem to want natural autonomy to swallow up rational autonomy, seeking instead to maintain a moral distinction, with hierarchical implications, between persons and other living things.

The conceptual and proliferation problems that affected rights-based deontological theories are present in Taylor's theory. The analogy be-tween rational autonomy and natural autonomy might well founder on the fact that so much of the latter involves no consciousness of prefer-ences or desires. Although we might well see the point of allowing that non-sentient living things have a kind of autonomy, we might think the conceptual distance between the autonomy of, say, an orchid and that of a primate is too great to sustain the mooted ethical extension. Moreover, the theory runs into problems of ranking claims based on natural autonomy. How, for instance, do we adjudicate situations in which human welfare is promoted, or rational autonomy protected, at the cost of destroying entities, such as plants or microbes, that have natural autonomy? One response to these problems is to try to render Taylor's insights in a non-Kantian form. Thus we might accept that there is something ethically significant about natural autonomy but suggest that its significance is best articulated through the concept of intrinsic value. We can say that natural autonomy is a basis of intrinsic value and either plug that into a consequentialist framework or into a non-Kantian, non-rights-based deontological framework.

There is a final problem that should be sketched. Taken literally, deontological ethics apparently render impermissible actions that do not seem impermissible and that may even be obligatory. For instance, the degradation of some small area of the natural environment in order to create a firebreak may be necessary to ensure the protection of an extensive area. If what we value is wild nature, then surely it is permis-sible to make the firebreak even though it involves the destruction of items of value. Thus a strict deontology is likely to deliver normative conclusions that are difficult to accept. One response, not unproblem-atic, is to suggest a mixed ethic, containing both consequentialist and deontological components. If enough of value is at stake, then it may be judged permissible to act in a way that a strict deontology would proscribe. By the same token, the deontological component would act as a brake on consequentialist justifications of environmental degradation (Sylvan and Bennett 1994). [...]

References

Feinberg, J. (1974) 'The rights of animals and unborn generations', in *Philosophy and Environmental Crisis*, ed. W. Blackstone (Athens, Ga.: University of Georgia Press).

Naess, A. (1986) 'The deep ecological movement: some philosophical aspects', *Philosophical Inquiry* (8).

Sylvan, R. and Bennett, D. (1994) *The Greening of Ethics: From Human Chauvinism to Deep-Green Theory* (Cambridge: Whitehorse Press).

Taylor, P. (1986) *Respect for Nature* (Princeton: Princeton University Press).

Robert Elliot

7 | The virtues of ecological citizenship

JAMES CONNELLY

In this reading, James Connelly presents a case for applying virtue ethics to environmental action and links this to the emerging debate on ecological citizenship. Rather than developing an account of virtue ethics that rigidly applies Aristotle's ideas to the present, he explores how virtues are both private and social – arguing that virtues are dispositions of character but also contribute to the collective good. As a result, he does not see virtue ethics as necessarily opposed to other ethical approaches but as compatible with them. On this basis, Connelly develops an account of the duties of ecological citizenship as self-imposed rather than through a reciprocal contract – duties can exist without corresponding rights. The remainder of this extract explores the role of agency and motive in promoting eco-virtues and explores how citizens can use these to understand the reasons for acting responsibly.

§ [...] The starting point is the simple question, What are the appropriate responses to environmental problems? Clearly, externally motivated environmental actions are necessary but not sufficient. If flights are cheap, we will fly; if gas is cheap, we will drive. Some eco-citizens, already keen practitioners of environmental virtue, deliberately limit their choice of transport to what they deem environmentally sustainable; but most of us, most of the time, will act only in response to the external motivations of price, punishment, or prohibition. The use of legal or economic instruments is therefore a necessary part of the environmentally sustainable whole. Although these measures are valuable in their own way, however, they do not constitute the whole answer because they are all alike in providing a motive extrinsic to the desired goal or effect. External motivation will continue to be required for some purposes, especially to break through the deadlock of collective action problems, but legal instruments and economic incentives need to be supplemented by appropriate environmental virtues. Virtuous eco-citizens will internalize the purpose and value of good environmental practices, and their obedience will thus transcend mere compliance, going beyond it toward autonomous virtuous activity.[1] [...]

Considering virtues

To assert the relevance of the virtues to green politics and citizenship is not in itself to endorse virtue ethics as such. Virtues might be taken to be important without this necessarily entailing a commitment to a particular claim in metaethics. The position defended here is the first-order claim that consideration of the virtues is a crucial part of green ethics and politics because exercise of the virtues is practically efficacious. On this account, virtues concerning the environment are directed outward toward the realization of environmental goods (and justified by their success in producing those goods) rather than human well-being or happiness (eudaemonia) in the Aristotelian sense. It might therefore be said that an eco-virtue ethics as presented here is impure because the virtues, traditionally understood, are situated within a conception of human flourishing and presuppose an account of what it is to be fully human. In this, a virtue is a character trait that a human being needs to achieve eudaemonia; virtues are thus teleological, the telos being internal to a conception of human flourishing. The account presented below, however, takes the telos to be primarily outwardly directed and consequential, and the account of the virtues is accordingly couched in instrumental terms. To that extent, our use of the virtues has to be justified according to their success in achieving environmental goods; the corollary is that if they fail to achieve these goods, we would have no interest in promoting them. Of course, we could always square the circle by making the bold claim that what is good for the environment is ipso facto good for human flourishing – but having to argue particular ontological claims prior to putting the virtues to good use is not my preferred starting point. For my purposes, then, a virtue is a character trait a human being needs to realize environmental ends; if eudaemonia is also achieved, so much the better, but that is not the direct focus. So let us accept that our use of the virtues is, in terms of virtue ethics per se, impure; but then, we *are* dealing with the 'dirty' virtues. Here we can follow Mill, who suggests that virtue although 'not naturally and originally part of the end, is capable of becoming so; and in those who love it disinterestedly it has become so, and is desired and cherished, not as a means to happiness, but as a part of their happiness' (1949, 200). In order to use the language of virtue, we are not restricted only to the Aristotelian idiom.

Virtues go beyond their bearers; they are not private but social, and their exercise therefore requires a conception of the common good. This point was made clear by Green: 'All virtues are really social; or, more properly, the distinction between social and self-regarding duties is a false one. Every virtue is self-regarding in the sense that it is a disposition, or habit of will, directed to an end which the man presents to himself as his good; every virtue is social in the sense that unless the good to which the will is directed is one in which the well-being of society in some form or other is involved, the will is not virtuous at all' (1966: §247). In the case of the eco-virtues, this common good (which I shall term 'sustainable common environmental good') needs to be further developed and specified. It is also important to remember that the conception of the good is not a pregiven entity but something itself in the process of being defined, molded, and brought into being. One of the key virtues will thus need to be the virtue of deliberating on what the sustainable common environmental good itself is. In the phrase sustainable common environmental good, the word *sustainable* appears at first glance simply to be added to an already-accepted idea of a common good. But it is rather more than a mere addition: it is an emergent feature arising out of a reflection on what the common good requires at this point in our history. We can be sure that if we are deliberating on the common good at all, then we will at the same time be including within it considerations of sustainability and related goals. [...]

The analysis of virtue

We need, then, to develop internally motivated, environmentally sensitive dispositions – virtues. These virtues constitute a key part of ecological citizenship. A virtue, fully formed, transcends mere compliance with law or policy, because it includes as part of itself the appropriate motivation and intentionality. Nevertheless, my focus here is primarily on consequences, not the internal features of moral character, and my claim is that environmental virtue is more practically environmentally effective than the alternatives. I am here not considering virtue as an intrinsic good but as an efficacious set of dispositions. My account is, to this extent, compatible with at least some versions of utilitarianism and is not dependent on an Aristotelian conception of virtue. I leave open the question of whether or not in the end environmental virtue has to be grounded in something like an Aristotelian account. My claim, then, is based on the intuition that virtues work; it avoids the necessity of adopting a strong view of the unity of humans and nature in human flourishing. This is because for the sake of environmental action, it is better to move forward with the resources we already know we possess, rather than wait for confirmation of stronger ethico-ontological claims around which it is harder to secure consensus.

What is a virtue? By contrast with the state of affairs in which the motivation for action does not necessarily coincide with the intention to do good, for a virtue approach motivation and intention are brought together. A virtue is a settled disposition to act in a certain sort of way. The formula for virtuous action is: I am *motivated* to do environmental good for the sake of the environment (or humanity) and I *intend* to do that environmental good. My motivation stretches back before the individual action and looks ahead beyond the action; I have a settled disposition to act in certain ways (including a disposition to consider my actions in a certain way) and this settled disposition is environmental virtue. When I act, I act intentionally, taking the environment as either the direct or indirect object of my action. Of course, not all action is explicitly intentional where 'intention' implies deliberation; the whole point of a virtue is that it becomes second nature, albeit a nature that (unlike the natural world) is affected by being known, and is in principle malleable to our intellectual touch.

Virtues are not merely habits, although they include elements of the habitual. They are habits critically reflected on and reflection habituated. A virtue is also the mean between two extremes or vices. This requires judgment, which is reflective; hence, the exercise of virtue must be reflective. Virtues are therefore critical dispositions – or at least, dispositions of which we can and should become critically aware, although we shouldn't be aware of them to the detriment of action. They cannot literally *be* second nature; they have to be reason naturalized through emotion and emotion rationalized through reason. Virtues cannot be acquired once for all. They are (and have to be) in constant flux; they exist only in use and there is no virtue at an instant. Over time, even the same disposition, which in one sense never alters, is nevertheless undergoing constant change as the agent deals with different problems in unique circumstances of judgment. Virtues are character traits, dispositions of character, but more than just dispositions – they are excellences of character. [...]

The duties of ecological citizenship

Ecological citizenship is characterized not by rights but by the self-imposed duties of the citizen. Duties are commitments that require the free exercise of the virtues to identify and perform them. Liberal theories of citizenship tend to focus on the granting and maintaining of rights; civic republican views focus on a deeper reciprocity between rights and duties. Ecological citizenship is different from the former in focusing its concern on duties, not rights, and it is different from the latter in being nonterritorial. This claim can be challenged on the grounds that citizenship is necessarily territorial, thereby making a nonterritorial citizenship a contradiction in terms. This is a powerful point. Nevertheless, we have to act *as if* (at the very least) we have global citizenship responsibilities for the simple reason that environmental problems are not locally containable. And we can go further by suggesting that if our responsibilities extend as far as the bounds of our community and if our community is increasingly globalized both politically and commercially, then the claim that citizenship is nonterritorial in the traditional sense seems a reasonable one to make. Ecological citizenship thus conceived embraces duties that are not limited in scope to time or place, and that are voluntarily self-imposed. The source of the duties is not the product of a reciprocal, contractual, social set of arrangements. Rather, it is the outcome of a recognition of the fact that we are already affecting (or have affected) others. The leading proponent of the view just articulated, Dobson, suggests that 'while this is a citizenship with international and intergenerational dimensions, its responsibilities are asymmetrical. Its obligations fall on those, precisely, with the capacity to "always already" act on others' (2003, 49–50). Those affected, that is, feel the heavy tread of others' ecological footprint; relationships thus arise with those on whom it impacts. These impacts will be asymmetrical because of the differential size of ecological footprints. As Dobson notes, 'The relevant cleavage is that between "globalizing" and "globalized" individuals, where the former is taken to refer to those whose action can "impact at a distance," and the latter to those whose actions cannot' (115).

In short, ecological citizenship is not so much about rights as about obligations. Bur can there be self-imposed duties without corresponding rights? That depends. Duties and rights are not necessarily symmetrical. In this they differ from reciprocally defined concepts such as *winner* and *loser* and *winning* and *losing*, each of which implies the other. Of course it is true that if I have a right, someone else (or some agency) has a corresponding duty; and again, if I, as a citizen, have rights, we might expect that I will be required to assume the duties of citizenship (this view would be typical of a civic republican perspective). But if I have a duty, it does not necessarily follow that there is a corresponding right. There is no difficulty in saying that we have duties toward people, animals, or things where we don't suppose that they have a corresponding right, merely that they are the object of our dutiful concern. In eco-citizenship, then, it might be said that we have duties to other people; they in turn have corresponding rights. But should we understand this literally or rhetorically? Everyone, as claimed above, has an equal right to an equal share of environmental goods. It seems reasonable to proceed to the conclusion that everyone therefore has an equal duty to maintain those rights or at least not to act so as to knowingly violate them. This position could, however, leave us with moral demands that are impossible to fulfill if it is taken to imply that we should always be acting positively so as to maintain rights, and it is wise to avoid making unreasonable and excessive demands. It might be that not a great deal is lost if we adopt the position that we have duties toward those who have had less than their share of the world's environmental goods – a duty that does not require reciprocity. But this is a moot point: to deny the applicability of rights in such a context might be taken to imply the relative lack of importance of the duties thus specified. On a related point, consider the nonhuman natural world. I suggest that we have a duty toward it, but that it has no rights per se – rights being conceptually difficult to ascribe to beings incapable, even in principle, of being part of a rights-making and rights-maintaining community. [...]

Ecological citizenship comprises the ecological duties together with the virtues appropriate to their fulfillment. This includes the duty of deliberating on duties: we have a duty to ask what our duty is. And even where our duty seems obvious – for example, to reduce the size of our environmental footprint – we should still question this and ask exactly how it might be translated into specific actions. Here, we should perhaps distinguish between duties as general goals or aspirations and specific duties appropriate to particular occasions. The latter cannot be determined in advance even where the general features are known. A concrete duty only becomes actual at the moment of acting, and the content of that duty at that point is a combination of the circumstances, ideals, principles, character, and virtues of the actor.[2] An eco-virtue is an internally motivated ecological thoughtfulness leading to action. The virtue of rational deliberation, avoiding the twin vices of insufficient thoughtfulness and too much thought at the expense of action, is essential to the proper formulation and understanding of our eco-duties. For example, the general duty to reduce the size of our eco-footprint is refined both by investigating expedient practical responses, and through reflection on our place in the world and differential use of its resources. An eco-duty is derived from an assessment of the size of our eco-footprint and the extent of our departure from equality in the way we tread the earth. Ecological duties are therefore not equal; they vary between individuals and between groups and nations. Those who have already consumed (and continue to consume) most have correspondingly greater duties.

Agency and action: promoting virtue?

To what extent is it possible to promote the life of eco-virtue? What role can the state have in this? Or are we forced to conclude that (virtue being voluntary) it cannot be promoted by the state and that attempts to promote the voluntary through the means available to the state are by their very nature self-stultifying?

The exercise of the virtues, even at its most developed, does not imply that we cease to need rules and regulation: they cannot be dispensed with, but neither are they primary. To merely live by rule is no virtue; but without rules there can be no virtues. Rules are refreshed by active virtuous action and reflection, and a framework of supporting legislation is desirable as a reminder to those who ought to develop the virtues, as a guide to those who are developing the virtues, or as a coherent and reliable underpinning and support for the actions of the already virtuous. Although virtues are private responsibilities, their possession is a public good, and their development and reinforcement is a public as well as private duty.

How are people to be drawn into the practice of environmental virtue? One answer might lie in designing deliberative institutions. But deliberative and other intellectualist approaches are not enough. They need to be part of something bigger in which people are drawn in by doing. The idea of 'enabling environmental practice' explored by Weston (1994) is relevant here. This includes but goes beyond tax and charge paying (although this is important in not only changing behavior but also encouraging people to reflect on their behavior). Practical participation can induce virtuous action; when reflected on, the virtue thus induced can become conscious of itself as such. *Being virtuous precedes virtuous being.* Virtue cannot be theorized into being; one must participate in a practice to discover its internal goods and goals.

It should be remembered, however, that we are not looking for moral perfection but merely virtue enough to achieve our environmental ends. We need sufficient virtue, not perfect virtue, and here we reopen the question of the state's role. A virtue-centered approach must include a consideration of both agency and motive. In the case of prohibition, the agent is the state compelling action through the threat of external compulsion. In the case of economic incentives, agency is shared in that the state facilitates action through external incentive rather than internal motivation. And in the case of duty or virtuous action, the action is internally motivated and the state cannot directly promote this; but can it be promoted *indirectly*?

Everyone must make their character for themselves. State action cannot directly make a person moral because acts done under compulsion tend to lose their character as moral acts. [...] Participation in certain sorts of activity encourages the development of appropriate ways of thinking and doing, and the state can encourage this. Again, the existence of a sense of approval or disapproval toward certain actions and ends as expressed in policy statements, legislation, differential taxation, charges, and appropriate intervention (for example, facilitating recycling through the provision of separate bins and collections) is influential in encouraging people to act in ways that become habitual and might become virtuous. [...]

Conclusion: some eco-virtues

Up to this point I have discussed virtues in general, but few in particular. Perhaps I should give some clues as to which virtues are the eco-virtues? Faith, hope, and charity seem appropriate to any list of virtues, as do the four cardinal virtues of courage, wisdom, justice, and moderation. If justice is the key virtue, the others will be subordinate to it, but it is not part of my present purpose to establish a hierarchy of environment virtues, merely to indicate what some of them might be.

Frugality might be considered a candidate as a central environmental virtue, with care, patience, righteous indignation, accountability, asceticism, commitment, compassion, concern, and cooperation making up the numbers. Of course, not all these virtues are specifically environmental – but we acknowledged earlier that environmental and nonenvironmental virtues would overlap, with old ones typically being put to new uses, and extending their scope and reference. This follows from the fact that we are seeking to generate a practical conception of a sustainable common environmental good, which is a modification of the common good, not an entirely new aspiration unrelated to all our previous goals and ideals. It might be suggested that not all these virtues are citizenship virtues, that some are private not public virtues. But this objection is invalid because one important difference flowing from the character of the eco-virtues is precisely that in the environmental context, the distinction between public and private virtues (and the related issue of what are often referred to as masculine and feminine virtues) has to be reconsidered. Feminine virtues are typically those associated with domesticity and the private realm, and masculine virtues with the public realm. On this understanding, many eco-virtues such as care, love, compassion, and so on, are cast as feminine virtues. This might be so, but we need to recognize that they should apply both in the public and private realms because their end lies in their contribution to sustaining and preserving the natural environment.

Whatever their precise nature, any putative list of virtues and vices could be extended a tremendously long way – for example, Wensveen identifies 189 virtues and 174 vices in the post-1970 environmental litera-ture. If we now turn to vice, we can perhaps agree with her that hubris or pride is first on the traditional list of sins, and should also be regarded as one of the major eco-sins (Wensveen 2000, 98). It is notable how many sins translate easily into eco-sins – envy, anger, sloth, greed, and gluttony being good examples, with their avoidance obviously necessary for any sustainable future. Other eco-sins clearly include exploitation, cruelty, willful ignorance, cynicism, and despair. Yet the point of this chapter was not to provide a definitive list of virtues so much as to argue for the importance of the virtue approach within environmen-tal citizenship. So I conclude with the comment that environmental virtues are continuous and reliable dispositions, internally motivated, but that a sustainable society will continue to require law, regulation, and economic incentives whose presence serves as a moral indicator of values and goals. The environmentally conscientious will internalize this awareness and consider how best to act on it; others won't, but at least their actions will be circumscribed by the law and public policy – and the possibility of choosing the good for its own sake remains open to them. Virtue is about doing those things that we should all do and yet that we can easily forget to do. This might be turning off lights, switch-ing off the car engine when waiting in a line of traffic, or minimizing our consumption of much-traveled and overly packaged out-of-season goods.[3] The virtuous are already minded to do what should be done; they remember. The potentially eco-virtuous life is characterized by a need for reminding. It is in the gap between minding and being reminded that encouraging the virtues of environmental citizenship can make an important difference.

Notes

1 For a related discussion of virtue and self-motivated compli-ance, see Pellikaan and van der Veen (2002, 28–46).

2 For a fuller account of this understanding of the nature of duty, see Connelly (2003).

3 For example, it is worth remem-bering (and acting on the knowledge) that 'a kiwi fruit flown from New Zealand to Britain emits five times its own weight in greenhouse gases' (Williams 2004, 286).

References

Connelly, J. 2003. *Metaphysics, Method, and Politics: The Political Philosophy of R. G. Collingwood.* Exeter, UK: Imprint Academic.

Dobson, A. 2003. *Citizenship and the Environment.* Oxford: Oxford University Press.

Green, T. H. 1966. *Lectures on the Principles of Political Obligation.* London: Longmans.

Mill, J. S. 1949. 'Utilitarianism'. In *The English Utilitarians*, ed. J. Plamenatz. Oxford: Blackwell.

Pellikaan, H., and R. J. van der Veen. 2002. *Environmental Dilemmas and Policy Design*. Cambridge: Cambridge University Press.

Wensveen, L. Van. 2000. *Dirty Virtues: The Emergence of Ecological Virtue Ethics*. New York: Humanity Books.

Weston, A. 1994. *Back to Earth: Tomorrow's Environmentalism*. Philadelphia: Temple University Press.

Williams, J. 2004. *Fifty Facts that Should Change the World*. Cambridge: Icon Books.

James Connelly

Summary of part one

MARTIN REYNOLDS, CHRIS BLACKMORE
AND MARK J. SMITH

The readings in this part follow a trajectory from an emphasis on concern for less formalized notions regarding care for the environment towards more formalized ideas about being accountable for any harm and wrong done to the environment. Some significant points of relevance for policy and action on environmental responsibility can be briefly summarized:

- Expressing an attitude of care – however alien it may seem in a prevailing cultural context – can have significant impacts, both geographically and across generations. The continuing significance of contributions from over fifty years ago – as well as the great philosophies of ancient Greece, the Eastern traditions of Taoism and Buddhism, and the many indigenous cultural traditions belonging especially to countries of the global South (countries conventionally regarded as having less global economic power and wealth) – is testament to a lasting legacy. In environmental responsibility there are rich traditions to inform our learning and nurturing with regard to caring for the environment.

- Ethics is not just a fixed body of knowledge relevant to environmental responsibility which is reserved for academia, but a wider tradition that invites action in terms of normative ideas regarding *what* ought to be a better way of living in and with our natural world and *how* best to act responsibly through appropriate moral agency. Ethics also invites political questions regarding appropriate space for deliberating on environmental issues, raising questions regarding *why* some issues are deemed more important than others, *why* some agents or means of agency are deemed more important than others and *why* citizens should understand the reasons for being environmentally responsible.

The three authors chosen to represent the three ethical traditions relating to environmental responsibility were selected on the basis of their appreciation of the need for complementarities rather than competition between ethical traditions. The consequentialist tradition would appear to particularly invite action based on scientific inquiry and the need for policy to be informed by appropriate measures of success, reflecting the intrinsic value of nature. This raises questions regarding what measures of success are important and who establishes those measures. The deontological tradition focuses more on the rules, laws and regulations informing environmental decision-making. How can appropriate constraints and obligations be codified by contracts and agreements to inhibit wrongdoing? What are the consequences of such decision-making based on behavioural rules and regulations, and to what extent should these anticipated consequences be attended to as part of the decision-making process? How might we better engage with the natural world, affording rights and autonomy to non-human nature? Finally, the tradition of virtue ethics invites questions regarding the different ways of supporting eco-virtuous behaviour – ways of transcending the dualistic bridge between living by rules alone and living without rules, both of which may be seen as non-virtuous. More specifically, what is the individual citizen's and state's role in promoting virtuous action?

TWO | **Nature matters**

Introduction to part two

MARTIN REYNOLDS

Asking the question 'what matters?' in relation to environmental responsibility can elicit a range of responses at different levels of engagement.
Clearly *nature* matters, but nature can matter directly, in terms of, say,
protecting threatened species or vulnerable ecosystems such as a tropical
rainforest or a whole continent like Antarctica, or indirectly through the
various forums of human deliberation on what matters, such as local
environmental protest groups or intergovernmental panels. Whatever
level of engagement is deemed relevant, as humans we may acknowledge that we are integral parts of the natural world. The flourishing
of planet Earth is dependent on the way in which our human social
worlds integrate with the biophysical natural world. Our engagement
with non-human nature, either directly or indirectly, circumscribes how
we care for nature and bear accountability for our impacts on nature in
the past, present and future. The chapters in this part explore different
manifestations of this engagement and their implications for improving
environmental responsibility.

The first reading, from Stephen Talbott, suggests the metaphor of
'conversation' as being helpful in thinking about the integral relationship between human and non-human nature. He regards the notion of
ecological conversation as being relevant to two perspectives on nature,
preservationist and managerialist – perspectives that align respectively
with the two dimensions of environmental responsibility discussed in
the Introduction, caring and accountability.

The next two readings explore two types of conversation – ethics and
science – in drawing out issues of importance for environmental responsibility. Andrew Light describes four key debates in environmental ethics
that have shaped the way in which nature is valued. While dialogues are
important for creating respect for the non-human natural world, Light
adds a note of caution regarding the need for a more relevant pragmatic
language so as to inform policy design and action. Eric Higgs is similarly
cautious about the language of science in ecological restoration initiatives. He argues for a distinction between the more focused scientific
endeavours of restoration ecology and the wider conversations concerning
ecological restoration in drawing out issues that matter.

The language used in any conversation is clearly shaped and limited by the way in which we frame nature and our involvement in the natural world. Ronald Moore identifies an apparent paradox in framing nature – that while we inevitably use framing devices to value nature, a core attribute or value of nature is that it is essentially unframed. As implied by Moore, the framing devices themselves suggest an arena of importance for environmental responsibility. The way in which environmental issues are framed can prompt different levels of responsibility. In the next chapter, two authors explore the concept of systems thinking as a purposeful way of framing. Fritjof Capra regards systems thinking as ecological thinking and argues for this to be the basis of a more relevant language for environmental responsibility. He describes this in terms of ecoliteracy – a language that reflects essential interrelationships and interdependencies among entities. On the other hand, Werner Ulrich signals the importance of applying a more precise systems language embodying a critical perspective, particularly when engaging with important issues of sustainability. According to Ulrich, a critical systems perspective offers humility in accepting the limitations of holistic approaches – the impossibility of framing all interrelationships and interdependencies – and a more explicit ethical dimension in appreciating multiple perspectives on what matters.

The last two chapters in this part focus more on the type of conversational space necessary for appropriate policy design and eco-citizenship. Picking up from Andrew Light's argument on the need for a more publicly engaged environmental philosophy, Robyn Eckersley explores the value and some limitations of environmental pragmatism as a more inclusive language for informing policy design, suggesting the need also to allow space for less formalized rationales and grassroots activism. Finally, in calling for cognitive justice, Shiv Visvanathan argues the need to continually develop and renegotiate appropriate conversational space in which scientists and lay citizens are recognized as legitimate co-contributors.

8 | Toward an ecological conversation

STEPHEN TALBOTT

The essay from which this edited extract comes reaches the core of environmental responsibility. Stephen Talbott argues from an explicitly human-centred perspective, challenging us to explore the relationship with the ecological world – the Other – in terms of human conversation. After putting forward two contrasting perspectives on environment – the radical preservationist and scientific management – the author illustrates the impoverishment of both in terms of mystifying or technically alienating non-human nature. 'Conversation' is used as a metaphor for identifying, bringing to light and engaging with what matters in environmental responsibility. The author is a senior researcher at the Nature Institute and published the original version of this article in NetFuture #27 (10 January 2002), available at netfuture.org/2002/Jan1002_127.html.

§ The chickadee was oblivious to its surroundings and seemed almost machine-like, if enfeebled, in its single-minded concentration: take a seed, deliver a few futile pecks, then drop it; take a seed, peck-peck-peck, drop it; take a seed ... The little bird, with its unsightly, disheveled feathers, almost never managed to break open the shell before losing its talons' clumsy grip on the seed. I walked up to its feeder perch from behind and gently tweaked its tail feathers. It didn't notice.

My gesture was, I suppose, an insult, although I felt only pity for this creature – pity for the hopeless obsession driving it in its weakened state. There were several sick chickadees at my feeder that winter a few years ago, and I began to learn why some people view feeding stations themselves as an insult to nature. A feeder draws a dense, 'unnatural' population of birds to a small area. This not only encourages the spread of disease, but also evokes behavioral patterns one might never see in a less artificial habitat. [...]

But by what right do I encourage tameness in creatures of the wild? The classic issue here has to do with how we should assess our impacts upon nature. Two views, if we drive them to schematic extremes for purposes of argument, conveniently frame the debate:

On one side, with an eye to the devastation of ecosystems worldwide, we can simply try to rid nature of all human influence. The sole ideal is pristine, untouched wilderness. The human being, viewed as a kind of disease organism within the biosphere, should be quarantined as far as possible. Call this 'radical preservationism.'

On the other side, impressed by our society's growing technical sophistication, we can urge the virtues of scientific management to counter the various ongoing threats to nature. Higher-yielding, genetically engineered vegetables, fruits, grains, livestock, fish, and trees – intensively monocropped and cultivated with industrial precision – can, we're told, supply human needs on reduced acreages, with less environmental impact. [...]

The problem with scientific management, founded as it is on the hope of successful prediction and control, is that complex natural systems have proven notoriously unpredictable and uncontrollable. [...]

[T]he real solution to the dispute between radical preservationists and scientific managers requires us to escape the assumptions common to both. Why, after all, does [one grant] that acceptable 'messing' with ecosystems would have to be grounded in successful prediction and control?

Once we make this assumption, of course, we are likely either to embrace such calculated control as a natural extension of our technical reach, or else reject it as impossible. And yet, when I sit with the chickadees, messing with their habitat, it does not feel like an exercise in prediction and control. My aim is to get to know the birds, and to understand them. Maybe this makes a difference.

It is certainly true, in one sense or another, that 'the limits of our knowledge should define the limits of our practice.' But we need to define the sense carefully. By what practice can we extend our knowledge, if we may never act without already possessing perfect knowledge?

Our inescapable ignorance mandates great caution – a fact our society has been reluctant to accept. Yet we cannot make any principle of caution absolute. The physician who construes the precept, 'First, do no harm,' as an unambiguous and definitive rule can no longer act at all, because only perfect prediction and control could guarantee the absence of harm. Those of us who urge precaution must not bow before the technological idols we are trying to smash. We can never perfectly know the consequences of our actions because we are *not* dealing with machines. We are called to live between knowledge and ignorance, and it is as dangerous to make ignorance the excuse for radical inaction as it is to found action upon the boast of perfect knowledge.

There is an alternative to the ideal of prediction and control. It helps, in approaching it, to recognize the common ground beneath scientific managers and those who see all human 'intrusion' as pernicious. Both camps regard nature as a world in which the human being cannot meaningfully participate. To the advocate of pristine wilderness untouched by human hands, nature presents itself as an inviolable and largely unknowable Other; to the would-be manager, nature is a collection of objects so disensouled and unrelated to us that we can take them as a mere challenge for our technological inventiveness. Both stances deprive us of any profound *engagement* with the world that nurtured us.

My own hope for the future lies in a third way. Perhaps we have missed this hope because it is too close to us. Each of us participates in at least one domain where we grant the autonomy and infinite worth of the Other while also acting boldly to affect and sometimes even rearrange the welfare of the Other. I mean the domain of human relations.

We do not view the sovereign individuality and inscrutability of our fellows as a reason to do nothing that affects them. But neither do we view them as mere objects for a technology of control.

How *do* we deal with them? We engage them in conversation.

We converse to become ourselves

I would like to think that what all of us, preservationists and managers alike, are really trying to understand is how to conduct an ecological conversation. We cannot predict or control the exact course of a conversation, nor do we feel any such need – not, at least, if we are looking for a *good* conversation. Revelations and surprises lend our exchanges much of their savor. We don't want predictability; we want respect, meaning, and coherence. A satisfying conversation is neither rigidly programmed nor chaotic; somewhere between perfect order and total surprise we look for a creative tension, a progressive and mutual deepening of insight, a sense that we are getting somewhere worthwhile.

The movement is essential. This is why we find no conclusive resting place in Aldo Leopold's famous dictum. 'A thing is right when it tends to preserve the integrity, stability, and beauty of the biotic community. It is wrong when it tends otherwise' (1970, p. 262).

Integrity and beauty, yes. But in what sense stability? Nature, like us, exists – preserves its integrity – only through continual self-transformation. Mere preservation would freeze all existence in an unnatural stasis, denying the creative destruction, the urge toward self-transcendence, at the world's heart. Scientific management, on the other hand, reduces evolutionary change to arbitrariness by failing to respect the independent character of the Other, through which all integral change arises. [...]

[C]onsider what it might mean to engage nature in respectful conversation. One can venture a few reasonably straightforward observations.

In any conversation it is, in the first place, perfectly natural to remedy one's ignorance by putting *cautious* questions to the Other. Every experimental gardening technique, every new industrial process, every different kind of bird feeder is a question put to nature. And, precisely because of the ignorance we are trying to remedy, there is always the possibility that the question itself will prove indelicate or otherwise an occasion for trouble. (My bird feeder was the wrong kind, conducive to the spread of disease. And you can quite reasonably argue that I should have investigated the issues and risks more thoroughly before installing my first feeder.)

In a respectful conversation such lapses are continually being committed and assimilated, becoming the foundation for a deeper, because more knowledgeable, respect. The very fact that we recognize ourselves as putting questions to nature rather than asserting brash control encourages us to anticipate the possible responses of the Other before we act, and to be considerate of the actual response, adjusting ourselves to it, when it comes.

This already touches on a second point: in a conversation we are always compensating for past inadequacies. As every student of language knows, a later word can modify the meaning of earlier words. The past can in this sense be altered and redeemed. We all know the bitter experience of words blurted out unwisely and irretrievably, but we also know the healing effects of confession and penance.

This in turn points us to a crucial third truth. At any given stage of a conversation, there is never a single right or wrong response. We can legitimately take a conversation in any number of healthy directions, each with different shades of meaning and significance.

Moreover, coming up with my response is not a matter of choosing among a range of alternatives already there, already defined by the current state of the exchange. My responsibility is creative; what alternatives exist depends in part on what new alternatives I can bring into being. Gandhi engendered possibilities for nonviolent resistance that were not widely known before his time, and the developers of solar panels gave us new ways to heat our homes. If we have any 'fixed' obligation, it is the obligation not to remain fixed but freely to transcend ourselves.

All conversation, then, is inventive, continually escaping its previous bounds. Unfortunately, our modern consciousness wants to hypostatize nature – to grasp clearly and unambiguously what this 'thing' is so that we can preserve it. But the notorious difficulties in defining what nature is – what we need to preserve – are no accident. There is no such thing as a nature wholly independent of our various acts to preserve (or destroy) it. You cannot define any ecological context over against one of its creatures – least of all over against the human being. If it is true that the creature becomes what it is only by virtue of the context, it is also true that the context becomes what it is only by virtue of the creature.

This can be a hard truth for environmental activists to accept, campaigning as we usually are to save 'it,' whatever 'it' may be. In conversational terms, the Other does not exist independently of the conversation. We cannot seek to preserve 'it,' because there is no 'it' there; we can only seek to preserve the integrity and coherence of the conversation through which both it and we are continually transforming ourselves. Hypostatization is always an insult because it removes the Other from the conversation, making an object of it and denying the living, shape-changing, conversing power within it.

Finally, conversation is always particularizing. I cannot converse with an abstraction or stereotype – a 'democrat' or 'republican,' an 'industrialist' or an 'activist,' or, for that matter, a 'preservationist' or a 'scientific manager.' I can converse only with a specific individual, who puts his own falsifying twist upon every label I apply. Likewise, I cannot converse with a 'wetland' or 'threatened species.' I may indeed *think about* such abstractions, but this thinking is not a conversation, just as my discoursing upon children is not a conversation with my son.

Permission and responsibility

How, then, shall we act? There will be many rules of thumb, useful in different circumstances. But I'm convinced that, under pressure of intense application, they will all converge upon the most frightful, because most exalted, principle of all. It's a principle voiced, albeit with more than a little trepidation, by my colleague at The Nature Institute, Craig Holdrege: 'You can do anything as long as you take responsibility for it' (2001).

Frightful? Yes. The first thing to strike most hearers will be that impossibly permissive *anything*. What environmentalist would dare speak these words at a convention of American industrialists?

But hold on a minute. How could this principle sound so irresponsibly permissive when its whole point is to frame permission in terms of responsibility? Apparently, the idea of responsibility doesn't carry that much gravity for us – and isn't this precisely because we are less accustomed to think of nature in the context of responsible conversation than of technological manipulation? Must we yield in this to the mindset of the managers?

If we do take our responsibility seriously, then we have to live with it. It means that a great deal depends on us – which also means that a great power of abuse rests on us. Holdrege's formulation gives us exactly what any sound principle must give us: the possibility of a catastrophic misreading in either of two opposite directions. We can accept the permission without the responsibility, or we can view the responsibility as denying us the permission. Both misreadings pronounce disaster. The only way to get at any balanced rule of behavior, any principle of organic wholeness, is to enter into conversation with it, preventing its diverse movements from running off in opposite directions, but allowing them to weave their dynamic and tensive unity through our own flexible thinking.

'You can do anything if you take responsibility for it.' An ill-intentioned one-sidedness can certainly make of this a mere permission without responsibility. But then, too, as we have seen, taking on the burden of responsibility without the permission ('First, do no harm – never, under any circumstance; do not even risk it') renders us catatonic.

Permission and responsibility must be allowed to play into each other. When we deny permission by being too assiduous in erecting barriers against irresponsibility, we are also erecting barriers against the exercise of responsibility. The first sin of the ecological thinker is to forget that there are no rigid opposites. There is no growth without decay, and no decay without growth. So, too, there is no opportunity for responsible behavior without the risk of irresponsible behavior.

'But doesn't all this leave us dangerously rudderless, drifting on relativistic seas? Surely we need more than a general appeal to responsibility! How can we responsibly direct ourselves without an understanding of the world and without the guidelines provided by such an understanding?'

Yes, understanding is the key. We need the guidelines it can bring. But these must never be allowed to freeze our conversation. This is evident enough in all human intercourse. However profound my understanding of the other person, I must remain open to the possibilities of his (and my) further development – possibilities that our very conversation may serve. [...]

The Nature Institute where I work sits amid the pastures of a biodynamic farm. The cows in these pastures have not been de-horned – a point of principle among biodynamic farmers. Recently I asked Holdrege whether he thought one could responsibly de-horn cows, a nearly universal practice in American agriculture.

'How does de-horning look from the cow's perspective? That's the first thing you have to ask,' he replied. When you observe the ruminants, he went on, you see that they all lack upper incisors, and they all possess horns or antlers, a four-chambered stomach, and cloven hooves.

If you look carefully at the animals, you begin to sense the significance of these linked elements even before you fully understand the relation between them. They seem to imply each other. Do you understand the nature of the implication? So here already an obligation presses upon you if you want to de-horn cattle: you must investigate how the horns relate to the entire organism.

Given his own observations of the cow (Holdrege 1997) and given his discussions with farmers who have noted the different behavior of cows with and without horns – and given also the lack of any compelling reason for de-horning when the cows are raised in a healthy manner – Holdrege's own conclusion is: 'Unusual situations aside, I don't see how we can responsibly de-horn cows.' [...]

The question of what *belongs* to an animal or a plant or a habitat is precisely the question of wholeness and integrity. It is a question foreign and inaccessible to conventional thinking simply because we long ago quit asking it. We had to have quit asking it when we began feeding animal remains to herbivores such as cows, and when we began raising chickens, with their beaks cut off, in telephone-book-sized spaces.

Most dramatically, we had to have quit asking it by the time genetic engineers, borrowing from the philosophy of the assembly line, began treating organisms as arbitrary collections of interchangeable mechanisms. There is no conversing with a random assemblage of parts. So it is hardly surprising, even if morally debilitating, that the engineer is not required to live alongside the organisms whose destiny he casually scrambles. He is engaged, not in a conversation, but a mad, free-associating soliloquy.

Approaching mystery

Our refusal of the ecological conversation arises on two sides. We can, in the first place, abandon the conversation on the assumption that whatever speaks through the Other is wholly mysterious and beyond our ken. This all too easily becomes a positive embrace of ignorance.

I do not see how anyone can look with genuine openness at the surrounding world without a sense of mystery on every hand. Reverence toward this mystery is the prerequisite for all wise understanding. But 'mysterious' does not mean 'unapproachable.' After thirty-two years of marriage my wife remains a mystery to me – in some ways a deepening mystery. Yet she and I can still converse meaningfully, and every year we get to know each other better.

There is no such thing as absolute mystery. Nearly everything is unknown to us, but nothing is unknowable *in principle*. Nothing we could want to know refuses our conversational approach. A radically unknowable mystery would be completely invisible to us – so we couldn't recognize it as unknowable.

Moreover, the world itself is shouting the necessity of conversation at us. Our responsibility to avoid destroying the earth cannot be disentangled from our responsibility to sustain the earth. We cannot heal a landscape without a positive vision for what the landscape might become – which can only be something it has never been before. There is no escaping the expressive consequences of our lives.

Our first conversational task may be to acknowledge mystery, but when you have prodded and provoked that mystery into threatening the whole planet with calamity, you had better hope you can muster a few meaningful words in response, if only words of apology. And you had better seek at least enough understanding of what you have prodded and provoked to begin redirecting your steps in a more positive direction.

But claiming incomprehension of the speech of the Other is not the only way to stifle the ecological conversation. We can, from the side of conventional science, deny the existence of any speech to be understood. We can say, 'There is no one there, no coherent unity in nature and its creatures of the sort one could speak with. Nature has no interior.'

But this will not do either. To begin with, we ourselves belong to nature, and we certainly communicate with one another. So already we can hardly claim that nature lacks a speaking interior. (How easy it is to ignore this most salient of all salient facts!) Then, too, we have always communicated in diverse ways with various higher animals. If we have construed this as a monologue rather than a conversation, it is not because these animals offer us no response, but only because we prefer to ignore it.

But beyond this, whenever we assume the organic unity of *anything*, we necessarily appeal to an immaterial 'something' that informs its parts, which otherwise remain a mere disconnected aggregate. You may refer to this something as spirit, archetype, idea, essence, the nature of the thing, its being, the 'cowness of the cow.' (Some of these terms work much better than others.) But without an interior and generative aspect – without something that speaks through the organism as a whole, something of which all the parts are a qualitative expression – you have no organism and no governing unity to talk about, let alone to converse with. [...]

What those who *are* receptive to the world's qualities consistently discover is a conversational partner.

Where does the wild live?

To foreclose on the possibility of ecological conversation, whether due to reticence in the presence of the mystery of the Other or simple denial of both mystery and Other, is to give up on the problem of nature's integrity and our responsibility. It is to forget that we ourselves stand within nature, bringing, like every creature, our own contributions to the ecology of the whole. Most distinctively, we bring the potentials of conscious understanding and the burden of moral responsibility. [...]

[W]hile we live *in* our environment, we are not wholly *of* it. We can detach ourselves from our surroundings and view them objectively. This is not a bad thing. What is disastrous is our failure to crown this achievement with the selfless, loving conversation that it makes possible. Only in encountering an Other separate from myself can I learn to love. The chickadee does not love its environment because it is – much more fully than we – an expression of its environment.

The willfulness and waywardness – the wildness – that has enabled us to stand apart and 'conquer' nature is also what enables us to give nature a voice. The miracle of selflessness through which a human being today can begin learning to 'speak for the environment' – a remarkable thing! – is the other face of our power to destroy the environment. So we now find ourselves actors in a grave and compelling drama rooted in the conflicting tendencies of our own nature, with the earth itself hanging in the balance. Given the undeniable facts of the situation, it would be rash to deny that this drama both expresses and places at risk the *telos* of the entire evolution of earth. But to accept the role we have been thrust into, and to sense our nearly hopeless inadequacy, is at the same time to open ourselves to the wisdom that would speak through us.

We do as much damage by denying our profound responsibilities toward nature as by directly abusing them. If you charge me with anthropocentrism, I accept the label, though on my own terms. If there is one creature that may not healthily scorn anthropocentrism, surely it is *anthropos*. How should we act, if not from our own center and from the deepest truth of our own being? But it is exactly this truth that opens us to the Other. We are the place within nature where willing openness to the Other becomes the necessary foundation of our own life.

The classicist Bruno Snell somewhere remarked that to experience a rock anthropomorphically is also to experience ourselves petromorphically – to discover what is rock-like within ourselves. It is the kind of discovery we have been making, aided by nature and the genius of language, for thousands of years. It is how we have come to know what we are – and what we are is (to use some old language) a microcosm of the macrocosm. Historically, we have drawn our consciousness of ourselves from the surrounding world, which is also to say that this world has awakened, or begun to awaken, within us (Barfield 1965; Barfield 1977).

In general, my observations of nature will prove valuable to the degree I can, for example, balance my tendency to experience the chickadee anthropomorphically with an ability to experience myself 'chickamorphically.' In the moment of true understanding, those two experiences become one, reflecting the fact that my own interior and the world's interior are, in the end, one interior.

The well-intentioned exhortation to replace anthropocentrism with biocentrism, if pushed very far, becomes a curious contradiction. It appeals to the uniquely human – the detachment from our environment that allows us to try to see things from the Other's point of view – in order to deny any special place for humans within nature. We are asked to make a philosophical and moral principle of the idea that we do not differ decisively from other orders of life – but this formulation of principle is itself surely one decisive thing we cannot ask of those other orders.

There is no disgrace in referring to the 'uniquely human.' If we do not seek to understand every organism's unique way of being in the world, we exclude it from the ecological conversation. To exclude ourselves in this way reduces our words to gibberish, because we do not speak from our own center.

But nothing here implies that humans possess greater 'moral worth' (whatever that might mean) than other living things. What distinguishes us is not our moral worth, but the fact that we bear the burden of moral responsibility. That this burden has risen to consciousness at one particular locus within nature is surely significant for the destiny of nature! [...]

Toward creative responsibility

[...] When Thoreau told us, 'In wildness is the preservation of the world' (1947), the wildness he referred to was at least in part *our* wildness. If humankind fails to embrace with its sympathies and understanding – which is to say, within our own being – every wild thing, then both we and the world will to that extent be diminished. This is true even if our refusal goes no further than the withdrawal from conversation.

Our failure to reckon adequately with the wild Other is as much a feature of human social relations as of our relations with nature, and as much a feature of our treatment of domesticated landscapes as of wilderness areas. In its Otherness, the factory-farmed hog is no less a challenge to our sympathies and understanding than the salmon, the commonplace chickadee no less than the grizzly bear. We do not excel in the art of conversation. If the grizzly is absent from the distant mountains, perhaps it is partly because we have lost sight of, or even denigrated, the wild spirit in the chickadee outside our doors.

If we really believed in the saving grace of wildness, we would not automatically discount habitats bearing the marks of human engagement. We would not look down upon the farmer whose love is the Other he meets in the soil and whose struggle is to draw out, in wisdom, the richness and productive potential of his farm habitat. Nor, thrilling to the discovery of a cougar track in the high Rockies, would we disparage the cultivated European landscape which, at its best, serves a far greater diversity of wild things than the primeval northern forest.

The point is not to pronounce any landscape good or bad, but to ask after the integrity of the conversation it represents. None of us would want to see the entire world reduced to someone's notion of a garden, but neither would we want to see a world where no humans tended reverently to their surroundings (Suchantke 2001). We should not set the creativity of the true gardener against the creativity at work in our oversight of the Denali wilderness. They are two very different conversations, and both ought to be – can be – worthy expressions of the wild spirit. [...]

References

Barfield, Owen (1965). *Saving the Appearances*. New York: Harcourt, Brace, Jovanovich. Originally published in 1957.

Barfield, Owen (1977). *The Rediscovery of Meaning, and Other Essays*. Middletown CT: Wesleyan University Press.

Holdrege, Craig (1997). 'The Cow: Organism or Bioreactor?' *Orion* (Winter), pp. 28–32.

Holdrege, Craig (2001). Personal communication.

Leopold, Aldo (1970). *A Sand County Almanac: With Essays on Conservation from Round River*. New York: Ballantine.

Suchantke, Andreas (2001). *Eco-Geography: What We See When We Look at Landscapes*. Great Barrington MA: Lindisfarne.

Thoreau, Henry David (1947). 'Walking.' In *The Portable Thoreau*, ed. Carl Bode. New York: Viking.

Stephen Talbott

9 | Contemporary environmental ethics

ANDREW LIGHT

This extract is from the first half of a paper outlining four debates surfacing 'intrinsic value of nature' as being an important matter in environmental ethics. Whereas 'conversation' (as understood in Reading 8) can leave space for 'creative responsibility', debates are centred more around competition between two opposing (human) positions. As Andrew Light acknowledges, whilst these debates can at times be debilitating, they might also be mobilized for a better course of action towards a more publicly engaged model of applied philosophy. In the second half of the paper, Light goes on to present a model based upon environmental pragmatism. The general attributes of environmental pragmatism are discussed a little more critically in Reading 13. But issues around valuing nature are nevertheless important to appreciate in pursuing any model or endeavour of environmental responsibility.

§ Since the inception of environmental ethics in the early 1970s, the principal question that has occupied the time of most philosophers working in the field is how the value of nature could best be described such that nature is directly morally considerable, in and of itself, rather than only indirectly morally considerable, because it is appreciated or needed by humans. Nature might be indirectly morally considerable because it is the source of things that humans need, such as natural resources used to provide the foundations for building and sustaining human communities. Nature might be directly morally considerable if it possesses some kind of value (for example, some kind of intrinsic value or inherent worth) demonstrable through a subjective or objective metaethical position. If nature is the sort of thing that is directly morally considerable, then our duties – for example, to preserve some natural park from development – would not be contingent on articulating some value that the park has for humans but would instead be grounded in a claim that the park has some kind of value that necessarily warrants our protection (for example, because it is a wild place or because it is the home of endangered species) without needing further appeal. [...]

The metaethical debates of environmental ethics

There are many ways to parse out the various metaethical and metaphysical schools of thought that have shaped the development of contemporary environmental ethics. My preference is to track this development in terms of a series of debates, with the first and most important one involving the rejection of anthropocentrism. Tim Hayward defines ethical anthropocentrism as the view that prioritizes those attitudes, values, or practices that give 'exclusive or arbitrarily preferential consideration to human interests as opposed to the interests of other beings' or the environment (1997, 51). [...]

[T]he notion of what anthropocentrism meant, and in consequence what overcoming anthropocentrism entailed, often relied on very narrow, straw-man definitions of anthropocentrism. Anthropocentrism was equated with forms of valuation that easily, or even necessarily, led to nature's destruction (rather than anthropocentric values, such as aesthetic values, which might count as reasons to preserve nature). Therefore, a corollary assumption of this dogma has been that even a limited endorsement of anthropocentric forms of valuation of nature would necessarily give credence to those anthropocentric values that prefer development over preservation.

[...] [T]he first divide among environmental ethicists is between those who accept the rejection of anthropocentrism as a necessary prerequisite for establishing a unique field of environmental ethics and those who do not accept this position, arguing that 'weaker' forms of anthropocentrism (for example, those that admit humanly based values to nature other than mere resource value) are sufficient to generate an adequate ethic of the environment (see Norton 1984). But even the general picture of this divide is more complicated. If environmental ethics was to start with a rejection of anthropocentrism, then the next step was to come up with a description of the value of nonhumans, or the nonhuman natural world, in nonanthropocentric terms. The preferred description of this form of value has generally been as some form of intrinsic value, thought to mean that nonhumans or ecosystems possessed some sort of value in and of themselves (as opposed to only possessing instrumental value to the achievement of human ends). Nonanthropocentrists have long argued that anthropocentrism cannot justify a basis for the intrinsic value of nature and so should be rejected (see Callicott 1996). [...]

[T]he debate between anthropocentrists and nonanthropocentrists in environmental ethics has long been entwined with debates over the validity of ascribing intrinsic value either to nonhuman animals or to species or ecosystems.

Andrew Light

If we are to persist with some form of nonanthropocentrism, the next relevant question becomes how to define the scope and limits of our descriptions of the intrinsic (or at least noninstrumental) value of nature. [...] [A] new debate very quickly emerged between 'individualists' and 'holists,' or 'sentientists' and 'holists,' which wound up largely excluding animal liberationists [such as Peter Singer 1974] from the domain of environmental ethics.

Individualists are those who argue that the extension of moral consideration beyond humans should be limited to other individuals, namely, those individuals who could be argued to have interests, or in the case of sentientists, were sentient, such as other animals. Primarily these arguments, no matter what their normative foundations (for example, consequentialist, nonconsequentialist, or virtue based), result in moral arguments for vegetarianism and against industrial animal agriculture, arguments questioning scientific experimentation on animals (especially of the more frivolous variety, such as for testing cosmetics), and sometimes arguments against hunting.

Holists argue in contrast that individualism or sentientism is inadequate for an environmental ethic because it fails to offer directly reasons for the moral consideration of ecosystems, wilderness, and endangered species – all top priorities for the environmental movement. Because conservationists and environmental scientists evaluate the workings of nature at the ecosystemic level (without much worry about the welfare of individuals so long as a species is not in danger), an ethic covering the same ground should also try to describe the value of nature and the priorities for preservation at the same level sometimes without regard for the welfare of individuals. At times, it is argued, the ends of individualism and holism conflict, as in the case of therapeutic hunting, where holists have maintained that killing individual members of a nonendangered species is justified whenever the numbers of that species produce a threat to endangered species or fragile ecosystems.

The debate between individualists and holists has evolved similarly to the debates between anthropocentrists and nonanthropocentrists. For example, sentientists argue that there is no clear defensible grounds for describing the noninstrumental value of nature per se without appeal to things in nature that can be considered to have interests, such as animals. Thus, trees, rocks, and whole ecosystems cannot be directly morally considerable, even though it is arguably the case that the health and welfare of whole systems and of endangered species could be covered indirectly by some combination of concern for the interests of nonhumans and of future human generations. Other individualists, most notably Tom

Regan (1983), one of the leading deontologists working on animal rights, have gone on to press harder still, arguing that holism entails a form of 'environmental fascism,' whereby the strong likelihood is raised that the welfare of individuals will often, if not always, be sacrificed to the needs of the greater biotic good

Somewhat in between these two camps are biocentric individualists, such as Paul Taylor and Gary Varner, who have pushed the boundaries of individualism beyond sentientism, arguing for a coherent individualism extended to cover the value of the capacity for flourishing of nonsentient organisms. For Taylor there is broadly speaking a sense in which all natural entities flourish, and so what is good or bad for them is a matter of what is good or bad for this flourishing, a claim that is not dependent on human interests. This expansion of individualism in part helps to bridge the gap between holists and individualists, even though biocentric individualists are adamant that holism in itself must be rejected. Not all interests among all living individual things are granted equal status on such views, with various arguments put forward for which some interests count more than others (for example, the interests of individuals capable of desires might be considered more important than those of individuals not capable of desires).

Nonetheless, despite such compromising positions, holists, such as J. Baird Callicott (especially Callicott 1980) and Holmes Rolston III, have prevailed in staking a claim for environmental ethics in some form of holism, most forcefully by recourse to the argument that many forms of individualism encounter problems in their plausible extension to species and ecosystems. [...]

Among holists there are still further debates, though not so much over the proper scope of environmental ethics. These debates largely cut along the lines of whether a case for the noninstrumental or intrinsic value of nature can best be made on subjectivist or on objectivist grounds. Leading subjectivists include Robert Elliot (1997) and Callicott, the latter best known for developing a Humean, and what he refers to as a 'communitarian,' line of reasoning out of the work of the forester and conservationist Aldo Leopold. Leopold is best known for his 1949 posthumously published memoir, *A Sand County Almanac*, in which he developed a holist 'land ethic' (see Callicott 1989 and 1999).

For Callicott, while value for him is subjective (as value is always a verb and can only be engaged in by those beings with the capacity to value, namely, humans, though perhaps some nonhumans as well), there are things in the world that can be subjectively considered to be intrinsically valuable (valued by a valuer for their own sake) through an evolutionary extension of what counts as inclusively important among a community of valuers. In the past what has been considered valuable for us has been restricted to other members of the human community (which has progressed from the empathetic bonds of the family to the clan to the tribe to the town, and so forth); the next progression of this evolution should be to consideration of nonhumans and ecosystems as similarly valuable. In Leopold's words, the next evolution of ethics should be to human–land relations. For Callicott, sorting out conflicts in value among competing demands from different communities that warrant our attention (for example, duties to our immediate families versus duties to ecosystems) requires adopting two second-order principles, ranking as higher our obligations to more intimate communities (such as our families in many cases) and to 'stronger interests' (such as duties to the preservation of endangered species).

In contrast, Rolston (see Rolston 1988, 1989, and 1994) argues that intrinsic values in nature are objective properties of the world. He does not claim that individual animals are unimportant (though he does not have strong qualms against the production and consumption of other animals; indeed, he even claims that meat eating is necessary to maintain our identity as a species). Rolston takes a position that is, initially at least, compatible with some form of individualism, arguing, similarly to Taylor, that every living organism has a *telos* from which we may derive a baseline form of intrinsic value. But different characteristics, such as the capacity for conscious reflection, add value to each organism. Along with this scheme of value he also offers arguments for the intrinsic value of species as well as ecosystems. For Rolston, there is a conceptual confusion involved in the claim that we could value individual organisms without valuing the larger wholes that produced them through evolutionary processes.

A further debate, brought on by the scope of holism, has evolved over the question of whether preservation of the environment should be grounded in a monistic foundation or whether a coherent ethical view of it can tolerate pluralism. Monists in environmental ethics generally argue that a single scheme of valuation is required to anchor our various duties and obligations in an environmental ethic (see, for example, Callicott 1990). This would mean that one ethical framework would have to cover the range of diverse objects of moral concern included under holism: other humans, other animals, living organisms, ecosystems, species, and perhaps even Earth itself. Such a view would have the advantage of generating a cleaner methodology for resolving disputes over conflicting obligations to and among these objects – itself a very worrisome problem, as an environmental ethic has a mandate covering many more competing claims for moral consideration than a traditional ethic.

Pluralists counter that it cannot be the case that we could have one ethical theory that covered this range of objects, either because the sources of value in nature are too diverse to account for in any single theory or because the multitude of contexts in which we find ourselves in different kinds of ethical relationships with both humans and nature demand a plurality of approaches for fulfilling our moral obligations (see, for example, Brennan 1988 and 1992). Accordingly, for Andrew Brennan, there is 'no one set of principles concerning just one form of value that provides ultimate government for our actions' (1992, 6). Such claims lead Callicott to charge pluralists with moral relativism.

While less a dogma than nonanthropocentrism and holism, argument over moral monism continues to push the evolution of the field, particularly over the issue of the relationship between theory and practice in environmental ethics. The debate over pluralism raises the question of how appeals concerning the welfare of the environment cohere with other issues in moral philosophy in particular situations. Many, if not most, cases of potential harm to the value of ecosystems are also cases of moral harm to human communities, which can be objected to for independent anthropocentric moral reasons. The literature on 'environmental justice,' the concern that minority communities often bear a disproportionate burden of environmental harms, such as exposure to toxic waste, is based on linking concerns about human health and well-being to environmental protection (see Schlosberg 1999). A truly pluralist environmental ethic would not be terribly concerned with whether the claims of harm to the interests of a minority community by the siting of a toxic-waste dump could or could not be based on the same scheme of value that would describe the harm done to the ecosystem by the dump. A pluralist ethic would be open to describing the harm to the ecosystem and to the human community in different though compatible terms for purposes of forming a broader coalition for fighting the dump (see Light 2002).

To conclude this section, a key set of debates – anthropocentrism versus nonanthropocentrism, individualism versus holism, subjective versus objective holism, and monism versus pluralism – have largely shaped the development of contemporary environmental ethics. At a minimum, the field is most clearly defined, though not always adequately defended, through its rejection of anthropocentrism and its commitment to holism. But the portrayal here of the varieties of this exchange has been far from complete. Consistent with the connection to broader questions in social and moral philosophy raised by the monism–pluralism debate, an extensive literature has developed connecting environmental ethics to feminism (for an overview of ecofeminism see Davion 2001), as have more restricted literatures on humanism (Brennan 1988), virtue theory (O'Neill 1993; Welchman 1999), pragmatism (Light and Katz 1996), communitarianism (de-Shalit 2000), and more nuanced understandings of human self-interest (Hayward 1998). All of these alternative directions in the field have presented new challenges in metaethics and normative ethics, but they have also done something more. In their own ways they have all moved beyond the more abstract questions of the metaethical debates concerning nonanthropocentric intrinsic value in nature to provide, in John O'Neill's words, 'more specific reason-giving concepts and corresponding claims about the ways in which natural objects are a source of wonder, the sense of proportion they invoke in us of our place within a wider history' (2001, 174). [...]

Nonanthropocentrism and environmental policy

With this variety of views in the field, how should environmental ethics proceed? One answer would be that it will simply proceed, whether it should or not, as a new set of debates between the more traditional nonanthropocentric views and the biocentric, anthropocentric, or other alternative views briefly mentioned at the end of the previous section. Many anthropocentric environmental ethicists seem determined to do just that (see Norton 1995 and Callicott 1996). There is, however, an alternative: in addition to continuing the tradition of most environmental ethics as philosophical sparring among philosophers, we could turn our attention to the question of how the work of environmental ethicists could be made more useful in taking on the environmental problems to which environmental ethics is addressed as those problems are undertaken in policy terms. The problems with contemporary environmental ethics are arguably more practical than philosophical, or at least their resolution in more practical terms is more important than their resolution in philosophical terms at the present time. For even though there are several dissenters from the dominant traditions in environmental ethics, the more important consideration is the fact that the world of natural-resource management (in which environmental ethicists should hope to have some influence, in the same way that medical ethicists have worked for influence over the medical professions) takes a predominantly anthropocentric approach to assessing natural value, as do most other humans. [...] Environmental ethics appears more concerned with overcoming human interests than redirecting them toward environmental concerns. As a consequence, a nonanthropocentric form of ethics has limited appeal to such an audience, even if it were true that this literature provides the best reasons for why nature has value (de-Shalit 2000). And not to appeal to such an audience arguably means that we are not having an effect either on the formation of better environmental polices or on the project of engendering public support for them. As such, I would argue, environmental ethics is not living up to its promise as a field of philosophy attempting to help resolve environmental problems. It is instead evolving mostly as a field of intramural philosophical debate. [...]

References

Attfield, Robin. 1987. *A Theory of Value and Obligation.* London: Croom Helm.

Brennan, Andrew. 1988. *Thinking about Nature.* Athens, Ga.: University of Georgia Press.

— 1992. 'Moral Pluralism and the Environment.' *Environmental Values* 1: 15–33.

Callicott, J. Baird. 1980. 'Animal Liberation: A Triangular Affair.' *Environmental Ethics* 2: 311–38.

— 1989. *In Defense of the Land Ethic.* Albany: State University of New York Press.

— 1990. 'The Case against Moral Pluralism.' *Environmental Ethics* 12: 99–124.

— 1996. 'On Norton and the Failure of Monistic Inherentism.' *Environmental Ethics* 18: 219–21, 461–5.

— 1999. *Beyond the Land Ethic.* Albany: State University of New York Press.

Davion, Victoria. 2001. 'Ecofeminism.' In *A Companion to Environmental Philosophy*, edited by D. Jamieson, 231–47. Maiden, Mass.: Blackwell Publishers.

de-Shalit, Avner. 2000. *The Environment between Theory and Practice.* Oxford: Oxford University Press.

— 2001. 'Ten Commandments of How to Fail in an Environmental Campaign.' *Environmental Politics* 10: 111–37.

Elliot, Robert. 1997. *Faking Nature.* London: Routledge.

Hayward, Tim. 1997. 'Anthropocentrism: A Misunderstood Problem.' *Environmental Values* 6: 49–63.

— 1998. *Political Theory and Ecological Values.* New York: St. Martin's Press.

Light, Andrew. 2002. 'The Case for a Practical Pluralism.' In *Environmental Ethics: An Anthology*, edited by A. Light and H. Rolston III, 229–47. Maiden, Mass.: Blackwell Publishers.

Light, Andrew, and Katz, Eric. 1996. *Environmental Pragmatism.* London: Routledge.

Naess, Arne. 1973. 'The Shallow and the Deep: Long-Range Ecology Movements.' *Inquiry* 16: 95–100.

Norton, Bryan G. 1984. 'Environmental Ethics and Weak Anthropocentrism.' *Environmental Ethics* 6: 131–48.

— 1995. 'Why I Am Not a Nonanthropocentrist: Callicott and the Failure of Monistic Inherentism.' *Environmental Ethics* 17: 341–58.

O'Neill, John. 1993. *Ecology, Policy, and Politics.* London: Routledge.

— 2001. 'Meta-ethics.' In *A Companion to Environmental Philosophy*, edited by D. Jamieson, 163–76. Maiden, Mass.: Blackwell Publishers.

Andrew Light

Regan, Tom. 1983. *The Case for Animal Rights.* Berkeley: University of California Press.

Rolston, Holmes III. 1975. 'Is There an Ecological Ethic?' *Ethics* 85: 93–109.

— 1988. *Environmental Ethics.* Philadelphia: Temple University Press.

— 1989. *Philosophy Gone Wild.* Buffalo, N.Y.: Prometheus Books.

— 1994. *Conserving Natural Value.* New York: Columbia University Press.

Routley (later Sylvan), Richard. 1973. 'Is There a Need for a New, an Environmental Ethic?' *Proceedings of the XVth World Congress of Philosophy,* 205–10.

Routley (later Sylvan), Richard, and Routley (later Plumwood), Val. 1979. 'Against the Inevitability of Human Chauvinism.' In *Ethics and Problems of the 21st Century,* edited by K. E. Goodpaster and K. M. Sayre, 36–59. Notre Dame,

Ind.: University of Notre Dame Press.

Schlosberg, David. 1999. *Environmental Justice and the New Pluralism.* Oxford: Oxford University Press.

Singer, Peter. 1974. 'All Animals Are Equal.' *Philosophical Exchange* 1: 103–16.

Taylor, Paul. 1984. 'Are Humans Superior to Animals and Plants?' *Environmental Ethics* 6: 149–60.

— 1986. *Respect for Nature.* Princeton: Princeton University Press.

Varner, Gary. 1998. *In Nature's Interests.* Oxford: Oxford University Press.

— 2001. 'Sentientism.' In *A Companion to Environmental Philosophy,* edited by D. Jamieson, 192–203. Maiden, Mass.: Blackwell Publishers.

Welchman, Jennifer. 1999. 'The Virtues of Stewardship.' *Environmental Ethics* 19: 411–23.

10 | The two-culture problem: ecological restoration and the integration of knowledge

ERIC HIGGS

Ecological restoration provides an arena in which values regarding what matters in the environment are contested among practitioners from a variety of disciplinary traditions. Whereas Andrew Light (Reading 9) examines four debates within the essentially non-scientific tradition of environmental ethics, Eric Higgs takes a broader perspective in re-examining a single divide: that between science and non-science. He suggests that the divide remains as relevant in contemporary times as when C. P. Snow first expressed the division in terms of 'two cultures' in the early 1950s. As a complement to the science of 'restoration ecology', the wider more non-science notion of 'ecological restoration' prompts a sense of responsibility as being a conversation (between science and non-science) rather than a 'debate' and chimes well with the idea of responsibility as a *creative* force.

Introduction

The terms 'ecological restoration' and 'restoration ecology' are frequently interchanged. Most of the students I teach, for example, think initially that these terms are synonyms, and certainly widespread conflation of the terms in the literature would support such a view. Restoration ecology, as I argue, is the suite of scientific practices that constitute an emergent subdiscipline of ecology and comprises what we consider typical of a contemporary natural science: hypotheses, conjectures, testing, experiments, field observations, publications, and debate. Ecological restoration is the ensemble of practices that constitute the entire field of restoration, including restoration ecology as well as the participating human and natural sciences, politics, technologies, economic factors, and cultural dimensions. [...]

This paper is motivated by the concern that the broader practice of restoration may become narrowed over the next decade as a result of zealous attention to scientific and technological considerations as well as our intrigue with larger and larger projects. Scientific and technological acumen is necessary for successful restoration, but insufficient. Durable restoration projects enjoy support by local communities, effective poli-cies, appropriate legislation, long-term financing, and a host of intangible factors that contribute to turning what might be a transitory initiative into something that, like the Curtis and Greene Prairies at the Univer-sity of Wisconsin-Madison Arboretum, which are arguably the earliest comprehensive ecological restoration projects in North America (Mills 1995), will leave positive legacies for future generations. Such success will require vigilance and care to ensure that the authority of science and our fascination with technology do not produce austere and ultimately fragile restorations in the future.

My concern originates in the observation that it remains difficult to construct the intellectual and practical bridges that link the divide be-tween the natural and human sciences (and humanities). Within colleges and universities there exists a schism that is perpetuated in research and teaching. Those who study restoration ecology have difficulty finding or incorporating broader perspectives in their studies. Likewise, those who take interest in restoration from a social perspective find it challenging to cross the gulf to the natural sciences (there are many fewer of these students). Some research and training programs are interdisciplinary by intent or leave room for flexible study, but interdisciplinarity has not sufficiently inoculated most academic institutions effectively to create integrated learning opportunities for aspiring restorationists. For the most part those who pursue restoration are formally trained in ecology, natural resource management, or any one of the allied natural sciences. Lest my arguments are construed as antagonistic to natural science, this is definitely not the case: what I propose instead is a more ambi-tious integration of learning and research in restoration that combines insights from both the natural and human sciences. The challenge lies in creating opportunities that emphasize integration within institutions that are largely inimical to such change and a larger culture that abets the split between science and culture.

The problem of separation is scarcely new. It is no easier now to have commerce between science and culture than it was almost 50 years ago when Sir Charles Percy Snow coined his controversial 'two cultures' hypothesis. Snow, a man of letters, inflamed controversy over the place of science in mid-century England and gave rise to the convenient notion of separate cultures guiding natural and human sciences (or science and humanities). The debate proved a complicated one. Snow argued that scientific literacy was appallingly low and that most so-called educated people operated in woeful ignorance of basic scientific concepts. No doubt he was right at some level, although his critics have taken him to task for his motivations. Judging by contemporary standards of scientific and mathematical literacy, for example test scores from high schools in North America, the problem persists. Care is needed, however, in separating out issues of scientific literacy from scientific authority, the former in shorter supply than the latter. The point made here is that the authority and structure of science constrain a broader notion of restoration.

In this essay I use Snow's term of convenience, two cultures, to illustrate a worrisome separation in restoration, one that threatens to undermine a broader participatory approach. I begin with the story of a restoration project that depends on science and culture for success and then move on to propose two reasons why the separation of science and culture is apparent: (1) the increasingly technological constitution of restoration; and (2) the authority of science. The conclusion is a plea for redoubling our efforts to provide restoration education that integrates across the natural and human sciences and humanities, and in so doing extends the interdisciplinary ambitions that are widespread if only partially effective in most contemporary universities. Ecological restoration could be an ideal locus for a liberal education (Jordan 2003). These arguments are applicable to estuarine restoration as much as any other type of restoration. My intention is to make a general case, although estuarine restoration, especially within urban and urbanizing regions, typically demands such an integrated approach.

Discovery Island

In July 2000 the first harvest in more than a century of Blue camas (*Camassia quamash*) bulbs took place on Discovery Island (near Victoria, British Columbia, Canada) by a team of ethnobotanists and Lekwungen indigenous peoples. Camas bulbs are a rich source of carbohydrates that were used historically as a major food source and trade good by the Coast Salish speaking indigenous peoples in the region around the Strait of Juan de Fuca, southern Vancouver Island, and the archipelago of islands between the very southwestern part of Canada and the northwest of the United States, as well as farther afield in the interior plateau of what is now the province of British Columbia (Canada) and the state of Washington (U.S.A.). Camas grows in meadows and savannas (associated locally with the regionally threatened Garry oak [*Quercus garryana*] ecosystem), both ecosystem types that have undergone extensive alteration and loss in this region over the past century.

The camas harvest of 2000 was culturally and ecologically significant. The Lekwungen people (or Songhees First Nation) occupied for roughly 4,000 years lands in what is now the City of Victoria. With British colonization of southern Vancouver Island in the 1840s, a series of purchases and agreements resulted in the loss of use of almost all traditional lands. Two forced relocations away from what would now be considered prime real estate in Victoria have provided a smaller urban reservation of less than 100 ha. Disease, especially smallpox in the late nineteenth century, reduced the community from several thousand to a low point around 1900 of just 100 individuals. Despite deprivations, the community rebounded to over 400 by the year 2000. It is difficult to imagine the scale of cultural loss and dislocation experienced by the Lekwungen people.

Cheryl Bryce, a member of the Lekwungen Nation, approached ethnobotanists Nancy Turner and Brenda Beckwith (School of Environmental Studies, University of Victoria, Canada) to advise on the traditional harvest and cooking of camas. A site on Discovery Island, a small island less than 2 km off the coast of Victoria, with extant camas meadow was selected for the initial harvest (part of Discovery Island is owned by the Lekwungen). In traditional times successful harvesting of camas depended on elaborate management, including selective harvesting of camas bulbs, weeding (especially Death camas [*Zigadenus venenosus*]), and annual prescribed burning. After a century of inattention, bulb production was low, weedy native and exotic plants had invaded the meadow, and the absence of fire had allowed a thick thatch to form on the meadow. Despite this, sufficient bulbs were harvested on this initial occasion to create a ceremonial harvest and pit cook (a traditional cooking method in which foods are placed in a small pit and heated using hot rocks).

This marked the beginning of revitalization through a cultural keystone species (Garibaldi and Turner 2004): camas. Seeds were harvested and replanted on nearby sites, weeding programs instituted, and prescribed fire re-introduced. Whether or not camas becomes a dietary mainstay for the Lekwungen in the future is less significant than the symbolic importance of the harvest. Keeping camas populations healthy depends on ecological restoration, which combines common contemporary techniques for maintaining a specific community of native plants with recognition of cultural objectives. It is a vital part of the project that camas harvesting respects the ecological fragility and significance of ecosystems. The historical continuity with the harvesting sites is what anchors the restoration project; it would be an utterly different prospect to contemplate a commercial, technological harvest of camas, although this, too, might become part of a Lekwungen cultural and economic revitalization.

Indigenous peoples worldwide are searching for ways of respecting tradition and living with modernity, and adaptations are required that may seem strange to those of us who live already within modern industrial economies. Inuit hunters in Nunavut (Canada), for example, use snowmobiles and geographic position systems in their hunts and at the same time maintain significant features of traditional hunting culture; the balance is sometimes difficult and always changing (Aporla 2003). Simplified monolithic models of indigenous engagement with ecosystems – original ecologists or despoilers – are incapable of capturing either contemporary realities faced by devastated peoples or the diversity of cultural practices and viewpoints. Ecological restoration in the case of the Lekwungen is also – and equally – cultural restoration. A crucial factor in the success of this project was that ethnobotanists trained to straddle botany and anthropology were principal advisors. This serves as an exemplar for the argument that successful restoration depends on ecological insights as well as cultural knowledge and support.

The technological constitution of restoration

In earlier work I suggested that we are approaching a fork in the road of restoration (Higgs 2003). Along one fork is the bumpy, experimental, community-engaged practice of restoration that has typified the growth of the field so far. Another path has opened, along which we find restoration megaprojects and increasingly well-refined, technically adept projects. We should not choose one or the other, but need to recognize that the well-paved road threatens to divert traffic from traditional approaches to restoration and to change fundamentally what counts as good restoration.

We live in a technological society, one thoroughly saturated with artifacts and processes aimed at convenience and efficiency. Some have described a basic pattern underlying technological society in which things that matter to us – music, art, celebration, knowledge – are increasingly rendered as commodities for consumption (Borgmann 1984; Higgs et al. 2000). What is worrisome is that we lose touch with the condition of authenticity with which we cherish traditional experience: contrast, for example, the live performance of music, especially music produced by oneself and friends, with recorded music. The latter is a reflection, more or less pale, of the direct experience.

The same pattern holds for ecosystems and restoration. Ecosystems can be rendered as commodities under the conditions of mitigation banking, real estate, and a propensity to fix problems that emanate from misuse. It is one thing to restore the damage wrought by heedless action as an act of historical reconciliation and quite another to despoil an ecosystem with the knowledge that there is a technology of reparation.

Eric Higgs

There is a risk we are increasingly influenced by the latter worldview, and this turns back to earlier concerns voiced by critics of restoration in the 1980s. Restoration itself can also become a commodity, and this is precisely glimpsed in the popularity of corporate restoration projects in which restoration becomes a symbol of environmental commitment. And, as restoration becomes more popular, it will be subject to the same constraints of efficiency that motivate other technological practices. At one level it is difficult to complain about efficiency because presumably it yields more restoration. The salient question is: What kind of restoration is being procured?

If ecological restoration is about the restoration of ecosystems and the human communities that sustain and are sustained by these ecosystems, then we should worry about the broader implications of ever more efficient technological restoration. What we want instead is the road less traveled, the one along which we find participatory restoration that manifests the best of science and culture. The challenge is in maintaining the meandering route in a society largely given over to a straight-line technological approach to life.

The authority of science

Several years ago Soule and Lease (1995) kicked off a furious debate about the meaning of nature with their book *Reinventing Nature? Responses to Postmodern Deconstruction*. They were unsettled by claims from social scientists and humanists that nature is entirely a cultural construct and that ecosystems will lose significance in an advanced technological society. The ensemble of essays in that volume, written by philosophers, literary critics, historians, and ecologists, painted not a simple negative view of postmodernism and the tendency to see nature as a cultural projection, but rather a complicated, ambiguous portrayal of how nature is represented. All contributors opposed a radical postmodernism in which nature is purely an artifact of human consciousness, but quite a few admitted that a complete understanding of nature depends on an interchange between so-called objective observations via science and the subjective knowledge that comes from memory, social position, and personal experience. Hence, along a line between nature-as-objective-fact and nature-as-cultural-construction the truth lies somewhere in the middle.

I think Soule and Lease were keen on exposing the frailties of postmodernism and championing the authority of science. In doing so, however, they threatened to submerge knowledge that falls outside of conventional science: personal testimony based on experience, for example, and creative knowledge derived from art, music, and poetry. Restorationists should take note, because they have until now thrived upon the mix of science and practical knowledge. Moreover, every time an ecosystem is restored, a particular view of nature is expressed. Restorationists are central players in defining and redefining how nature is defined and interpreted.

One risks making a too obvious claim by suggesting that restoration is practiced by people who hold particular values about what counts as an appropriate ecosystem, and this in turn is conditioned by our contemporary and changing views of nature and wilderness. Soule and Lease were concerned that these cultural values were being taken too seriously and at the expense of ecological verities. The concern, then, is that restoration would become a practice given over to human motivations alone and would result in what some have termed designer ecosystems (Palmer et al. 2004). A related objection is that any model of ecological restoration that embodies cultural awareness misses the significance of true wilderness: areas that have little or no sustained human involvement. Examples abound of wilderness restoration, but such projects are based to some extent on an acknowledgment of human engagement with the landscape. Moreover, the idea of wilderness has been impaled in a number of important ways, not the least by acknowledgment of a systemic underrepresentation of long-standing if subtle human practices (Cronon 1995; Higgs 2003). This being the case, there is danger in suggesting that either ecology or culture should trump one another. Both deserve attention. Although it is fair to suggest that cultural values, especially those of indigenous people, have been underplayed, it would be dangerous to swing to a kind of restoration that would submerge the ecological significance of a place.

Successful restoration depends on science and local knowledge (or traditional ecological knowledge as it is sometimes known, or experience; the knowledge of testimony and pattern). The ability to conduct controlled experiments and understand nutrient cycling is complemented by practical knowledge such as the history of planting on a particular site, organizing volunteers to water seedlings, with whom to speak in smoothing regulatory tangles, and where the best local supplies are obtained. Although both forms of knowledge are important, typically only scientists are considered experts. [...]

[A]n overreliance on science can deform the work of restorationists, first by pushing other forms of knowledge to the sidelines. Landscape architects, for example, who are trained to think in several different ways, often alternate between scientific or technical knowledge that accounts for why some plantings work better than others and aesthetic judgment

Eric Higgs

that indicates why one planting will appear better than another. Science also tends to reify nature, which is to take an abstraction and make it seem real. This brings us back to the beginning of this section and to debates over the objectivity with which we regard nature. In taking too strong a view of nature – which after all is an abstract notion if for no other reason than it is expressed through language – more weight than appropriate is often given to our particular view of things instead of understanding this view as historically and culturally conditioned. Humility is difficult to achieve when the challenge of restoration is reduced to putting the right pieces into place. We do see the world through our social filters, for example, in the way we have tended to systematically exclude people from our understanding of ecological history. Cultural contingency matters for restorationists because we need to understand that people make sense of a place in different ways. In the end, science matters, but as one of many rather than the only form of knowledge that makes up the practice of ecological restoration. Relying on science alone or as the highest form of knowledge steers us away from a broader view of restoration toward an exclusive focus on restoration ecology. When science is vaulted to primary position and combined with the ethos of a technological society, as described in the previous section, the basics are in place for the ascendance of restoration ecology over ecological restoration.

Two cultures

The title of this paper hints at resolution of the two-culture problem, one in which the separated estates of science and culture are joined or rejoined. The two-culture formulation compelled me to dig into the debates around a lecture given by Lord C. P. Snow in 1959 at Cambridge (Snow 1993). Snow, a novelist and influential mid-century public man in England, spoke and later published his account of a growing gulf between humanistic and scientific thinking. He argued that the rise of scientific thinking had not been adequately assessed and understood by those in an academy still profoundly shaped by humanistic traditions. If there is such a thing as cultural literacy, then Snow argued that scientific literacy counted, too. Snow was not so much inventing the idea of a gulf between humanistic and scientific thinking but giving popular expression to it. Snow ignited a storm of controversy that raged on both sides of the Atlantic in the early 1960s, and his phrase, two cultures, became an emblem for the gulf separating scientific from other forms of knowledge. [...]

What Snow misses, as pointed out by Kimball, is the recognition that what science needs is a moral center, and this center is and will always be extrinsic to the practice of science.

By moral center I mean the orientation that forms over time in a society by which conventions of appropriate practice are brought to common and widely agreeable understanding. The moral center changes over time to represent new conventions, and as Aldo Leopold famously observed, expands to include a wider range of moral responsibility (Leopold 1949). It anchors our understanding of what is right and wrong at any given time, although arbitrating issues at the outer reaches of social convention is fraught with difficulty in a civil society. This is felt acutely in pluralistic societies that are working with multiple cultural perspectives on what matters most and what values are central to a good life. The existence of a moral center allows for recognition, respect, and incorporation of different points of view.

Scientific knowledge and practice are crucial ingredients in the mixture that constitutes a moral center, but by no means either the defining or deterministic character of it. This is a main clue for understanding the gulf separating the two cultures. In a society that gives privilege to scientific and technological knowledge, the moral center upon which science and technology must ultimately be based is obscured. The kinds of knowledge that most effectively open up the moral center to understanding – primarily humanistic knowledge but also the human sciences – are pushed to the sidelines. Thus, at a time when we most need moral direction we have the fewest available resources with which to work.

This creates a sharp problem for ascertaining the best conduct for restoring ecosystems and what the proper ends for restoration ought to be, especially knowing that our values toward those ecosystems will shift over time as they have been doing throughout history. The solution will not come from regression analyses or replicated studies, but the deep, searching, intelligent, humble inquiries into the human past and prospect, to the varieties of human experience, value and creativity, and of course to the many ways we have both loved and despoiled nature. To confront the moral challenges of science requires that we respect those things unknowable through scientific inquiry and that we avoid replacing moral inquiry with unreconstructed rationalism and a relentless consumptive mood.

I witness this daily at my university and know that it is widespread in other institutions of higher learning. The humanities and arts are pushed aside or slowly starved by the 'can do,' moneyed practicality of contemporary science. We have forgotten mostly that what allows us to be good citizens and excellent restorationists is our capacity for judgment,

Eric Higgs

wisdom, and good conduct. Although scientific training is vital, it will never be more than a necessary condition to good restoration. [...]

My antidote to the two-culture problem is to ensure that those who train to be restorationists understand the moral center of their work, which is anchored to a compassionate understanding of place. Restoration education must reflect the traditions of interdisciplinarity inside ecological restoration, secure these for the future, and thereby serve as a beacon of integrative practice. No restoration program should be sanctioned without courses that include environmental philosophy, economics, sociology, and so on. A well-rounded student, a concept that flies to a certain extent in the face of modern training, will in the end be exactly what restoration practice needs. Not everyone will be equally competent and rounded. Much like the grand tradition of liberal arts education, restoration education must draw from all corners of learning. This is the surest way of honoring the broad promise of *ecological restoration.*

References

Aporta, C. 2003. 'Old routes, new trails: contemporary Inuit travel and orienting in Igloolik, Nunavut'. Ph.D. dissertation. University of Alberta, Canada.

Borgmann, A. 1984. *Technology and the Character of Contemporary Life*. University of Chicago Press, Illinois.

Cairns, J. Jr. 1995. 'Ecosocietal-restoration: reestablishing humanity's relationship with natural systems'. *Environment* 37: 4–33.

Cronon, W., editor. 1995. *Uncommon Ground: Toward Reinventing Nature*. Norton, New York.

Garibaldi, A., and N. Turner. 2004. 'Cultural keystone species: implications for ecological conservation and restoration'. *Ecology and Society* 9: 1 [online edition].

Higgs, E. S. 1994. 'Expanding the scope of restoration ecology'. *Restoration Ecology* 2: 137–46.

Higgs, E. S. 2003. *Nature by Design: People, Natural Process, and Ecological Restoration*. MIT Press, Cambridge, Massachusetts.

Higgs, E. S., A. Light, and D. Strong, editors. 2000. *Technology and the Good Life?* University of Chicago Press, Illinois.

House, F. 1999. *Totem Salmon: Life Lessons from Another Species*. Beacon Press, Boston, Massachusetts.

Janzen, D. H. 1988. 'Tropical ecological and biocultural restoration'. *Science* 239: 243–4.

Jordan, W. R. III 2003. *The Sunflower Forest: Ecological Restoration and the New Communion with Nature*. University of California Press, Berkeley.

Kimball, R. 1994. '"The two cultures" today'. *The New Criterion* 12.

Leopold, A. 1949. *A Sand County Almanac and Sketches Here and There*. Oxford University Press, New York.

Mills, S. 1995. *In Service of the Wild: Restoring and Reinhabiting Damaged Land*. Beacon Press, Boston, Massachusetts.

Palmer, M. et al. 2004. 'Ecology for a crowded planet'. *Science* 304: 1251–2.

Rogers-Martinez, D. 1992. 'The Sinkyone Intertribal Park Project'. *Restoration and Management Notes* 10: 64–9.

Snow, C. P. 1993. *The Two Cultures*. Cambridge University Press, London, United Kingdom.

Soule, M., and G. Lease, editors. 1995. *Reinventing Nature? Responses to Postmodern Deconstruction*. Island Press, Covelo, California.

Eric Higgs

11 | The framing paradox

RONALD MOORE

The paradox alluded to in this extract concerns (i) the appreciation that our framing devices actually create aesthetic experience, in much the same way as a simple picture frame, in counterpart to (ii) the intuitive appreciation of nature's aesthetic, holistic value (beauty) as being essentially unframed. Ronald Moore's suggestion that we regard frames as references of *focus* rather than *confinement* prompts questions regarding how we frame what matters in environmental responsibility. In his conclusion, Moore makes reference to the influential American educational reformer and philosophical pragmatist John Dewey (1859–1952), an influence evident particularly in the development of environmental pragmatism (Reading 13).

Introduction

A standard feature of most artworks that contributes importantly to our aesthetic experience of them is the frame. A traditional easel painting is bounded by a frame that sets limits on our range of visual attention and makes it possible to see the contents within it as intelligibly organized. Even unframed paintings are bounded by their canvas edges. Similarly, dramas, operas, dances, and various other performances are framed by the confines of their theatrical context (the proscenium arch, the amphitheater setting, the architectural backdrop of the Baths of Caracalla, etc.). Analogously, works of literature may be seen as framed by their covers, works of music by the temporal limits on their performance, sculptures by the dimensions of their material form, and so on. By contrast with all of these, however, nature can seem strikingly and importantly unframed. When I admire the display of stars in a desert night sky, for example, there is no boundary that guides or limits my perception except the extreme boundary of the visual horizon (and that turns out to be no boundary at all, provided I am willing to travel far enough). When I wander through a forest, finding this or that of its myriad features beautiful, I am not conscious of any frame that organizes them. Even if, for a moment, I notice the way the path opens upon a lovely mountain vista, caught between dense shrubbery and overhanging limbs, in the next moment I am free to walk through this apparent frame into a never-ending sequence of changing scenes. The same limitlessness of objective and malleability of perception characterize our aesthetic experience of nature from the microscopic to the telescopic scale, and from the wilderness setting to the urban setting. Art is framed, and nature is not.

But is this really so? The claim that nature – or our experience of nature – is importantly and distinctively unframed is an entrenched dogma [...]

Nature framed

[...] We habitually organize parts and wholes in our experience, whether we are dealing with natural objects or artifacts. The part-and-whole sorting is done through words and concepts. This is a that. This goes in that file. No one calls it that; we call it this. And so on. We don't live life as a vast undifferentiated panorama of experience. We frame what we experience as we go along. Framing is an important and inevitable aspect of our common human endeavor to make experience intelligible. The worker in the automobile factory has to frame his particular methodical procedure to make it sensible to him as part of the larger operation. The minister charged with coming up with a sermon every week has to frame her ideas in a way that will be received by her parishioners as a coherent message. The lawyer defending his client's interests must frame an argument that will win over the jury.

My point is that framing in the aesthetic sense is a lot different from framing in the physical sense. Frames around pictures are simply emblems of the wider business of framing that we engage in all the time. If I see the thistle-head as a thistle-head rather than as a miscellaneous weed or as a piece of trash, that will be because I can call up a category, or frame, within which I can regard it. The categories Kendall Walton identified as importantly determinative of our aesthetic judgments about art are examples of the carving-up process that is involved in all aesthetic experience (see Walton, 1970, pp. 334–67). But they are not the most prevalent examples. Many of the ways we isolate natural objects for aesthetic regard are inarticulate. Some natural objects we deem beautiful are bounded by their names. This, for example, is a beautiful gladiolus. And it is beautiful as a gladiolus. It isn't a lily, and wouldn't be beautiful as a lily. So, the very classification into which the object falls puts us in a position to decide what features count toward its being correctly deemed beautiful. But many other natural objects of aesthetic attention are not bounded by names or categories. The gentle pit-a-pat of water dripping from dozens of springlets into a narrow gorge. The odd soft-hard feel

Ronald Moore

of tiny zeolite crystals in the fissure of a sea-ledge. The way silhouetted forms interplay and overlap in a forested horizon at twilight. Odd catches of sea-marsh fragrance. The taste left by a weed stem one has been idly chewing on. And so on and on. Even if we should agree that it is an aesthetic mistake and a denigration of nature to think of environmental beauty as nothing other than a series of scenes, framed and composed for our enjoyment as quasi-artworks, we needn't deny that we often gather together the elements of our experience of nature into wholes as a way of focusing attention on them, experiencing them against their background. Sometimes this does amount to looking at nature in the way we look at art. Sometimes it doesn't. The occasional act of seeing a mountain setting as the very thing that might make for a great landscape painting is no more injurious to our sense of the beauty of the natural environment than the occasional act of thinking how much a certain birdsong is like one of the recorder parts in a Telemann quartet. [...]

The business of setting boundaries [...] can be accomplished in a great many ways. The most obvious, of course, is the way the landscape painter employs when she holds up an empty frame, or her hands, determining that just this much and no more will be the range of her aesthetic attention. This is a familiar means of converting the experience of unorganized natural phenomena into scenery, or a scene. But we are also selecting a range of objects for aesthetic attention and setting boundaries when we simply decide that this cloud mass and not that, this tree and not that, this section of the pond surface and not that is what we want to have as the focus of our experience. When we do this, scene and scenery may be the last things in our minds. We want to take aesthetic stock of the natural objects that capture our attention, and nothing more.

How do we do it? We draw upon memory, imagination, and our culturally acquired capacity to direct attention in such a way as to put some things in the foreground of awareness and others in the background. A fern frond can be made to stand out from a crowd of similar fronds on a cliff face just by deciding to pay close attention to it and not the others. One could equally decide to pay attention to a cluster of five fronds, or only to their stalks, or to the way they are swaying in the breeze, or the intensity of the color in their veins. In deliberate acts of selective attention, we informally frame and reframe natural objects of sensory awareness all the time. Not every informal act of framing, of course, will produce an aesthetic experience. The frame is only a precondition of the processes of reflection and delectation that can take place within it.

[...] 'A landscape to be seen has to be composed' (Santayana, 1936, p. 101). The subtle truth behind this gnomic statement is that some measure of bounding and interpretation is needed if the observer is to turn the restless, endless sensory field into appreciable wholes. Here we may wish to recall that Aristotle, who never spoke of the beauty of landscapes, insisted that the possibility of beauty turns on the concept of limitation. Limit, as he saw it, is what makes it possible to take natural objects as wholes, so that their parts may be regarded as composed, or not. If well composed, according to the canons of suitability specific to it, a natural object might be beautiful, and otherwise not. Drawing on this thought, we can generalize the point Santayana was making: To be seen as beautiful, a natural object has to be composed. And to be composed, it must be bounded, so that its parts can be parts of a whole.

Carlson's (2000) attack on what he calls the 'scenery cult' portrays its proponents as busy converting raw environmental beauty into framed scenes that charm in the way picture postcards charm, by articulating what is essentially limitless into compositions whose formal character-istics (balance, unity, etc.) can then be admired. In his most compelling illustration of this mistake, a guest in a cabin with a picture window looks out upon a mountain-ringed lake and admires what he sees en-compassed by the window-frame as a splendid scene. But, by moving back into the cabin, he can spoil the effect of the 'picture' by adopting a perspective from which the characteristic of balance is lost as the top of a mountain is lopped off by the frame, as in a bad snapshot. To get the beauty straight and free from forced composition, all he has to do is step outside the cabin and look about (see Carlson, 2000, p. 36). But look about and see what? It seems to me that, outside the cabin, the guest is indeed freer to look first here and then there, taking stock of this and then that aspect of his surroundings. Yet, if he is to see beauty in nature (and not just gather a general sense of the beauty of nature), he may well see it as inhering in a beautiful something – a thing, a feature of a thing, a combination of features, or the interplay of some features with others. And for there to be a something there to see, some limitation of his awareness must be imposed.

It is not, contrary to what Carlson suggests, simply to facilitate aware-ness of formal qualities in nature (which he thinks are destined to be a relatively insignificant aspect of aesthetic appreciation of the environment in any case) that the guest in front of the cabin will frame, or focus, his awareness as he looks at the mountains, the lake, and so on. Rather, he must do something of this sort in order to see what he sees as anything at all, let alone as a possible subject of beauty. One can imagine him gazing out at the natural splendor and saying under his breath 'how beautiful!' This exclamation is overheard by another guest, who asks,

Ronald Moore

'What is beautiful?' To which he responds 'Well, all of this,' sweeping his arm before him. But gestures of this kind are notoriously ambiguous and uninformative. So his companion presses him for clarification. 'Do you mean the mountain? The lake? The play of light on the water? What, exactly?' And at this point we have reached a crucial fork in the theoretic road. If we go in one direction, the inarticulate gestures continue, and there cannot be any prospect of communicating the character or content of his aesthetic experience to his correspondent. In this case the most we can say is that the beauty he perceives seems to be out there in a general perfusion of the sensible environment. If we go in the other direction, he considers just what feature or features of the sensible environment present themselves as beautiful – not, or not only, scenic, but beautiful. And in that case, he will abandon the frameless awareness indicated by the sweep of his arm in favor of a more focused, more considered judgment about what counts in a particular beauty judgment. The first path preserves the sense that natural beauty is best understood as unframed, but it does so at the cost of focus and communicability. The second path embraces the idea that beauty judgments require some form of limitation or focal conspectus to make them comprehensible, but it does so at the cost of the dynamic, engaged appreciation of a limitless environment.

The paradox and its resolution

The paradox of framing derives from the tension that this divergence of paths engenders. We can formulate it this way: On the one hand, it seems that nothing can be comprehended as an object of appreciation unless it is framed or bounded in some way. On the other hand, it seems that appreciative experience of natural environments requires the dissolving and penetrating of all boundaries in favor of a dynamic and engaged experience. Thus, in one sense, frames seem indispensable to aesthetic experience as a precondition of comprehensible appreciation while, in another, they seem destined to impair proper regard for natural beauty, converting limitless sensible subjects into mere scenes or compositions.

The usual strategy for resolving paradoxes involves taking a closer look at apparently incompatible premises to see whether they really do imply what they are usually taken to imply. If it can be shown that the way in which the premises are formulated disguises ambiguities or possibilities of reinterpretation, then re-reading the premises in one way rather than another does away with their apparent incompatibility. That is exactly how we need to resolve the framing paradox. The source of the problem, as I see it, lies in an overly narrow conception of 'frame' that has been assumed throughout the debate. Both framists and anti-framists speak of frames as enclosing their aesthetic contents and helping to compose those contents, making possible an appreciation of their balance, unity, harmony, and so on. Framists think this a virtue. Anti-framists think it a vice, at least as it is applied to nature. But neither side fully appreciates the nuanced way in which the other deals with the line between inside and outside.

Although it is certainly true that picture frames facilitate form appreciation in a way that is relatively rigid and impermeable, our experience of paintings, for example, often penetrates the frame by taking stock of undisclosed elements that are part of the painting as much as is the paint on the canvas. To take an obvious example, a proper appreciation of most medieval paintings will require familiarity with the iconographic code that lends significance to some of their elements. That code is not within the frame; it is instead a part of the work that the framed composition calls up. The aesthetic experience one may have in contemplating such a painting – the beauty one might find in it, say – is focused, but not confined, by the frame. And the same is true of many other features of paintings in all periods and places. Irony, parody, homage, political message, and so on, are important parts of artworks not presented on their framed surface. Nor are such elements of response as the way in which a particular painting resonates with recent world events. Or the way it unintentionally echoes work done in another age or place. Or the way its display in a particular museum space creates harmony or tension between it and other paintings, and so on. Yet all of these factors can properly contribute to one's aesthetic experience of the painting as it is presented.

The same contrast between focus and confinement is obviously true of other artistic media as well. The novels we most want to read are those that refuse to stay resolutely within their covers. When we buy tickets to watch plays, we hope and expect our experience will transcend the limits of the stage to connect up with other valuable things in our lives. And the same is obviously true of dance, opera, sculpture, gardens, and other artforms. Even though the various ways in which works in all of these artforms are framed do the important work of focusing our regard on a definite this to be appreciated, it is nearly never the artist's intent to restrict the audience's attention to what is displayed within the frame.

In the natural environment, the notion of what is framed and what is not is equally malleable. [...]

[The] fortunate propensity of nature to stimulate our imaginations profitably is an asset bestowed on it by its unframedness (Hepburn,

1966). Artworks are, relatively speaking, bound in their meaning by the frames and interpretive guides and the like that explain what those frames compose. But I am suggesting that this way of putting things both over-states the controlling function of the frame in art and understates the attention-focusing function of informal framing devices in our experience of nature. [...]

If we think of framing simply as concentration of attention within limits – not concerning ourselves with the question of the potential of those limits to control the elements it confines into a composition – we must concede that every aesthetic experience of nature is framed. It is framed because it depends first and foremost upon the senses, and each of these has a limited range. It is easy to make too much of this condition. This sort of framing is a limitation that is, like many other essentially human limitations, generally indiscernible in the conduct of life. But it is also easy to make too little of it. Whether one is standing outside the cabin looking at the vast panorama or standing within it looking through the window, one is looking at what is necessarily only a selection from the great inventory of natural phenomena. It obviously follows that nature as a whole cannot be appreciated aesthetically, and that we are therefore stuck with finding beauty, sublimity, etc., in parts of nature rather than in a limitless and therefore insensible whole. To this plain fact of limitation, we may add the fact that our limited capacities of attention and comprehension, let alone culturally inculcated limitations on what we may become aware of, inevitably circumscribe our ability to experience natural phenomena. This conclusion flies in the face of at least the most ambitious forms of 'aesthetic integralism,' the notion that natural beauty emerges when, and only when, we regard the whole of nature (just as the beauty of a poem emerges when, and only when, we regard the whole of the poem). [...]

In the end, the framing controversy is about the variety of limits on attention. Everyone admits that our sensory exposure to the world is limited and that our way of making sense of, or appreciating, the world to which we are exposed is also limited. Not only are the limits inevit-able, they are basic conditions of the intelligibility of our sensory world. One person walks along a mountain path turning his head this way and that, listening to the wind, smelling the faint fragrance of high pine needles, feeling the gusts of frigid air on his cheeks. His awareness of all these natural qualities is informally framed, re-framed, and re-framed again as he continues his hike. If his sensory experience were utterly unframed it would be chaotic and unintelligible. Certainly it would be unappreciable. Another person peers through a microscope to examine a volvox colony. She locates it in a dense biotic soup of other animate and inanimate matter, and she isolates it for attention simply by seeing it as a volvox colony, taking its physical limits as the limits of her regard, and pushing all the rest of what appears in her optical field into the background. She has framed the volvox colony for attention – and if she finds it aesthetically interesting, as a potential focus of aesthetic experience, she does so simply by allowing one set of frames (names and physical dimensions of the named objects) to subtend the larger frames of sensory awareness. A third person stops in the course of clearing a debris-clogged gutter to admire the way the oil-runoff, surface froth, and slow-moving mud are catching the low-angled winter light to produce a luminous, rhythmic swirl. As he gathers this in, he turns to his fellow laborer and, looking through his hands with thumbs at right angles, says, 'I wish I had a camera!'

I would insist that each of these persons (and of course the roster of similar examples could be indefinitely extended) is in a position to have an aesthetic experience involving a natural object, and hence to be in a position to appreciate natural beauty (or other natural aesthetic qualities). [...] Appreciation doesn't just rove endlessly and haphazardly across the sensory panorama. It must be trained on this or that, focused by our interest in taking in objects or qualities in various assortments. We can't help limiting our experience of nature by selecting various objects for attention at various times.

Taking an aesthetic interest in a particular natural object is an act of selective attention occurring within other selections of attention that don't disappear in the moment of particular appreciation. They just become temporarily extraneous to the appreciation at hand. [...]

Conclusion

[...] [T]he framing paradox is easily resolved in the context of appreciative practice. If by 'frame' what is really implied is the selection of this or that object or constellation of objects for aesthetic attention, rival claims about nature being framed and unframed can be seen as no more than variable markers on the endless scale of aesthetic selectivity. To frame a piece of the vast environmental whole need not be to convert the selected portion into a quasi-artwork. At one point on the scale, it can be to do precisely what the conceptualists like Allen Carlson and Marcia Eaton have said we should do, namely to regard natural things as what they are, employing the appropriate categories of natural science. Categories of this sort function quite ably as frames, locating what it is that we are observing and presenting it as an integral object against its larger background. Names are also frames. To see the dandelion as a dandelion is to use its name to draw its qualities into focal awareness. At another point on the scale, to frame a natural object can be to form a nameless experiential conspectus rather than a scene or nature-portrait. In such a coalescence of awareness, whatever composition occurs should not be thought of as a forced integration of component elements, but rather as a realization of their relations in a situation of focused aesthetic awareness. In a way, this view is simply an application to the context of natural objects of the central point of John Dewey's doctrine of aesthetic value. Dewey, it will be recalled, maintained that aesthetic value of any kind emerges in the course of converting undifferentiated experience into experiences. Experiences are, in his account, units, or wholes of lived awareness with distinctive beginnings, middles, and ends. Dewey's way of putting the point has seemed to his latter-day critics to put too much emphasis on organic unity. But his fundamental assertion that aesthetic value invariably arises out of experiences rendered whole and comprehensible by being articulated, i.e., by being separated out from the run of the rest of experience by acts of focal attention, correctly and powerfully expresses the importance of framing in aesthetic living. [...]

References

Aristotle (1450b, 1451a) *Poetics.* Available online at: perseus. uchicago.edu/hopper/toc.jsp? doc¼ Perseus:text:1999.01.0056: section¼ 1447a (accessed 26 July 2006).

Carlson, A. (2000) *Aesthetics and the Environment* (New York: Routledge).

Carroll, N. (1995) 'On Being Moved by Nature', in: S. Kemal and I. Gaskell (eds) *Landscape, Natural Beauty, and the Arts*, p. 251 (Cam-bridge: Cambridge University Press).

Hepburn, R. (1966) 'Contemporary Aesthetics and the Neglect of Natural Beauty', in: B. Williams and A. Montefiore (Eds) *British Analytical Philosophy*, p. 290 (Lon-don: Routledge & Kegan Paul).

Santayana, G. (1936) *The Sense of Beauty* (New York: Scribner's).

Walton, K. (1970) 'Categories of Art', *Philosophical Review*, 79, pp. 334–67.

12 | Systems thinking for environmental responsibility

FRITJOF CAPRA, WERNER ULRICH

The three readings in this chapter are extracts relating to
systems thinking and its potential for framing what matters in
environmental responsibility. What is systems thinking? How is it
done? What's more, why is it frequently invoked as a helpful way
of addressing environmental issues? There are two key features of
systems thinking that take constructive framing to a level where
we might take responsibility for our framing devices. First is an
appreciation of the interrelationships and interdependencies
between all entities. Second is the awareness that systems are
human conceptual constructs, and so systems thinking necessarily invites and celebrates contrasting perspectives on issues.
Fritjof Capra, an American physicist, writer and environmental
activist, is a passionate advocate of systems thinking in promoting
(i) a more holistic/ecological worldview and (ii) the need for a
change in values through taking on a new perspective – adopting
what he calls a new paradigm. The two readings from Capra
convey these basic ideas on systems thinking respectively.

But the two systems ideas prompt questions. First, how far can
any framing device claim to be comprehensive or holistic – incorporating every interrelationship and interdependence? Second,
while advocating a new paradigm based on a present understanding of life and society, what basis is there for claiming this as being
the 'right' view, or universal and timeless? Paradigms, like systems,
are ultimately frameworks, determined culturally by time and
place. Systems thinking ought to be a way of making our inevitable
framing devices explicit and open to critique and transformation.

The third reading in this chapter comes from a critical systems
philosopher from Switzerland with experience in government planning. In extracts from a revised paper by Werner Ulrich, homage
is paid to his mentor – another great systems philosopher, C. W.
Churchman. Ulrich outlines a third important feature of systems
thinking: an essential critical dimension to address our continual
responsibility in making claims of being 'holistic' and/or practising

respect for different value positions. Space in this volume does not permit a description of Ulrich's own endeavours in addressing these issues through his 'critical systems heuristics', though references might be followed up, including many available on open access from Ulrich's own website, www.geocities.com/csh_home/.

Reading 12a: Fritjof Capra, The web of life
Chapter 1: Deep ecology – a new paradigm
[...] The more we study the major problems of our time, the more we come to realize that they cannot be understood in isolation. They are systemic problems, which means that they are interconnected and interdependent. For example, stabilizing world population will only be possible when poverty is reduced worldwide. The extinction of animal and plant species on a massive scale will continue as long as the Southern Hemisphere is burdened by massive debts. Scarcities of resources and environmental degradation combine with rapidly expanding populations to lead to the breakdown of local communities, and to the ethnic and tribal violence that has become the main characteristic of the post-Cold War era.

Ultimately, these problems must be seen as just different facets of one single crisis, which is largely a crisis of perception. It derives from the fact that most of us, and especially our large social institutions, subscribe to the concepts of an outdated worldview, a perception of reality inadequate for dealing with our overpopulated, globally interconnected world.

There are solutions to the major problems of our time; some of them even simple. But they require a radical shift in our perceptions, our thinking, our values. And, indeed, we are now at the beginning of such a fundamental change of worldview in science and society, a change of paradigms as radical as the Copernican Revolution. But this realization has not yet dawned on most of our political leaders. The recognition that a profound change of perception and thinking is needed if we are to survive has not yet reached most of our corporate leaders either, nor the administrators and professors of our large universities. [...]

The paradigm that is now receding has dominated our culture for several hundred years, during which it has shaped our modern Western society and has significantly influenced the rest of the world. This paradigm consists of a number of entrenched ideas and values, among them the view of the universe as a mechanical system composed of elementary building-blocks, the view of the human body as a machine, the view of life in society as a competitive struggle for existence, the belief in unlimited material progress to be achieved through economic and technological growth, and – last, not least – the belief that a society in which the female is everywhere subsumed under the male is one that follows a basic law of nature. [...]

Chapter 2: From the parts to the whole

[...] The emergence of systems thinking was a profound revolution in the history of Western scientific thought. The belief that in every complex system the behaviour of the whole can be understood entirely from the properties of its parts is central to the Cartesian paradigm. This was Descartes' celebrated method of analytic thinking, which has been an essential characteristic of modern scientific thought. In the analytic, or reductionist, approach, the parts themselves cannot be analysed any further, except by reducing them to still smaller parts. Indeed, Western science has been progressing in that way, and at each step there has been a level of fundamental constituents that could not be analysed any further.

The great shock of twentieth-century science has been that systems cannot be understood by analysis. The properties of the parts are not intrinsic properties, but can be understood only within the context of the larger whole. Thus the relationship between the parts and the whole has been reversed. In the systems approach, the properties of the parts can be understood only from the organization of the whole. Accordingly, systems thinking does not concentrate on basic building-blocks but rather on basic principles of organization. Systems thinking is 'contextual', which is the opposite of analytical thinking. Analysis means taking something apart in order to understand it; systems thinking means putting it into the context of a larger whole. [...]

Chapter 3: Systems theories

[...] It is perhaps worthwhile to summarize the key characteristics of systems thinking at this point. The first, and most general, criterion is the shift from the parts to the whole. Living systems are integrated wholes whose properties cannot be reduced to those of smaller parts. Their essential, or 'systemic', properties are properties of the whole, which none of the parts have. They arise from the 'organizing relations' of the parts, i.e. from a configuration of ordered relationships that is characteristic of that particular class of organisms, or systems. Systemic properties are destroyed when a system is dissected into isolated elements.

Another key criterion of systems thinking is the ability to shift one's attention back and forth between systems levels. Throughout the living world, we find systems nesting within other systems, and by applying the same concepts to different systems levels – e.g. the concept of stress to an organism, a city, or an economy – we can often gain important insights. On the other hand, we also have to recognize that, in general, different systems levels represent levels of differing complexity. At each level the observed phenomena exhibit properties that do not exist at lower levels. The systemic properties of a particular level are called 'emergent' properties, since they emerge at that particular level.

In the shift from mechanistic thinking to systems thinking, the relationship between the parts and the whole has been reversed. Cartesian science believed that in any complex system, the behaviour of the whole could be analysed in terms of the properties of its parts. Systems science shows that living systems cannot be understood by analysis. The properties of the parts are not intrinsic properties, but can be understood only within the context of the larger whole. Thus systems thinking is 'contextual' thinking; and since explaining things in terms of their context means explaining them in terms of their environment, we can also say that all systems thinking is environmental thinking.

Ultimately – as quantum physics showed so dramatically – there are no parts at all. What we call a part is merely a pattern in an inseparable web of relationships [...]

Reading 12b: Fritjof Capra, Hidden connections
Changing the game

As this new century unfolds, it, becomes increasingly apparent that the neo-liberal 'Washington Consensus' and the policies and economic rules set forth by the Group of Seven and their financial institutions – the World Bank, the IMF and the World Trade Organization (WTO) – are consistently misguided. Analyses by scholars and community leaders cited throughout this book show that the 'new economy' is producing a multitude of interconnected harmful consequences – rising social inequality and social exclusion, a breakdown of democracy, more rapid and extensive deterioration of the natural environment, and increasing poverty and alienation. The new global capitalism has also created a global criminal economy that profoundly affects national and international economies and politics; it has threatened and destroyed local communities around the world; and with the pursuit of an ill-conceived biotechnology it has invaded the sanctity of life by attempting to turn diversity into monoculture, ecology into engineering and life itself into a commodity.

State of the world

Despite new environmental regulations, the increasing availability of ecofriendly products and many other encouraging developments championed by the environmental movement, the massive loss of forests and the greatest extinction of species in millions of years has not been reversed.[1] By depleting our natural resources and reducing the planet's biodiversity we damage the very fabric of life on which our well-being depends, including the priceless 'ecosystem services' that nature provides for free – processing waste, regulating the climate, regenerating the atmosphere and so on.[2] These vital processes are emergent properties of nonlinear living systems, that we are only beginning to understand, and they are now seriously endangered by our linear pursuits of economic growth and material consumption. [...]

[T]he current form of global capitalism is ecologically and socially unsustainable, and hence politically unviable in the long run. More stringent environmental regulations, better business practices and more efficient technologies are all necessary, but they are not enough. We need a deeper systemic change.

Such deep systemic change is already under way. Scholars, community leaders and grassroots activists around the world are forming effective coalitions and are raising their voices not only to demand that we must 'change the game', but also to suggest concrete ways of doing so.

Globalization by design

Any realistic discussion of changing the game must begin with the recognition that, although globalization is an emergent phenomenon, the current form of economic globalization has been consciously designed and *can* be reshaped [...] [T]oday's global economy is structured around networks of financial flows in which capital works in real time, moving rapidly from one option to another in a *relentless* search for investment opportunities.[3] The global market is really a network of machines – an automaton that imposes its logic on all human participants. However, in order to function smoothly, this automaton has to be programmed by human actors and institutions. The programmes that give rise to the new economy consist of two essential components – values and operational rules.

The global financial networks process signals that assign specific financial value to every asset in every economy. This process is far from straightforward. It involves economic calculations based on advanced mathematical models; information and opinions provided by market valuation firms, financial gurus, leading central bankers and other influential analysts; and, last but not least, information turbulences that are largely uncontrolled.[4]

In other words, the tradable financial value of any asset (which is subject to continual adjustments) is an emergent property of the automaton's highly nonlinear dynamics. However, underlying all evaluations is the *basic* principle of unfettered capitalism: that money-making should always be valued higher than democracy, human rights, environmental protection or any other value. Changing the game means, first and foremost, changing this basic principle.

In addition to the complex process of assessing tradable values, the programmes of the global financial networks contain operational rules that must be followed by markets around the world. These are the free-trade rules that the World Trade Organization imposes on its member states. To ensure maximum profit margins in the global casino, capital must be allowed to flow freely through its financial networks so that it can be invested anywhere in the world at a moment's notice. These free-trade rules, together with increasing deregulation of corporate activities, are designed to guarantee the *free* movement of capital. The impediments to unrestricted trade that are removed or curtailed by this new legal framework are usually environmental regulations, public health laws, food safety laws, workers' rights and laws giving nations control over investments on their territory and ownership of their local culture.[5]

The resulting integration of economic activities goes beyond purely economic aspects; it extends to the cultural domain. Countries around the world with vastly different cultural traditions are increasingly homogenized through relentless proliferation of the same restaurant franchises, hotel chains, high-rise architecture, superstores and shopping malls. The result, in Vandana Shiva's apt phrase, is an increasing 'monoculture of the mind'. [...]

Ecoliteracy and ecodesign

Ecological sustainability is an essential component of the core values that form the basis for reshaping globalization. Accordingly, many of the NGOs, research institutes, and centres of learning in the new global civil society have chosen sustainability as their explicit focus. Indeed, creating sustainable communities is the great challenge of our time,

The concept of sustainability was introduced in early 1985 by Lester Brown, founder of the Worldwatch Institute, who defined a sustainable society as one that is able to satisfy its needs without diminishing the chances of future generations.[6] Several years later, the report of the World Commission on Environment and Development (the 'Brundtland Report') used the same definition to present the notion of sustainable development: 'Humankind has the ability' to achieve sustainable development – to meet the needs of the present without compromising the ability of future generations to meet their own needs.[7] These definitions of sustainability are important moral exhortations. They remind us of our responsibility to pass on to our children and grandchildren a world with as many opportunities as the one we inherited. However, this definition does not tell us anything about how to build a sustainable society. This is why there has been much confusion about the meaning of sustainability, even within the environmental movement.

The key to an operational definition of ecological sustainability is the realization that we do not need to invent sustainable human communities from scratch but can model them after nature's ecosystems, which are sustainable communities of plants, animals and microorganisms. Since the outstanding characteristic of the Earth household is its inherent ability to sustain life, a sustainable human community is one designed in such a manner that its ways of life, businesses, economy, physical structures and technologies do not interfere with nature's inherent ability to sustain life. Sustainable communities evolve their patterns of living over time in continual interaction with other living systems, both human and nonhuman. Sustainability does not mean that things do not change: it is a dynamic process of co-evolution rather than a static state.

The operational definition of sustainability implies that the first step in our endeavour to build sustainable communities must be to become 'ecologically literate', i.e. to understand the principles of organization, common to all living systems, that ecosystems have evolved to sustain the web of life.[8] [...] [L]iving systems are self-generating networks organizationally closed within boundaries but open to continual flows of energy and matter. This systemic understanding of life allows us to formulate a set of principles of organization that may be identified as the basic principles of ecology and used as guidelines for building sustainable human communities. Specifically, there are six principles of ecology that are critical to sustaining life: networks, cycles, solar energy, partnership, diversity and dynamic balance (see table).

These principles are directly relevant to our health and well-being. Because of our vital need to breathe, eat and drink, we are always embedded in the cyclical processes of nature. Our health depends upon the purity of the air we breathe and the water we drink, and it depends on the health of the soil from which our food is produced. In the coming decades the survival of humanity will depend on our ecological literacy – our ability to understand the basic principles of ecology and to live accordingly. Thus, ecological literacy, or 'ecoliteracy', must become a critical skill for politicians, business leaders and professionals in all spheres, and should be the most important part of education at all levels – from primary and

Fritjof Capra

secondary schools to colleges, universities and the continuing education and training of professionals.

[...] Ecoliteracy – the understanding of the principles of organization that ecosystems have evolved to sustain the web of life – is the first step on the road to sustainability. The second step is to move towards ecodesign. We need to apply our ecological knowledge to the fundamental redesign of our technologies and social institutions, so as to bridge the current gap between human design and the ecologically sustainable systems of nature. [...]

Principles of ecology

Networks

At all scales of nature, we find living systems nesting within other living systems – networks within networks. Their boundaries are not boundaries of separation but boundaries of identity. All living systems communicate with one another and share resources across their boundaries.

Cycles

All living organisms must feed on continual flows of matter and energy from their environment to stay alive, and all living organisms continually produce waste. However, an ecosystem generates no net waste, one species' waste being another species' food. Thus, matter cycles continually through the web of life.

Solar Energy

Solar energy, transformed into chemical energy by the photosynthesis of green plants, drives the ecological cycles.

Partnership

The exchanges of energy and resources in an ecosystem are sustained by pervasive co-operation. Life did not take over the planet by combat but by co-operation, partnership, and networking.

Diversity

Ecosystems achieve stability and resilience through the richness and complexity of their ecological webs. The greater their biodiversity, the more resilient they will be.

Dynamic Balance

An ecosystem is a flexible, ever-fluctuating network. Its flexibility is a consequence of multiple feedback loops that keep the system in a state of dynamic balance. No single variable is maximized; all variables fluctuate around their optimal values.

Design, in the broadest sense, consists in shaping flows of energy and materials for human purposes. Ecodesign is a process in which our human purposes are carefully meshed with the larger patterns and flows of the natural world. Ecodesign principles reflect the principles of organization that nature has evolved to sustain the web of life. To practise industrial design in such a context requires a fundamental shift in our attitude towards nature. In the words of science writer Janine Benyus, it 'introduces an era based not on what we can *extract* from nature, but on what we can *learn* from her'.[9]

Epilogue: Making sense

[...] As this new century unfolds, there are two developments that will have major impacts on the well-being and ways of life of humanity. Both have to do with networks, and both involve radically new technologies. One is the rise of global capitalism; the other is the creation of sustainable communities based on ecological literacy and the practice of ecodesign. Whereas global capitalism is concerned with electronic networks of financial and informational flows, ecodesign is concerned with ecological networks of energy and material flows. The goal of the global economy is to maximize the wealth and power of its elites; the goal of ecodesign to maximize the sustainability of the web of life.

These two scenarios – each involving complex networks and special advanced technologies – are currently on a collision course. We have seen that the current form of global capitalism is ecologically and socially unsustainable. The so-called 'global market' is really a network of machines programmed according to the fundamental principle that money-making should take precedence over human rights, democracy, environmental protection or any other value.

However, human values can change; they are not natural laws. The same electronic networks of financial and informational flows *could* have other values built into them. The critical issue is not technology, but politics. The great challenge of the twenty-first century will be to change the value system underlying the global economy, so as to make it compatible with the demands of human dignity and ecological sustainability [...]

Notes

1 See Brown et al. (2001).
2 See Hawken, Lovins and Lovins (1999), p. 3.
3 See Castells (2000).
4 Castells (2000).
5 See Barker and Mander (1999), Wallach and Sforza (2001).
6 Brown (1981).
7 World Commission on Environment and Development (1987).

Fritjof Capra

8 See Orr (1992), Capra (1996), Callenbach (1998).

9 Benyus (1997), p. 2.

References

Barker, Debi and Jerry Mander, 'Invisible Government', International Forum on Globalization, October 1999.

Benyus, Janine, *Biomimicry*, Morrow, New York, 1997.

Brown, Lester, *Building a Sustainable Society*, Norton, New York, 1981.

Brown, Lester et al., *State of the World 2001*, Worldwatch Institute, Washington, DC, 2001.

Callenbach, Ernest, *Ecology: A Pocket Guide*, University of California Press, Berkeley, 1998.

Capra, Fritjof, *The Web of Life*, Anchor/Doubleday, New York, 1996.

Castells, Manuel, 'Information Technology and Global Capitalism', in Hutton and Giddens (2000).

Hawken, Paul, Amory Lovins and Hunter Lovins, *Natural Capitalism*, Little, Brown, New York, 1999.

Hutton, Will and Anthony Giddens (eds), *Global Capitalism*, The New Press, New York, 2000.

Orr, David, *Ecological Literacy*, State University of New York Press, 1992.

Wallach, Lori and Michelle Sforza, *Whose Trade Organization?*, Public Citizen, 2001.

World Commission on Environment and Development, *Our Common Future*, Oxford University Press, New York, 1987.

Reading 12c: Werner Ulrich, Can we secure future-responsive management through systems thinking and design?

The epistemological crux: comprehensiveness

How can we design improvement without appreciating the totality of conditions that will determine the quality of our decisions, for example, risks and chances, future opportunities, and expected distributions of different benefits and costs? In Churchman's [1968: 3] words, 'How can we design improvement without understanding the whole system?' To Churchman, the question implies that conventional analytic patterns of decision making and problem solving need to be complemented by a 'sweep-in' process [Singer 1957; Churchman 1982: 117 and 125–32], a systematic and self-critical attempt to consider ever more aspects of the larger system – ideally, the totality of relevant conditions. [...]

The ethical crux: conflict

Once we begin to understand management as the art of designing improvement, we can hardly escape the question of what really constitutes an improvement, that is, what ought to be our standards of improvement. Even if the epistemological challenge could be met satisfactorily, so that some kind of holistic understanding of the world we live in were possible, improvement would hardly ever mean improvement for everyone concerned or affected. Management inescapably implies judgment about whose needs are to be served and what costs are to be imposed on those who are not served but are affected. How can we justify the value implications of decisions in the face of conflicting values, needs and interests? [...]

What is future-responsive management? Three concerns

[...] Churchman has shown a strong concern for what more recently – particularly in developmental and environmental studies as well as in future research – has come to be designated the ideal of sustainability.

According to this ideal, we should consider our policies and designs for improvement critically with regard to long-term environmental and developmental implications, so as to make sure that they promote ecologically viable and socioeconomically as well as socioculturally desirable conditions. [...]

I will suggest three main concerns that I link to the idea of future-responsive management [...]

Concern no. 1: ... toward a different kind of future discourse

[...] [T]he sweep-in process seems to become a hopeless undertaking, as much as it appears epistemologically necessary. Need we conclude that if we take the systems idea seriously, we are bound to end up with inaction, if not mental breakdown, and ultimately with a bottomless epistemological and ethical skepticism?

The answer for me is no, although I confess that Churchman's 'heroic' stance sometimes leaves me dismayed. It is such a tall order! But I think it is only so long as we try to sweep in the future in terms of a forecasting approach (that is, in terms of empirical science) that the quest for future-responsive management must remain chimerical. Apart from the usual focus on this empirical-predictive dimension of the future discourse, there are other ways to conceive of future-responsive management.

I think, first of all, of what might be called the cultural dimension of the future discourse, namely, the cultural assumptions on which depend our perceptions of the present as well as our conceptions of the future. Challenging cultural assumptions is no less important for conceiving of possible futures than is the technical side of forecasting. As an illustration, a 1925 forecast of the American Petroleum Institute on oil use in the United States projected 50 million automobiles in the US by 1975. The actual number turned out to be 120 million. The forecast had presumed that the number of cars would be equivalent to one fourth of the US population, as this was the fraction of white males over 20 in the population.

By challenging cultural assumptions, we make the sweep-in process meaningful without losing practicability. We can then pursue the quest for comprehensiveness by uncovering alternative contexts of meaning (interpreting 'facts') rather than by extending our knowledge in an empirical-predictive sense (technical scope of forecasting). No impossible cognitive requirements are involved in such an effort, for it aims not at all-encompassing knowledge but only at better (mutual) understanding. That is to say, it requires not so much an unbounded exploration of an ever-growing larger system over time but rather a sincere effort to ensure authentic and unhampered communication. [...]

Concern no. 2: ... toward a new ethic of future-responsive management
An increased consideration of the cultural dimension of the future discourse, though it may help us to uncover alternative future visions, does not automatically secure improvement in an ethical sense, for it has no way of distinguishing ethically defensible from ethically unacceptable consensus. [...]

A future-responsive ethics must consider the harm or improvement caused in the whole system. Churchman's concept of a whole systems ethics is apt in this context, as it reminds us of the intrinsic connection between ethical and systems thinking. Table 1 contrasts some of the mentioned limitations of the old ethics with the requirements of a new, future-responsive ethics. [...]

Concern no. 3: ... toward a critical turn in systems thinking and design
[...] A critical turn of our understanding of systems rationality is in order. In *The Systems Approach and Its Enemies*, Churchman [1979] taught us essential lessons about such a critical turn. I understand the book's basic message thus: The concept of systems rationality that will help us to secure improvement is one that clearly acknowledges its own lack of comprehensiveness as a necessary condition of critically tenable practice.

This notion of a nonrationalistic, because self-limiting, concept of rationality for me marks an important turning point in the recent history of systems theory: it represents a shift from 'precritical' hard and soft systems thinking to critical systems thinking. From this new perspective, the implication of the systems idea is not that we must understand the whole system but rather that we need to deal critically with the fact that we never do. As I tried to show in *Critical Heuristics* [Ulrich 1983], the systems idea, once we begin to understand it in this sense, will remind us of the unholy character of our systems maps and designs. It can also

TABLE 1 The old ethics are based on the notion that the acting individual can judge the moral quality of his or her action from experience ('conscience') while in the new ethics, understanding the whole system (acting 'con scientia') becomes a crucial moral requirement.

Aspect	Old ethics	New ethics
Focus (object of ethical judgment)	Individualistic ethics: The moral quality of an agent's individual action is evaluated.	Whole systems ethics: The improvement of the whole system is evaluated.
Critical instance of ethical judgment	Volitional ethics: Good will and personal responsibility ('conscience') are the crucial issues of moral competence.	Cognitivist ethics: Understanding based on knowledge ('con scientia') of the total relevant system is the crucial issue of moral competence.
Cognitive requirements	Low: Can be met by all people of good will without requiring any special expertise ('knowledge-free' ethics of certainty).	High: A sweep-in process is needed to appreciate the whole-systems implications of an action from different viewpoints; collective expertise is required (knowledge-based ethics of uncertainty).
Reach with respect to the future	Ethics of immediacy: The consequences of an action can be known and judged from experience, as the agent and those affected or concerned share a present, geographical space and social life-world.	Ethics of remoteness: The consequences of an action may not be known from experience; the agent and those affected or concerned need not share a present, geographical space and social life-world.
Reach with respect to environmental concerns	Anthropocentric ethics: Nature is not an object of human responsibility, it is beyond the reach of human intervention and cares for itself.	Universal ethics: Nature has become an object of human responsibility, as the causal scale of our policies and technologies has become global.

provide a methodological basis for developing tools of critical reflection – conceptual tools that can help us systematically to uncover the inevitable incomprehensiveness or selectivity of designs. To this purpose, critical systems heuristics offers both a conceptual framework and forms of cogent argumentation. (For introductory overviews see Ulrich [1987 and 1993].)

Conclusion

Can we secure future-responsive management through systems thinking and design? The answer, it seems to me, must be a self-critical 'no,' followed by a challenging 'however.'

No, because the systems idea, by helping us to better understand the crucial epistemological and ethical difficulties of securing improvement that persists, does not automatically remove these difficulties. The difficulties in question – the epistemological necessity of the quest for comprehensiveness, the ethical problem of dealing with conflicts of interests, and the subsequent methodological difficulty of defining clear and valid standards of improvement – are not introduced by the systems approach but reflect genuine qualities of the world we live in, in which complex interconnections and conflicts are typical. The idea of future-responsive management raises these difficulties in a particularly acute form by facing us with the impossible cognitive requirements of an empirical-predictive future discourse and with difficult ethical conflicts between the interests of future and present generations.

However, skepticism provides no solution. It merely serves to immunize mistaken claims to rationality against critical debate. The fact that reason cannot secure comprehensive rationality provides no sound argument against a systematic effort to promote critical awareness with respect to our failure to be comprehensively rational. In particular, it will not help to reject the systems idea because of its difficult implications, as if it caused the difficulties of which it reminds us. The systems idea is neither the cause nor the solution of the problem, it is only the messenger. Accusing the messenger of the bad news will help as little as ignoring the news.

The only reasonable response is to take the messenger seriously and to listen carefully to what it has to say, so as to understand its message as well as possible. To the extent that we take the systems idea seriously, we will begin to understand its critical implications and will thereby gain awareness of our failure to be comprehensive. Such awareness may ultimately be the only method available for ordinary planners and decision makers to become more future-responsive. Uncovering the lack of comprehensiveness – the unavoidable selectivity – of our designs and then systematically tracing the practical implications of that selectivity is perhaps the only way to prevent the difficulties in question from becoming a source of systematic deception! [...]

References

Churchman, C. West 1968, *Challenge to Reason*, McGraw-Hill, New York.

Churchman, C. West 1979, *The Systems Aproach and Its Enemies*, Basic Books, New York.

Churchman, C. West 1982, *Thought and Wisdom*, Intersystems Publications, Seaside, California.

Singer, Edgar A., Jr 1957, *Experience and Reflection*, ed. C. W. Churchman, University of Pennsylvania Press, Philadelphia, Pennsylvania.

Ulrich, Werner 1983, *Critical Heuristics of Social Planning: A New Approach to Practical Philosophy*, Paul Haupt Academic Publishers, Bern, Switzerland, and Stuttgart, Germany.

Ulrich, Werner 1987, 'Critical heuristics of social systems design,' *European Journal of Operational Research*, Vol. 31, No. 3, pp. 276–83.

Ulrich, Werner 1993, 'Some difficulties of ecological thinking considered from a critical systems perspective: A plea for critical holism,' *Systems Practice*, Vol. 6, No. 6, pp. 583–611.

13 | Environmental pragmatism, ecocentrism and deliberative democracy

ROBYN ECKERSLEY

How might our framing devices – both informal (through aesthetic judgements) and formal (for example, through systems thinking) – help to provide space in relaying understanding and support for more effective policy design? The question is taken up in the second half of the original reading by Andrew Light (Reading 9) in pursuing the fourth debate in environmental ethics – between monists and pluralists. Robyn Eckersley takes as her point of departure the same debate in an attempt to identify how particular approaches to valuing nature – considering nature 'matters' – might influence policy and action. She regards monists as ecocentric 'advocates' and pluralists as 'mediators' associated with environmental pragmatism. While Light is regarded as a 'mediator', Eckersley adopts a more circumscribed view of environmental pragmatism – providing 'a sympathetic critique'. As a political theorist, Eckersley identifies three weaknesses of the pragmatist tradition and delineates circumstances where such framing can be of value and where other more challenging monist-based approaches might be more appropriate. The reading makes reference to ideas of social learning and deliberative democracy picked up subsequently in Parts Three and Four of this anthology, but more immediately invites attention to the kind of cognitive space required for citizen involvement referred to in Reading 14.

Introduction

[...] [E]cocentric philosophers (most notably J. Baird Callicott) have argued that the pragmatists' embrace of moral pluralism carries with it the danger of lapsing into indecisive relativism. In particular, the refusal by environmental pragmatists to privilege any substantive environmental values in advance of policy dialogue is seen as problematic insofar as it can lead to philosophical contradictions and dubious political outcomes that may not necessarily protect the environment.[1] According to this construction, ecocentric theorists and activists are the fearless environmental justice advocates, standing up for the interests of the environmental victims of economic development, including both humans and nonhuman species. [...]

In this chapter, I seek to defend the democratic credentials of eco-centrism and offer a sympathetic critique of environmental pragmatism. I also suggest that the different philosophical approaches and strategic practices preferred by environmental pragmatism and ecocentrism may be understood as two different and necessary 'democratic moments' in the processes of environmental policy making, which carry with them different purposes, strengths and weaknesses. I shall call the pragmatists 'the mediators' and ecocentric theorists and activists the 'advocates'. (I apply these labels equally to theorists and activists in each camp, on the view that public philosophical reflection and communication is no less political than practical political engagement and activism.) The environmental mediators are good listeners who are flexible and open-minded. They are respectful of the diversity of different human modes of interacting with and valuing ecological communities and they seek to reduce conflict by focusing on immediate, practical environmental problem solving. Often this may require deftly side-stepping intractable and heated moral conflicts in order to concentrate the minds of the parties on common practical problems. In contrast, the environmental advocates are the relentless critics of the status quo who are deeply committed to particular environmental values, worldviews and policy goals. They are the activists and long-term visionaries who seek to inspire, move, persuade and cajole others in order to shift cultural understandings by a variety of different forms of political communication and engagement (such as political rhetoric, satire, science, logic, poetry, literature, art and practical example). They are prepared to challenge and disrupt conventional norms and policy discourses, generate political conflict and sometimes they may refuse to engage in formalized democratic deliberation if it is likely to compromise their values and goals.

These distinctions may be understood as two different ideal types, which means that not all environmental pragmatists and ecocentrics would necessarily conform exactly to the respective criteria. Moreover, these ideal types are not entirely mutually exclusive, in that both the mediator and the advocate support democratic deliberation, at least in principle. However, as we shall see, there are tensions associated with how democratic deliberation is understood and best realized. I therefore enlist the figures of the pragmatic mediator and the activist advocate in order to draw out these differences and illuminate the necessary and potentially productive tensions between these different types of democratic engagement. Indeed, these tensions resonate with a more general tension in political thought and practice about the relative importance of, and relationship between, justice and democracy. On the one hand, we are familiar with the claim that justice should be the 'first virtue' of political thought and practice and therefore prior to, or at least determinative of, democracy while, on the other hand, we find claims that justice is simply that which emerges from a fair democratic dialogue. Posing the tension in these stark terms would suggest that ecocentrics understand environmental justice to be the necessary starting point of political inquiry and practice, while environmental pragmatists would accord this status to democracy since it provides the fairest means of reconciling value pluralism. However, this is not meant to suggest that ecocentrics are necessarily undemocratic nor that environmental pragmatists are not concerned about environmental justice. Rather, the different starting points merely illuminate different entry points and objectives that inform different understandings of the *relationship* between justice and democracy. In any event, in recent debates in political theory there seems to be a growing acknowledgment that neither justice nor democracy should be understood as the prior virtue, that justice and democracy presuppose each other and are therefore mutually defining (Gould 1988; Young 1990; Kingwell 1995; Benhabib 1996). The real debate, as we shall see, concerns how environmental justice and democracy are mutually related, in theory and practice. [...]

Environmental pragmatism

The environmental pragmatists' commitment to open-ended inquiry and practical democratic engagement is grounded in the insights of the classical American pragmatists, the chief pioneers of whom were C. S. Peirce (1839–1914), William James (1842–1910) and especially John Dewey (1859–1952). As a philosophical movement, the early pragmatists were concerned 'to improve the methods by which human beings can acquire new knowledge and understanding of their environment, both in an ordinary life context and, in a more organized way, through science'.[2] Common and related themes developed by the 'classical pragmatists' included an emphasis on the tentative and provisional character of knowledge, the self-corrective character of inquiry as an ongoing experiential process, and the interpretation of ideas, meaning and truth through their practical consequences. According to this radical empiricist approach, truth is interpreted not in any abstract or absolutist way but rather from the standpoint of particular agents in relation to their experience of particular problems, an experience which includes agents' beliefs and utilities. John Dewey, in particular, reinterpreted pragmatism as instrumentalism and interpreted truth as 'warranted assertability'.

Socially and politically, the classical pragmatists were humanists and democrats who emphasized the importance of the social construction of knowledge, and social learning through democratic inquiry. [...]

For some environmental pragmatists, the human perspective is the only thing we know as humans and therefore the human perspective becomes the measure of all things by default.[3] For committed Deweyians, it is meaningless to talk about the value of something in the absence of a human valuer, although this need not rule out the valuing of nonhuman entities for their own sake by human subjects. Indeed, respect for moral pluralism necessarily entails respect for those cultures and traditions that value nonhuman nature in moral, aesthetic or spiritual terms. But it also necessarily entails respect for those cultures and traditions which do not. [...]

Just solutions to social and ecological problems must be understood as provisional, dialogical and context specific in relation to a particular community of inquirers rather than fixed, monological and universal.

Although I have so far introduced environmental pragmatism as essentially a method of environmental policy making rather than as a substantive environmental philosophy, there are some environmental pragmatists, such as Bryan Norton, who have developed pragmatism in a more substantive direction, insofar as they have defended the principle of sustainability as philosophically consistent with environmental pragmatism. That is, sustainability is defended on the grounds that it keeps open options and opportunities for future generations and is consistent with a Darwinian emphasis on practical survival and a pragmatic conception of truth. For Norton, pursuing the practical path of sustainability is more likely to guarantee the survival of the community of inquirers and their descendants than any rival philosophy, and is therefore 'destined, in the terms of Pierce, to be adopted as the conclusion of all rational inquirers, as they struggle through many experiments to make coherent sense of human experience'.[4] The principle of sustainability is also defended as especially amenable to social learning: it is open-ended and therefore requires social interpretation and experimentation before it can find expression in practical policies in response to practical problems.

However, for Andrew Light and Eric Katz, environmental pragmatism is defended primarily as a methodology rather than a substantive environmental philosophy.[5] This approach involves starting with existing environmental problems and conflicts, and understanding and working with the experience, beliefs, values and 'baggage' that real people carry with them in particular contexts. [...]

Deliberation, creative conflict mediation and social learning thus replace any quest for ethical perfection. For Bryan Norton, moral monism (such as nonanthropocentric environmental ethics) and applied philosophy typically go together. That is, moral monists are 'armchair philosophers' who develop and defend particular universal principles from which policy makers and others are expected to 'derive' particular policy options. In contrast, practical philosophers seek to generate workable principles from practice rather than work out practical policies from general principles.[6] [...]

The limitations of 'practical problem-solving'

So far, we have outlined the environmental pragmatist understanding of how a 'genuine environmental democracy' ought to function. That is, environmental pragmatists hold to a regulative ideal of democratic deliberation that is respectful, ecumenical and directed toward practical problem solving. As appealing as this regulative ideal may be, I nonetheless want to highlight three major, interrelated limitations and/or undeveloped dimensions of environmental pragmatism. The first is that its narrow focus on problem solving makes it insufficiently critical and emancipatory when examined from the perspective of oppressed and marginal groups and classes or nonhuman species. From this perspective, environmental pragmatism runs the risk of being too accommodating of the existing constellation of social forces that drive environmental degradation. The second limitation is that it is too instrumentalist in the way that it seeks to close off noninstrumental democratic encounters and the opportunity for the parties to engage in dialogue for dialogue's sake – a possibility that can sometimes work to build mutual respect and trust as much as it can deepen antagonisms. Moreover, although environmental pragmatists seek to avoid moral reductionism, their *method* of inquiry is reductionist in the sense that it seeks to filter out arguments that do not address questions of practical necessity – effectively reducing collective deliberation to deliberation about competing utilities. The third criticism is that there is ultimately nothing especially *environmental* about the kind of democratic inquiry defended by environmental pragmatists, in the sense that environmental pragmatism ultimately rests on a liberal humanist moral premise rather than any explicit environmental values. And as we shall see, many ecocentric political theorists have taken issue with the moral foundations of liberal democracy on the ground that it is not pluralist or inclusive enough.

Too accommodating, not critical enough

To remain consistent with their methodological approach, we would expect environmental pragmatists to approach environmental conflicts by recommending practically oriented deliberation and mediation among the parties or their representatives. We would also expect them to counsel against anything that might lead to an escalation of conflict, since conflict stands in the way of practical problem solving. Now there certainly are many circumstances when such a strategy is likely to be prudent and effective. Indeed, the concern to unify disparate political actors around a common problem is one of the greatest strengths of environmental pragmatism, which has suggested some tactful and creative methods that might, in some instances, serve to soften or shelve such deeply held moral convictions in order to achieve practical outcomes.[7]

However, deeply held moral, religious and/or cultural convictions may not be the only reasons why the respectful and practical democratic disposition hoped for by pragmatists may be found in short supply. In real world democracies, differences in income, wealth, status, knowledge and 'communicative power' are widespread. In their effort to acknowledge and work with *moral* pluralism, environmental pragmatists have tended to neglect a wider range of *other* reasons for conflict, intransigence or non-cooperation by particular parties to environmental disputes. For example, it may be because of poverty and economic necessity brought about by capital flight, debt or corruption. It may be because certain parties have other, more 'effective' means of force at their disposal to achieve their goals other than the force of argumentative persuasion, such as the public coercive power of the state, the private power to make threats or inducements or even the more subtle power that comes with simply belonging to the dominant cultural or ethnic group in a particular society. Or it may be because certain parties or their advocates do not believe they will achieve a fair or meaningful hearing precisely because the forces arrayed against them are more powerful and/or because the outcome of any cooperative dialogue may serve to deflect attention away from deeper and more systemic 'background injustices', including social and economic structures and the social dispositions they foster. This is a situation that regularly confronts the unemployed, indigenous peoples, women, people of color and those advocates who seek the protection of endangered and threatened species and their habitats. In their otherwise laudable practical concern to work creatively with the diverse moral orientations of the parties in particular policy dialogues in response to particular problems, structural injustices and the powerful social agents and dominant discourses that serve to reproduce them are necessarily placed in the background. Of course, environmental pragmatists would doubtless be aware of, and troubled by, such structural problems.

143

However, my point is that there is nothing in their practical *method* of problem solving that would encourage or facilitate a shift toward a more general political or economic critique precisely because such a move would detract from reaching a practical agreement in response to particular and immediate problems. [...]

Now some environmental pragmatists may well object to my argument by pointing out that environmental pragmatism has the potential to develop in a much more critical direction. After all, if economic and political structural inequalities stand in the way of a more robust democracy, then as democrats, pragmatists ought to challenge those structural inequalities and therefore incline toward a more critical pragmatism. Indeed, Dewey emphasized the need for institutional criticism. [...]

[N]one of these points represent insuperable barriers for environmental pragmatism, although if it took a more critical turn it would need to change its 'marketing'. That is, it cannot claim to offer a method of environmental problem solving that is efficacious from an instrumental point of view while also remaining consistently critical of broader social structures. Indeed, I do not believe any political theory can reasonably make such a claim!

Too instrumentalist

Even where environmental pragmatists are at their strongest in suggesting that intractable debates about deeply held moral convictions might be deftly side-stepped in order to focus on the practical problems at hand, I have suggested that this is a recipe that is likely to work only some of the time. One of the reasons for this is that not all environmental conflicts can or ought to be reduced to a simple question of incompatible *use* of nonhuman nature by differently situated humans. This is because environmental conflicts are also manifestations of deeper social and political controversies concerning lifestyle, identity, cultural dispositions and modes of relating to others. Under these circumstances, practical conflicts cannot and ought not to be isolated from these deeper social and political conflicts because any resolution of particular problems usually serves as a precedent for future policy making, in which case much more is at stake than merely solving the *particular* practical problem at hand. In such circumstances, what Thompson calls 'the force of necessity' is therefore unlikely to bring together the relevant community of inquirers and allow them to let go of their fundamental convictions in order to reach an effective pragmatic resolution of the immediate environmental problem/conflict.

Yet there is a deeper, and somewhat ironic, point to be made against the instrumentalist, problem-solving orientation of environmental pragmatism. For those sympathetic with the work of Hannah Arendt and also the Frankfurt School, keeping the dialogue alive in order to ask more and deeper questions is ultimately more valuable and important than resolving immediate, narrowly defined practical problems. From an Arendtian perspective, democratic exchange is an intrinsically valuable end in itself rather than a mere means to other ends while for the Frankfurt School the challenge is merely to prevent instrumental reason from dwarfing or displacing other forms of human reason.[8] The irony here is that approaching deliberation in a less goal-directed way may turn out to be more 'instrumental' in fostering mutual trust and mutual understanding of difference *precisely because the pressure of practical imperatives is lifted*. After all, it is difficult *simultaneously* to listen and open oneself outwards in order to understand differently situated others while also making instrumental assessments and calculations of one's environmental claims in relation to others. [...]

[T]he resort to the language of 'rights', 'intrinsic value' or 'inherent dignity' of nature may be understood, among other things, as a strategic attempt [by environmental pragmatists] to tap into an emancipatory vocabulary. Historically, the successive struggles to extend rights have been struggles to deepen and extend recognition to hitherto excluded social classes and groups (slaves, working class, women, ethnic minorities). Such struggles have also been struggles over social power and the 'social construction of reality', including the power to define what is 'real' and who/what should count as 'normal' and morally considerable. More recently, however, new social movements and a diverse range of linguistic, ethnic and religious minorities have introduced an identity/difference politics which has challenged the liberal democratic 'color-blind constitution' along with homogenizing models of political identity and citizenship.[9] Such movements and groups have challenged the idea of 'extending' political recognition on the basis of criteria that do not reflect their own experiences and identities.

Similar problems arise with the method of 'humane extensionism' that has been employed by many environmental philosophers and activists, which seeks to incorporate nonhuman others and ecosystems into human moral frameworks by analogy with humans. Despite well-meaning intentions, such a method serves to privilege similarity with humans over difference.[10] This sets artificial limits on the range of values and reasons why we might respect nature, creating a web of incorporations and inclusions that leaves us unable to respect 'unassimilated otherness'.[11] [...]

Liberal humanism, not pluralist enough?

As we have seen, environmental pragmatists purport to celebrate moral pluralism and reject nonanthropocentric theory as monistic and reductionistic. Yet if the environmental pragmatists' embrace of moral pluralism is to avoid arbitrary or indecisive relativism then pragmatists must ultimately privilege *some* moral values over others, if only to justify their pragmatic democratic procedures. Any approach that understands justice in dialogic terms – as fair dialogue – necessarily presupposes a prior moral theory of what is fair. As we have seen, environmental pragmatism ultimately comes to rest on the basic (monistic?) liberal humanistic principle of respect for individuals and their right to participate in the determination of their collective fate. Ecocentric democratic theory may be understood not as rejecting this principle but rather as seeking to extend it [...], on the ground that the moral pluralism of environmental pragmatism is not quite pluralist enough. That is, it calls for a more inclusive moral and procedural framework that acknowledges and seeks to reconcile not just conflicting human values and interests but also conflicts between human and nonhuman interests in ways that ensure special advocacy on behalf of nonhuman interests. If this is still monism, as pragmatists aver, then it is at least a more encompassing monism than liberal humanism. [...]

Indeed, it is this epistemological question about how we come to *know* nature that has been central to the general resistance to ecocentric efforts to transcend anthropocentrism or human chauvinism in policy making. To borrow Kate Soper's terminology, are we seeking to emancipate 'nature' or Nature?[12] That is, are we seeking to liberate the 'nature' we have constructed, or Nature as extra-discursive reality? [...]

The distinctive political project of ecocentrism, as I understand it, is to enable the flourishing of Nature in the knowledge that we must always necessarily grapple with the fact that we only have access to Nature through our own discursive maps (whether based on scientific or customary/vernacular knowledge), which are approximate, provisional understanding of so-called 'real' Nature. If we understand the problem in this way, then there ought to be no necessary *moral* objection to proceeding with the project of enabling and promoting a flourishing nonhuman Nature. Indeed, the acknowledgment that the only Nature we know is a provisional, socially constructed 'map' that is at best an approximation of the 'real territory' provides the basis of a number of cautionary tales as to how the 'emancipatory project' might be pursued. Such an argument might run as follows: if we want to enable the nonhuman to flourish and if it is acknowledged that our understanding of nature is incomplete, culturally filtered and provisional *then* we ought to proceed with care, caution and humility rather than with recklessness and arrogance in our interactions with 'nature'. In short, we must acknowledge that our knowledge of Nature and its limits is itself limited (and contested). Practically, these arguments provide support for a risk-averse posture in environmental and technology impact assessment and in environmental policy making generally.

If the foregoing arguments are accepted, then we have reason to question the pluralist credentials of environmental pragmatism. [...]

Conclusion

[...] *[B]oth* pragmatist mediators and ecocentric activists must operate in a political context that falls short of their mutually informing ideals of justice and democracy (albeit in different ways) – a brute fact that requires difficult strategic political choices about where to direct intellectual focus and political energy. In this context, the choice as to whether to 'weigh in' as an advocate (and therefore become a relentless critic of those who disagree) or a mediator (in an effort to generate respect and trust and find common ground) is always a difficult one. However, in view of the respective strengths and limitations of critical advocacy and pragmatic mediation, I suspect we would find our 'real world democracy' even poorer if it were made up of only mediators, or only advocates. This is because the tension between the advocate and the mediator ought to be understood as a healthy, constitutive tension in any democratic society because, among other things, it serves to steer democratic deliberation away from policy paralysis, on the one hand, and policy complacency, on the other. Democracy is about *arguing* as well as *making decisions* and advocates and mediators play different but invaluable roles in each of these phases. Now, in theory, the tensions between environmental pragmatism and ecocentrism might be narrowed or possibly even resolved by the development of a more *critical* pragmatism if some of my criticisms are taken on board. However, ultimately – in practice – I do not believe they can, or ought, to be eliminated in any 'real world' democracy.

Notes

1 Callicott (1990; 1995).
2 Magee (1987, p. 29).
3 Parker (1996, p. 33).
4 Norton (1996, pp. 122–3).
5 'For us, environmental pragmatism is an open-ended inquiry into the specific real-life problems of humanity's relationship to the environment', Light and Katz (1996, 'Introduction').

6 Norton (1996, p. 108). Similarly, Daniel Farber has argued that 'A convincing analysis should be like a web, drawing on the coherence of

many sources, rather than a tower, built on a single unified foundation' (Farber 1999, p. 10).

7 Cass Sunstein (1997) has also defended agreements on outcomes and narrow or low-level principles on which people can converge from diverse foundations. He argues that such 'incompletely theorised agreements' are a distinctive solution to social pluralism (p. 115). As Andrew Light (2000) has shown, Arne Naess has also defended the deep ecology platform along these lines.

8 See, for example, Hannah Arendt (1958), Theodor Adorno and Max Horkheimer (1979) and Jurgen Habermas (1971).

9 As Benhabib (1996, p. 5) explains, 'Contemporary Western liberal democracies are being challenged by groups who insist upon their unassimilatable difference and who want to use their experience of alterity to demystify the rationalist and identitary illusions of these liberal democracies.'

10 See, for example, Rodman (1977) and Luke (1997).

11 Plumwood (1993).

12 Soper (1995).

References

Adorno, Theodor and Max Horkheimer. *The Dialectic of Enlightenment.* Translated by John Cummings. London: Verso, 1979.

Arendt, Hannah. *The Human Condition.* Chicago: University of Chicago Press, 1958.

Benhabib, Seyla (ed.). *Democracy and Difference: Contesting the Boundaries of the Political.* Princeton, New Jersey: Princeton University Press, 1996.

Callicott, J. Baird. 'The Case Against Moral Pluralism.' *Environmental Ethics* 12, no. 2 (1990): 999–1024.

Callicott, J. Baird. 'Environmental Philosophy is Environmental Activism: The Most Radical and Effective Kind.' Pp. 19–35 in *Environmental Philosophy and Environmental Activism*, edited by Don E. Marrietta Jr and Lester Embree. Lanham, Maryland: Rowman and Littlefield, 1995.

Farber, Daniel. *Ecopragmatism: Making Environmentally Sensible Decisions in an Uncertain World.* Chicago: University of Chicago Press, 1999.

Gould, Carol. *Rethinking Democracy.* Cambridge: Cambridge University Press, 1988.

Habermas, Jurgen. *Toward a Rational Society; Student Protest, Science and Society.* Translated by Jeremy Shapiro. London: Heinemann Educational Books, 1971.

Kingwell, Mark. *A Civil Tongue: Justice, Dialogue, and the Politics of Pluralism.* University Park, Pennsylvania: Pennsylvania State University Press, 1995.

Light, Andrew. 'Callicott and Naess on Pluralism.' Pp. 125–8 in *Beneath the Surface: Critical Essays on the Philosophy of Deep Ecology*, edited by Andrew Light and David Rothenburg. Cambridge, MA: MIT Press, 2000.

Light, Andrew and Eric Katz (eds). *Environmental Pragmatism.* London: Routledge, 1996.

Luke, Brian. 'Solidarity Across Diversity: A Pluralistic Rapprochement of Environmentalism and Animal Liberation' in *The Ecological Community: Environmental Challenges for Philosophy, Politics, and Morality*, edited by Roger S. Gottlieb. New York: Routledge, 1997.

Magee, Bryan. *The Great Philosophers: An Introduction to West-*

ern Philosophy. Oxford: Oxford University Press, 1987.

Norton, Bryan. 'Integration or Reduction: Two Approaches to Environmental Values.' Pp. 105–38 in *Environmental Pragmatism*, edited by Andrew Light and Eric Katz. London: Routledge, 1996.

Parker, Kelley A. 'Pragmatism and Environmental Thought.' Pp. 21–37 in *Environmental Pragmatism*, edited by Andrew Light and Eric Katz. London: Routledge, 1996.

Plumwood, Val. *Feminism and the Mastery of Nature*. London: Routledge, 1993.

Rodman, John. 'The Liberation of Nature?' *Inquiry* 20 (1977): 83–145.

Soper, Kate. *What is Nature?* Oxford: Blackwell, 1995.

Sunstein, Cass. 'Deliberation, Democracy and Disagreement.' Pp. 93–117 in *Justice and Democracy: Cross-Cultural Perspectives*, edited by Ron Bontekoe and Marietta Stepaniants. Honolulu: University of Hawaii Press, 1997.

Young, Iris Marion. *Justice and the Politics of Difference*. Princeton, New Jersey: Princeton University Press, 1990.

Robyn Eckersley

14 | Knowledge, justice and democracy

SHIV VISVANATHAN

The final reading of Part Two is taken from the second half of
a paper by Shiv Visvanathan, an anthropologist of science and
technology and a human rights researcher in India. The author
has worked on and been influenced by the aftermath of the
Bhopal gas disaster of 1984 – an industrial accident involving a
pesticide subsidiary plant of the American-owned Union Carbide
which resulted in the deaths of some twenty thousand people. The
experience prompted an interest in alternative bio-environmental
practices based on diverse understandings of nature and society
which might lead to innovative ways of mutual learning. In this
extract, he explores the political space required for enabling
different frameworks of thinking (cognitive structures) to converse
with each other in more meaningful and purposeful ways. The
reading comes from an anthology that attempts to bridge the
divide between work focused mostly in the global North on
science and technology studies and development-studies work
focused in the global South. Visvanathan's idea of 'cognitive
justice' challenges mainstream authoritarian culture of science
and technology and associated attempts at patronizing localized
knowledge systems through the rhetoric of participation and
ethnoscience, in search of an alternative, more legitimate form of
dialogue. The notion of democratizing knowledge is appropriately
contextualized in India – one of the largest democracies.

A grass-roots critique of science

Science in India 'began as a positivist celebration wherein Indian
scientists such as Meghnad Saha literally dreamt of a society based on
the scientific method' (Visvanathan 1984). India was a society as proud
of its sample surveys and its science policy as it was of its flag. A society
that dreamt of its laboratories and dams as the new temples of modern
India witnessed the fact that the sacrilege began with science. We faced a
set of science projects that were difficult to understand within a positivist
science or the old dualism between good science/bad science policy. We
had to face the following facts:

1 Our dams had produced not only energy but an ethnicity of over 40 million refugees. One needs a common base to audit development and displacement within the same discourse (Parsuraman and Unnikrishnan 2000).

2 Our scientific Forest Acts threatened both animals and people, creating a debate between scientific and social forestry threatening one-seventh of our population.

3 The Bhopal gas tragedy created thousands of victims who were subject to the scientific gaze but received neither compensation nor healing.

4 The Green Revolution produced the paradox of an official India self-sufficient in food while increasing the salinity of our soils and decreasing the diversity of our agriculture (Shiva 1989).

5 The only dictatorship India had was between 1975 and 1977 and it was justified in terms of scientific metaphors that legitimitized compulsory sterilization in family planning and forced demolitions in the name of scientific urban planning.

6 India today is a nuclear state where science has driven the move towards nuclearization. What is troubling is not just nuclearization but the terms of discourse within which scientific debates are carried out.

The question the grass-roots movements in science had to face as a philosophical and political conundrum was whether the above crises were because of bad science, bad politics and bad technology or was the problem also inherent in the logic of science and technology. This political drama in what I called the politics of knowledge took place at four levels.

- What are the rules for a scientific controversy in a democracy that includes tribals, marginal fishing groups, shifting cultivators, slums, industrial refugees and a middle class demographically the size of Europe? How does one make decisions about science and technology in a society that is undergoing the first, second and third industrial revolutions simultaneously?

- How does one frame an interaction between science and democracy which looks systematically at the 'scientization' of democracy and the 'democratization' of science? How does one phenomenologically bracket them so that one can re-examine these taken-for-granted worlds?

- How does one create a framework of controversy which neither economizes science by instrumentalizing it or reduces it to a battle between

151

scientific fundamentalism (positivism and reductionism) and religious fundamentalism?

- What concepts do we need which go beyond rights, cost–benefit, objectivity and efficiency? What one hopes to present is the framework and the repertoire of tactics and concepts generated.

One realizes, of course, that a wide variety of movements is grouped under the same rubric here, but it is important to capture the unity of this great parliament of science whereby civil society – particularly grass-roots groups and dissenting academics – built a more democratic framework for science. What emerges is not only a great exercise in democratic theory, but also a contribution to the philosophy and history of science.

The initial critical moves emphasized the latter half of the innovation chain. The first major critiques came both from the Bernalians within the state and from left-leaning movements such as the Kerala Sastra Sahitya Parishad (KSSP)[1] and the Delhi Science Forum. Their dream of democracy was still diffusionist. It was a dream of taking science to the villages. What was invented was the idea of the scientific temper, a pedagogic vision that a scientific world-view could be induced in a people. Unfortunately the radical scientist often visualized the scientific temper as an intellectual vaccine that could eliminate superstition, magic and religious fundamentalism. The left-leaning movements carried this same scientific view through science quizzes celebrating Newton, Bernal and Darwin. Here civil society and the progressive state shared a common vision of a positivist science. But in the later debates there came a split between the science policy of the state and the critiques of science by civil society. It was a science war, which emphasized that the citizenship provided by the new social contract was inadequate because it was a citizenship based on an industrial premise, which saw the citizen as a consumer and not an inventor of knowledge. It also realized that both science in India and the Indian constitution were disembedded knowledges.

The critique of science began as a human rights problem because development projects either marginalized or cannibalized the culture of tribes, slums or the peasantry. The standard notion of human rights did not work because, while it was adequate at the level of the individual, it was unavailable at the level of the group. Second, what one needed was a science that realized that nature was not just an object of an experiment or a resource but part of a way of life. As Tom Kocherry, leader of the Kerala Fishers Forum, claimed: 'Seventy per cent of India depends on nature for its livelihood.' Nature was thus not only a mode of production but a mode of thought. The movements realized that there were few life-affirming notions of nature within science. The concept of wilderness used in American ecology was inadequate because for the American the wilderness was an unpopulated monument. One needed something beyond the American dialectic of wilderness and frontier or the British obsession with gardens. The world-view of the Bishnois[2] or the Chipko[3] movement came from their religious cosmology. It was not anti-science but a critique only of a statist science, which saw the pulp and paper industry as a more eligible citizen than the tribes foraging for food and medicines. In the new model of development as an enclosure movement not only were tribals and marginal peasants displaced, they were rendered illegal. What was destroyed was not only the forest but a common body of knowledge about trees, fodder, forest produce, seeds, medicines, building. This was not merely a resource pool but a way of life that sustained a way of knowledge (see also Wynne 2005).

The movements were confronted with two facts. First, the idea of rights was adequate for torture but helpless against science-induced displacement, obsolescence or even genocide. Second, they realized that in the battle called development the idea of nature itself had changed. It was not just farm, fish and fowl, it was also hybridized with technology. The citizen lives simultaneously in a natural, technological, biotechnological and information environment (Whiteside 2002). One had to confront these different hybridities simultaneously. One needs not only a new ethic for nature in science but a new ethic of technology. They also sensed the iatrogenic nature of science policy, created particularly by the reductionist nature of scientific expertise. But the answer was not Luddism. The modern Luddite cannot smash the abstract machine, only rework the classifications behind abstract thought. S/he must become futurologist, epistemologist and constitutionalist, and must also realize that the new politics of science is created by dissenting imaginations within and alternative imaginations without. A critique of science as an ongoing exercise cannot be located in fundamentalisms, only in competing and reciprocal criticalities. For every Shiva or Medha Patkar there is a Chipko and a Narmada movement. Further, there is no one construction of Chipko, Narmada or Balliapal, any more than there can be one master narrative of science. The power of the movements lay in the fact that they realized that politics is not just a protest against a dam or a forest bill. It must extend a challenge to official narratives of science and to the epistemologies that underlie it. Or, to put it bluntly, how do non-violent movements search for a non-violent science?

The movements realized that the politics of time was crucial at three levels of science: first, the politics of the history of science; second, the politics of memory; and finally the politics of multiple time.

The history of science has always constructed itself as a rational, cumulative, continuous exercise. Science as an exoteric internalist narrative constructs itself in linear and progressive time. Science is conducted in victorious time, which has no place for defeated knowledges. While science deals with a diversity of times – mechanical, historical, evolutionary and quantum (nanosecond) – its own narratives are constructed in the impoverished time of unilinear narratives. For the movements, science fails as a narrative and as an act of storytelling, and yet they realize that it is the very unilinearity of time which provides its cognitive power. As Kuhn (1970) remarked, the textbook as a reflection of a cognitive regime rewrites histories where defeated or alternative hypotheses have little place.

The politics of memory is a close corollary to the first because the progressive rhetoric of science is an amnesiacal one. It museumizes other forms of knowledge in the name of progress. It also renders obsolescent ways of life, which are abandoned because of the changing nature of technology. The innovations of science take place in standardized time. Science understands the grammar of progress but not the logic of obsolescence as a lived world. The paradigm as a monoparadigmatic space comes with an indifference about certain forms of time. Within the innovation chain, Socrates becomes a Schumpeterean idiot.

Democracy needs a multiplicity of times. A tribesperson involved in shifting cultivation operates in a world of over twenty different kinds of time, which emanates from the way s/he deals with soil, seed, seasons, rituals, fast, feast, rest, work, domestic and communal space. Farmers, women, patients and tribespeople live in a variety of times, which they need access to and which science denies them. It is within this context that ecology is as vital to science as quantum physics. What ecology smuggles into science is a notion of memory as a thesaurus of times. What the movements emphasized is that a democracy based on standard factory time is literally an oxymoron. At this point one must emphasize the difference and overlap between the different politics of memory. Ian Hacking talks of three forms of Foucaultian politics (Hacking 1995). The first dealt with the politics of the body, the second with the politics of populations. Hacking adds that the third form of hegemony is the politics of memory as an act of scientization. But the politics of the second idea of memory deals with a liberation from history as the only form of memory with a plurality of times. The trouble with the official idea of sustainability is that it lacks such a repertoire of times.

Once the framework of multiple time is established, the abstractness of science is challenged. Science, as the movements and the dissenting academics suggest, is not merely an object of production created through the optical gaze of the Enlightenment but a subject of consumption and validation. The tacit division of labour between an expert who produces knowledge and a citizen who consumes it has to be rendered less asymmetrical by understanding the citizen as a person of knowledge. The worker, the peasant and the craftsman are all citizens of knowledge about science. This understanding cannot be devalued as 'ethnoscience' while expert understanding is 'philosophy of science'. Such a hierarchy or devaluation creates the possibility of the museumization or appropriation of these other knowledges. Strangely, even at a time when science is appropriating and patenting peasant knowledges, there is no epistemic acknowledgement of their status. Science begins a form of strip mining, where knowledge about local drugs, therapeutics, soils and seeds is abstracted without considering the philosophies they are embedded in.

Beyond participation: the challenge of cognitive justice

Given the tendency of science and technological projects towards displacement, obsolescence and erasure, the movements believe that the externalist idea of community involvement, participation and use of local materials is not enough. These are externalist measures. Even the subaltern emphasis on 'voice' is a trifle sentimental. These become mere epicycles that the scientific panopticon throws out to humanize itself. They do not touch the normal science of a discipline. The movements understand that participation does not constitute an epistemic challenge. It can merely add to the popularization of science or to an increasing awareness about decision-making. But the politics of an epistemic challenge requires a different set of constitutional or legislative guarantees. Probably the best way to explain it is by relating an anecdote.

A few months back, representatives of what are now called denotied tribes – tribes once classified as criminal by the British – came to meet us. These tribes, which are over a few million strong, face a devastating medical situation: sickle cell anaemia, a condition of which they have little understanding. They also face mental trauma from the everydayness of police torture and harassment. The community goes to the government primary health centres and to the herbal doctors. Their representatives had come with a suggestion. What they wanted was a dialogue, a seminar wherein patients, victims, medical practitioners of various persuasions, public health specialists, psychiatrists and human rights activists met and listened to their testimonies of health, illness and well-being. What they

155

hoped would emerge from it was a new kind of health policy which they would present to the local legislature. They wanted a dialogic health policy which saw health and development together: not in the language of expertise but in terms of a new notion of health politics.

What they wanted was not just participation. They wanted *presence* of two kinds, participation and *cognitive representation*. They wished that, when a policy was decided, the tribal doctor and the Western health expert were both present and that the policy should represent the language of this dialogue. Such a presence goes beyond participation and ethno-science to cognitive empowerment. The political economy and ecology of the tribal situation demand access to a variety of medical systems. Plurality is necessary for true access to a system because one cannot have choice without alternatives. What one needs is the idea of cognitive justice: the constitutional right of different systems of knowledge to exist as part of dialogue and debate. The movement's critiques of science and technology thus realized that the challenge to the expertises of technology required a stronger framework of participation. The idea of participation fundamentally accepts the experts' definition of knowledge. It seeks only to modify or soften it. It seeks a blend of expert knowledge and ethnoscience. But it is a world where expert knowledge is presented as high theory and the layperson's ideas as a pot-pourri of practices, local ideas and raw material. There is no principle of equivalence. Cognitive justice, however, recognizes the plurality of knowledge systems. It also recognizes the relation between knowledge and livelihood and lifestyle. It is in this context that it holds that policy must not be articulated within one monochromatic frame of knowledge but within an existential plurality of them. For example, a medical policy in India should be formulated recognizing the presence of a variety of medical systems and defining a patient as one open to this medical body of knowledge and its ideas of pain, healing, suffering, sickness and death. Cognitive justice goes beyond voice or resistance to recognizing constitutionally the body of knowledge within which an individual is embedded.

The idea of cognitive justice suggests that there is a link between survival and forms of knowledge. It includes not only the rights of dissenting scientists within a dominant paradigm, but also the rights of alternative epistemologies and alternative sciences. The debate on alternative sciences cannot be exhausted by Lysenkoism and the racialism of Nazi science. Alternative sciences existed long before as traditional agriculture or alternative medical systems. A plea for cognitive justice also establishes the understanding that democracy within knowledge is crucial. The opposition of expert and layperson disguises to a certain extent the opposition between science and alternative sciences. One needs instead a parliament of epistemic debates, but also the ecologies that would let these forms of knowledge survive and thrive not in a preservationist sense but as active practices. The idea of cognitive justice thus visualizes a body of knowledge that citizens, especially in subsistence cultures, have access to as consumers, critics, practitioners and philosophers. As a tactic it renders irrelevant the hierarchical contempt implicit in the notion of ethnoscience as a lesser life form or model of being.

In search of plural visions

What the movements and their critique of science sought was not anti-science but a plural vision that allowed for both the wisdom of normal science and the vision of the eccentric, the dissenter, the marginal, the vulnerable and alternative world-views. The playfulness, the new concepts and new reciprocity between science and social worlds created through novelty by combination, was extended by grass-roots politics and philosophers to a wider domain. They forced the democratic imagination to contend with science by inventing new methodologies beyond boy scout calls for participation and empowerment [...]. Programmes for open societies offer science as an image and model for democracy but they do little to add to the democratization of science or its imagination. A science that seeks only consumers' or citizens' approval is a disguised demagoguery that will work against the grass-roots innovators.

Notes

1 The Kerala Sastra Sahitya Parishad (the Kerala literary and scientific association) was a forum established by Malyali science writers. It is today a movement with over 40,000 members dedicated to the popularization of science and to utilizing science for progressive ends.

2 The Bishnois are followers of the fifteenth-century saint Guru Jambeshwar, who instructed his followers to protect plant and animal life. A cattle-rearing and agricultural community, the Bishnois do not allow hunting or felling on their land.

3 The Chipko movement arose as a protest against logging abuses in the state of Uttar Pradesh in India. The word 'chipko' literally means 'embrace'. The movement's name derives from the non-violent practice of women who hugged trees, interposing themselves between the tree and the contractors.

References

Hacking, I. (1995) *Rewriting the Soul: Multiple Personality and the Sciences of Memory*, Princeton, NJ: Princeton University Press.

Kuhn, T. (1970). *The Structure of Scientific Revolutions*, Chicago, University of Chicago.

Parsuraman, S. and Unnikrishnan, P. V. (eds) (2000) *India Disasters Report: Towards a Policy Initiative*, New Delhi: Oxford University Press.

Shiv Visvanathan

Shiva, V. (1989) *The Violence of the Green Revolution: Third World Agriculture, Ecology and Politics*, Vandana Shiva Third World Network and Zed Books.

Visvanathan, S. (1984) *Organising for Science: The Making of an Individual Research Laboratory*, New Delhi: Oxford University Press.

Whiteside, K. H. (2002) *Divided Natures*, Cambridge, MA: MIT Press.

Wynne, B. (2005) 'Risk as globalizing 'democratic' discourse? Framing subjects and citizens'. In M. Leach, I. Scoones and B. Wynne (eds), *Science and Citizens: Globalization and the Challenge of Engagement*, London and New York: Zed Books, pp. 66–82.

Summary of part two

MARTIN REYNOLDS

What matters in environmental responsibility is what might widely be referred to as nature. Nature *matters* in many disciplines, professions and daily endeavours. A theme underlying many of the readings in this part is the more specific matter of communication – both communication between human and non-human nature, and communication among humans deliberating on the natural world. Put in another way, for environmental responsibility what matters most is the quality of conversation.

Issues of environmental responsibility might therefore be better conceived in terms of our integral relationship with the natural world, including human deliberation on this world. The readings express concerns about the challenges of engaging directly or indirectly with the natural world in order to foster greater responsibility. Three concerns of particular relevance for progressing appropriate policy and action can be summarized:

- Giving expression to what's at stake in any situation of environmental responsibility requires acknowledgement not only of our integral relationship with other stakeholders in the non-human natural world (providing expressions of care), but also of our own peculiar stakeholding role as agents of moral responsibility (providing expressions of accountability).
- Debates among scientists, ethicists and many others with a professional stakeholding interest in environmental issues can be helpful in delineating issues of responsibility, but they might also act as a constraint by confining conversation within academic or other professional cloisters and by entrenching existing viewpoints rather than allowing viewpoints to develop and co-evolve.
- Although questions regarding what matters in environmental responsibility can vary depending on the context, and be disputed from different perspectives, there are always opportunities to frame issues in a more constructive and creative manner to foster greater response abilities.

Attending responsibly to an ever-changing natural world invites different ways of listening and seeing, as well as talking and writing (among other expressions of feedback). A conversation is not just a record of words being exchanged, but rather an experience – between poles of well-being and suffering – gained. Several of the authors allude to the importance of embracing the experiential world more, in order to bridge the divide between natural and social worlds. Such an endeavour requires critical space to do justice to the ecological world, and experiential tools such as those offered by systems thinking and environmental pragmatism to support more purposeful and responsible environmental policy and action.

THREE | **Individual and collective responsibility**

Introduction to part three

CHRIS BLACKMORE

Working out just where responsibilities lie in relation to our environment can be challenging. Who is accountable for environmental harms such as pollution of our air or water, destruction of habitats for wildlife or what some would consider abuse of natural resources? Who cares for our environment and ensures that we 'do the right thing', both for now and in terms of our obligations to future generations? What constitutes environmentally responsible behaviour? Addressing such questions requires an understanding of how individual and collective responsibilities work together. The chapters in this part offer a range of different perspectives on individual and collective responsibility and the relationship between them. Different kinds of responsibilities are considered, operating at different levels and in contexts ranging from human groups and human behaviour to future generations, 'the commons', corporations and different kinds of communities, environmental policies and science. Some of the chapters focus on rights, contracts and duties, thus contributing to a deontological view, but others take a broader perspective in considering obligations, thinking, learning and behaviour, which draw on a range of other theories and practices.

The first two readings focus on individuals in their contexts. Sir Geoffrey Vickers looks at the relationship between autonomy and responsibility, arguing that they can be complementary. His focus is on the nature of individuals' obligations and how these relate to culture and standards. Michael Maniates, on the other hand, is concerned with how responsibility for environmental problems has become individualized, limiting our collective imagination in terms of engaging meaningfully with doing things differently in order to address issues of consumption. He asks how this trend might be reversed.

Next, Martin P. Golding addresses our obligations to future generations, considering also both rights and duties. He challenges assumptions about whom we have obligations to and the nature of those obligations. Extracts from Garrett Hardin's influential article on 'the tragedy of the commons' then provide an example of how people act in relation to each other, in this case in situations of using and managing shared resources ('commons'). Thomas Dietz, Elinor Ostrom and Paul Stern's more recent perspective on commons such as climate and oceans focuses on multilevel governance and adaptive institutions. Corporations are a part of this picture, and some of the issues relating to their social and environmental responsibilities and how others should engage with them are covered in Jonathon Porritt and Claire Fauset's debate.

The last two readings of this part focus on collective processes, specifically on social learning as a means of enabling different groups of stakeholders to work together to take responsibility for the effects of their actions on their environment. Chris Blackmore considers some of the principles and practices of social learning, such as the kind of multilevel, multi-stakeholder interaction that can lead to effective 'concerted action' in managing our natural resources. Social learning can work alongside other mechanisms to enable engagement in practice, which she argues can lead to environmental responsibility. Finally, Robin Grove-White charts the course of environmental issues and policies and the changing role of science. He identifies an urgent need for new learning capacities in environmental and technological policy- and decision-making, and he calls for a better understanding of how social learning relates to action in the face of uncertainty.

15 | Autonomous yet responsible?

GEOFFREY VICKERS

This chapter is one of several written by Geoffrey Vickers around 1980 about responsibility, using as his main sources experiences of his long lifetime spent largely in the UK – in the legal profession, as a wartime soldier and in public administration. He participated in much collective and personal decision-making that he described as 'heavy with responsibility'. He raises here questions about the nature of the obligations individuals sometimes feel, the relationship between this sense of obligation and shared cultural norms and the standards revealed.

§ To many people today the word 'responsibility' suggests being answerable to someone for what one does, submissive to orders, liable to correction, subject to another man's judgement. The word autonomy suggests being answerable only to oneself and therefore 'free'. And yet we continually act on the confident assumption that other people will do what we expect of them, although they are not answerable to us in any formal way. And if asked why, we would answer that we believe them to be responsible people; and we expect other people to believe the same of us. We also find that being answerable only to ourselves can involve commitments and constraints at least as tough as those involved by being responsible to other people. So there must be something foggy about these two words and the relation between them, something worth clearing up, especially today when people are so fearful of losing their autonomy and so chary of accepting responsibility.

I find it useful to begin by asking in what circumstances we use the word 'ought' in regard to our own behaviour.

Take an extreme case. I am ordering lunch in a restaurant. I cannot eat all the things I like. Which shall I choose? I choose what I prefer. I have a biological need for food. I enjoy some tastes more than others. I might find it hard to explain why I chose what I did, even though it may seem an important decision. (Suppose this is my first freely chosen meal after years in prison.) Yet even so it will not involve any 'ought's.

But suppose I am training for a race or I am on a medical diet, or I am trying to economize or even just trying to keep my weight down.

Now there are things on that list which I 'ought not' to choose. And if I do, I shall have a feeling, however slight, that I have let someone down. And that someone will be me. I may also have broken an understanding with my trainer or with my doctor or even with my creditors but they need none of them know. The basic trouble will be that I have ignored a commitment which I had previously taken, because I could not tolerate the constraint which it imposed. And I shall feel diminished by this even though it affects no one but me.

I think this elementary example makes clear some important things about human motivation. There is an area in which people's choices of what to do are influenced by their sense of what they ought to do or be, and this in turn derives from internal standards which they have developed, defining what they will regard for themselves as success in doing and being. These standards organize their personalities and their actions. They often conflict with and sometimes overcome simpler forms of motivation such as instinctive or conditioned responses or even proposals for purposeful action where the means proposed would not 'match' these inbuilt standards.

Of course the standards can change, they are always being either changed or confirmed simply by being used. But they resist change, especially as they grow more coherent and comprehensive. And it is they which give to a human personality whatever character and coherence it may possess.

Note that I have said nothing so far about good and bad or right and wrong. These standards may be wildly different from what society expects. I knew a young man who felt it would be out of character for him to pay any debt until he had to. All I am out to establish now is something which you will not readily find stressed in text books on psychology – that we develop standards of what we expect of ourselves and that these affect what we do and define what we are for others as well as ourselves.

Of course these two pictures may differ widely and both may be deceptive. We may refuse to recognize differences between our standards and the way we are actually performing. Others are likely to judge our standards by our performance since they have no other access to our standards. That is why we are taught as children – or used to be taught – to say 'we're sorry' when we violate a standard so that the other party may not judge us wholly by generalizing from what we have just done.

Now let us look at it from the side of other people – not (yet) of 'society' or 'the government' or 'the State' but simply other people. It is very important to all of us that other people should be for some purposes reliable and in these areas we judge them by standards of 'ought'. We probably do not mind whether they are vegetarians. We may not mind whether they are Christians. But we do mind whether they are muggers. We think they ought not to be, we try to get them to internalize this standard for themselves, and in so far as we do not succeed, we try to prevent or deter them from mugging us.

Of course if someone is not reliable, trustworthy, responsible, it is a help to know it; but we need far more predictability than that. If there were no social interaction except confrontation and trade-off and mutual deceit the place would blow up or break down within days. It runs on trust. No con-man could make a living if it didn't. Even trade-off would be impossible if no one could be trusted to keep a bargain. And this trust is an aggregate of specific trusts – the assurance that other people share the same standards as we do of what to expect of themselves in various specific circumstances, where what they do and what they are matter to us.

A great deal of these expectations is embodied in laws and regulations which are there to be read; and many people obey many of these because it would not pay them not to. They could not afford to be caught in default. And lots of other rules too, rules of courtesy for example and conventions of speech, cannot be broken without invoking 'sanctions' of some kind. You offend the other party, you lose his confidence, you damage your reputation. There is a whole net of feedback mechanisms for keeping the rules, apart from the visible ones of the law. And these work on us whether we are also acting in breach of our own standards or in accordance with them or in some area where we have no standards at all, only a prudential judgement of risks and outcomes.

But keeping rules is no simple matter, whether they be our own or someone else's. They have to be applied in particular cases and contexts by particular people and this often involves resolving conflicts between the rules, as well as conflicts with the other parties. Playing roles is much more than keeping rules. The criminal law, for example, is not much use unless both judges and policemen can be trusted to play their roles 'responsibly'. And 'responsibly' means in accordance with standards shared by the role player and by those who rely on him. In applying the law to a specific case a bench of judges, though sharing the same training and experience and working on the same facts, may reach differing conclusions; yet no one supposes that either the dissentients or the others are shown thereby to be 'irresponsible'. On the contrary, their willingness to differ is seen as exemplifying their sense of personal responsibility; and the reasons which they give for their judgements support this and further both the growth and the continuing coherence of the law. On the other hand, a known maverick is unlikely to be appointed a judge.

It seems to me therefore to be clear why every human group, however large or small, develops a net of shared expectations, standards of what they expect of themselves as well as what they expect of each other and of what they assume others to expect of themselves. I would not expect it to cover the whole area of behaviour or to be wholly shared even in the area which it covers. But it has to be sufficiently wide in scope and sufficiently fully shared to enable a 'society' to hang together in so far as it needs to and yet to allow its members enough flexibility in setting their own standards to allow for differences in their make-up and their life experiences. And when I say 'society' in that context, I mean any group of people from two upwards, whatever brings them together. And this flexibility is needed also to allow for growth and change in what comes to be fully shared, as well as to allow for personal differences.

Nor is there any doubt about how these standards become internalized. From birth onwards, we are both socialized into and differentiated out from the society into which we are born. We are socialized in by all the pressures of our elders (and soon our peer group also) persuading us by example and precept to adopt their standards. We are differentiated out by applying our own minds both to making sense of our own experience and to seeing how far the code we are being taught is actually practised by others, and is actually acceptable to ourselves. Whether we accept it or reject it, we shall be affected by it – revolutionaries are children of their times, no less than conservatives. But it is not a question of 'either-or'. The heritage of mankind is not so barren as to include nothing which today's babies will grow up to prize. If it were, it would be a bad prospect for today's babies.

On this showing then, responsibility is the state of having accepted a commitment, and autonomy means the right to choose our commitments and the ability to live by them and accept the constraints which they always impose. So responsibility and autonomy are not antitheses; they are complementary. And yet each qualifies the other. Eichmann was not excused for his lack of autonomy because he 'responsibly' did what he was told to do. Nor was Hitler's 'autonomy' accepted as a justification for 'commitments' which he accepted. We are social animals, each acculturated in its own cultural tradition and our fellows in each of our cultural groups have a right to constrain our individual artistry if it plays too much havoc with the cultural pattern. Hence the ambivalence and tragedy of human life. Who fails to know by now that it is ambivalent and tragic by its very nature and that an essential part of its nature is the moral artistry which I have been describing?

Who fails? Many 'natural scientists' and many of those whom the culture of science has distorted. The 'scientific' approach has blurred our understanding of the moral dimension for understandable historical reasons which I have no space to summarize here. These have done their work, they are out of date and they should now be dismissed. As a critical method a scientific approach is still capable of being harnessed to the criticism and clarification of human standards, individual and collective; and its current impotence or adverse effect is partly due to influences far beyond its control, notably to the form of individualism which has become established in Western societies over the last two centuries. But it is a failure we cannot afford.

The laws of the natural world are as they are and we cannot change them, but we can learn about them and use our knowledge to change the natural world, though often in ways which we neither intend nor desire. The world of men (equally subject to these natural laws) has also its own laws, far more important for us men and far less stable, depending for their stability and their change on us. They *are* these structures of self and mutual expectation and their nature requires us not only to know them but to share the responsibility both for changing them and for preserving them. They are works of art at all levels from the personal to the planetary in so far as any human mind commits itself to reshaping or preserving them and accepts the constraints which every such commitment imposes. Autonomy is the claim to participate however humbly in this process. The current results are awful, the prospects are worse, but the process is human and ennobling and gives meaning to human effort even when it does not give shape to human life.

The shaping and preserving of these standards is also what politics is about – in the totalitarian world and in the Westernized world. It is not the whole story, or even the whole conscious story. But it is the major field of activity conscious and unconscious. It is the activity of defining and redefining, explicitly or by implication, the standards of good and bad, of right and wrong.

And now, having at last allowed those almost tabu words to appear, I shall be asked whether I am arguing that they are purely relative or purely arbitrary norms or purely rationalizations of actions taken for quite different reasons. And I shall reject all these questions as being inappropriately expressed. I claim to have pointed to the process by which we develop commitments and corresponding constraints and to the processes continually at work to build upon them a sufficiently shared net of self and mutual expectations – and equally to change one set for another. I have pointed to a number of in-built conflicts within the individual, between one individual and another and between an

169

individual and any or all of the societies to which he belongs. None of these takes place in vacuo. They take place in a specific context and that context includes the context of history, the individual's history and the history of his society. Autonomy would not be interpreted as it is or prized as it is in the West today except for features of Western history which reach back at least two centuries. The struggle to give form to human life, whether individual or collective, is inconceivable except in a social and an historical context which defines for men and societies at each time and place what are the commitments and constraints which they must accept or deny and which are the ones which are of most common concern. We start from wherever we are with whatever constraints and enablements we may then have. And each of us is engaged not merely in giving form to an individual life, but also in playing his part in taking over and passing on the whole human heritage to another generation, knowing that it will in some degree be not merely different but better or worse for passing through him, if only because he will have contributed something to preserving or changing the contemporary standards of better and worse.

I have personally a hope – though only a hope, not quite a faith – that there is to be seen in human history what I would call a trans-cultural vector, a direction in which in any given context, it is most human or least inhuman to move. One of the near-imperatives of this view is the importance of raising the level of trust and the quality (no, not the quantity) of human communication. For it seems to me that our humanity resides in some real degree in our ability to maintain through change the net of self and mutual expectations which creates a culture. Hopes of this kind may be encouraging, but they are not necessary. The task of being human need not rely on them. The field of knowledge most likely to throw light on it is history, the history of individuals, of societies and of cultures. History is significantly not classed as a science, partly because too many theories compete for our acceptance, but chiefly because it is itself a human artefact, a future constantly being created in the present by men guided by interpretations of their own past. It is not subject to scientific validation. It is in some degree open to human creation. And its criteria are necessarily moral.

We do not need to recombine genes. We do need to combine as human beings in cultural forms fit to sustain their dual human function – to survive and to maintain and raise their standards of human living. These standards are ethical as well as economic and they will become more so as the human environment becomes increasingly the human and the man-made, rather than the natural world. Ethics are not a trimming to be added when economic demands are satisfied. They are the distinctive character of human life, ever more demanding as economic interaction grows. They involve commitment to personal as well as collective standards and the endless resolution of the conflicts within them and between them. They should be the prime concern of men sufficiently responsible to deserve a corresponding measure of autonomy.

I have raised in a most summary way three questions which are of great practical importance to all of us today. One concerns the nature of the sense of obligation which some individuals sometimes feel even today as commitment and constraint in some specific situation. The second concerns the relationship between this personal sense of obligation and the norms of the culture which the individual shares with others. The third concerns the quality of the standards revealed by both individual and social mores and the criteria by which these standards can themselves be judged better or worse. They are important because, as I shall maintain, no individual personality and no human society can cohere and survive unless such standards are sufficiently comprehensive, sufficiently cogent and sufficiently shared; and because the quality of individual and social life depends on the quality of the standards. [...]

Geoffrey Vickers

16 | Individualization: plant a tree, buy a bike, save the world?

MICHAEL MANIATES[1]

This reading has been written from a North American perspective, but Michael Maniates's account of the individualization of responsibility for environmental problems that drives a narrowing of our collective imagination could easily apply in other areas of the world, e.g. in parts of Europe. He suggests we act largely as individual consumers doing what is familiar rather than embarking on meaningful social action that could lead to radically new ways of living. Challenging the forces that lead to this individualization would require different frameworks of thinking and talking and the author suggests one by way of illustration. (Note: this reading has been extracted from a longer paper where further analysis was included, including about what led to individualization of responsibility in the United States.)

§ *'But now,' says the Once-ler, 'now that you're here, the word of the Lorax seems perfectly clear. UNLESS someone like you cares a whole awful lot, nothing is going to get better. It's not. SO ... catch!' calls the Once-ler. He lets something fall. 'It's a Truffula seed. It's the last one of all! You're in charge of the last of the Truffula seeds. And Truffula Trees are what everyone needs. Plant a new Truffula. Treat it with care. Give it clean water. And feed it fresh air. Grow a forest. Protect it from axes that hack. Then the Lorax and all of his friends may come back.'* (Dr Seuss)[2]

Most people are eagerly groping for some medium, some way in which they can bridge the gap between their morals and their practices. (Saul Alinsky)[3]

One of the most successful modern-day children's stories is *The Lorax*, Dr Seuss's tale of a shortsighted and voracious industrialist who clear-cuts vast tracks of Truffula trees to produce 'Thneeds' for unquenchable consumer markets. The Lorax, who 'speaks for the trees' and the many animals who make the Truffula forest their home, politely but persistently challenges the industrialist, a Mr Once-ler, by pointing out again and again the terrible toll his business practices are taking on the natural landscape. The Once-ler remains largely deaf to the Lorax's protestations. 'I'm just meeting consumer demand,' says the Once-ler; 'if I didn't, someone else would.' When, finally, the last Truffula tree is cut and the landscape is reduced to rubble, the Once-ler – now out of business and apparently penniless – realizes the error of his ways. Years later, holed up in the ruins of his factory amidst a desolate landscape, he recounts his foolishness to a passing boy and charges him with re-planting the forest.

The Lorax is fabulously popular. Most of the college students with whom I work – and not just the ones who think of themselves as environmentalists – know it well and speak of it fondly. My children read it in school. There is a 30-minute animated version of the book, which often finds its way onto television. The tale has become a beloved organizing touchstone for environmentalists. In years past, for example, the EcoHouse on my campus has aired it as part of its Earth Day observations, as did the local television station. A casual search through the standard library databases reveals over 80 essays or articles in the past decade that bear upon or draw from the book. A more determined search of popular newspapers and magazines would no doubt reveal additional examples of shared affection for the story.

All this for a tale that is, well, both dismal and depressing. The Once-ler is a stereotypical rapacious businessman. He succeeds in enriching himself by laying ruin to the landscape. The Lorax fails miserably in his efforts to challenge the interlocking processes of industrial capitalism and consumerism that turn his Eden into a wasteland. The animals of the story are forced to flee to uncertain futures. At the end of the day the Lorax's only satisfaction is the privilege of being able to say 'I told you so,' but this – and the Once-ler's slide into poverty – has got to be small consolation. The conclusion sees a small boy with no evident training in forestry or community organizing unpromisingly entrusted with the last seed of a critical species. He's told to 'Plant a new Truffula. Treat it with care. Give it clean water. And feed it fresh air. Grow a forest. Protect it from axes that hack. Then the Lorax and all of his friends may come back.' His chances of success are by no means high.

So why the amazing popularity of *The Lorax*? Why do so many find it to be 'the environmental book for children' – and, seemingly, for grown-ups too – 'by which all others must be judged?'[4] One reason is its overarching message of environmental stewardship and faith in the restorative powers of the young. The book recounts a foolish tragedy that can be reversed only by a new and, one hopes, more enlightened generation. Surely another reason is the comfortable way in which the book – which adults can easily trivialize as *children*'s literature – permits us to look squarely at a set of profoundly uncomfortable dynamics we know to be operating but find difficult to confront: consumerism, the concentration of economic power, the mindless degradation of the environment, the seeming inability of science (represented by the fact-spouting Lorax himself) and objective fact to slow the damage. The systematic undermining of environmental systems fundamental to human well-being is scary stuff, though no more so than one's own sense of personal impotence in the face of such destruction. Seuss's clever rhyming schemes and engaging illustrations, wrapped around the 20th-century tale of economic expansion and environmental degradation, provide safe passage through a topic we know is out there but would rather avoid.

There's another reason, though, why the book is so loved. By ending with the charge to plant a tree, *The Lorax* both echoes and amplifies an increasingly dominant, largely American response to the contemporary environmental crisis. This response half-consciously understands environmental degradation as the product of *individual* shortcomings (the Once-ler's greed, for example), best countered by action that is staunchly *individual* and typically *consumer-based* (buy a tree and plant it!) It embraces the notion that knotty issues of consumption, consumerism, power and responsibility can be resolved neatly and cleanly through enlightened, uncoordinated consumer choice. Education is a critical ingredient in this view – smart consumers will make choices, it's thought, with the larger public good in mind. Accordingly, this dominant response emphasizes (like the Lorax himself) the need to speak politely, and individually, armed only with facts.

For the lack of a better term, call this response the *individualization of responsibility*. When responsibility for environmental problems is individualized, there is little room to ponder institutions, the nature and exercise of political power, or ways of collectively changing the distribution of power and influence in society – to, in other words, 'think institutionally.'[5] Instead, the serious work of confronting the threatening socio-environmental processes that *The Lorax* so ably illuminates falls to individuals, acting alone, usually as consumers. We are individualizing responsibility when we agonize over the 'paper or plastic' choice at the checkout counter, knowing somehow that neither is right given larger institutions and social structures. We think aloud with the neighbor over the back fence about whether we should buy the new Honda or Toyota hybrid-engine automobile now or wait a few years until they work the kinks out, when really what we wish for is clean, efficient, and effective public transportation of the sort we read about in science fiction novels when we were young – but which we can't vote for with our consumer dollars since, for reasons rooted in power and politics, it's not for sale. So we ponder the 'energy stickers' on the ultra-efficient appliances at Sears, we diligently compost our kitchen waste, we try to ignore the high initial cost and buy a few compact-fluorescent lightbulbs. We read spirited reports in the *New York Times Magazine* on the pros and cons of recycling while sipping our coffee,[6] study carefully the merits of this and that environmental group so as to properly decide upon the destination of our small annual donation, and meticulously sort our recyclables. And now an increasing number of us are confronted by opportunistic green-power providers who urge us to 'save the planet' by buying their 'green electricity' – while doing little to actually increase the quantity of electricity generated from renewable resources.

The Lorax is not why the individualization of responsibility dominates the contours of contemporary American environmentalism. Several forces, described later in this article, are to blame. They include the historical baggage of mainstream environmentalism, the core tenets of liberalism, the dynamic ability of capitalism to commodify dissent, and the relatively recent rise of *global* environmental threats to human prosperity. Seuss's book simply has been swept up by these forces and adopted by them. Seuss himself would probably be surprised by the near deification of his little book; and his central character, a Lorax who politely sought to hold a corporate CEO accountable, surely would be appalled that his story is being used to justify individual acts of planting trees as the primary response to the threat of global climate change.[7]

Mark Dowie, a journalist and sometimes historian of the American environmental movement, writes about our 'environmental imagination,' by which he means our collective ability to imagine and pursue a variety of productive responses (from individual action to community organization to whole-scale institutional change) to the environmental problems before us.[8] My claim in this is that an accelerating individualization of responsibility in the United States is narrowing, in dangerous ways, our 'environmental imagination' and undermining our capacity to react effectively to environmental threats to human well-being. Those troubled by overconsumption, consumerism and commodification should not and cannot ignore this narrowing. Confronting the consumption problem demands, after all, the sort of institutional thinking that the individualization of responsibility patently undermines. It calls too for individuals to understand themselves as citizens in a participatory democracy first, working together to change broader policy and larger social institutions, and as consumers second. By contrast, the individualization of responsibility, because it characterizes environmental problems as

175

the consequence of destructive consumer choice, asks that individuals imagine themselves as consumers first and citizens second. Grappling with the consumption problem, moreover, means engaging in conversation both broad and deep about consumerism and frugality and ways of fostering the capacity for restraint. But when responsibility for environmental ills is individualized, space for such conversation disappears: the individually responsible consumer is encouraged to purchase a vast array of 'green' or 'eco-friendly' products on the promise that the more such products are purchased and consumed, the healthier the planet's ecological processes will become. 'Living lightly on the planet' and 'reducing your environmental impact' becomes, paradoxically, a consumer-product growth industry. [...]

A dangerous narrowing?

A few years back Peter Montague, editor of the internet-distributed *Rachel's Environmental and Health Weekly*, took the Environmental Defense Fund (EDF) to task for its annual calendar, which this powerful and effective organization widely distributes to its more than 300,000 members and many non-members too. What drew Montague's ire was the final page of EDF's 1996 calendar, which details a 10-point program to 'save the Earth' (EDF's phrase):

1 Visit and help support our national parks;
2 Recycle newspapers, glass, plastic and aluminum;
3 Conserve energy and use energy-efficient lighting;
4 Keep tires properly inflated to improve gas mileage and extend tire life;
5 Plant trees;
6 Organize a Christmas tree recycling program in your community;
7 Find an alternative to chemical pesticides for your lawn;
8 Purchase only those brands of tuna marked 'dolphin-safe';
9 Organize a community group to clean up a local stream, highway, park, or beach; and
10 Become a member of EDF.

Montague's reaction was terse and pointed:

What I notice here is the complete absence of any ideas commensurate with the size and nature of the problems faced by the world's environment. I'm not against recycling Christmas trees – if you MUST have one – but who can believe that recycling Christmas trees – or supporting EDF as it works overtime to amend and re-amend the Clean Air Act – is part of any serious effort to 'save the Earth'? I am forced to conclude once again that the mainstream environmental movement in the U.S. has run out of ideas and has no worthy vision.[9]

Shortly after reading Montague's disturbing and, for me, surprising rejection of 10 very sensible measures to protect the environment, I walked into an introductory course on environmental problems that I often team-teach with colleagues in the environmental science department. The course challenges students to consider not only the physical cause-and-effect relationships that manifest themselves as environmental degradation, but also to think critically about the struggles for power and influence that underlie most environmental problems. That day, near the end of a very productive semester, my colleague divided the class of about 45 students into smaller 'issue groups' (energy, water, agriculture, etc.) and asked each group to develop a rank-order list of 'responses' or 'solutions' to environmental threats specific to that issue. He then brought the class back together, had each group report, and tabulated their varied 'solutions.' From this group of 45, the fourth most recommended solution to mounting environmental degradation was to ride a bike rather than drive a car. Number three on the list was to recycle. The second most preferred action was 'plant a tree' and the top response was, again, 'plant a tree' (the mechanics of tabulating student preference across the issue groups permitted a singularly strong preference to occupy two slots).

When we asked our students – who were among the brightest and best prepared of the many with whom we'd worked over the years – why, after thirteen weeks of intensive study of environmental problems, they were so reluctant to consider as 'solutions' broader changes in policy and institutions, they shrugged. Sure, we remember studying these kinds of approaches in class, they said, but such measures were, well, fuzzy, mysterious, messy, and 'idealistic.' [...]

In our struggle to bridge the gap between our morals and our practices, we stay busy – but busy doing that with which we're most familiar and comfortable: consuming our way (we hope) to a better America and a better world. When confronted by environmental ills – ills many confess to caring deeply about – Americans seem capable of understanding themselves only as consumers who must buy 'environmentally sound' products (and then recycle them), rather than as citizens who might come together and develop political muscle sufficient to alter institutional arrangements that drive a pervasive consumerism.[10] The relentless ability of contemporary capitalism to commodify dissent and sell it back to dissenters is surely one explanation for the elevation of consumer over citizen.[11] But another factor, no doubt, is the growing suspicion of and unfamiliarity with processes of citizen-based political action among masses of North Americans. The interplay of State and Market after World War II has whittled the obligations of citizenship down to the singular and highly individualized act of voting in important elections. The increasing fragmentation and mobility of everyday life undermines our sense of neighborhood and community, separating us from the small arenas in which we might practice and refine our abilities as citizens. We build shopping malls but let community playgrounds deteriorate and migrate to sales but ignore school-board meetings. Modern-day advances in entertainment and communication increasingly find us sitting alone in front of a screen, making it all seem fine. We do our political bit in the election booth, then get back to 'normal.'[12]

Given our deepening alienation from traditional understandings of active citizenship, together with the growing allure of consumption-as-social-action, it's little wonder that at a time when our capacity to imagine an array of ways to build a just and ecologically resilient future must expand, it is in fact narrowing. At a moment when we should be vigorously exploring multiple paths to sustainability, we are obsessing over the cobblestones of but one path. This collective obsessing over an array of 'green consumption' choices and opportunities to recycle is noisy and vigorous, and thus comes to resemble the foundations of meaningful social action. But it isn't, not in any real and lasting way that might alter institutional arrangements and make possible radically new ways of living that seem required.

Environmentalism and the flight from politics

[...] Throughout the 20th century, in fact, mainstream environmentalism has demonstrated an ability to foster multiple and simultaneous interpretations on where we are and where we are heading.

But that ability has, today, clearly become impaired. Although public support for things environmental has never been greater, it is so because the public increasingly understands environmentalism as an individual, rational, cleanly apolitical process that can deliver a future that works without raising voices or mobilizing constituencies. As individual consumers and recyclers we are supplied with ample and easy means of 'doing our bit.' The result, though, is often dissonant and sometimes bizarre: consumers wearing 'save the earth' T-shirts, for example, speak passionately against recent rises in gasoline prices when approached by television news crews; shoppers drive all over town in their gasoline-guzzling SUVs in search of organic lettuce or shade-grown coffee; and diligent recyclers expend far more fossil-fuel energy on the hot water spent to meticulously clean a tin can than is saved by its recycling.

Despite these jarring contradictions, the technocratic, sanitary and individualized framing of environmentalism prevails, largely because it is continually reinforced. Consider, for example, recent millennial issues of *Time* and *Newsweek* that look to life in the future.[13] They paint a picture of smart appliances, computer-guided automobiles, clean neighborhoods, eco-friendly energy systems, and happy citizens. How do we get to this future? Not through bold political leadership or citizen-based debate within enabling democratic institutions – but rather via consumer choice: informed, decentralized, apolitical, individualized. Corporations will build a better mousetrap, consumers will buy it, and society will be transformed for the better. A struggle-free eco-revolution awaits, one made possible by the combination of technological innovation and consumer choice with a conscience.

[...] Shocking images of a 'hole' in the ozone layer in the late 1980s, ubiquitous video on rainforest destruction, media coverage of global climate change and the warming of the poles: all this and more have brought the public to a new state of awareness and concern about the 'health of the planet.' What, though, is the public to do with this concern? Academic discussion and debate about global environmental threats focuses on distant international negotiations, complicated science fraught with uncertainty that seems to bedevil even the scientists, and nasty global politics. This is no place for the 'normal' citizen. Environmental groups often encourage people to act, but recommended action on global environmental ills is limited to making a donation, writing a letter, or – yes – buying an environmentally friendly product. The message on all fronts seems to be 'Act ... but don't get in the way.' Confronted by a set of global problems that clearly matter and seeing no clear way to attack them, it is easy to imagine the lay public gravitating to individualistic, consumer-oriented measures.

[...] A privatization and individualization of responsibility for environmental problems shifts blame from State elites and powerful producer groups to more amorphous culprits like 'human nature' or 'all of us.' State elites and the core corporations upon which they depend to drive economic growth stand to benefit from spreading the blame and cranking the rotary of consumption.[14]

[...] Mainstream conversations about global sustainability advance the 'international conference' as the most meaningful venue for global environmental problem-solving. It is here that those interests best able to organize at the international level – States and transnational corporations – hold the advantage in the battle to shape the conversation of sustainability and craft the rules of the game. And it is *precisely* these actors who benefit by moving mass publics toward private, individual, well-intentioned consumer choice as *the* vehicle for achieving 'sustainability.'

It's more than coincidental that as our collective perception of environmental problems has become more global, our prevailing way of framing environmental problem-solving has become more individualized. In the end, individualizing responsibility does not work – you can't plant a tree to save the world – and as citizens and consumers slowly come to discover this fact their cynicism about social change will only grow: 'you mean after fifteen years of washing out these crummy jars and recycling them, environmental problems are still getting worse – geesh, what's the use?' Individualization, by implying that any action beyond the private and the consumptive is irrelevant, insulates people from the empowering experiences and political lessons of *collective* struggle for social change and reinforces corrosive myths about the difficulties of public life.[15] By legitimating notions of consumer sovereignty and a self-balancing and autonomous market, it also diverts attention from political arenas that matter. In this way, individualization is both a symptom and a source of waning citizen capacities to participate meaningfully in processes of social change. If consumption, in all its complexity, is to be confronted, the forces that systematically individualize responsibility for environmental degradation must be challenged.

IPAT, and beyond

But how? One approach would focus on undermining the dominant frameworks of thinking and talking that make the individualization of responsibility appear so natural and 'common sense.' Among other things, this means taking on 'IPAT.'

At first glance it would seem that advocates of a consumption angle on environmental degradation should naturally embrace IPAT (impact = population × affluence × technology). The 'formula' argues, after all, that one cannot make sense of, much less tackle, environmental problems unless one takes into account all three of the proximate causes of environmental degradation. Population growth, resource-intensive and highly polluting technologies, and affluence (that is, levels of consumption) together conspire to undermine critical ecological processes upon which human well-being depends. Focusing on one or two of these three factors, IPAT tells us, will ultimately disappoint.

IPAT is a powerful conceptual framework, and those who would argue the importance of including consumption in the environmental-degradation equation have not been reluctant to invoke it. They note, correctly so, that the 'A' in IPAT has for too long been neglected in environmental debates and policy action.[16] However, although IPAT provides intellectual justification for positioning consumption center-stage, it also comes with an underlying set of assumptions – assumptions that reinforce an ineffectual Loraxian flight from politics.

A closer look at IPAT shows that the formula distributes widely all culpability for the environmental crisis [...]. Population size, consumption levels, and technology choice are all to blame. Responsibility for environmental degradation nicely splits, moreover, between the so-called developed and developing world: if only the developing world could get its population under control and the developed world could tame its overconsumption and each could adopt green technologies, then all would be well. Such a formulation is, on its face, eminently reasonable, which explains why IPAT stands as such a tempting platform from which advocates of a consumption perspective might press their case.

In practice, however, IPAT amplifies and privileges an 'everything is connected to everything else' biophysical, ecosystem-management understanding of environmental problems, one that obscures the exercise of power while systematically disempowering citizen actors. When everything is connected to everything else, knowing how or when or even why to intervene becomes difficult; such 'system complexity' seems to overwhelm any possibility of planned, coordinated, effective intervention.[17] Additionally, there is not much room in IPAT's calculus for questions of agency, institutions, political power, or collective action.

[...] Proponents of a consumption angle on environmental degradation must cultivate alternatives to IPAT and conventional development models that focus on, rather than divert attention from, politically charged elements of commercial relations. Formulas like IPAT are handy in that they focus attention on key elements of a problem. In that spirit, then, I propose a variation: 'IWAC,' which is environmental Impact = quality of Work × meaningful consumption Alternatives × political Creativity. If ideas have power, and if acronyms package ideas, then alternative formulations like IWAC could prove useful in shaking the environmentally-inclined out of their slumber of individualization. And this could only be good for those who worry about consumption.

Take 'work' for example. IPAT systematically ignores work while IWAC embraces it. As *The Atlantic Monthly* senior editor Jack Beatty notes, 'radical talk' about work – questions about job security, worker satisfaction, downsizing, overtime, and corporate responsibility – is coming back strong into public discourse.[18] People who might otherwise imagine themselves as apolitical care about the state of work, and they do talk about it. IWAC taps into this concern, linking it to larger concerns about environmental degradation by suggesting that consumeristic impulses are linked to the routinization of work and, more generally, to the degree of worker powerlessness within the workplace. The more powerless one feels at work, the more one is inclined to assert power as a consumer. The 'W' in IWAC provides a conceptual space for asking difficult questions about consumption and affluence. It holds out the possibility of going beyond a critique of the 'cultivation of needs' by advertisers to ask about social forces (like the deadening quality of the workplace) that make citizens so susceptible to this 'cultivation.'[19] Tying together two issues that matter to mass publics – the nature of work and the quality of the environment – via something like IWAC could help revitalize public debate and challenge the political timidity of mainstream environmentalism.

Likewise, the 'A' in IWAC, 'alternatives,' expands IPAT's 'T' in new directions by suggesting that the public's failure to embrace sustainable technologies has more to do with institutional structures that restrict the aggressive development and wide dissemination of sustainable technologies than with errant consumer choice. The marketplace, for instance, presents us with red cars and blue ones, and calls this consumer choice, when what sustainability truly demands is a choice between automobiles and mass transit systems that enjoy a level of government support and subsidy that is presently showered upon the automotive industry.[20] With 'alternatives,' spirited conversation can coalesce around questions like: Do consumers confront real, or merely cosmetic choice? Is absence of choice the consequence of an autonomous and distant set of market mechanisms? Or is the self-interested exercise of political and economic power at work? And how would one begin to find out? In raising these uncomfortable questions, IWAC focuses attention on claims that the direction and pace of technological development is far from autonomous and is almost always political.[21] Breaking down the widely held belief (which is reinforced by IPAT) that technical choice is 'neutral' and 'autonomous' could open the floodgates to full and vigorous debate over the nature and design of technological choice. Once the veil of neutrality is lifted, rich local discourse can, and sometimes does, follow.[22]

And then there is the issue of public imagination and collective creativity, represented by the 'C' in IWAC. 'Imagination' is not a word one often sees in reflections on environmental politics; it lies among such terms as love, caring, kindness, and meaning that raise eyebrows when introduced into political discourse and policy analysis.[23] This despite the work of scholars like political scientist Karen Litfin that readily shows how ideas, images, categories, phrases and examples structure our collective imagination about what is proper and what is possible. Ideas and images, in other words, and those who package and broker them, wield considerable power.[24] [...]

Conclusion

IWAC is more illustrative than prescriptive. It draws into sharp relief the fact that prevailing conceptualizations of the 'environmental crisis' drive us towards an individualization of responsibility that legitimizes existing dynamics of consumption and production. The recent globalization of environmental problems – dominated by natural-science diagnoses of global environmental threats that ignore critical elements of power and institutions – accelerates this individualization, which has deep roots in American political culture. To the extent that commonplace language and handy conceptual frameworks have power, in that they shape our view of the world and tag some policy measures as proper and others as far-fetched, IWAC stands as an example of how one might go about propagating an alternative understanding of why we have environmental ills, and what we ought to be doing about them.

A proverbial fork in the road looms large for those who would seek to cement consumption into the environmental agenda. One path of easy walking leads to a future where 'consumption' in its environmentally undesirable forms – 'overconsumption,' 'commodification,' and 'consumerism' – has found a place in environmental debates. Environmental groups will work hard to 'educate' the citizenry about the need to buy green and consume less and, by accident or design, the pronounced asymmetry of responsibility for and power over environmental problems will remain obscure. Consumption, ironically, could continue to expand as the privatization of the environmental crisis encourages upwardly spiraling consumption, so long as this consumption is 'green.'[25] This is the path of business-as-usual.

The other road, a rocky one, winds toward a future where environmentally concerned citizens come to understand, by virtue of spirited debate and animated conversation, the 'consumption problem.' They would see that their individual consumption choices *are* environmentally important, but that their control over these choices is constrained, shaped, and framed by institutions and political forces that can be remade only through collective citizen action, as opposed to individual consumer behavior. This future world will not be easy to reach. Getting there

Michael Maniates

183

means challenging the dominant view – the production, technological, efficiency-oriented perspective that infuses contemporary definitions of progress – and requires linking explorations of consumption to politically charged issues that challenge the political imagination. Walking this path means becoming attentive to the underlying forces that narrow our understanding of the possible.

To many, alas, an environmentalism of 'plant a tree, save the world' appears to be apolitical and non-confrontational, and thus ripe for success. Such an approach is anything but, insofar as it works to constrain our imagination about what is possible and what is worth working toward. It is time for those who hope for renewed and rich discussion about 'the consumption problem' to come to grips with this narrowing of the collective imagination and the growing individualization of responsibility that drives it, and to grapple intently with ways of reversing the tide.

Notes

1 I thank Thomas Princen, Benjamin Slote, Richard Bowden, and Brian Hill for their helpful comments on earlier drafts of this article.

2 Geisel 1971.

3 Alinksy 1969, p. 94.

4 Larsen 1998, p. 39.

5 Bellah et al. 1991.

6 See, for example, John Tierney, 'Recycling is Garbage,' *New York Times Magazine*, 30 June 1996, pp. 24–30; 48–53.

7 See for example, 'Plant Trees in Dr. Seuss's Honor,' *Instructor*. Primary Edition vol. 108, no. 1, August 1998, p. 9.

8 Dowie 1996.

9 Montague 1996.

10 Coleman 1994; and Smith 1998.

11 Frank 1997; and Frank and Weiland 1997.

12 Freie 1998.

13 *Time*, for example, has run a five-part 'Visions of the 21st Century' series covering the following topics: Health and the Environment (vol. 154, no. 19, November 8, 1999); How We Will Live (vol. 155, no. 7,

February 21, 2000); Science (vol. 155, no. 14, April 10, 2000); Our World, Our Work (vol. 155, no. 21, May 22, 2000); and Technology (vol. 155, no. 25, June 19, 2000). Each special issue provides a large dose of technological utopianism.

14 See, for example, Reich 1991.

15 See Lappé and DuBois 1994 for a discussion of the 'ten myths of power' that dominate US public life.

16 Kates 2000, pp. 10–19; and Holdren 2000, pp. 4–5.

17 Costanza and Cornwell 1992, pp. 12–20, 42.

18 Beatty 1996, p. 20.

19 Bookchin 1980; Gorz 1980; Schor 1999; Schor et al. 2000; and Durning 1992.

20 Roodman 1996.

21 Galbraith 1985; Noble 1986; and Winner 1977.

22 Sclove, Scammell and Holland 1998.

23 Wapner 1996, pp. 21–4, 76.

24 Litfin 1994.

25 Plant and Plant 1991; Smith 1998; Carson and Moulden 1991; and Coddington 1993.

References

Alinksy, Saul. 1969. *Reveille for Radicals.* New York: Vintage Books.

Beatty, Jack. 1996. 'The Year of Talking Radically.' *The Atlantic Monthly* 277 (6): 20.

Bellah, Robert, et al. 1991. 'Introduction: We Live Through Institutions.' In *The Good Society.* New York: Alfred A. Knopf.

Bookchin, Murray. 1980. *Toward an Ecological Society.* Montreal: Black Rose Books.

Cahn, Matthew. 1995. *Environmental Deceptions: The Tension Between Liberalism and Environmental Policymaking in the United States.* Albany, N.Y.: State University of New York Press.

Carson, Patrick, and Julia Moulden. 1991. *Green Is Gold: Business Talking to Business About the Environmental Revolution.* New York: Harper Business.

Coddington, Walter. 1993. *Environmental Marketing: Positive Strategies for Reaching the Green Consumer.* New York: McGraw-Hill.

Coleman, Daniel. 1994. *Ecopolitics: Building a Green Society.* New Brunswick: Rutgers University Press.

Costanza, Robert, and Laura Cornwell. 1992. 'The 4P Approach to Dealing with Scientific Uncertainty.' *Environment* 34 (9): 12–20, 42.

Dowie, Mark. 1996. *Losing Ground: American Environmentalism at the Close of the Twentieth Century.* Cambridge, MA: MIT Press.

Durning, Alan. 1992. *How Much Is Enough?* New York: W. W. Norton and Company.

Fairlie, Simon. 1992. 'Long Distance, Short Life: Why Big Business Favours Recycling.' *The Ecologist* 22 (5): 276–83.

Frank, Thomas. 1997. *The Conquest of Cool.* Chicago: The University of Chicago Press.

Frank, Thomas, and Matt Weiland, eds. 1997. *Commodify Your Dissent: Salvos from the Baffler.* New York: W. W. Norton and Company.

Freie, John. 1998. *Counterfeit Community: The Exploitation of Our Longing for Connectedness.* Lanham, Md.: Rowman & Littlefield.

Galbraith, John K. 1985. *The New Industrial State,* 4th edition. Boston: Houghton Mifflin.

Geisel, Theodore Seuss (Dr Seuss). 1971. *The Lorax.* New York: Random House.

Gorz, Andre. 1980. *Ecology as Politics.* Boston: South End Press.

Gottlieb, Robert. 1995. *Forcing the Spring: The Transformation of the American Environmental Movement.* Washington D.C.: Island Press.

Holdren, John. 2000. 'Environmental Degradation: Population, Affluence, Technology and Sociopolitical Factors.' *Environment* 42 (6): 4–5.

Hunter, J. Robert. 1997. *Simple Things Won't Save the Earth.* Austin: The University of Texas Press.

Kates, Robert. 2000. 'Population and Consumption: What We Know, What We Need to Know.' *Environment* 42 (3): 10–19.

Lappé, Frances Moore, and Paul DuBois. 1994. *The Quickening of America.* San Francisco: Jossey-Bass Publishers.

Larsen, Jonathan. 1998. 'Holy Seuss!' *Amicus Journal* 20 (2): 39.

Litfin, Karen. 1994. *Ozone Discourses.* New York: Columbia University Press.

Montague, Peter. 1996. 'Review: More Straight Talk.' *Rachel's Environmental and Health Weekly.*

December 19, number 525. Available at www.rachel.org.

Noble, David. 1986. *Forces of Production: A Social History of Industrial Automation.* New York: Oxford University Press.

Plant, Christopher and Judith Plant, eds. 1991. *Green Business: Hope or Hoax?* Philadelphia: New Society Publishers.

Reich, Robert. 1991. *The Work of Nations.* New York: Alfred A. Knopf.

Roodman, David. 1996. *Paying the Piper: Subsidies, Politics, and the Environment.* Worldwatch Paper 133. Washington D.C.: The Worldwatch Institute.

Roszak, Theodore, Mary E. Gomes, and Allen D. Kanner. 1995. *Ecopsychology.* San Francisco: Sierra Club Books.

Sale, Kirtpatrick. 1993. *The Green Revolution: The American Environment Movement 1962–1992.* New York: Hill and Wang.

Schor, Juliet. 1999. *The Overspent American: Upscaling, Downshifting,* *and the New Consumer.* New York: HarperCollins.

Schor, Juliet, et al. 2000. *Do Americans Shop Too Much?* Boston: Beacon Press.

Sclove, Richard, Madeleine Scammell, and Breena Holland. 1998. *Community-Based Research in the United States: An Introductory Reconnaissance Including Twelve Organizational Case Studies and Comparison with the Dutch Science Shops and with the Mainstream American Research System.* Amherst, MA: The Loka Institute, July.

Smith, Toby. 1998. *The Myth of Green Marketing: Tending Our Goats at the Edge of Apocalypse.* Toronto: University of Toronto Press.

Wapner, Paul. 1996. 'Toward a Meaningful Ecological Politics.' *Tikkum* 11 (3): 21–2.

Winner, Langdon. 1977. *Autonomous Technology: Technics-out-of-Control as a Theme in Political Thought.* Cambridge, MA: MIT Press.

17 | Obligations to future generations

MARTIN P. GOLDING

A note from Martin P. Golding that accompanied this 1972 paper explained that it was highly speculative and an attempt to extend the author's article on a theory of human rights. Yet its explorations still have much relevance today, several decades later. It is another exploration of the nature of obligations, this time to future people. Questions of claims, moral communities, contracts and how far we can and should look into the future are all explored.

§ [...] [T]he notion of obligations to future generations [...] finds increasing use in discussions of social politics and programs, particularly as concerns population distribution and control and environment control. Thus, it may be claimed, the solution of problems in these areas is not merely a matter of enhancing our own good, improving our own conditions of life, but is also a matter of discharging an obligation to future generations.

Before I turn to the question of the basis of such obligations – the necessity of the plural is actually doubtful – there are three general points to be considered: (1) Who are the individuals in whose regard it is maintained that we have such obligations, to whom do we owe such obligations? (2) What, essentially, do obligations to future generations oblige us to do, what are they aimed at? and (3) To what class of obligation do such obligations belong, what kind of obligation are they? [...]

[...] Obligations to future generations are distinct from the obligations we have to our presently living fellows, who are therefore excluded from the purview of the former, although it might well be the case that *what* wc owe to future generations is identical with (or overlaps) what we owe to the present generation. However, I think we may go further than this and also exclude our most immediate descendants, our children, grandchildren and great-grandchildren, perhaps. What is distinctive about the notion of obligations to future generations is, I think, that it refers to generations with which the possessors of the obligations cannot expect in a literal sense to share a common life. [...]

But if their inner boundary be drawn in this way, what can we say about their outer limits? Is there a cut-off point for the individuals in whose

regard we have such obligations? Here, it seems, there are two alternatives. First, we can flatly say that there are no outer limits to their purview:
all future generations come within their province. A second and more
modest answer would be that we do not have such obligations towards
any assignable future generation. In either case the referent is a broad and
unspecified community of the future, and I think it can be shown that we
run into difficulties unless certain qualifications are taken into account.
Our second point concerns the question of what it is that obligations
to future generations oblige us to do. The short answer is that they
oblige us to do many things. But an intervening step is required here,
for obligations to future generations are distinct from general duties to
perform acts which are in themselves intrinsically right, although such
obligations give rise to duties to perform specific acts. Obligations to
future generations are essentially an obligation to produce – or to attempt
to produce – a desirable state of affairs *for* the community of the future,
to promote conditions of good living for future generations. [...] If we
think we have an obligation to transmit our cultural heritage to future
generations it is because we think that our cultural heritage promotes,
or perhaps even embodies, good living. In so doing we would hardly
wish to falsify the records of our civilization, for future generations must
also have, as a condition of good living, the opportunity to learn from
the mistakes of the past. [...]

To come closer to contemporary discussion, consider, for example,
population control, which is often grounded upon an obligation to future
generations. It is not maintained that population control is intrinsically
right – although the rhetoric frequently seems to approach such a claim
– but rather that it will contribute towards a better life for future generations, and perhaps immediate posterity as well. (If population control
were intrinsically anything, I would incline to thinking it intrinsically
wrong.) On the other hand, consider the elimination of water and air
pollution. Here it might be maintained that we have a definite duty to
cease polluting the environment on the grounds that such pollution is
intrinsically bad[1] or that it violates a Divine command. Given the current mood of neo-paganism, even secularists speak of the despoilment
of the environment as a sacrilege of sorts. When the building of a new
dam upsets the ecological balance and puts the wildlife under a threat,
we react negatively and feel that something bad has resulted. And this
is not because we necessarily believe that our own interests or those of
future generations have been undermined. Both views, but especially
the latter (Divine command), represent men as holding sovereignty over
nature only as trustees to whom not everything is permitted. Neverthe-

less, these ways of grounding the duty to care for the environment are distinguishable from a grounding of the duty upon an obligation to future generations, although one who acknowledges such an obligation will also properly regard himself as a trustee to whom not everything is permitted. Caring for the environment is presumably among the many things that the obligation to future generations obliges us to do because we thereby presumably promote conditions of good living for the community of the future.

The obligation [...] is not an immediate catalogue of specific duties. It is in this respect rather like the responsibility that a parent has to see to the welfare of his child. Discharging one's parental responsibility requires concern, seeking, and active effort to promote the good *of* the child, which is the central obligation of the parent and out of which grow the specific parental obligations and duties. The use of the term 'responsibility' to characterize the parent's obligation connotes, in part, the element of discretion and flexibility which is requisite to the discharging of the obligation in a variety of antecedently unforeseeable situations. Determination of the specific duty is often quite problematic even – and sometimes especially – for the conscientious parent who is anxious to do what is good for his child. And, anticipating my later discussion, this also holds for obligations to future generations. There are, of course, differences, too. Parental responsibility is enriched and reinforced by love, which can hardly obtain between us and future generations.[2] (Still, the very fact that the responsibility to promote the child's good is an obligation means that it is expected to operate even in the absence of love.) Secondly, the parental obligation is always towards assignable individuals, which is not the case with obligations to future generations. There is, however, an additional feature of likeness between the two obligations which I shall mention shortly.

The third point about obligations to future generations – to what class of obligation do they belong? – is that they are *owed*, albeit owed to an unspecified, and perhaps unspecifiable, community of the future. Obligations to future generations, therefore, are distinct from a general duty, when presented with alternatives for action, to choose the act which produces the greatest good. Such a duty is not owed to anyone, and the beneficiaries of my fulfilling a duty to promote the greatest good are not necessarily individuals to whom I stand in the moral relation of having an obligation that is owed. But when I owe it to someone to promote his good, he is never, to this extent, merely an incidental beneficiary of my effort to fulfill the obligation.

He has a presumptive *right* to it and can assert a claim against me for it. Obligations to future generations are of this kind. There is something which is due to the community of the future from us. The moral relation between us and future generations is one in which they have a claim against us to promote their good. Future generations are, thus, possessors of presumptive rights.

This conclusion is surely odd. How *can* future generations – the not-yet-born – *now* have claims against us? This question serves to turn us finally to consider the basis of our obligations to future generations. I think it useful to begin by discussing and removing one source of the oddity.

It should first be noticed that there is no oddity in investing present effort in order to promote a future state of affairs or in having an owed obligation to do so. The oddity arises only on a theory of obligations and claims (and, hence, of rights) that virtually identifies them with acts of willing, with the exercise of sovereignty of one over another, with the pressing of demands – in a word, with *making* claims. But, clearly, future generations are not now engaged in acts of willing, are not now exercising sovereignty over us, and are not now pressing their demands. Future generations are not now making claims against us, nor will it be *possible* for them to do so. (Our immediate posterity is in this last respect in a different case.) [...]

[...] [T]here is a distinction to be drawn between *having* claims and *making* claims. The mere fact that someone claims something from me is not sufficient to establish it as his right, or that he has a claim relative to me. On the other hand, someone may have a claim relative to me whether or not he makes the claim, demands, or is even able to make a claim. (This is not to deny that claiming plays a role in the theory of rights.) Two points require attention here. First, some claims are frivolous. What is demanded cannot really be claimed as a matter of right. The crucial factor in determining this is the *social ideal*, which we may provisionally define as a conception of the good life for man. It serves as the yardstick by which demands, current and potential, are measured.[3] Secondly, whether someone's claim confers an entitlement upon him to receive what is claimed *from me* depends upon my moral relation to him, on whether he is a member of my *moral community*. It is these factors, rather than any actual demanding, which establish whether someone has a claim relative to me. [...]

Who are the members of my moral community? (Who is my neighbor?) The fact is that I am a member of more than one moral community, for I belong to a variety of groups whose members owe obligations to one another. And many of the particular obligations that are owed vary from group to group. As a result my obligations are often in conflict and I experience a fragmentation of energy and responsibility in attempting to meet my obligations. What I ought to desire for the members of one of these groups is frequently in opposition to what I ought to desire for the members of another of these groups. Moral communities are constituted, or generated, in a number of ways, one of which is especially relevant to our problem. Yet these ways are not mutually exclusive, and they can be mutually reinforcing. This is a large topic and I cannot go into its details here. It is sufficient for our purpose to take brief notice of two possible ways of generating a moral community so as to set in relief the particular kind of moral community that is requisite for obligations to future generations.

A moral community may be constituted by an explicit contract between its members. In this case the particular obligations which the members have towards each other are fixed by the terms of their bargain. Secondly, a moral community may be generated out of a social arrangement in which each member derives benefits from the efforts of other members. As a result a member acquires an obligation to share the burden of sustaining the social arrangement. Both of these are communities in which entrance and participation are fundamentally a matter of self-interest, and only rarely will there be an obligation of the sort that was discussed earlier, that is, a responsibility to secure the good of the members. In general the obligations will be of more specialized kinds. It is also apparent that obligations acquired in these ways can easily come into conflict with other obligations that one may have. Clearly, a moral community comprised of present and future generations cannot arise from either of these sources. We cannot enter into an explicit contract with the community of the future. And although future generations might derive benefits from us, these benefits cannot be reciprocated. (It is possible that the [biologically] dead do derive *some* benefits from the living, but I do not think that this possibility is crucial. Incidentally, just as the living could have obligations to the distant unborn, the living also have obligations to the dead. If obligation to the past is a superstition, then so is obligation to the future.)[4] Our immediate posterity, who will share a common life with us, is in a better position in this respect; so that obligations towards our children, born and unborn, conceivably *could* be generated from participation in a mutually beneficial social arrangement. This, however, would be misleading.

It seems, then, that communities in which entrance and participation are fundamentally matters of self-interest do not fit our specifications. [...]

So far, in the above account of the generation of my moral community, the question of membership has been discussed solely in reference to those towards whom I initially have the sentiments that are identified with fellow-feeling. But we can go beyond this. Again we take our clue from the history of the development of rights. For just as the content of a system of rights that are possessed by the members of a moral community is enlarged over time by the pressing of claims, demanding, so also is the moral community enlarged by the pressing of claims by individuals who have been hitherto excluded. The claiming is not only a claim for something, but may also be an assertion; 'Here I am, I count too.' The struggle for rights has also been a counter-struggle. The widening of moral communities has been accompanied by attempts at exclusion. It is important for us to take note of one feature of this situation.

The structure of the situation is highlighted when a stranger puts forward his demand. The question immediately arises, shall his claim be recognized as a matter of right?[5] Initially I have no affection for him. But is this crucial in determining whether he ought to count as a member of my moral community? The determination depends rather on what he is like and what are the conditions of his life. One's obligations to a stranger are never immediately clear. If a visitor from Mars or Venus were to appear, I would not know what to desire for him. I would not know whether my conception of the good life is relevant to him and to his conditions of life. The good that I acknowledge might not be good for him. Humans of course are in a better case than Martians or Venusians. Still, since the stranger appears as strange, different, what I maintain in my attempt to exclude him is that my conception of the good is not relevant to him, that 'his kind' do not count. He, on the other hand, is in effect saying to me: Given your social ideal, you must acknowledge my claim, for it *is* relevant to me given what I am; your good is my good, also.[6] If I should finally come to concede this, the full force of my obligation to him will be manifest to me quite independently of any fellow-feeling that might or might not be aroused. The *involuntary* character of the obligation will be clear to me, as it probably never is in the case of individuals who command one's sympathy. And once I admit him as a member of my moral community, I will also acknowledge my responsibility to secure this good for him even in the absence of any future claiming on his part.

With this we have completed the account of the constitution of the type of moral community that is required for obligations to future generations. I shall not recapitulate its elements. The step that incorporates future generations into our moral community is small and obvious. Future generations are members of our moral community because, and insofar as, our social deal is relevant to them, given what they are and their conditions of life. I believe that this account applies also to obligations towards our immediate posterity. However, the responsibility that one has to see to the welfare of his children is in addition buttressed and qualified by social understandings concerning the division of moral labor and by natural affection. The basis of the obligations is nevertheless the same in both instances.[7] Underlying this account is the important fact that such obligations fall into the area of the moral life which is independent of considerations of explicit contract and personal advantage. Moral duty and virtue also fall into this area. But I should like to emphasize again that I do not wish to be understood as putting this account forward as an analysis of moral virtue and duty in general.

As we turn at long last specifically to our obligations to future generations, it is worth noticing that the term 'contract' has been used to cover the kind of moral community that I have been discussing. It occurs in a famous passage in Burke's *Reflections on the Revolution in France*:

> Society is indeed a contract. Subordinate contracts for objects of mere occasional interest may be dissolved at pleasure – but the state ought not to be considered as nothing better than a partnership agreement in a trade of pepper and coffee, calico or tobacco, or some other such low concern, to be taken up for a little temporary interest, and to be dissolved by the fancy of the parties. It is to be looked upon with other reverence; because it is not a partnership in things subservient only to the gross animal existence of a temporary and perishable nature.
>
> It is a partnership in all science; a partnership in all art; a partnership in every virtue and in all perfection. As the ends of such a partnership cannot be obtained in many generations, it becomes a partnership not only between those who are living, but between those who are living, those who are dead and those who are to be born.
>
> Each contract of each particular state is but a clause in the great primaeval contract of eternal society, linking the lower with the higher natures, connecting the visible and invisible world according to a fixed compact sanctioned by the inviolable oath which holds all physical and all moral natures, each in their appointed place.[8]

The contract Burke has in mind is hardly an explicit contract, for it is 'between those who are living, those who are dead and those who are to be born.' He implicitly affirms, I think, obligations to future generations. In speaking of the 'ends of such a partnership,' Burke intends a conception of the good life for man – a social ideal. And if I do not misinterpret

193

him, I think it also plain that Burke assumes that it is relatively the same conception of the good life whose realization is the object of the efforts of the living, the dead, and the unborn. They all revere the same social ideal. Moreover, he seems to assume that the conditions of life of the three groups are more or less the same. And, finally, he seems to assume that the same general characterization is true of these groups ('all physical and moral natures, each in their appointed place').

Now I think that Burke is correct in making assumptions of these sorts if we are to have obligations to future generations. However, it is precisely with such assumptions that the notion of obligation to future generations begins to run into difficulties. My discussion, until this point, has proceeded on the view that we *have* obligations to future generations. But do we? I am not sure that the question can be answered in the affirmative with any certainty. I shall conclude this note with a very brief discussion of some of the difficulties. They may be summed up in the question: Is our conception – 'conceptions' might be a more accurate word – of the good life for man relevant[9] to future generations?

It will be recalled that I began by stressing the importance of fixing the purview of obligations to future generations. They compromise the community of the future, a community with which we cannot expect to share a common life. It appears to me that the more *remote* the members of this community are, the more problematic our obligations to them become. That they are members of our moral community is highly doubtful, for we probably do not know what to desire for them. [...]

[...] One might go so far as to say that if we have an obligation to distant future generations it is an obligation not to plan for them. Not only do we not know their conditions of life, we also do not know whether they will maintain the same (or a similar) conception of the good life for man as we do. Can we even be fairly sure that the same general characterization is true both of them and us?

The [...] more distant the generation we focus upon, the less likely it is that we have an obligation to promote its good. We would be both ethically and practically well-advised to set our sights on more immediate generations, and perhaps solely upon our immediate posterity. After all, even if we do have obligations to future generations, our obligations to immediate posterity are undoubtedly much clearer. The nearer the generations are to us, the more likely it is that our conception of the good life is relevant to them. There is certainly enough work for us to do in discharging our responsibility to promote a good life for them. But it would be unwise, both from an ethical and a practical perspective, to seek to promote the good of the very distant.

And it could also be *wrong*, if it be granted – as I think it must – that our obligations towards (and hence the rights relative to us of) near future generations and especially our immediate posterity are clearer than those of more distant generations. By 'more distant' I do not necessarily mean 'very distant.' We shall have to be highly scrupulous in regard to anything we do for any future generation that also could adversely affect the rights of an intervening generation. Anything else would be 'gambling in futures.' We should therefore be hesitant to act on the dire predictions of certain extreme 'crisis ecologists' and on the proposals of those who would have us plan for mere survival. In the main, we would be ethically well-advised to confine ourselves to removing the obstacles that stand in the way of immediate posterity's realizing the social ideal. This involves not only the active task of cleaning up the environment and making our cities more habitable, but also implies restraints upon us. Obviously, the specific obligations that we have cannot be determined in the abstract. This article is not the place for an evaluation of concrete proposals that have been made. I would only add that population limitation schemes seem rather dubious to me. I find it inherently paradoxical that we should have an obligation to future generations (near and distant) to determine in effect the very membership of those generations.[10] [...] It appears that whether we have obligations to future generations in part depends on what we do for the present.

Notes

1 See the remarks of Russell E. Train (Chairman of the Council on Environmental Quality), quoted in *National Geographic*, 138 (1970), p. 780: 'If we're to be responsible we must accept the fact that we owe a massive debt to our environment. It won't be settled in a matter of months, and it won't be forgiven us.'

2 Cf. the discussion of *Fernstenliebe* (Love of the Remotest) in Nicolai Hartmann, *Ethics*, trans. by Coit, 11 (New York: Macmillan Co., 1932), pp. 317ff.

3 There is also another factor relevant to determining whether what is demanded can be claimed as a matter of right, namely, the availability of resources of goods. But I am suppressing this for purposes of this discussion.

4 Paraphrasing C. S. Lewis, *The Abolition of Man* (New York: Macmillan Co., paperback ed. 1969), p. 56: 'If my duty to my parents is a superstition, then so is my duty to posterity.'

5 When Sarah died Abraham 'approached the children of Heth, saying: I am a stranger and a sojourner with you; give me a possession of a burying-place with you, that I may bury my dead out of my sight' (Genesis 23:3, 4). A classical commentary remarks that Abraham is saying: If I am a stranger, I will purchase it, but if I am a sojourner it is mine as a matter of right.

6 Cf. T. H. Green, *Lectures on the*

Martin P. Golding

Principles of Political Obligation (New York and London: Longmans, 1959; Ann Arbor: University of Michigan Press, 1967), Sec. 140. I here acknowledge my debt to Green, in which acknowledgment I was remiss in my article on Human Rights.

7 I think it is an interesting commentary on our times that the rhetoric of obligation to future generations is so much used just when the family bond has become progressively tenuous.

8 *Reflections on the Revolution in France* (London: Dent, 1910), pp. 93–4.

9 The author at last begs pardon for having to use such an abused word.

10 On this and other arguments relating to the problem, see Martin P. Golding and Naomi H. Golding, 'Ethical and Value Issues in Population Limitation and Distribution in the United States,' *Vanderbilt Law Review*, 24 (1971), pp. 495–523.

18 | The tragedy of the commons

GARRETT HARDIN

Extracts from Garrett Hardin's original 1968 article are included here with the intention of retaining its main narrative. In focus are the effects of increasing population and certain kinds of self-interested human behaviour on the world's shared 'commons', such as public land, air and water. Suggestions are made for safeguarding the commons, such as increasing private property and relinquishing some individual freedoms. This work can be seen as an example of contemporary contract theory, which offers explanations about why and how we can or should act responsibly in relation to others. This paper influenced much subsequent work on population and resource utilization, policy and governance, including that detailed in the next reading, from Dietz et al.

§ At the end of a thoughtful article on the future of nuclear war, Wiesner and York[1] concluded that: 'Both sides in the arms race are ... confronted by the dilemma of steadily increasing military power and steadily decreasing national security. *It is our considered professional judgment that this dilemma has no technical solution.* If the great powers continue to look for solutions in the area of science and technology only, the result will be to worsen the situation.'

I would like to focus your attention not on the subject of the article (national security in a nuclear world) but on the kind of conclusion they reached, namely that there is no technical solution to the problem. An implicit and almost universal assumption of discussions published in professional and semi-popular scientific journals is that the problem under discussion has a technical solution. A technical solution may be defined as one that requires a change only in the techniques of the natural sciences, demanding little or nothing in the way of change in human values or ideas of morality. [...]

Recall the game of tick-tack-toe. Consider the problem, 'How can I win the game [...]?' It is well known that I cannot, if I assume (in keeping with the conventions of game theory) that my opponent understands the game perfectly. [...]

The class of 'No technical solution problems' has members. My thesis is that the 'population problem,' as conventionally conceived, is a member of this class. How it is conventionally conceived needs some comment. It is fair to say that most people who anguish over the population problem are trying to find a way to avoid the evils of overpopulation without relinquishing any of the privileges they now enjoy. They think that farming the seas or developing new strains of wheat will solve the problem – technologically. I try to show here that the solution they seek cannot be found. The population problem cannot be solved in a technical way, any more than can the problem of winning the game of tick-tack-toe.

What shall we maximize?

Population, as Malthus said, naturally tends to grow 'geometrically,' or, as we would now say, exponentially. In a finite world this means that the per capita share of the world's goods must steadily decrease. Is ours a finite world?

A fair defence can be put forward for the view that the world is infinite; or that we do not know that it is not. But, in terms of the practical problems that we must face in the next few generations with the foreseeable technology, it is clear that we will greatly increase human misery if we do not, during the immediate future, assume that the world available to the terrestrial human population is finite. 'Space' is no escape.[2]

A finite world can support only a finite population; therefore, population growth must eventually equal zero. [...] When this condition is met, what will be the situation of mankind? Specifically, can Bentham's goal of 'the greatest good for the greatest number' be realized?

No – for two reasons, each sufficient by itself. The first is a theoretical one. It is not mathematically possible to maximize for two (or more) variables at the same time. This was clearly stated by von Neumann and Morgenstern[3] [...]

The second reason springs directly from biological facts. To live, any organism must have a source of energy (for example, food). This energy is utilized for two purposes: mere maintenance and work. For man, maintenance of life requires about 1600 kilocalories a day ('maintenance calories'). Anything that he does over and above merely staying alive will be defined as work, and is supported by 'work calories' which he takes in. Work calories are used not only for what we call work in common speech; they are also required for all forms of enjoyment, from swimming and automobile racing to playing music and writing poetry. If our goal is to maximize population it is obvious what we must do: We must make the work calories per person approach as close to zero as possible. No gourmet meals, no vacations, no sports, no music, no literature, no art.

[...] I think that everyone will grant, without argument or proof, that maximizing population does not maximize goods. Bentham's goal is impossible. [...]

We want the maximum good per person; but what is good? To one person it is wilderness, to another it is ski lodges for thousands. To one it is estuaries to nourish ducks for hunters to shoot; to another it is factory land. Comparing one good with another is, we usually say, impossible because goods are incommensurable. Incommensurables cannot be compared.

Theoretically this may be true; but in real life incommensurables *are* commensurable. Only a criterion of judgment and a system of weighting are needed. [...]

We can make little progress in working toward optimum population size until we explicitly exorcize the spirit of Adam Smith in the field of practical demography. In economic affairs, *The Wealth of Nations* (1776) popularized the 'invisible hand,' the idea that an individual who 'intends only his own gain' is, as it were, 'led by an invisible hand to promote ... the public interest.'[4] Adam Smith did not assert that this was invariably true, and perhaps neither did any of his followers. But he contributed to a dominant tendency of thought that has ever since interfered with positive action based on rational analysis, namely, the tendency to assume that decisions reached individually will, in fact, be the best decisions for an entire society. If this assumption is correct it justifies the continuance of our present policy of laissez-faire in reproduction. If it is correct we can assume that men will control their individual fecundity so as to produce the optimum population. If the assumption is not correct, we need to re-examine our individual freedoms to see which ones are defensible.

Tragedy of freedom in a commons

The rebuttal to the invisible hand in population control is to be found in a scenario first sketched in a little-known pamphlet[5] in 1833 by a mathematical amateur named William Forster Lloyd (1794–1852). We may well call it 'the tragedy of the commons,' using the word 'tragedy' as the philosopher Whitehead used it:[6] 'The essence of dramatic tragedy is not unhappiness. It resides in the solemnity of the remorseless working of things.' He then goes on to say, 'This inevitableness of destiny can only be illustrated in terms of human life by incidents which in fact involve unhappiness. For it is only by them that the futility of escape can be made evident in the drama.'

The tragedy of the commons develops in this way. Picture a pasture open to all. It is to be expected that each herdsman will try to keep as many cattle as possible on the commons. Such an arrangement may work reasonably satisfactorily for centuries because tribal wars, poaching, and disease keep the numbers of both man and beast well below the carrying capacity of the land. Finally, however, comes the day of reckoning, that is, the day when the long-desired goal of social stability becomes a reality. At this point, the inherent logic of the commons remorselessly generates tragedy.

As a rational being, each herdsman seeks to maximize his gain. Explicitly or implicitly, more or less consciously, he asks, 'What is the utility to me of adding one more animal to my herd?' This utility has one negative and one positive component.

1) The positive component is a function of the increment of one animal. Since the herdsman receives all the proceeds from the sale of the additional animal, the positive utility is nearly +1.

2) The negative component is a function of the additional overgrazing created by one more animal. Since, however, the effects of overgrazing are shared by all the herdsmen, the negative utility for any particular decision-making herdsman is only a fraction of 1.

Adding together the component partial utilities, the rational herdsman concludes that the only sensible course for him to pursue is to add another animal to his herd. And another; and another ... But this is the conclusion reached by each and every rational herdsman sharing a commons. Therein is the tragedy. Each man is locked into a system that compels him to increase his herd without limit – in a world that is limited. Ruin is the destination toward which all men rush, each pursuing his own best interest in a society that believes in the freedom of the commons. Freedom in a commons brings ruin to all. [...]

In an approximate way, the logic of the commons has been understood for a long time, perhaps since the discovery of agriculture or the invention of private property in real estate. But it is understood mostly only in special cases which are not sufficiently generalized. Even at this late date, cattlemen leasing national land on the western ranges demonstrate no more than an ambivalent understanding, in constantly pressuring federal authorities to increase the head count to the point where overgrazing produces erosion and weed-dominance. Likewise, the oceans of the world continue to suffer from the survival of the philosophy of the commons. Maritime nations still respond automatically to the shibboleth of the 'freedom of the seas.' Professing to believe in the 'inexhaustible resources of the oceans,' they bring species after species of fish and whales closer to extinction.[7]

The National Parks present another instance of the working out of the tragedy of the commons. At present, they are open to all, without limit. The parks themselves are limited in extent – there is only one Yosemite Valley – whereas population seems to grow without limit. The values that visitors seek in the parks are steadily eroded. Plainly, we must soon cease to treat the parks as commons or they will be of no value to anyone.

What shall we do? We have several options. We might sell them off as private property. We might keep them as public property, but allocate the right to enter them. The allocation might be on the basis of wealth, by the use of an auction system. It might be on the basis of merit, as defined by some agreed-upon standards. It might be by lottery. Or it might be on a first-come, first-served basis, administered to long queues. These, I think, are all the reasonable possibilities. They are all objectionable. But we must choose – or acquiesce in the destruction of the commons that we call our National Parks.

Pollution

In a reverse way, the tragedy of the commons reappears in problems of pollution. Here it is not a question of taking something out of the commons, but of putting something in – sewage, or chemical, radioactive, and heat wastes into water; noxious and dangerous fumes into the air, and distracting and unpleasant advertising signs into the line of sight. The calculations of utility are much the same as before. The rational man finds that his share of the cost of the wastes he discharges into the commons is less than the cost of purifying his wastes before releasing them. Since this is true for everyone, we are locked into a system of 'fouling our own nest,' so long as we behave only as independent, rational, free-enterprisers.

The tragedy of the commons as a food basket is averted by private property, or something formally like it. But the air and waters surrounding us cannot readily be fenced, and so the tragedy of the commons as a cesspool must be prevented by different means, by coercive laws or taxing devices that make it cheaper for the polluter to treat his pollutants than to discharge them untreated. We have not progressed as far with the solution of this problem as we have with the first. Indeed, our particular concept of private property, which deters us from exhausting the positive resources of the earth, favors pollution. The owner of a factory on the bank of a stream – whose property extends to the middle of the stream – often has difficulty seeing why it is not his natural right to muddy the waters flowing past his door. The law, always behind the times, requires elaborate stitching and fitting to adapt it to this newly perceived aspect of the commons.

The pollution problem is a consequence of population. It did not much matter how a lonely American frontiersman disposed of his waste. 'Flowing water purifies itself every 10 miles,' my grandfather used to say, and the myth was near enough to the truth when he was a boy, for there were not too many people. But as population became denser, the natural chemical and biological recycling processes became overloaded, calling for a re-definition of property rights.

How to legislate temperance?

Analysis of the pollution problem as a function of population density uncovers a not generally recognized principle of morality, namely: *the morality of an act is a function of the state of the system at the time it is performed.*[8] Using the commons as a cesspool does not harm the general public under frontier conditions, because there is no public; the same behavior in a metropolis is unbearable. A hundred and fifty years ago a plainsman could kill an American bison, cut out only the tongue for his dinner, and discard the rest of the animal. He was not in any important sense being wasteful. Today, with only a few thousand bison left, we would be appalled at such behavior. [...]

That morality is system-sensitive escaped the attention of most codifiers of ethics in the past. 'Thou shalt not ...' is the form of traditional ethical directives which make no allowance for particular circumstances. The laws of our society follow the pattern of ancient ethics, and therefore are poorly suited to governing a complex, crowded, changeable world. Our epicyclic solution is to augment statutory law with administrative law. Since it is practically impossible to spell out all the conditions under which it is safe to burn trash in the back yard or to run an automobile without smog-control, by law we delegate the details to bureaus. The result is administrative law, which is rightly feared for an ancient reason – *Quis custodiet ipsos custodes?* – 'Who shall watch the watchers themselves?' [...]

Prohibition is easy to legislate (though not necessarily to enforce); but how do we legislate temperance? Experience indicates that it can be accomplished best through the mediation of administrative law. We limit possibilities unnecessarily if we suppose that the sentiment of *Quis custodiet* denies us the use of administrative law. We should rather retain the phrase as a perpetual reminder of fearful dangers we cannot avoid. The great challenge facing us now is to invent the corrective feedbacks that are needed to keep custodians honest. We must find ways to legitimate the needed authority of both the custodians and the corrective feedbacks.

Freedom to breed is intolerable

The tragedy of the commons is involved in population problems in another way. In a world governed solely by the principle of 'dog eat dog' – if indeed there ever was such a world – how many children a family had would not be a matter of public concern. Parents who bred too exuberantly would leave fewer descendants, not more, because they would be unable to care adequately for their children. David Lack and others have found that such a negative feedback demonstrably controls the fecundity of birds.[9] But men are not birds, and have not acted like them for millenniums, at least.

If each human family were dependent only on its own resources; *if* the children of improvident parents starved to death; *if*, thus, overbreeding brought its own 'punishment' to the germ line – then there would be no public interest in controlling the breeding of families. But our society is deeply committed to the welfare state,[10] and hence is confronted with another aspect of the tragedy of the commons.

In a welfare state, how shall we deal with the family, the religion, the race, or the class (or indeed any distinguishable and cohesive group) that adopts overbreeding as a policy to secure its own aggrandizement?[11] To couple the concept of freedom to breed with the belief that everyone born has an equal right to the commons is to lock the world into a tragic course of action. [...]

Conscience is self-eliminating

It is a mistake to think that we can control the breeding of mankind in the long run by an appeal to conscience. Charles Galton Darwin made this point when he spoke on the centennial of the publication of his grand father's great book. The argument is straightforward and Darwinian.

People vary. Confronted with appeals to limit breeding, some people will undoubtedly respond to the plea more than others. Those who have more children will produce a larger fraction of the next generation than those with more susceptible consciences. The difference will be accentuated, generation by generation. [...]

We hear much talk these days of responsible parenthood; the coupled words are incorporated into the titles of some organizations devoted to birth control. [...] But what is the meaning of the word responsibility in this context? Is it not merely a synonym for the word conscience? When we use the word responsibility in the absence of substantial sanctions are we not trying to browbeat a free man in a commons into acting against his own interest? Responsibility is a verbal counterfeit for a substantial *quid pro quo*. It is an attempt to get something for nothing. [...]

Mutual coercion mutually agreed upon

The social arrangements that produce responsibility are arrangements that create coercion, of some sort. Consider bank-robbing. The man who takes money from a bank acts as if the bank were a commons. How do we prevent such action? Certainly not by trying to control his behavior solely by a verbal appeal to his sense of responsibility. Rather than rely on propaganda we follow Frankel's lead and insist that a bank is not a commons; we seek the definite social arrangements that will keep it from becoming a commons. That we thereby infringe on the freedom of would-be robbers we neither deny nor regret.

The morality of bank-robbing is particularly easy to understand because we accept complete prohibition of this activity. [...] But temperance also can be created by coercion. Taxing is a good coercive device. To keep downtown shoppers temperate in their use of parking space we introduce parking meters for short periods, and traffic fines for longer ones. We need not actually forbid a citizen to park as long as he wants to; we need merely make it increasingly expensive for him to do so. Not prohibition, but carefully biased options are what we offer him. A Madison Avenue man might call this persuasion; I prefer the greater candor of the word coercion.

Coercion is a dirty word to most liberals now, but it need not forever be so. [...] To many, the word coercion implies arbitrary decisions of distant and irresponsible bureaucrats; but this is not a necessary part of its meaning. The only kind of coercion I recommend is mutual coercion, mutually agreed upon by the majority of the people affected.

To say that we mutually agree to coercion is not to say that we are required to enjoy it, or even to pretend we enjoy it. Who enjoys taxes? We all grumble about them. But we accept compulsory taxes because we recognize that voluntary taxes would favor the conscienceless. We institute and (grumblingly) support taxes and other coercive devices to escape the horror of the commons. [...]

Recognition of necessity

Perhaps the simplest summary of this analysis of man's population problems is this: the commons, if justifiable at all, is justifiable only under conditions of low-population density. As the human population has increased, the commons has had to be abandoned in one aspect after another.

First we abandoned the commons in food gathering, enclosing farm land and restricting pastures and hunting and fishing areas. These restrictions are still not complete throughout the world.

Somewhat later we saw that the commons as a place for waste disposal would also have to be abandoned. Restrictions on the disposal of domestic sewage are widely accepted in the Western world; we are still struggling to close the commons to pollution by automobiles, factories, insecticide sprayers, fertilizing operations, and atomic energy installations.

[...] Every new enclosure of the commons involves the infringement of somebody's personal liberty. Infringements made in the distant past are accepted because no contemporary complains of a loss. It is the newly proposed infringements that we vigorously oppose; cries of 'rights' and 'freedom' fill the air. But what does 'freedom' mean? When men mutually agreed to pass laws against robbing, mankind became more free, not less so. Individuals locked into the logic of the commons are free only to bring on universal ruin; once they see the necessity of mutual coercion, they become free to pursue other goals. [...]

The most important aspect of necessity that we must now recognize is the necessity of abandoning the commons in breeding. No technical solution can rescue us from the misery of overpopulation. Freedom to breed will bring ruin to all. [...]

The only way we can preserve and nurture other and more precious freedoms is by relinquishing the freedom to breed, and that very soon. 'Freedom is the recognition of necessity' – and it is the role of education to reveal to all the necessity of abandoning the freedom to breed. Only so can we put an end to this aspect of the tragedy of the commons.

Notes

1 J. B. Wiesner and H F York, *Sci. Amer.* 211 (No. 4), 27 (1964).

2 G. Hardin, *J. Hered.* 50, 68 (1959); S. von Hoernor, *Science* 137, 18 (1962).

3 J. von Neumann and O. Morgenstern, *Theory of Games and Economic Behavior* (Princeton Univ. Press, Princeton, N.J., 1947), p. 11.

4 A. Smith, *The Wealth of Nations* (Modern Library, New York, 1937), p. 423.

5 W. F. Lloyd, *Two Lectures on the Checks to Population* (Oxford Univ. Press, Oxford, England, 1833), reprinted (in part) in *Population, Evolution, and Birth Control*, G. Hardin,

Ed. (Freeman, San Francisco, 1964), p. 37.

6 A. N. Whitehead, *Science and the Modern World* (Mentor, New York, 1948), p. 17.

7 S. McVay, *Sci. Amer.* 216 (No. 8), 13 (1966).

8 J. Fletcher, *Situation Ethics* (Westminster, Philadelphia, 1966).

9 D. Lack, *The Natural Regulation of Animal Numbers* (Clarendon Press, Oxford, 1954).

10 H. Girvetz, *From Wealth to Welfare* (Stanford Univ. Press, Stanford, Calif., 1950).

11 G. Hardin, *Perspec. Biol. Med.* 6, 366 (1963).

Garrett Hardin

19 | The struggle to govern the commons

THOMAS DIETZ, ELINOR OSTROM AND
PAUL STERN

This paper was originally published as part of a special issue of
Science magazine that, some thirty-five years after Garrett Hardin's
highly influential article 'The tragedy of the commons' (extracts
of which appear in Reading 18), charted some alternatives to
Hardin's choices for managing the commons of centralized
government and private property. From an environmental
responsibility perspective, this article is rich in examples of
relevant individual and collective actions taken at different levels.
It also discusses principles, requirements and diverse practices
of governance that have enabled people to take responsibility for
environmental resources. (Note: Two graphs that appeared in the
original work and their related references do not appear here and
a couple of notes have been reduced, but in other ways the article
is complete.)

§ *Human institutions – ways of organizing activities – affect the resilience
of the environment. Locally evolved institutional arrangements governed
by stable communities and buffered from outside forces have sustained
resources successfully for centuries, although they often fail when rapid
change occurs. Ideal conditions for governance are increasingly rare. Critical
problems, such as transboundary pollution, tropical deforestation, and climate change, are at larger scales and involve nonlocal influences. Promising
strategies for addressing these problems include dialogue among interested
parties, officials, and scientists; complex, redundant, and layered institutions; a mix of institutional types; and designs that facilitate experimentation, learning, and change.*

In 1968, Hardin[1] drew attention to two human factors that drive environmental change. The first factor is the increasing demand for natural
resources and environmental services, stemming from growth in human
population and per capita resource consumption. The second factor is
the way in which humans organize themselves to extract resources from
the environment and eject effluents into it – what social scientists refer to

as institutional arrangements. Hardin's work has been highly influential[2] but has long been aptly criticized as oversimplified.[3, 4, 5, 6]

Hardin's oversimplification was twofold: He claimed that only two state-established institutional arrangements – centralized government and private property – could sustain commons over the long run, and he presumed that resource users were trapped in a commons dilemma, unable to create solutions.[7, 8, 9] He missed the point that many social groups, including the herders on the commons that provided the metaphor for his analysis, have struggled successfully against threats of resource degradation by developing and maintaining self-governing institutions[3, 10, 11, 12, 13] Although these institutions have not always succeeded, neither have Hardin's preferred alternatives of private or state ownership.

In the absence of effective governance institutions at the appropriate scale, natural resources and the environment are in peril from increasing human population, consumption, and deployment of advanced technologies for resource use, all of which have reached unprecedented levels. For example, it is estimated that 'the global ocean has lost more than 90% of large predatory fishes' with an 80% decline typically occurring 'within 15 years of industrialized exploitation.'[14] The threat of massive ecosystem degradation results from an interplay among ocean ecologies, fishing technologies, and inadequate governance.

Inshore fisheries are similarly degraded where they are open access or governed by top-down national regimes, leaving local and regional officials and users with insufficient autonomy and understanding to design effective institutions.[15, 16] For example, the degraded inshore ground fishery in Maine is governed by top-down rules based on models that were not credible among users. As a result, compliance has been relatively low and there has been strong resistance to strengthening existing restrictions. This is in marked contrast to the Maine lobster fishery, which has been governed by formal and informal user institutions that have strongly influenced state-level rules that restrict fishing. The result has been credible rules with very high levels of compliance.[17, 18, 19] [...] The rules and high levels of compliance related to lobster appear to have prevented the destruction of this fishery. [...]

Resources at larger scales have also been successfully protected through appropriate international governance regimes such as the Montreal Protocol on stratospheric ozone and the International Commission for the Protection of the Rhine Agreements.[20, 21, 22, 23, 24] [...] The Montreal Protocol, the centerpiece of the international agreements on ozone depletion, was signed in 1987. Before then, ODS concentrations were increasing faster than those of CO_2; the increases slowed by the early 1990s and the concentration appears to have stabilized in recent years. The international treaty regime to reduce the anthropogenic impact on stratospheric ozone is widely considered an example of a successful effort to protect the global commons. In contrast, international efforts to reduce greenhouse gas concentrations have not yet had an impact.

Knowledge from an emerging science of human–environment interactions, sometimes called human ecology or the 'second environmental science',[25, 26] is clarifying the characteristics of institutions that facilitate or undermine sustainable use of environmental resources under particular conditions.[6, 27] The knowledge base is strongest with small-scale ecologies and institutions, where long time series exist on many successes and failures. It is now developing for larger-scale systems. In this review, we address what science has learned about governing the commons and why it is always a struggle.[28]

Why a struggle?

Devising ways to sustain the earth's ability to support diverse life, including a reasonable quality of life for humans, involves making tough decisions under uncertainty, complexity, and substantial biophysical constraints as well as conflicting human values and interests. Devising effective governance systems is akin to a coevolutionary race. A set of rules crafted to fit one set of socioecological conditions can erode as social, economic, and technological developments increase the potential for human damage to ecosystems and even to the biosphere itself. Furthermore, humans devise ways of evading governance rules. Thus, successful commons governance requires that rules evolve.

Effective commons governance is easier to achieve when (i) the resources and use of the resources by humans can be monitored, and the information can be verified and understood at relatively low cost (e.g., trees are easier to monitor than fish, and lakes are easier to monitor than rivers);[29] (ii) rates of change in resources, resource-user populations, technology, and economic and social conditions are moderate;[30, 31, 32] (iii) communities maintain frequent face-to-face communication and dense social networks – sometimes called social capital – that increase the potential for trust, allow people to express and see emotional reactions to distrust, and lower the cost of monitoring behavior and inducing rule compliance;[33, 34, 35, 36] (iv) outsiders can be excluded at relatively low cost from using the resource (new entrants add to the harvesting pressure and typically lack understanding of the rules); and (v) users support effective monitoring and rule enforcement.[37, 38, 39] Few settings in the world are characterized by all of these conditions. The challenge is to devise institutional arrangements that help to establish such conditions or, as we discuss below, meet the main challenges of governance in the absence of ideal conditions.[6, 40, 41]

Selective pressures

The characteristics of resources and social interaction in many subsistence societies present favorable conditions for the evolution of effective self-governing resource institutions.[13] Hundreds of documented examples exist of long-term sustainable resource use in such communities as well as in more economically advanced communities with effective, local, self-governing rights, but there are also many failures.[6, 11, 42, 43, 44] As human communities have expanded, the selective pressures on environmental governance institutions increasingly have come from broad influences. Commerce has become regional, national, and global, and institutions at all of these levels have been created to enable and regulate trade, transportation, competition, and conflict.[45, 46] These institutions shape environmental impact, even if they are not designed with that intent. They also provide mechanisms for environmental governance (e.g., national laws) and part of the social context for local efforts at environmental governance. Larger-scale governance may authorize local control, help it, hinder it, or override it.[47, 48, 49, 50, 51, 52] Now, every local place is strongly influenced by global dynamics.[48, 53, 54, 55, 56, 57]

The most important contemporary environmental challenges involve systems that are intrinsically global (e.g., climate change) or are tightly linked to global pressures (e.g., timber production for the world market) and that require governance at levels from the global all the way down to the local.[48, 58, 59] These situations often feature environmental outcomes spatially displaced from their causes and hard-to-monitor, larger-scale economic incentives that may not be closely aligned with the condition of local ecosystems. Also, differentials in power within user groups or across scales allow some to ignore rules of commons use or to reshape the rules in their own interest, such as when global markets reshape demand for local resources (e.g., forests) in ways that swamp the ability of locally evolved institutions to regulate their use.[60, 61, 62]

The store of governance tools and ways to modify and combine them is far greater than often is recognized.[6, 63, 64, 65] Global and national environmental policy frequently ignores community-based governance and traditional tools, such as informal communication and sanctioning, but these tools can have significant impact.[63, 66] Further, no single broad type of ownership – government, private, or community – uniformly succeeds or fails to halt major resource deterioration, as shown for forests in multiple countries (supporting online material text, figs S1 to S5, and table S1).

Requirements of adaptive governance in complex systems

Providing information Environmental governance depends on good, trustworthy information about stocks, flows, and processes within the re-source systems being governed, as well as about the human–environment interactions affecting those systems. This information must be congruent in scale with environmental events and decisions.[48, 67] Highly aggregated information may ignore or average out local information that is important in identifying future problems and developing solutions.

For example, in 2002, a moratorium on all fishing for northern cod was declared by the Canadian government after a collapse of this valuable fishery. An earlier near-collapse had led Canada to declare a 200-mile zone of exclusive fisheries jurisdiction in 1977.[68, 69] Considerable optimism existed during the 1980s that the stocks, as estimated by fishery scientists, were rebuilding. Consequently, generous total catch limits were established for northern cod and other ground fish, the number of licensed fishers was allowed to increase considerably, and substantial government subsidies were allocated for new vessels.[70] What went wrong? There were a variety of information-related problems including: (i) treating all northern cod as a single stock instead of recognizing distinct populations with different characteristics, (ii) ignoring the variability of year classes of northern cod, (iii) focusing on offshore-fishery landing data rather than inshore data to 'tune' the stock assessment, and (iv) ignoring inshore fishers who were catching ever-smaller fish and doubted the validity of stock assessments.[70, 71, 72] This experience illustrates the need to collect and model both local and aggregated information about resource conditions and to use it in making policy at the appropriate scales.

Information also must be congruent with decision makers' needs in terms of timing, content, and form of presentation.[73, 74, 75] Informational systems that simultaneously meet high scientific standards and serve ongoing needs of decision makers and users are particularly useful. Information must not overload the capacity of users to assimilate it. Systems that adequately characterize environmental conditions or human activities with summary indicators such as prices for products or emission permits, or certification of good environmental performance, can provide valuable signals as long as they are attentive to local as well as aggregate conditions.[76, 77, 78]

Effective governance requires not only factual information about the state of the environment and human actions but also information about uncertainty and values. Scientific understanding of coupled human–biophysical systems will always be uncertain because of inherent unpredictability in the systems and because the science is never complete.[79] Decision makers need information that characterizes the types and magnitudes of this uncertainty, as well as the nature and extent of scientific ignorance and disagreement.[80] Also, because every environmental decision requires tradeoffs, knowledge is needed about individual and social values and about the effects of decisions on various valued outcomes. For many environmental systems, local and easily captured values (e.g., the market value of lumber) have to be balanced against global, diffuse, and hard-to-capture values (e.g., biodiversity and the capability of humans and ecosystems to adapt to unexpected events). Finding ways to measure and monitor the outcomes for such varied values in the face of globalization is a major informational challenge for governance.

Dealing with conflict Sharp differences in power and in values across interested parties make conflict inherent in environmental choices. Indeed, conflict resolution may be as important a motivation for designing resource institutions as is concern with the resources themselves.[81] People bring varying perspectives, interests, and fundamental philosophies to problems of environmental governance,[74, 82, 83, 84] and their conflicts, if they do not escalate to the point of dysfunction, can spark learning and change.[85, 86]

For example, a broadly participatory process was used to examine alternative strategies for regulating the Mississippi River and its tributaries.[87] A dynamic model was constructed with continuous input by the Corps of Engineers, the Fish and Wildlife Service, local landowners, environmental groups, and academics from multiple disciplines. After extensive model development and testing against past historical data, most stakeholders had high confidence in the explanatory power of the model. Consensus was reached over alternative management options, and the resulting policies generated far less conflict than had existed at the outset.[88]

Delegating authority to environmental ministries does not always resolve conflicts satisfactorily, so governments are experimenting with various governance approaches to complement managerial ones. They range from ballots and polls, where engagement is passive and participants interact minimally, to adversarial processes that allow parties to redress grievances through formal legal procedures, to various experiments with intense interaction and deliberation aimed at negotiating decisions or allowing parties in potential conflict to provide structured input to them through participatory processes.[89, 90, 91, 92, 93]

Inducing rule compliance Effective governance requires that the rules of resource use are generally followed, with reasonable standards for tolerating modest violations. It is generally most effective to impose modest sanctions on first offenders, and gradually increase the severity of sanctions for those who do not learn from their first or second encounter.[39, 94] Community-based institutions often use informal strategies for achieving compliance that rely on participants' commitment to rules and subtle social sanctions. Whether enforcement mechanisms are formal or informal, those who impose them must be seen as effective and legitimate by resource users or resistance and evasion will overwhelm the commons governance strategy.

Much environmental regulation in complex societies has been 'command and control.' Governments require or prohibit specific actions or technologies, with fines or jail terms possible for punishing rule breakers. If sufficient resources are made available for monitoring and enforcement, such approaches are effective. But when governments lack the will or resources to protect 'protected areas,'[95, 96, 97] when major environmental damage comes from hard-to-detect 'nonpoint sources,' and when the need is to encourage innovation in behaviors or technologies rather than to require or prohibit familiar ones, command and control approaches are less effective. They are also economically inefficient in many circumstances.[98, 99, 100]

Financial instruments can provide incentives to achieve compliance with environmental rules. In recent years, market-based systems of tradable environmental allowances (TEAs) that define a limit to environmental withdrawals or emissions and permit free trade of allocated allowances under those limits have become popular.[76, 101, 102] TEAs are one of the bases for the Kyoto agreement on climate change.

Economic theory and experience in some settings suggest that these mechanisms have substantial advantages over command and control.[103, 104, 105, 106] TEAs have exhibited good environmental performance and economic efficiency in the U.S. Sulfur Dioxide Allowance Market intended to reduce the prevalence of acid rain[107, 108] and the Lead Phasedown Program aimed at reducing the level of lead emissions.[109] Crucial variables that differentiate these highly successful programs from less successful ones, such as chlorofluorocarbon production quota trading and the early EPA emission trading programs, include: (i) the level of predictability of the stocks and flows, (ii) the number of users or producers who are regulated, (iii) the heterogeneity of the regulated users, and (iv) clearly defined and fully exchangeable permits.[110]

TEAs, like all institutional arrangements, have notable limitations.

TEA regimes tend to leave unprotected those resources not specifically covered by trading rules (e.g., by-catch of noncovered fish species)[111] and to suffer when monitoring is difficult (e.g., under the Kyoto protocol, the question of whether geologically sequestered carbon will remain sequestered). Problems can also occur with the initial allocation of allowances, especially when historic users, who may be called on to change their behavior most, have disproportionate power over allocation decisions.[76, 101] TEAs and community-based systems appear to have opposite strengths and weaknesses,[101] suggesting that institutions that combine aspects of both systems may work better than either approach alone. For example, the fisheries tradable permit system in New Zealand has added comanagement institutions to complement the market institutions.[102, 112]

Voluntary approaches and those based on information disclosure have only begun to receive careful scientific attention as supplements to other tools.[63, 77, 113, 114, 115] Success appears to depend on the existence of incentives that benefit leaders in volunteering over laggards and on the simultaneous use of other strategies, particularly ones that create incentives for compliance.[77, 116, 117, 118] Difficulties of sanctioning pose major problems for international agreements.[119, 120, 121]

Providing infrastructure The importance of physical and technological infrastructure is often ignored. Infrastructure, including technology, determines the degree to which a commons can be exploited (e.g., water works and fishing technology), the extent to which waste can be reduced in resource use, and the degree to which resource conditions and the behavior of human users can be effectively monitored. Indeed, the ability to choose institutional arrangements depends in part on infrastructure. In the absence of barbed-wire fences, for example, enforcing private property rights on grazing lands is expensive, but with barbed-wire fences, it is relatively cheap.[122] Effective communication and transportation technologies are also of immense importance. Fishers who observe an unauthorized boat or harvesting technology can use a radio or cellular phone to alert others to illegal actions.[123] Infrastructure also affects the links between local commons and regional and global systems. Good roads can provide food in bad times but can also open local resources to global markets, creating demand for resources that cannot be used locally.[124] Institutional infrastructure is also important, including research, social capital, and multilevel rules, to coordinate between local and larger levels of governance.[48, 125, 126]

Be prepared for change Institutions must be designed to allow for adaptation because some current understanding is likely to be wrong, the required scale of organization can shift, and biophysical and social systems change. Fixed rules are likely to fail because they place too much confidence in the current state of knowledge, whereas systems that guard against the low probability, high consequence possibilities and allow for change may be suboptimal in the short run but prove wiser in the long run. This is a principal lesson of adaptive management research.[31, 127]

Strategies for meeting the requirements of adaptive governance

The general principles for robust governance institutions for localized resources (Fig. 3) are well established as a result of multiple empirical studies.[13, 39, 128, 129, 130, 131, 132, 133, 134, 135, 136, 137] Many of these also appear to be applicable to regional and global resources,[138] although they are less well tested at those scales. Three of them seem to be particularly relevant for problems at larger scales.

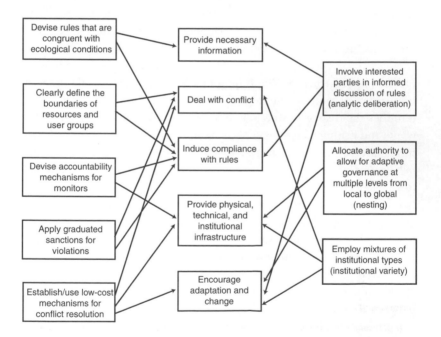

FIGURE 3 General principles for robust governance of environmental resources ([...] left and right columns) and the governance requirements they help meet ([...] center column).[(13, 158)] Each principle is relevant for meeting several requirements. Arrows indicate some of the most likely connections between principles and requirements. Principles in the right column may be particularly relevant for global and regional problems.

Analytic deliberation Well-structured dialogue involving scientists, re-source users, and interested publics, and informed by analysis of key information about environmental and human-environment systems, appears critical. Such analytic deliberation[74, 139, 140] provides improved information and the trust in it that is essential for information to be used effectively, builds social capital, and can allow for change and deal with inevitable conflicts well enough to produce consensus on governance rules. The negotiated 1994 U.S. regulation on disinfectant by-products in water that reached an interim consensus, including a decision to collect new information and reconsider the rule on that basis,[74] is an excellent example of this approach.

Nesting Institutional arrangements must be complex, redundant, and nested in many layers.[32, 141, 142] Simple strategies for governing the world's resources that rely exclusively on imposed markets or one-level, central-ized command and control and that eliminate apparent redundancies in the name of efficiency have been tried and have failed. Catastrophic failures often have resulted when central governments have exerted sole authority over resources. Examples include the massive environmental degradation and impoverishment of local people in Indonesian Borneo,[95] the increased rate of loss and fragmentation of high-quality habitat that occurred after creating the Wolong Nature Reserve in China,[143] and the closing of the northern cod fishery along the eastern coast of Canada partly attributable to the excessive quotas granted by the Canadian gov-ernment.[70]

Institutional variety Governance should employ mixtures of institutional types (e.g., hierarchies, markets, and community self-governance) that employ a variety of decision rules to change incentives, increase informa-tion, monitor use, and induce compliance.[6, 63, 117] Innovative rule evaders can have more trouble with a multiplicity of rules than with a single type of rule.

Conclusion

Is it possible to govern such critical commons as the oceans and the climate? We remain guardedly optimistic. Thirty-five years ago it seemed that the 'tragedy of the commons' was inevitable everywhere not owned privately or by a government. Systematic multidisciplinary research has, however, shown that a wide diversity of adaptive governance systems have been effective stewards of many resources. Sustained research coupled to an explicit view of national and international policies as experiments can yield the scientific knowledge necessary to design appropriate adaptive institutions.

Sound science is necessary for commons governance, but not sufficient. Too many strategies for governance of local commons are designed in capital cities or by donor agencies in ignorance of the state of the science and local conditions. The results are often tragic, but at least these tragedies are local. As the human footprint on the Earth enlarges,[144] humanity is challenged to develop and deploy understanding of large-scale commons governance quickly enough to avoid the large-scale tragedies that will otherwise ensue.

Notes

1 G. Hardin, *Science* 162, 1243 (1968).

2 See (6, 145). It was the paper most frequently cited as having the greatest career impact in a recent survey of biologists (146). [...]

3 B. J. McCay, J. M. Acheson, *The Question of the Commons: The Culture and Ecology of Communal Resources* (Univ. of Arizona Press, Tucson, 1987).

4 P. Dasgupta, *Proc. Br. Acad.* 90, 165 (1996).

5 D. Feeny, F. Berkes, B. McCay, J. Acheson, *Hum. Ecol.* 18, 1 (1990).

6 Committee on the Human Dimensions of Global Change, National Research Council, *The Drama of the Commons*, E. Ostrom *et al.*, Eds (National Academy Press, Washington, DC, 2002).

7 J. Platt, *Am. Psychol.* 28, 642 (1973).

8 J. G. Cross, M. J. Guyer, *Social Traps* (Univ. of Michigan Press, Ann Arbor, 1980).

9 R. Costanza, *Bioscience* 37, 407 (1987).

10 R. McC. Netting, *Balancing on an Alp: Ecological Change and Continuity in a Swiss Mountain Community* (Cambridge Univ. Press, Cambridge, 1981).

11 National Research Council, *Proceedings of the Conference on Common Property Resource Management* (National Academy Press, Washington, DC, 1986).

12 J.-M. Baland, J.-P. Platteau, *Halting Degradation of Natural Resources: Is There a Role for Rural Communities?* (Clarendon Press, Oxford, 1996).

13 E. Ostrom, *Governing the Commons: The Evolution of Institutions for Collective Action* (Cambridge Univ. Press, New York, 1990).

14 R. A. Myers, B. Worm, *Nature* 423, 280 (2003).

15 A. C. Finlayson, *Fishing for Truth: A Sociological Analysis of Northern Cod Stock Assessments from 1987 to 1990* (Institute of Social and Economic Research, Memorial Univ. of Newfoundland, St Johns, Newfoundland, 1994).

16 S. Hanna, in *Northern Waters: Management Issues and Practice*, D. Symes, Ed. (Blackwell, London, 1998), pp. 25–35.

17 J. Acheson, *Capturing the Commons: Devising Institutions to Manage the Maine Lobster Industry* (Univ. Press of New England, Hanover, NH, 2003).

18 J. A. Wilson, P. Kleban, J. Acheson, M. Metcalfe, *Mar. Policy* 18, 291 (1994).

19 J. Wilson, personal communication.

20 S. Weiner, J. Maxwell, in *Dimensions of Managing Chlorine in the Environment*, report of the MIT/ Norwegian Chlorine Policy Study (MIT, Cambridge, MA, 1993).

21 U. Weber, *UNESCO Courier*, June 2000, p. 9.

22 M. Verweij, *Transboundary Environmental Problems and Cultural Theory: The Protection of the Rhine and the Great Lakes* (Palgrave, New York, 2000).

23 C. Dieperink, *Water Int.* 25, 347 (2000).

24 E. Parson, *Protecting the Ozone Layer: Science and Strategy* (Oxford Univ. Press, New York, 2003).

25 E. Ostrom, C. D. Becker, *Annu. Rev. Ecol. Syst.* 26, 113 (1995).

26 P. C. Stern, *Science* 260, 1897 (1993).

27 E. Ostrom, J. Burger, C. B. Field, R. B. Norgaard, D. Policansky, *Science* 284, 278 (1999).

28 We refer to adaptive governance rather than adaptive management (31, 127) because the idea of governance conveys the difficulty of control, the need to proceed in the face of substantial uncertainty, and the importance of dealing with diversity and reconciling conflict among people and groups who differ in values, interests, perspectives, power, and the kinds of information they bring to situations (139, 148–51). Effective environmental governance requires an understanding of both environmental systems and human–environment interactions (26, 82, 152, 153).

29 E. Schlager, W. Blomquist, S. Y. Tang, *Land Econ.* 70, 294 (1994).

30 J. H. Brander, M. S. Taylor, *Am. Econ. Rev.* 88, 119 (1998).

31 L. H. Gunderson, C. S. Holling, *Panarchy: Understanding Transformations in Human and Natural Systems* (Island Press, Washington, DC, 2001).

32 M. Janssen, *Complexity and Ecosystem Management* (Elgar, Cheltenham, UK, 2002).

33 R. Putnam, *Bowling Alone: The Collapse and Revival of American Community* (Simon and Schuster, New York, 2001).

34 A. Bebbington, *Geogr. J.* 163, 189 (1997).

35 R. Frank, *Passions within Reason: The Strategic Role of the Emotions* (Norton, New York, 1988).

36 J. Pretty, *Science* 302, 1912 (2003).

37 J. Burger, E. Ostrom, R. B. Norgaard, D. Policansky, B. D. Goldstein, Eds, *Protecting the Commons: A Framework for Resource Management in the Americas* (Island Press, Washington, DC, 2001).

38 C. Gibson, J. Williams, E. Ostrom, in preparation.

39 M. S. Weinstein, *Georgetown Int. Environ. Law Rev.* 12, 375 (2000).

40 R. Meinzen-Dick, K. V. Raju, A. Gulati, *World Dev.* 30, 649 (2002).

41 E. L. Miles *et al.*, Eds, *Environmental Regime Effectiveness: Confronting Theory with Evidence* (MIT Press, Cambridge, MA, 2001).

42 C. Gibson, M. McKean, E. Ostrom, Eds, *People and Forests* (MIT Press, Cambridge, MA, 2000).

43 S. Krech III, *The Ecological Indian: Myth and History* (Norton, New York, 1999).

44 For relevant bibliographies, see (147, 154).

45 D. C. North, *Structure and Change in Economic History* (North, New York, 1981).

46 R. Robertson, *Globalization: Social Theory and Global Culture* (Sage, London, 1992).

47 O. R. Young, Ed., *The Effectiveness of International Environmental Regimes* (MIT Press, Cambridge, MA, 1999).

48 O. R. Young, *The Institutional Dimensions of Environmental Change: Fit, Interplay, and Scale* (MIT Press, Cambridge, MA, 2002).

49 R. Keohane, E. Ostrom, Eds, *Local Commons and Global Interdependence* (Sage, London, 1995).

50 J. S. Lansing, *Priests and Programmers: Technologies of Power in the Engineered Landscape of Bali* (Princeton Univ. Press, Princeton, NJ, 1991).

51 J. Wunsch, D. Olowu, Eds, *The Failure of the Centralized State* (Institute for Contemporary Studies Press, San Francisco, CA, 1995).

52 N. Dolšak, E. Ostrom, Eds, *The Commons in the New Millennium: Challenges and Adaptation* (MIT Press, Cambridge, MA, 2003).

53 Association of American Geographers Global Change and Local Places Research Group, *Global Change and Local Places: Estimating, Understanding, and Reducing Greenhouse Gases* (Cambridge Univ. Press, Cambridge, 2003).

54 S. Karlsson, thesis, Linköping University, Sweden (2000).

55 R. Keohane, M. A. Levy, Eds, *Institutions for Environmental Aid* (MIT Press, Cambridge, MA, 1996).

56 O. S. Stokke, *Governing High Seas Fisheries: The Interplay of Global and Regional Regimes* (Oxford Univ. Press, London, 2001).

57 A. Underdal, K. Hanf, Eds, *International Environmental Agreements and Domestic Politics: The Case of Acid Rain* (Ashgate, Aldershot, England, 1998).

58 W. Clark, R. Munn, Eds, *Sustainable Development of the Biosphere* (Cambridge Univ. Press, New York, 1986).

59 B. L. Turner II *et al.*, *Global Environ. Change* 1, 14 (1991).

60 T. Dietz, T. R. Burns, *Acta Sociol.* 35, 187 (1992).

61 T. Dietz, E. A. Rosa, in *Handbook of Environmental Sociology*, R. E. Dunlap, W. Michelson, Eds (Greenwood Press, Westport, CT, 2002), pp. 370–406.

62 A. P. Vayda, in *Ecology in Practice*, F. di Castri *et al.*, Eds (Tycooly, Dublin, 1984).

63 Committee on the Human Dimensions of Global Change, National Research Council, *New Tools for Environmental Protection: Education, Information, and Voluntary Measures*, T. Dietz, P. C. Stern, Eds (National Academy Press, Washington, DC, 2002).

64 M. Auer, *Policy Sci.* 33, 155 (2000).

65 D. H. Cole, *Pollution and Property: Comparing Ownership Institutions for Environmental Protection* (Cambridge Univ. Press, Cambridge, 2002).

66 F. Berkes, J. Colding, C. Folke, Eds, *Navigating Social-Ecological Systems: Building Resilience for Complexity and Change* (Cambridge Univ. Press, Cambridge, 2003).

67 K. J. Willis, R. J. Whittaker, *Science* 295, 1245 (2002).

68 Kirby Task Force on Atlantic Fisheries, *Navigating Troubled Waters: A New Policy for the Atlantic Fisheries* (Department of Fisheries and Oceans, Ottawa, 1982).

69 G. Barrett, A. Davis, J. *Can. Stud.* 19, 125 (1984).

70 A. C. Finlayson, B. McCay, in *Linking Social and Ecological Systems*, F. Berkes, C. Folke, Eds (Cambridge Univ. Press, Cambridge, 1998), pp. 311–38.

71 J. A. Wilson, R. Townsend, P. Kleban, S. McKay, J. French, *Ocean Shoreline Manage.* 13, 179 (1990).

72 C. Martin, *Fisheries* 20, 6 (1995).

73 Committee on Risk Perception and Communication, National Research Council, *Improving Risk Communication* (National Academy Press, Washington, DC, 1989).

74 Committee on Risk Characterization and Commission on Behavioral and Social Sciences and Education, National Research Council, *Understanding Risk: Informing Decisions in a Democratic Society*, P. C. Stern, H. V. Fineberg, Eds (National Academy Press, Washington, DC, 1996).

75 Panel on Human Dimensions of Seasonal-to-Interannual Climate Variability, Committee on the Human Dimensions of Global Change, National Research Council, *Making Climate Forecasts Matter*, P. C. Stern, W. E. Easterling, Eds (National Academy Press, Washington, DC, 1999).

76 T. Tietenberg, in *The Drama of the Commons*, Committee on the Human Dimensions of Global Change, National Research Council, E. Ostrom *et al.*, Eds (National Academy Press, Washington, DC, 2002), pp. 233–57.

77 T. Tietenberg, D. Wheeler, in *Frontiers of Environmental Economics*, H. Folmer, H. Landis Gabel, S. Gerking, A. Rose, Eds (Elgar, Cheltenham, UK, 2001), pp. 85–120.

78 J. Thøgerson, in *New Tools for Environmental Protection: Education, Information, and Voluntary Measures*, T. Dietz, P. C. Stern, Eds (National Academy Press, Washington, DC, 2002), pp. 83–104.

79 J. A. Wilson, in *The Drama of the Commons*, Committee on the Human Dimensions of Global Change, National Research Council, E. Ostrom *et al.*, Eds (National Academy Press, Washington, DC, 2002), pp. 327–60.

80 R. Moss, S. H. Schneider, in *Guidance Papers on the Cross-Cutting Issues of the Third Assessment Report of the IPCC*, R. Pachauri, T. Taniguchi, K. Tanaka, Eds (World Meteorological Organization, Geneva, Switzerland, 2000), pp. 33–51.

81 B. J. McCay, in *The Drama of the Commons*, Committee on the Human Dimensions of Global Change, National Research Council, E. Ostrom *et al.*, Eds (National Academy Press, Washington, DC, 2002), pp. 361–402.

82 Board on Sustainable Development, National Research Council, *Our Common Journey: A Transition Toward Sustainability* (National Academy Press, Washington, DC, 1999).

83 Committee on Noneconomic and Economic Value of Biodiversity, National Research Council, *Perspectives on Biodiversity: Valuing Its Role in an Everchanging World* (National Academy Press, Washington, DC, 1999).

84 W. M. Adams, D. Brockington, J. Dyson, B. Vira, *Science* 302, 1915 (2003).

85 P. C. Stern, *Policy Sci.* 24, 99 (1991).

86 V. Ostrom, *Public Choice* 77, 163 (1993).

87 R. Costanza, M. Ruth, in *Institutions, Ecosystems, and Sustainability*, R. Costanza, B. S. Low, E. Ostrom, J. Wilson, Eds (Lewis Publishers, Boca Raton, FL, 2001), pp. 169–78.

88 F. H. Sklar, M. L. White, R. Costanza, *The Coastal Ecological Landscape Spatial Simulation (CELSS) Model* (U.S. Fish and Wildlife Service, Washington, DC, 1989).

89 O. Renn, T. Webler, P. Wiede-

Dietz, Ostrom and Stern

mann, Eds, *Fairness and Competence in Citizen Participation: Evaluating Models for Environmental Discourse* (Kluwer Academic Publishers, Dordrecht, Netherlands, 1995).

90 R. Gregory, T. McDaniels, D. Fields, *J. Policy Anal. Manage.* 20, 415 (2001).

91 T. C. Beierle, J. Cayford, *Democracy in Practice: Public Participation in Environmental Decisions* (Resources for the Future, Washington, DC, 2002).

92 W. Leach, N. Pelkey, P. Sabatier, *J. Policy Anal. Manage.* 21, 645 (2002).

93 R. O'Leary, L. B. Bingham, Eds, *The Promise and Performance of Environmental Conflict Resolution* (Resources for the Future, Washington, DC, 2003).

94 E. Ostrom, R. Gardner, J. Walker, Eds, *Rules, Games, and Common-Pool Resources* (Univ. of Michigan Press, Ann Arbor, 1994).

95 L. M. Curran *et al.*, in preparation.

96 J. Liu *et al.*, *Science* 300, 1240 (2003).

97 R. W. Sussman, G. M. Green, L. K. Sussman, *Hum. Ecol.* 22, 333 (1994).

98 F. Berkes, C. Folke, Eds, *Linking Social and Ecological Systems: Management Practices and Social Mechanisms* (Cambridge Univ. Press, Cambridge, 1998).

99 G. M. Heal, *Valuing the Future: Economic Theory and Sustainability* (Colombia Univ. Press, New York, 1998).

100 B. G. Colby, in *The Handbook of Environmental Economics*, D. Bromley, Ed. (Blackwell Publishers, Oxford, 1995), pp. 475–502.

101 C. Rose, in *The Drama of the Commons*, Committee on the Human Dimensions of Global Change, Na-

tional Research Council, E. Ostrom *et al.*, Eds (National Academy Press, Washington, DC, 2002), pp. 233–57.

102 T. Yandle, C. M. Dewees, in *The Commons in the New Millennium: Challenges and Adaptation*, N. Dolšak, E. Ostrom, Eds (MIT Press, Cambridge, MA, 2003), pp. 101–28.

103 G. Libecap, *Contracting for Property Rights* (Cambridge Univ. Press, Cambridge, 1990).

104 R. D. Lile, D. R. Bohi, D. Burtraw, *An Assessment of the EPA's SO₂ Emission Allowance Tracking System* (Resources for the Future, Washington, DC, 1996).

105 R. N. Stavins, *J. Econ. Perspect.* 12, 133 (1998).

106 J. E. Wilen, *J. Environ. Econ. Manage.* 39, 309 (2000).

107 A. D. Ellerman, R. Schmalensee, P. L. Joskow, J. P. Montero, E. M. Bailey, *Emissions Trading Under the U.S. Acid Rain Program* (MIT Center for Energy and Environmental Policy Research, Cambridge, MA, 1997).

108 E. M. Bailey, 'Allowance trading activity and state regulatory rulings' (Working Paper 98-005, MIT Emissions Trading, Cambridge, MA, 1998).

109 B. D. Nussbaum, in *Climate Change: Designing a Tradeable Permit System* (OECD, Paris, 1992), pp. 22–34.

110 N. Dolšak, thesis, Indiana University, Bloomington, IN (2000).

111 S. L. Hsu, J. E. Wilen, *Ecol. Law Q.* 24, 799 (1997).

112 E. Pinkerton, *Co-operative Management of Local Fisheries* (Univ. of British Columbia Press, Vancouver, 1989).

113 A. Prakash, *Bus. Strategy Environ.* 10, 286 (2001).

114 J. Nash, in *New Tools for Environmental Protection: Education, Information and Voluntary Measures*, T. Dietz, P. C. Stern, Eds (National

Academy Press, Washington, DC, 2002), pp. 235–52.

115 J. A. Aragón-Correa, S. Sharma, *Acad. Manage. Rev.* 28, 71 (2003).

116 A. Randall, in *New Tools for Environmental Protection: Education, Information and Voluntary Measures*, T. Dietz, P. C. Stern, Eds (National Academy Press, Washington, DC, 2002), pp. 311–18.

117 G. T. Gardner, P. C. Stern, *Environmental Problems and Human Behavior* (Allyn and Bacon, Needham Heights, MA, 1996).

118 P. C. Stern, *J. Consum. Policy* 22, 461 (1999).

119 S. Hanna, C. Folke, K.-G. Mäler, *Rights to Nature* (Island Press, Washington, DC, 1996).

120 E. Weiss, H. Jacobson, Eds, *Engaging Countries: Strengthening Compliance with International Environmental Agreements* (MIT Press, Cambridge, MA, 1998).

121 A. Underdal, *The Politics of International Environmental Management* (Kluwer Academic Publishers, Dordrecht, Netherlands, 1998).

122 A. Krell, *The Devil's Rope: A Cultural History of Barbed Wire* (Reaktion, London, 2002).

123 S. Singleton, *Constructing Cooperation: The Evolution of Institutions of Comanagement* (Univ. of Michigan Press, Ann Arbor, 1998).

124 E. Moran, Ed., *The Ecosystem Approach in Anthropology: From Concept to Practice* (Univ. of Michigan Press, Ann Arbor, 1990).

125 M. Janssen, J. M. Anderies, E. Ostrom, paper presented at the Workshop on Resiliency and Change in Ecological Systems, Santa Fe Institute, Santa Fe, NM, 25 to 27 October 2003.

126 T. Princen, *Global Environ. Polit.* 3, 33 (2003).

127 K. Lee, *Compass and Gyroscope* (Island Press, Washington, DC, 1993).

128 C. L. Abernathy, H. Sally, *J. Appl. Irrig. Stud.* 35, 177 (2000).

129 A. Agrawal, in *The Drama of the Commons*, Committee on the Human Dimensions of Global Change, National Research Council, E. Ostrom *et al.*, Eds (National Academy Press, Washington, DC, 2002), pp. 41–85.

130 P. Coop, D. Brunckhorst, *Aust. J. Environ. Manage.* 6, 48 (1999).

131 D. S. Crook, A. M. Jones, *Mt. Res. Dev.* 19, 79 (1999).

132 D. J. Merrey, in *Irrigation Management Transfer*, S. H. Johnson, D. L. Vermillion, J. A. Sagardoy, Eds (International Irrigation Management Institute, Colombo, Sri Lanka and the Food and Agriculture Organisation, Rome, 1995).

133 C. E. Morrow, R. W. Hull, *World Dev.* 24, 1641 (1996).

134 T. Nilsson, thesis, Royal Institute of Technology, Stockholm, Sweden (2001).

135 N. Polman, L. Slangen, in *Environmental Co-operation and Institutional Change*, K. Hagedorn, Ed. (Elgar, Northampton, MA, 2002).

136 A. Sarker, T. Itoh, *Agric. Water Manage.* 48, 89 (2001).

137 C. Tucker, *Praxis* 15, 47 (1999).

138 R. Costanza *et al.*, *Science* 281, 198 (1998).

139 T. Dietz, P. C. Stern, *Bioscience* 48, 441 (1998).

140 E. Rosa, A. M. McWright, O. Renn, 'The risk society: Theoretical frames and state management challenges' (Dept of Sociology, Washington State Univ., Pullman, WA, 2003).

141 S. Levin, *Fragile Dominion: Complexity and the Commons* (Perseus Books, Reading, MA, 1999).

142 B. Low, E. Ostrom, C. Simon, J. Wilson, in *Navigating Social-Ecological Systems: Building Resilience for Complexity and Change*, F. Berkes, J. Colding, C. Folke, Eds (Cambridge Univ. Press, New York, 2003), pp. 83–114.

143 J. Liu *et al.*, *Science* 292, 98 (2001).

144 R. York, E. A. Rosa, T. Dietz, *Am. Sociol. Rev.* 68, 279 (2003).

145 G. Hardin, *Science* 280, 682 (1998).

146 G. W. Barrett, K. E. Mabry, *Bioscience* 52, 28, 2 (2002).

147 C. Hess, *The Comprehensive Bibliography of the Commons*, database available online at www.indiana.edu/_iascp/Iforms/searchcpr.html.

148 V. Ostrom, *The Meaning of Democracy and the Vulnerability of Democracies* (Univ. of Michigan Press, Ann Arbor, 1997).

149 M. McGinnis, Ed., *Polycentric Governance and Development: Readings from the Workshop in Political Theory and Policy Analysis* (Univ. of Michigan Press, Ann Arbor, 1999).

150 M. McGinnis, Ed., *Polycentric Games and Institutions: Readings from the Workshop in Political Theory and Policy Analysis* (Univ. of Michigan Press, Ann Arbor, 2000).

151 T. Dietz, *Hum. Ecol. Rev.* 10, 60 (2003).

152 R. Costanza, B. S. Low, E. Ostrom, J. Wilson, Eds, *Institutions, Ecosystems, and Sustainability* (Lewis Publishers, New York, 2001).

153 Committee on the Human Dimensions of Global Change, National Research Council, *Global Environmental Change: Understanding the Human Dimensions*, P. C. Stern, O. R. Young, D. Druckman, Eds (National Academy Press, Washington, DC, 1992).

154 C. Hess, *A Comprehensive Bibliography of Common-Pool Resources* (CD-Rom, Workshop in Political Theory and Policy Analysis, Indiana Univ., Bloomington, 1999).

[...]

158 P. C. Stern, T. Dietz, E. Ostrom, *Environ. Pract.* 4, 61 (2002).

159 We thank R. Andrews, G. Daily, J. Hoehn, K. Lee, S. Levin, G. Libecap, V. Ruttan, T. Tietenberg, J. Wilson, and O. Young for their comments on earlier drafts; and G. Laasby, P. Lezotte, C. Liang, and L. Wisen for providing assistance. Supported in part by NSF grants BCS-9906253 and SBR-9521918, NASA grant NASW-01008, the Ford Foundation, and the MacArthur Foundation.

Supporting Online Material: www.sciencemag.org/cgi/content/full/302/5652/1907/ DC1 SOM Text, Figs. S1 to S5, Table S.

20 | The big debate: reform or revolution?

JONATHON PORRITT AND CLAIRE FAUSET

This reading is the *New Internationalist*'s edited version of a longer conversation about corporate responsibility. In debate style, opposing views are taken on whether to work with corporations to help them take social and environmental responsibility or to encourage people to take direct action to resist them.

§ **Jonathon Porritt** (JP) has pioneered a strategy of working with leading corporations to help them become more socially and environmentally responsible. As chair of the UK Sustainable Development Commission, he is a principal adviser to the British government. He sets out his vision for change in a recent book: *Capitalism as if the World Matters*.

Claire Fauset (CF) is part of a growing movement of people taking direct action to resist the corporations they see as standing in the way of a transition towards a fair, low-carbon future. She recently published *What's Wrong with Corporate Social Responsibility?* for Corporate Watch.

New Internationalist put the two of them together in a room, sat back, and watched the sparks fly.

JP You imply in your report that there is *nothing* that companies can do voluntarily to make a difference in this world, that regulation is the only way to bring about corporate change, that companies will *always* do the least that they can in order to prioritize the interests of shareholders and therefore will *never* give priority to other stakeholders. I think the evidence speaks strongly against that.

You quote only the bad stories (which *are* bad). There is a sense that you are demonizing companies. But when you peel away what that means, you are really demonizing the people who work for them. If I have learned anything from my 15 years working with companies it is that people care passionately about these issues and believe that if they get their company responding they are making a very big contribution.

CF I *do* think that the aim of Corporate Responsibility (CR) is to do the minimum possible, and is quite explicitly about avoiding regulation.

It tries to convince people that their best way of getting change is as a consumer, buying things and voting with their till receipts. That is fundamentally the opposite of democracy. It is disempowering.

JP Aren't you in danger of patronizing most people? I don't think people *have* been seduced into this passive, consumerist mindset. I think this is where we have just lurched out of indifference, ignorance, laziness ... Some companies are involved in CR to try and ward off regulation, no question about that. But some companies would welcome increased regulation. Not perhaps for reasons that you would like, but they want to see off the free-riders, the cowboys, the companies that do not give a shit about all this stuff.

CF They are for the kind of regulation that benefits them the most, they're fishing for market-based mechanisms ...

JP That's a different story. Market-based mechanisms can have teeth. And they are introduced by governments. They come with the same amount of legitimacy as another piece of regulation. I don't understand the difference.

CF The problem is that those who can pay benefit most from the market – for example with carbon trading, those who can pay for carbon emissions can emit more. There is no principle of justice or equality behind it.

JP But that depends on how you design your market instrument. Governments *can* design market instruments so they actually affect the better-off people more than the less well-off people. *If* they want to!

CF Exactly! I am not saying that government is much different from the corporate sector ...

JP Now we are getting down to it! You can't say that! (laughs)

CF What I mean is that the ideology is essentially the same. It is a neoliberal free-market ideology.

JP Yes. *Temporarily*. You and I are going to agree totally about this. It appals me how governments around the world have fallen in with this corporatist ideology. It's a disgraceful abnegation of their responsibility ...

CF Exactly. But we can't change this through reform, through engaging with governments and corporations. Social change doesn't happen as a result of parliamentary decisions. You have to have a process that devolves power to people rather than supports the existing power structures.

JP But if one gets to the state of mind where you say that nobody can ever trust government and politicians again, then we are stuffed. What are we meant to do? Make it all happen ourselves?

CF Well, yes! Increasing the number of people working on the inside is not going to create change. The most effective thing is to be out there talking to people, increasing mistrust of corporations and government, making people angry, making people want to take action.

JP The most effective thing would be to do *both*. A sort of pincer effect on government and on business.

CF But there are plenty of people working on the inside ...

JP Well, there are *now*. There never used to be, don't forget.

CF But that is part of the problem. The really good people get trained up in sustainable development, then go and work for the corporations and get sucked into the machine that grinds slowly along. Capitalism sucks up the collective genius around it into its own project. That is what has happened to the green movement.

JP Do you think the green NGOs like Friends of the Earth and Greenpeace have just been completely co-opted?

CF Significantly co-opted. I think that CR has been very effective in getting them into the boardroom instead of out on the streets, of isolating the radicals, cultivating the idealists into becoming realists, and then co-opting them into engaging so that the only change you can get is incremental. It is not a shift in the business model. I think that a lot of people working on the outside feel sold out by the people on the inside.

JP You are presenting this as an either/or. I have always said that direct action is a fundamental part of this movement for change. We need more of it, not less. But I think you are saying to me I should prioritize my time differently. I am often criticized for selling out. But I am doing what I believe works.

CF But don't you think that you are increasing corporations' legitimacy, whereas we are working to destroy their legitimacy?

JP Well, I don't want to destroy companies' legitimacy. We are going to need them, to ensure that wealth creators comply with the laws, have a proper relationship with government, consumers, and so on. I want to transform the way in which government mandates their legitimacy.

CF It's not government that gives legitimacy, it is people.

JP Well, we give legitimacy to companies through what we purchase. But with our vote, theoretically, we empower governments to regulate the structure of the economy. That's the bit that has gone terribly wrong. Governments are failing massively in their duty.

CF But you are assuming that corporations are wealth creators and not wealth concentrators.

JP Well, they are both.

CF Wealth exists within society, within the planet. To assume that the only way of distributing goods and services to meet people's needs is

225

through capitalism – that you need the profit motive to do that – ignores the idea that you could have any other system.

JP Don't we need markets to deliver goods and services?

CF I believe that a more co-operative system could meet people's needs in a more egalitarian way. We need to be putting our energy into thinking about the principles by which our society should be organized. The idea that is coming strongly through the media and through CR is that you don't have to think about these things – corporations share your values and your principles. And that really frustrates efforts to empower people.

JP You are implying a level of political awareness on the part of these companies that is miles from what I have discovered! It is with great difficulty that I can get any of these companies to talk about capitalism. Most of what they are doing is being done by default.

CF It's not that I think there's some secret club somewhere ...!

JP Maybe there is! (laughs)

CF But it is a strategy that evolves. Shell found CR to be a very effective mechanism and then it was adopted by other companies. Compare Shell to McLibel. McDonald's took out the biggest law suit in UK legal history against a couple of random people and their leaflets. But Shell ran a million-pound PR campaign: 'get people to engage', 'we want to hear', 'say whatever you want to about us'. Which was the most successful strategy? This is how CR evolved. I don't think that somebody sat down and wrote the whole project. Well, maybe the PR people! (laughs)

JP OK, but follow that logic through. Just say that all the different campaigns against Nestlé (which I think have actually been pretty effective) had such a profound impact that the company decided to completely change its product portfolio – to get rid of formula milk. Would you be satisfied with that? Or would you say that the whole company has to cease to exist because you just don't want multinationals in the world?

CF In that multinationals exist to concentrate wealth and power – no, they have no place in a just world. The structure is the problem, and so we need to find alternative ways of structuring things.

JP Every single survey tells you that, *absolutely*, people care about sweatshops and worry that their purchases might be adding to the exploitation of people elsewhere in the world. Does that mean that they change the way they buy clothes? A *little* bit. Does it mean that they want to restructure the whole clothes industry in the Western world? Not on your bloody life!

CF People do behave differently as consumers than they do as citizens. But climate change is a crux point at which we have to do things right or we are fucked. It requires an awful lot of people agitating, not just adjusting to the structures that exist.

JP The difficulty is persuading government to be more proactive. If you look at the speeches that have come out of the UK Government, we have got this huge disconnect between a rhetorical understanding of what the problem is and a policy delivery process which is pathetically inadequate.

But here's a question for you: the Business Environment Programme has a 'corporate leaders group' made up of the chief execs of 14 companies. Over the last two years it has been lobbying government to increase regulation to enable those companies to do a better job on climate change. This is the first time I know of a group of leading companies saying to government: you are failing in your job, which is to create markets, or structure markets so that wealth creators – which is what I like to call them, rather than pernicious parasites on the face of the earth ...

CF Wealth concentrators!

JP (laughs) ... so that business can get on and do a better job for the planet. Now I expect that you are going to say that this is just bullshit, this initiative is worthless.

CF I don't *know*, but I suspect that it is. Because these companies aren't in any way able to act altruistically. They have to be pursuing the best interests of their corporation, which I don't think is *ever* going to be in the best interest of society.

JP But eventually it must be.

CF Why?

JP Because there is no difference between the stakeholders of a company, including its shareholders, and society. Ultimately companies cannot work in societies that are imploding. They can't make money!

CF They can work in societies that are stable and also oppressive, unjust and unsustainable.

JP For a while. But that won't last long. The interests of society and the interests of corporations *must* converge eventually. I think you have to allow the oil, transport and aviation companies the possibility of a journey. Nobody has it in their power to stop them doing what they do because *people want to buy what they produce*. When someone goes and fills up their car – who actually is responsible for those emissions? I don't think it is the oil company, I think it is the person who owns the car and goes and fills it up with petrol. The need to drastically reduce CO_2 emissions is a new reality for many companies. We cannot just go after them! So I am interested in the efforts that BP and Shell are making towards alternative energy.

CF I think partly what they are relying on is that they will get the patent on something that is fundamental to the way that society is organized in the future, so that they will have a monopoly on that system of producing energy.

JP And there is a problem in that?

CF Yes! Our future sustainability is being ransomed out to corporations *now*.

JP But where else would research come from? If governments are not going to fund programmes for cutting-edge technologies then we have to rely on the big companies to do it.

CF But companies are also relying on consumption being as great in the future. And that is not sustainable. We do not have the renewable resources to keep consuming the amount we are now.

JP What if we *did* have enough renewable energy for nine billion people to consume at current levels with no damage to the physical environment?

CF Then they would have to go without food and water. We are hitting limits to growth in so many areas! That is one of the fundamental problems with capitalism. It relies on the increased consumption of all these resources. The forests and the fisheries and all the other renewable resources are running out, it is not just about carbon dioxide.

JP I couldn't agree more. Not a bad point to end on!

Further details

www.newint.org (for the longer conversation)
www.forumforthefuture.org.uk
www.sd-commission.org.uk
www.corporatewatch.org
www.climatecamp.org.uk

21 | Social learning and environmental responsibility

CHRIS BLACKMORE

This paper by Chris Blackmore was written specifically for this book both to explore the relationship between the two concepts and to help raise awareness of a substantial body of work on social learning of relevance to environmental responsibility.

Introduction

Social learning has been much in the spotlight at the start of the twenty-first century for those focused on managing contested resources and taking purposeful action to create a more sustainable world (Leeuwis and Pyburn 2002; SLIM 2004; Keen et al. 2005; Grove-White 2005; Ison et al. 2007; Wals 2007). Social learning has at various times been described as a policy instrument, a conceptual framework, a governance mechanism and a process of systemic change (SLIM 2004). One of the main ideas that such learning encompasses is one of learning our way together to a more sustainable future in dynamic multi-stakeholder situations of uncertainty and complexity.

The focus here is on the kinds of social learning most relevant to environmental responsibility – an equally slippery concept that builds on traditions of corporate social responsibility and the philosophical ground of environmental ethics. The main questions addressed are what is involved in social learning and how social learning, in whatever form, might help people to take responsibility for actions that adversely affect our interconnected biophysical and social environments.

What does social learning look like?

Two examples that could be interpreted both as social learning and taking environmental responsibility are as follows:

1 Jiggins et al. (2007) described how a search for a new approach to water management was triggered by a ban on sprinkler irrigation, imposed in the Netherlands in the Benelux middle area, when groundwater levels fell during a period of dry weather. Among the many stakeholders in this situation were water boards, farmers, horticulturalists,

conservationists and individual members of the public. While the sprinkler ban provided one solution, these stakeholders all articulated 'the problem' in different ways. The challenge was for stakeholders to act together in a way that conserved groundwater without cutting off essential supplies for farming and horticulture. With the help of a farmers' and horticulturalists' union a proactive multi-stakeholder collaboration was formed, based on shared learning and voluntary participation. They worked in awareness that the authorities could intervene if voluntary effort proved insufficient. Together those concerned learnt how to use water more efficiently, using feedback processes enabled by fixing measuring devices to sprinklers and, in two later projects, installing small weirs across field ditches so water could both be held longer and levels observed more easily. In these ways farmers could see how much water they were using and understand better how to keep a balance.

2   Willemsen et al. (2007) described multilevel social learning around local seed in a project in three Andean provinces in Ecuador. Community, facilitation team, NGO and individual learning took place through field visits, meetings, school activities, workshops, evaluation and documentation processes. Exchanges of experiences between the different levels took place with 'social interaction in which framing and reframing of concepts related to seeds and agriculture on the different levels played a key role. Social learning – learning that occurred with different stakeholders, in a setting in which people searched for solutions to the actual problem of seed erosion they experienced – helped to create a collective basis to start a project on Informal Seed Systems' (ibid.: 479). The seed erosion they refer to here is genetic erosion and the process of losing biodiversity, where traditional crops have largely been replaced by modern varieties of maize and potato threatening the sustainability of communities. The aim of the project was to find a way forward that would address seed erosion and be meaningful to farmers.

These examples could also be interpreted in other ways, for instance as managing water resources sustainably or sustainable agriculture. Social learning and environmental responsibility can be related to many different kinds of activity. In both of the above cases, dynamic processes of multi-stakeholder, multilevel and collective learning were facilitated in ways that valued different kinds of knowledge and understanding. This kind of social learning approach is different from other regulatory, educational or market instruments of policy or governance that can be used to encourage environmental responsibility, which tend to work with more fixed forms of knowledge and understandings of 'the problem' (Ison et al. 2007). Many of those mentioned at the start of this chapter are interested in how social learning can be used in ways that complement other instruments of policy and governance.

Individual, collective and social learning

What constitutes social learning varies a great deal, depending on what is considered social and how learning is theorized (Blackmore 2007). For instance, Wenger (1998) elaborated what he referred to as a social theory of learning, considering learning as a fundamentally social phenomenon and inevitable – an integral part of human nature. He distinguished this kind of learning, which defines learning as a social and historical process, from a theory of social learning that focuses primarily on collective learning. Others have focused more on collective learning (Daniels and Walker 1996; de Laat and Simons 2002; SLIM 2004). De Laat and Simons (2002) explained some of these individual and collective distinctions by plotting learning processes against learning outcomes at both individual and collective levels. They distinguished four kinds of learning as a result: (i) individual learning; (ii) individual learning processes with collective outcomes; (iii) learning in social interaction; and (iv) collective learning. In practice, different kinds of learning are likely to be ongoing at any time.

Two kinds of relationship are particularly significant when trying to link social learning and environmental responsibility. Neither of these relationships is simple but (in my view) they are worth trying to under stand, to avoid assumptions about where responsibilities lie and how individual and collective responsibilities might work together. The first relationship is between the individual and the collectives with which they identify.

Wenger (1998, 146) observed:

> [...] in everyday life it is difficult – and, I would argue, largely unnecessary – to tell exactly where the sphere of the individual ends and the sphere of the collective begins. Each act of participation or reification,[1] from the most public to the most private, reflects the mutual constitution between individuals and collectivities. Our practices, our languages, our artifacts, and our world views all reflect our social relations. Even our most private thoughts make use of concepts, images, and perspectives that we understand through our participation in social communities.
>
> Taken separately, the notions of individual and community are

reifications whose self-contained appearance hides their mutual constitution. We cannot become human by ourselves; hence a reified, physiologically based notion of individuality misses the interconnectedness of identity. Conversely, membership does not determine who we are in any simple way; hence generalizations and stereotypes miss the lived complexity of identity.

Two implications of individuals never being out of their social contexts of particular relevance here are that (i) *both* individual *and* collective thinking and action need to be considered, not just one or the other; and (ii) the 'mutual constitution between individuals and collectivities' that Wenger refers to is a highly dynamic process which can affect who can and, from different viewpoints, who should take responsibility. Boardman (2006) provided an example of how individual consumers, manufacturers and policies needed to work together differently to avoid unnecessary carbon dioxide emissions. She considered how to create a virtuous rather than a vicious circle where policies would encourage responsibility among both consumers and manufacturers. Boardman's example seems to recognize the interconnections and dynamics of individual and collective responsibility.

The second significant relationship that needs to be considered is between learning and action. Learning is not always manifest as action. Individuals may learn so that they have the potential to act but whether they do act depends on their context. Knowing how to, say, use water or energy efficiently doesn't mean these actions are taken. Economic, social and technological factors may need to work together in a different way to encourage or enable such savings to be made. Also, individual actions taken to try to make environmental improvements such as recycling glass jars or planting trees do not necessarily accumulate in ways that help as different ways of living might, as Maniates (2001) has argued. Ison et al. (2007) are among those whose main interest in social learning, in their case in the context of managing and using water, is with concerted action and with its potential as a complementary governance mechanism, i.e. where actions resulting from learning do harmonize in a constructive way.

In addition to considering these two relationships – between individuals and collectives and learning and action – there is a question that is addressed in the next section about how we develop relationships with nature that might lead to us taking responsibility. In what sense might this process be thought of as social rather than, say, environmental learning?

Engagement, identity and responsibility

Wenger focused strongly on *identity* when explicating his social theory of learning and writing about 'communities of practice' – which he sees as groups of people who share a concern or a passion for something they do and learn how to do it better as they interact regularly (Wenger 2008). Appleby (2008) commented that although Wenger did not talk specifically about the relationship between nature and issues of identity, he provided many of the links in the chain.

Wenger explains engagement as a source of identification: 'we build communities of practice through this process [of engagement in practice], we work out our relations with each other and with the world, and we gain a lived sense of who we are. Through engagement in practice, we see first-hand the effects we have on the world and how the world treats the likes of us.' Appleby suggests that

> A failure to take voluntary responsibility for environmental problems arises because, for many, our engagement in practice provides insufficient connection with the natural world for us 'to work out our relations' with the environment and with nature. Such is our separation from nature that we don't see the effects that, say, disposing of waste to landfill or heating our homes with oil or gas has on the world ... Individuals are far more likely to accept responsibility if they can clearly see the impact of the waste they create. Having your own landfill site in the community really would be 'engagement in practice'!

Engagement and identification are among a range of concepts that Wenger includes in his social theory of learning. Appleby's observations suggest that they also play an important part in taking responsibility.

Considering the earlier examples of social learning, the social interactions around the weirs in the Netherlands and the local seed in Ecuador could be seen as engagement in more sustainable practices. How individuals identified with the processes is not evident from the brief details included here, but it is not difficult to imagine that this kind of engagement could provide some of the missing connections that Appleby refers to which would enable responsibility for environmental problems to be taken.

Ison et al. (2007) concluded that 'social learning, in concert with other coordination mechanisms, has application in research and practice in natural resource management in general and more broadly in response to the current global environmental crisis, but [...] it needs to be better understood and institutionalised'. Better understanding of the role that

Chris Blackmore

social learning may have in enabling people to take environmental responsibility is certainly needed.

Note

1 Wenger considers participation and reification as an inseparable duality in his theory and as fundamental to negotiating meaning. Reification means making something into a thing. Wenger suggests that processes of participating might include living in the world, membership, interacting, etc., and linked processes of reification might be documents, points of focus, forms, etc.

References

Appleby, C. (2008) Personal communication.

Blackmore, C. (2007) 'What kinds of knowledge, knowing and learning are required for addressing resource dilemmas? – a theoretical overview', *Environmental Science and Policy*, 10: 512–25.

Boardman, B. (2006) 'Creating a virtuous circle for climate change with consumers, manufacturers and sufficiency', Conference paper, EEDAL (International Energy Efficiency in Domestic Appliances & Lighting Conference), 21–23 June, London.

Daniels, S., and G. Walker (1996) 'Collaborative learning: improving public deliberation in ecosystem-based management', *Environmental Impact Assessment Review*, 16: 71–102.

De Laat, M. F. and P. R. J. Simons (2002) 'Collective learning: theoretical perspectives and ways to support networked learning', *Vocational Training: European Journal*, 27: 13–24.

Grove-White, R. (2005) 'Uncertainty,

environmental policy and social learning', *Environmental Education Research*, 11(1): 21–4.

Ison, R. L., N. Röling and D. Watson (2007) 'Challenges to science and society in the sustainable management and use of water: investigating the role of social learning', *Environmental Science and Policy*, 10: 499–511.

Jiggins, J., E. van Slobbe and N. Röling (2007) 'The organisation of social learning in response to perceptions of crisis in the water sector of the Netherlands', *Environmental Science and Policy*, 10: 526–36.

Keen, M., V. Brown and R. Dyball (2005) *Social Learning in Environmental Management: Towards a Sustainable Future*, London and Sterling, VA: Earthscan.

Leeuwis, C. and R. Pyburn (eds) (2007) *Wheelbarrows Full of Frogs – Social Learning in Rural Resource Management*, Assen, The Netherlands: Royal Van Gorcum.

Maniates, M. F. (2001) 'Individualization: plant a tree, buy a bike, save the world?', *Global Environmental Politics*, 1(3): 31–52.

SLIM (2004) 'The role of learning processes in integrated catchment management and the sustainable use of water', SLIM Policy Briefing no. 6.

Wals, A. (2007) *Social Learning Towards a Sustainable World: Principles, Perspectives, and Praxis*, Wageningen, The Netherlands: Wageningen Academic Publishers.

Wenger, E. (1998) *Communities of Practice – Learning, Meaning and*

Identity, Cambridge: Cambridge University Press.

— (2008) *Communities of Practice: A Brief Introduction*, www.ewenger. com/theory/index.htm, accessed 31 July 2008.

Willemsen, M., J. B. Ochoa and C. Almekinders (2007) 'Multi-level social learning around local seed in Andean Ecuador', ch. 26 in A. Wals, *Social Learning Towards a Sustainable World: Principles, Perspectives, and Praxis*, Wageningen, The Netherlands: Wageningen Academic Publishers.

Chris Blackmore

22 | Uncertainty, environmental policy and social learning

ROBIN GROVE-WHITE

This piece was written to contextualize a special issue of *Environmental Education Research* on environmental policy developments of the preceding two decades. Robin Grove-White is based in the UK and has been closely involved in these developments. This piece has wider relevance for this book because of its focus on environmental policy and action, as both are related to environmental responsibility. Links are made between political and institutional problems concerning sustainable development, the role and authority of science and the role of social learning in relation to action in the face of uncertainty.

§ We have reached a stage where our societies need new thinking about the environment. That need goes deep.

There's now uneasy recognition, intellectually at least, that current trends in macro-economic development – unrelentingly energy-intensive, resource-hungry and damaging to non-human denizens of the globe – are sustainable only at an ever-more horrible environmental, and associated human, price. But the economic and political models which shape and govern everyday behaviour continue to corral most of us within patterns of expectation and dependency which make any serious change of direction all but unthinkable. Hence the widely observed 'value–action gap' in most of us: we know there's a serious problem, yet feel increasingly uneasy at our own personal inability to help mitigate it.

It is this *cultural* challenge to which, in my view, the research project providing the contents of this Special Issue was responding. Those involved were pursuing a richer understanding of the central environmental-economic concept of natural capital, as one specific and practical focus of the question: might it be possible to nurture fresh ways of thinking and feeling about the environment, of a kind which could foster practices encoding more authentically sustainable approaches within daily life?

For more than four decades, governments have been aware of the *problematique* of the environment. In the 1970s and 1980s, their efforts came to focus on a range of significant, but politically tractable, issues in the fields of pollution and land use. Air and water quality standards, new waste disposal practices, safeguarding of natural areas for wildlife and amenity protection, higher standards of energy efficiency, modest transport constraints and improvements, all were implemented relatively painlessly in many countries. This was what commentators like Burke (1997) have called the *'easy* politics' of the environment – largely win-win situations, with few losers and low political costs. Central to these approaches in countries like the UK was the authority of 'sound science', as a means of generating legitimacy for political intervention.

At an international level too, such science-based approaches assisted action. One high point came at the Earth Summit of 1992. Three global Conventions – on Climate, Biodiversity and Forestry – were agreed, all of them grounded in a particular shared, largely scientific understanding of what was now at stake.

Environmental non-governmental organisations (NGOs) helped build popular support for such measures. Having been agitating since the late 1960s for government action, but forced through experience to become progressively more 'realistic' about what they could expect governments to deliver, they helped crystallise a dominant discourse, or paradigm, of environmental improvement increasingly shared by government and in-dustry. In the UK, this took particularly graphic form in their participation in the various Sustainable Development Round Tables of the mid-1990s. Mainstream environmental NGOs, from having been radical standard-bearers, became part of an institutionalised policy community.

Meanwhile, beyond the Westminster village, the world rolled on. With the end of the Cold War, capitalism's vigour precipitated dynamic economic growth over a growing proportion of the globe. World trade burgeoned. Technological capacities multiplied. Populations in the de-veloping world continued to expand. And as wealth increased, so also did poverty. The gaps between rich and poor continued to widen, with growing environmental burdens falling on the latter.

By the late 1990s, the overall price of this worldwide dynamism was becoming clearer to many – and not just environmental activists: fossil fuel-induced climate change increasingly evident, the oceans depleting, the non-human natural world ever more squeezed, urbanisation appar-ently unstoppable, transport gridlock more and more probable. The tools and concepts of environmental policy approaches forged in the earlier period are beginning to look alarmingly ineffectual in the face of such inexorable pressures.

What this signals is that we are now well and truly into Burke's era of the *'hard* politics' of the environment – an era in which meaningful initiatives aimed at correcting destructive trends will incur costs to, and hence strong resistance from, major groups in society. Look no further than the UK's fuel protests of 2002, the proliferating local rows around wind energy development – or, most dishearteningly, the Labour Government's political *volte-face* on intelligent transport planning in 2000. The creation of political consensus around meaningful government action on matters of central environmental policy significance is becoming ever more difficult.

Compounding this difficulty is the shifting state of relations between science and contemporary society. In the present technological era, scientific innovation and its translation into ever-more pervasive goods and services have drawn government and scientists into increasingly ambiguous patterns of relationship. On the one hand, science-derived innovation is central to the country's material prosperity and competitive trade position, which is why governments fund it so generously. On the other, science continues to be relied on politically as the disinterested source of objective appraisal for regulatory purposes.

The tension between these two roles for science has become evident in the UK since the early 1990s. A series of science-related controversies – the Brent Spar oil terminal, BSE and GM crops – helped to bring into public focus the selectiveness and limited predictive power of scientific risk assessment, particularly (though not only) where leading-edge technological innovation is concerned. Social scientists have come to understand the extent to which the values and purposes of the bodies undertaking such assessments help shape and determine their findings – particularly with respect to the inevitable wider uncertainties and indeterminacies which may (or may not) come to be recognised.

Moreover, this is happening at a time when the potential *reach* of the new technologies – information technology, genomics, nanotechnology and who knows what else? – has become unprecedentedly great, and their pace and patterns of development all but impossible to anticipate, let alone for scientific experts confidently to 'assess'.

As a consequence, controversies like those surrounding GM crops in Britain over the period 1998–2004 have been leading to increasing focus on processes of 'public engagement' to assist political judgements in the face of uncertainty, rather than relying exclusively on the avowedly Olympian sound science of the recent past. In a growing number of fields of environmental policy significance – radioactive waste disposal, transport and biodiversity protection, as well as prospective new technologies – the confident certainties of the previous 'sound science' era are beginning to be replaced by a greater degree of humility towards the inevitable provisionalities and limitations of our knowledge.

This new realism about the strengths and limitations of science for public policy is deeply unsettling, but of great importance. It comes at a time when public disaffection from mainstream political institutions has reached new levels. Indeed, some would argue that these two phenomena are related – that past political claims for the comprehensiveness of scientific understanding in risk assessment have themselves contributed towards the public scepticism which now inhibits effective environmental governance. Be that as it may, there is now a new situation in which society's judgements about what courses of action will or will not prove to be 'sustainable' will demand more open public discussion and negotiation.

How well equipped are our public institutions – including our educational systems – for such developments? And more immediately, how well equipped are we as citizens for purposeful involvement in such processes of 'engagement'? There are grounds for concern. Difficulties over representation, discursive competence and democratic process beset many new deliberative fora, and their success in engaging the wider public with key issues around environment and sustainability remains questionable.

This points to an urgent need for the cultivation of new learning capacities across the full range of policy-making and decision-making about environment and technology. We need to generate more widely shared understandings, appropriate to the circumstances we now face, of how exploratory social learning relates to action in the face of future uncertainty. [...]

Reference

Burke, T. (1997, 20 June) 'The buck stops everywhere', *New Statesman*, 14–16.

Robin Grove-White

Summary of part three

CHRIS BLACKMORE

Most of the readings in this part focus to some extent on how both individuals and different collectives can bring about long-term changes leading to more sustainable ways of life. Some authors, such as Vickers, also tease out and challenge some of the distinctions and assumptions implicit in our use of language relating to responsibility and our environment. Recurring ideas brought forward that are of particular relevance to environmental responsibility can be summarized:

- People are deeply affected by their social and environmental contexts, but respond in more than one way. When considering responsibility it can be useful to think of individuals and collectives as dualities rather than dualisms.
- Individual freedoms can be, but are not necessarily, at odds with choosing to act responsibly at a collective level.
- We all have moral obligations to others, although we need to bear in mind that some see that as both a commitment and a constraint.
- There are choices to make about how we relate to other stakeholders in an environmental issue.
- We face a lot of uncertainty in relation to our future environments and need to develop learning capacities and engage meaningfully in more sustainable practices, using our collective imagination.
- Humans face major challenges and struggle in both individual and collective thinking and actions that can bring about radical changes that are needed for long-term sustainability.

The researchers and writers in this part of the book voice many concerns, including some about the kinds of obligations we have and who they extend to, rates of consumption of our natural resources, moral standards and the boundaries of our moral communities. Other concerns are about individual actions that avoid meaningful social action that could lead to new and more sustainable ways of living, a need to safeguard the commons (particularly in situations of high population density), a need for better governance of the commons and adaptive institutions, and a need to understand better how social learning may contribute to environmental responsibility.

A diversity of ideas for change are also elaborated, ranging from new models of environmental impact and corporate social responsibility to new modes of multilevel governance and institutions and an increased focus on learning processes. Evidence is also provided that highlights how some of these ideas can work in some situations. When considering all the readings in this part, there appears to be a tension between individual and collective responsibility which can be either destructive or creative. As individuals, we are never far away from many different forms of collective. The readings raise many questions about responsibility and our environment which explore how people can work together to produce sensible collective outcomes. Whether in terms of care or accountability, they also suggest that environmental responsibility needs to be not just attributed but also accepted, both by individuals and by collectives.

FOUR | Ecological citizenship

Introduction to part four

MARK J. SMITH

Since the 1990s, there has been an increased awareness of environmental injustices and, moreover, the connections between environmental and social injustices in both the developed and developing worlds as part of the movement for sustainable development. This coincided with the increased focus on urban as well as rural issues across all societies, breaking down the traditional distinction between the green and brown agendas. At the beginning of the twenty-first century, these changes in focus became even more salient, with half the world's population being urban dwellers.

The shift of focus from developed to developing societies is represented in the first reading of this part, by Joan Martinez-Alier, who highlights the parallels and differences between environmental justice movements in South Africa and the USA. The American environmental justice movement differs from accounts of environmental responsibility such as those of, for example, Aldo Leopold by stressing the social and urban consequences of environmental harm. In South Africa, it highlights the increased importance of transnational responsibility, particularly for global companies.

Next, in a seminal contribution, Andrew Dobson explores the meaning of ecological citizenship and how it differs from the assumptions of environmental citizenship informed by the liberal focus on rights. Dobson highlights the idea of ecological citizenship as a politics of obligation, duty and responsibility, and argues that we can have obligations for the effects of our actions even when those affected cannot easily be included in our immediate political community – in other words, that rights and duties are not always reciprocal. He proposes that environmental justice involves fair shares of ecological space in a global context and that this can be achieved through an ethical approach based on virtues.

Following up on the connections between social and environmental justice, Julian Agyeman provides concrete illustrations of solid waste management and residential energy use to indicate how 'just sustainabilities' can be developed. In the subsequent reading, Agyeman and Bob Evans develop a case for broad-focus civic environmentalism, where citizens and not-for-profit organizations address economic and social as well as environmental issues in a complementary way, and where policy-making arises from a bottom-up rather than a top-down process. This links concerns about equity and justice explicitly to governance and democracy.

Sherilyn MacGregor takes the implications of this farther to explore how feminist ecological citizenship fundamentally challenges liberal assumptions about what is political by suggesting, like Dobson, that we need to address environmental politics in private life and through governing institutions. MacGregor argues that ecological citizenship needs to integrate the perspectives and experiences of women – that environmental responsibility is more likely when informed by the feminist ethics of care. If we take civil society and private lives more seriously as spaces of ethical and political contestation then, as the reading by Gill Seyfang illustrates, environmental responsibilities can be developed through sustainable consumption strategies, whereby citizens and households (by understanding the reasons) can reduce their ecological footprint. This also poses the question of how to develop environmental responsibility in different cultural contexts, illustrated by Mark J. Smith and Piya Pangsapa's reading on Buddhist virtues and action in Southeast Asia linking community livelihoods and ecology.

The second reading by Smith and Pangsapa highlights another terrain for promoting social and environmental responsibility in civil society: the corporate or business sector. This reading also highlights how stakeholder participation in company decisions by all affected constituencies is an essential prerequisite when moving from corporate responsibility to corporate citizenship. In the final reading, Smith and Pangsapa reassess the approach of Andrew Dobson by suggesting that we need to focus on the contingent and complex conditions on the ground – *the strategic context* – in order to promote environmental responsibility. They conclude that each context will demand its own 'greenprint', drawing on specific *ethico-political* assumptions that speak to the culture, community traditions and governance institutions in each location – and, moreover, that different virtues will be more or less relevant to different environmental issues and different social contexts.

23 | Environmental justice in the United States and South Africa

JOAN MARTINEZ-ALIER

This reading by Joan Martinez-Alier, a key figure in the development of ecological economics and the field of political ecology, focuses on the role of environmental justice movements in both developed and developing countries. In particular, this reading highlights the fact that the importance of linking social and environmental justice in the Global South by exploring the environment is a necessity of the poor and not just a luxury for the rich. The focus of this extract is the 'environmentalism of the poor' in both the United States and South Africa in order to indicate the differences and similarities between environmental justice in developed and developing societies.

§ Since the late 1980s and early 1990s, 'environmental justice' has come to mean an organized movement against 'environmental racism'. [...] There are books on ethics with the title 'environmental justice' (Wenz, 1988) that discuss the norms to be applied to the allocation of environmental benefits and burdens among people including future generations, and between people and other sentient beings. The subject includes the extension of Rawls' principles of justice to future human generations (under the somewhat fanciful assumption that we are behind a veil of ignorance as to which generation we belong to), and the discussion on whether animals have 'rights'. However, 'environmental justice' is an expression which belongs more to environmental sociology and to the study of race relations than to environmental ethics or philosophy. [...] Environmental justice is the organized movement against 'environmental racism', that is the disproportionate allocation of toxic waste to Latino or African-American communities in urban-industrial situations and in the USA. It is also applied to Native American reservations, particularly in the context of uranium mining and nuclear waste. Indeed, 'environmental justice' could subsume historic conflicts on sulphur dioxide, the Chipko and Chico Mendes cases, the current conflicts on the use of carbon sinks and reservoirs, the conflicts on oustees from dams, the fight for the preservation of rainforests or mangroves for livelihood, and many other cases around the world which sometimes have to do with 'racism' and sometimes not.

Ecological distribution conflicts [...] are conflicts over the principles of justice applicable to the burdens of pollution and to access to environmental resources and services. For instance, are there moral and legal duties for greenhouse gas emissions beyond national borders (as there are duties regarding the 200-mile fishing zone, or for CFC emissions)? Do such duties arise only from ratified treaties, that is positive law, or are there general principles of international environmental justice? Do they apply to corporations such as Unocal or Texaco? For instance, could the allocation of CO_2 allowances inside the European Union be seen as an internal application of a principle of environmental distributive justice (by allowing increases per capita to Portugal, Spain, Greece and Ireland)? On the other hand, does the European Union total carbon allowance represent internationally an injustice because all countries, including Portugal, Spain, Greece and Ireland, are already much above the per capita world average for CO_2 emissions? [...]

Fighting 'environmental racism'

The environmental justice movement in the United States is different from the two previous currents of environmentalism in this country, namely, the efficient and sustainable use of natural resources (in the tradition of Gifford Pinchot), and the cult of wilderness (in the tradition of John Muir). As a self-conscious movement, environmental justice fights against the alleged disproportionate dumping of toxic waste or exposure to different sorts of environmental risk in areas of predominantly African-American, or Hispanic or Native American, populations. The language employed is not that of uncompensated externalities but rather the language of race discrimination, which is politically powerful in the USA because of the long Civil Rights struggle. In fact, the organized environmental justice movement is an outgrowth, not of previous currents of environmentalism, but of the Civil Rights movement. Some direct collaborators of Martin Luther King were among the 500 people arrested in the initial episode of the environmental justice movement, in the town of Afton in Warren County in North Carolina in 1982 (Bullard, 1993). Governor Hump had decided to locate a dump for PCB residues (polychlorinated biphenyls) in Warren County, which in 1980 had 16,000 inhabitants of whom 60 per cent were African-American, most of them under the poverty line. A NIMBY struggle escalated into a massive non-violent protest with nationwide support when the first trucks arrived in 1982. [...] Its roots are in the African-American Civil Rights movement of the 1960s, also in the United Farm Workers' movement of Cesar Chavez which had gone on strike in 1965 against grape growers (who used pesticides which are now banned) and which worked together in 1968 with the Environmental Defence Fund in a short marriage of convenience for the prohibition of DDT to the benefit of birds' and human health. Martin Luther King's last journey to Memphis, Tennessee in April 1968 had been related to the improvement of working conditions of garbage disposal workers subject to health risks. [...]

Why were black people so totally absent from the governing bodies of the Sierra Club and other main environmental organizations, collectively known as the 'big ten'? The 'people of colour' environmental justice movement, fed up with 'white' environmentalism, pronounced itself initially against slogans such as 'Save the Rainforest', insisting on urban issues, and ignoring the fact that many rainforests are civilized jungles. Only some mainstream organizations, such as Greenpeace and the Earth Island Institute (founded by David Brower in San Francisco), responded quickly and favourably to the challenge of the environmental justice movement. In 1987, the United Church of Christ Commission for Racial Justice published a study of the racial and socioeconomic characteristics of communities with hazardous waste sites. Subsequent studies confirmed that African-Americans, Native Americans, Asian Americans and Latinos were more likely than other groups to find themselves near hazardous waste facilities. Other studies found that the average fine for violations of environmental norms in low-income or people of colour communities was significantly lower than fines imposed for violations in largely white neighbourhoods. Under the banner of fighting 'environmental racism' low-income groups, members of the working class and people of colour constituted a movement for environmental justice, which connected environmental issues with racial and gender inequality, and with poverty.

There are many cases of local environmental activism in the USA by 'citizen-workers groups' (Gould et al., 1996) outside the organized environmental justice movement, some with a hundred years' roots in the many struggles for health and safety in mines and factories, perhaps also in complaints against pesticides in southern cotton fields, and certainly in the struggle against toxic waste at Love Canal in upstate New York led by Lois Gibbs (Gibbs, 1981, 1995) who also later led a nationwide 'toxics-struggles' movement showing that poor communities would not tolerate any longer being dumping grounds (Gottlieb, 1993; Hofrichter, 1993). In the 'official' environmental justice movement are included celebrated episodes of collective action against incinerators (because of the uncertain risk of dioxins), particularly in Los Angeles, led by women. Cerrell Associates had made known a study in 1984 in California on the political difficulties facing the siting of waste-to-energy conversion plants (such as incinerators of urban domestic waste), recommending areas of low environmental awareness and low capacity for mobilizing social resources in opposition. There were surprises when opposition arose in unexpected areas, such as the Concerned Citizens of South Central Los Angeles in 1985. Also in the 1980s, other environmental conflicts gave rise to groups such as People for Community Recovery in South Chicago (Altgeld Gardens), led by Hazel Johnson, and the West Harlem Environmental Action (WHEACT) in New York, led by Vernice Miller. In 1989, the South-West Network for Economic and Environmental Justice (SNEEJ), led by Richard Moore, was founded, with its main seat in Albuquerque, New Mexico, out of grievances felt by Mexican and Native American populations. Richard Moore was the first signatory of a famous letter sent to the 'big ten' environmental organizations in the USA in January 1990 by the leaders of organizations representing African-Americans and Hispanic Americans. The letter warned that the 'white' organizations would not be able to build a strong environmental movement unless they addressed the issue of toxic waste dumps and incinerators [...]

The insistence on 'environmental racism' is sometimes surprising to analysts from outside the USA. In fact, some foreign academics refuse to acknowledge the racial angle, and have boldly stated: 'If one were asked to date the beginning of the environmental justice movement in the United States, then 2 August 1978 might be the place to start. This was the day when the CBS and ABC news networks first carried news of the effect of toxic waste on the health of the people of a place called Love Canal' (Dobson, 1998: 18). However, the Love Canal people, led by Lois Gibbs, were not people of colour, they were white, as such categories are understood in the USA, and therefore were subject only to metaphorical, not real 'environmental racism'. [...] Bullard, who is both an academic and an activist, realizes the potential of the environmental justice movement beyond 'minority' populations, asserting in 1994:

> Grassroots groups, after decades of struggle, have grown to become the core of the multi-issue, multi-racial, and multi-regional environmental justice movement. Diverse community-based groups have begun to organize and link their struggles to issues of civil and human rights, land rights and sovereignty, cultural survival, racial and social justice, and sustainable development ... Whether in urban ghettos and barrios, rural 'poverty pockets', Native American reservations, or communities in

the Third World, grassroots groups are demanding an end to unjust and non-sustainable environmental and development policies.[1]

[...] As mining, logging, oil drilling and waste-disposal projects push into further corners of the planet, people all over the world are seeing their basic rights compromised, losing their livelihoods, cultures and even their lives. Environmental devastation globally and what we call 'environmental racism' in the United States, are violations of human rights and they occur for similar reasons.[2]

Louisiana is one of the best places for 'environmental racism'. It contains 'Cancer Alley' between New Orleans and Baton Rouge. There are communities in Louisiana such as Sunrise, Reveilletown and Morrison-ville, which were on the fence-lines of Placid Refinery, Georgia Gulf and Dow Chemical, respectively, and which 'were literally wiped off the map, and the people suffered the permanent loss of their homes after many years of struggles'.[3] [...] Granting the increasing internationalization of the US environmental justice movement, granting its awareness that environmental injustices are not only directed against African-Americans, why is Lois Gibbs not 'officially' credited within the environmental justice movement as being its founder in the 1970s in Love Canal, why is the official birth located in North Carolina in 1982? The answer is race, an important principle of the American social constitution.[4] In America there is racism, and there is also anti-racism. Race is of practical importance in order to explain not only the controversial geography of toxic dumps or incarceration rates but also residential and school patterns. Moreover, to establish a link between the non-violent Civil Rights movement of the 1960s and the increasing environmental awareness of the 1970s and 1980s proved attractive for instrumental reasons. The legislation against racism (such as Title VI of the Federal Civil Rights Act of 1964) forbids discrimination based on race. However, in order to establish the exist-ence of racism, it is not sufficient to prove that environmental impact is different[;] it must also be shown that there is an explicit intention to cause harm to a minority group. [This has] shifted the debate on environmentalism away from the emphasis on 'wilderness' (preservation) or the emphasis on 'eco-efficiency' (conservation) towards emphasis on social justice (Gottlieb, 1993). Though structured around a core of people of colour activists, it encompasses also conflicts on environmental risks affecting poor people of whatever colour. Internationally, it is slowly linking up with Third World environmentalism (Hofrichter, 1993). I have, then, only one minor quarrel with the 'official' environmental justice movement in the USA, and this is its emphasis on 'minority' groups.

The movement worked with the Clinton–Gore administration in order to diminish environmental threats to minority groups in the USA; becoming somewhat enmeshed in governmental commissions, it has not led a worldwide movement for environmental justice. [...]

Wilderness versus the environmentalism of the poor in South Africa?

In South Africa, race is even more important socially and politically than in the USA. The country also has a strong wilderness movement. These are common traits. But South Africa is very different from the USA. In South Africa, environmental justice is not a movement in defence of 'minority' populations, as it has evolved in the USA. On the contrary, the majority of the population is potentially concerned. An Environmental Justice Networking Forum in South Africa with substantial township and rural organizational membership (Bond, 2000: 60) is trying to mobilize a new constituency focusing attention on a range of urban, environmental health, and pollution-related problems, and also land and water management problems, which had not been considered by the 'wilderness' NGOs. In their view, good environmental management involves protecting people as well as plants and animals. [...] Attempts have been made in South Africa, as elsewhere, to discard the old colonial and post-colonial idea that preservation of Nature cannot be achieved unless indigenous people are removed, and instead to involve local people in managing reserves through offering them economic incentives, in the form of a share of eco-tourist (or even controlled hunting) revenues. Beyond this, a powerful environmental movement will perhaps emerge in the new South Africa which will link the struggle against racism, social injustice and the exploitation of people with the struggle against the abuse of the environment. For instance, land erosion is interpreted as a consequence of the unequal distribution of land, when African populations were crowded into 'homelands' under apartheid. The expansion of tree plantations for paper and paper pulp creates 'green deserts', in a country where a large proportion of the population depends on fuelwood for cooking (Cock and Koch, 1991: 176, 186).

Environmental conflicts in South Africa are often described in the language of environmental justice (Bond, 2000; McDonald, 2001). Thus a conflict in the late 1990s placed environmentalists and local populations against a project near Port Elizabeth for the development of an industrial zone, a new harbour and a smelter of zinc for export, owned by Billinton, a British firm, which would guzzle up electricity and water at cheap rates while poor people cannot get the small amounts of water and electricity they need, or in any case must pay increasing rates under current economic policies. The Billinton project had costs in terms of tourists' revenues because of the threats to a proposed national elephant park extension nearby, to beaches, estuaries, islands and whales (Bond, 2000: 47). There were also costs in terms of the displacement of people from the village of Coega. [...] The life of the people of Coega was already full of memories of displacements under the regime of apartheid. Although Billinton could no longer profit from the lack of voice of the people under apartheid, now – it was alleged – it sought 'to take advantage of the region's desperate need for employment to enable construction of a highly polluting facility that would never be allowed adjacent to a major population centre in the UK or any other European country'.[5] A small improvement in the economic situation of the people would be obtained at high social and environmental cost, because of displacement of people, and also because of increased levels of sulphur dioxide, heavy metals, dust and liquid effluents. [...] The environmental impacts which the apartheid regime left behind are now surfacing. There are large liabilities to be faced. Best known is the asbestos scandal, which includes international litigation initiated by victims of asbestosis against British companies, particularly Cape. Thousands of people asked for compensation because of personal damages as a result of Cape's negligence in supervising, producing and distributing asbestos products. The lawyers argue that Cape was aware of the dangers of asbestos at least from 1931 onwards, when in Britain asbestos regulations were introduced. Nevertheless, production continued in South Africa with the same low safety standards until the late 1970s. Medical researchers have found that 80 per cent of Penge's black miners (in Northern Province) who died between 1959 and 1964 had asbestosis. The average age of the victims was 48. Cape operated a mill for 34 years in Prieska, Northern Cape, where 13 per cent of workers' deaths were attributed to mesothelioma, a very painful asbestos-related cancer. Asbestos levels in this mill in 1948 were almost 30 times the maximum UK limit. [...]

Wilderness enthusiasts might come to recognize that economic growth implies stronger and stronger material impacts, and also the disproportionate appropriation of environmental resources and sinks, thus damaging poor and indigenous people whose struggles for livelihood are sometimes fought in idioms (such as the 'sacredness' of Nature) which should be attractive to the wilderness enthusiasts themselves. Such an alliance is not always easy, because often population growth, poverty and, possibly, cultural traditions which do not contain 'wilderness' values lead to encroaching upon and poaching the great wilderness reserves whose preservation has been so much a product of 'white' civilization, notably in eastern Africa and South Africa. [...] From what is still the opposite viewpoint, 'minority group campaigners against pollution accuse mainstream US environmental organizations of obsession with "elitist" goals such as wilderness preservation. A similar chasm has opened up in South Africa recently as radical activists influenced by the American environmental justice movement have rediscovered ecological issues' (Beinart and Coates, 1995: 107), such as the dangers of asbestos and herbicides, the health conditions in mines and the lack of water in black urban settlements. Thus the subaltern third current of environmentalism (environmental justice, the environmentalism of the poor) is consciously present nowadays both in the USA and in South Africa, First World and Third World, two countries whose dominant environmental tradition is the 'cult of wilderness' but where anti-racism and environmentalism are now walking together.

Notes

1 R. Bullard, Directory. People of Color Environmental Groups 1994–1995, Environmental Justice Resource Center, Clark Atlanta University, Georgia.

2 Deborah Robinson, executive director of International Possibilities Unlimited, Washington DC, 'Environmental Devastation at Home & Abroad: The Importance of Understanding the Link', 1999 (www. preamble.org/environmental-justice).

3 Kathryn Ka Flewellen and Damu Smith, 'Globalization: reversing the global spiral', 1999 (www.preamble.org/environmental-justice).

4 For instance, when asking for a Social Security card in the USA, one is asked to classify oneself in one racial group, and, at least until recently, only in one.

5 Letter from Norton Tennille and Boyce W. Papu to Peter Mandelson, 7 September 1998 (www.saep.org).

References

Beinart, W. and P. Coates (1995), *Environment and History: The Taming of Nature in the USA and South Africa*, Routledge, London and New York.

Bond, P. (2000), 'Economic growth, ecological modernization or environmental justice? Conflicting discourses in post-apartheid South Africa', *Capitalism, Nature, Socialism*, 11(1): 3–61.

Bullard, R. (1993), *Confronting Environmental Racism: Voices from the Grassroots*, South End Press, Boston.

Cock, J. and E. Koch (eds) (1991), *Going Green: People, Politics and the Environment in South Africa*, Oxford University Press, Cape Town.

Dobson, A. (1998), *Justice and the Environment: Conceptions of Environmental Sustainability and Dimensions of Social Justice*, Oxford University Press, Oxford.

Gibbs, L. M. (1981), *Love Canal: My Story*, State University of New York Press, Albany.

Gibbs, L. M. (1995), *Dying from Dioxin: A Citizen's Guide to Reclaiming our Health and Rebuilding Democracy*, South End Press, Boston.

Gottlieb, R. (1993), *Forcing the Spring: The Transformation of the American Environmental Movement*, Island Press, Washington DC.

Gould, K. A., A. Schnaiberg and A. Wienberg (1996), *Local Environmental Struggles: Citizen Activism in the Treadmill of Production*, Cambridge University Press, New York.

Hofrichter, R. (ed.) (1993), *Toxic Struggles: The Theory and Practice of Environmental Justice*, foreword by Lois Gibbs, New Society Publishers, Philadelphia.

McDonald, D. (ed.) (2001), *Environmental Justice in South Africa*, Ohio University Press, Athens.

Wenz, P. (1988), *Environmental Justice*, State University of New York Press, Albany.

Joan Martinez-Alier

24 | Ecological citizenship

ANDREW DOBSON

Andrew Dobson's seminal book *Citizenship and the Environment* (2003) provides a detailed exposition of different aspects of the debate on ecological citizenship. Dobson's contributions to environmental political theory and the ideology of 'ecologism' are designed to promote environmental awareness through citizens understanding the reasons for being responsible as well as through the citizenship curriculum in the education system. In this reading, Dobson offers a response to recent academic discussions of ecological citizenship and shows how the post-cosmopolitan approach can facilitate a more adequate account of obligations by drawing upon ecological footprint analysis. In the process, he distinguishes morality and politics in accounting for what he describes as the first virtue of ecological citizenship, the virtue of justice.

§ Hartley Dean makes some useful orientating remarks as far as the connections between environmental politics and citizenship are concerned:

> Green thinking has impacted on our understandings of citizenship in at least three different ways. First, environmental concerns have entered our understanding of the rights we enjoy as citizens. Second, the enhanced level of global awareness associated with ecological thinking has helped to broaden our understanding of the potential scope of citizenship. Third, emergent ecological concerns have added fuel to a complex debate about the responsibilities that attach to citizenship. (Dean 2001: 491)

[These] remarks might lead us to think that the citizenship–environment connection would be a well-explored one, so it is a major surprise to find how little systematic work has been done on the issue. John Barry (1999, 2002), Mark J. Smith (1998), and Peter Christoff (1996) have made important inroads, though, and Angel Valencia (2002) has given us a critically comprehensive survey of the territory. Mark J. Smith refers to a 'new politics of obligation', according to which 'human beings have obligations

TABLE 1 Three types of citizenship

Liberal	Civic republican	Post-cosmopolitan
Rights/entitlements (contractual)	Duties/responsibilities (contractual)	Duties/responsibilities (non-contractual)
Public sphere	Public sphere	Public and private spheres
Virtue-free	'Masculine' virtue	'Feminine' virtue
Territorial (discriminatory)	Territorial (discriminatory)	Non-territorial (non-discriminatory)

[Dobson, 2003, Chapter 2]

to animals, trees, mountains, oceans, and other members of the biotic community' (1998: 99). I am not sure that all of the obligations (or rather to whom or to what he says they are owed) are obligations of citizenship properly speaking, and I shall have more to say on this later. But the idea of obligation to which he refers is certainly central to what I would regard as a defensible articulation of ecological citizenship, and the word should immediately alert us to Table 1 (see above) where our three types of citizenship are set out. 'Obligation' and 'responsibility' are not, it will be remembered, the language of liberal citizenship, so it is unlikely that the type of citizenship to which Smith refers will lend itself to full expression in the liberal idiom. As he says, 'At the centre of this intellectual project is the firm conviction that conventional conceptions of justice and citizenship do not provide the human species with an adequate set of tools for resolving the difficulties created by ecological damage today' (1998: 91). I hope to build on Smith's valuable insights in what follows.

Another key contribution [...] made by Peter Christoff [...] is whether there can be a citizenship 'beyond the state'. We have seen that both cosmopolitans and post-cosmopolitans think that there can, and that the former believe that one of the reasons this is so is because citizenship is about participation in the public sphere, and that there is no reason to confine this sphere to the state. Christoff makes a useful contrast in this context: 'it is helpful to look at notions of citizenship from a completely different angle, and turn to conceptions of citizenship based on moral responsibility and participation in the public sphere rather than those defined formally by legal relationships to the state' (1996: 157). He picks up the transnational nature of many environmental problems and locates these in globalizing developments of which they are both a symptom and a cause. Such developments, he argues, 'emphasise the growing disjuncture or dislocation observed earlier between moral citizenship (as

Andrew Dobson

practised in individual and "community" action and moral responsibility) and legal citizenship as defined by the nation-state' (1996: 161). This dislocation survives in – and indeed nurtures – the idea of ecological citizenship. [...]

The value of Barry's, Smith's, and Christoff's work lies in seeing that there is more to be said about the relationship between citizenship and the environment than can be said from the dominant liberal and territorial point of view. Bart van Steenbergen, in contrast, has devoted a widely quoted essay to this relationship (van Steenbergen 1994). He builds on T. H. Marshall's influential three-fold typology of citizenship (civil, political, and social citizenship) in the following way: 'It is my intention to explore the possibility that at the edge of the twenty-first century, citizenship will gain a new and fourth dimension. I am referring here to the notion of ecological citizenship as an addition, but also as a correction, to the three existing forms of citizenship' (van Steenbergen 1994: 142). The idea of environmental rights in the citizenship context is indeed very important, but over-reliance on Marshall could prevent us from seeing what is genuinely interesting in the environment–citizenship relationship. As we know, Marshall's is notoriously a rights-based typo-logy, yet as Smith, for example, rightly points out, one of environmental politics' most crucial contributions to contemporary theorizing is its focus on duties and obligations. [...] Rights-talk can be a little *too* intoxicating in the context of the environment and citizenship. Van Steenbergen himself, for example, makes the giant leap from arguing sensibly for a different *type* of citizenship right to the following rather less convincing idea: 'in short, ecological citizenship ... has to do with the extension of citizenship rights to non-human beings' (1994: 146). [...] It is a mistake to try to extend the citizen community in this way [...] because I believe citizenship rights to be a matter of justice, and justice can only very arguably be predicated of non-human beings (Dobson 1998: 166–83). I do, though, think that such beings can be moral patients, and therefore must be regarded as members of the moral community. But then our relationships with them are humanitarian rather than citizenly, and so to regard ecological citizenship as extending *citizen* rights to non-human animals is a mistake. [...]

Environmental and ecological citizenship

I have been using the terms 'environmental citizenship' and 'ecological citizenship' more or less interchangeably. I want to now introduce a little more precision, and to have these terms refer to quite specific phenomena. From now on I shall take 'environmental citizenship' to refer to the way in which the environment–citizenship relationship can be regarded from a liberal point of view. This is a citizenship that deals in the currency of environmental rights [...] conducted exclusively in the public sphere, whose principal virtues are the liberal ones of reasonableness and a willingness to accept the force of the better argument and procedural legitimacy, and whose remit is bounded political configurations modelled on the nation-state. For the most rough-and-ready purposes, it can be taken that environmental citizenship here refers to attempts to extend the discourse and practice of rights-claiming into the environmental context. I shall reserve the term 'ecological citizenship', on the other hand, for the specifically ecological form of post-cosmopolitan citizenship. [...] Ecological citizenship deals in the currency of non-contractual responsibility, it inhabits the private as well as the public sphere, it refers to the source rather than the nature of responsibility to determine what count as citizenship virtues, it works with the language of virtue, and it is explicitly non-territorial. [...] Environmental and ecological citizenship are complementary in that while they organize themselves on different terrains, they can both plausibly be read as heading in the same direction: the sustainable society. Enshrining environmental rights in constitutions, for example, is as much a part of realizing the political project of sustainability as carrying out ecological responsibilities. [...] Environmental citizenship leaves citizenship unchanged, in that the environment–citizenship encounter can be exhaustively captured and described by its liberal variant. Ecological citizenship, on the other hand, obliges us to rethink the traditions of citizenship in ways that may, eventually, take us beyond those traditions. [...]

Liberal citizenship and the environment

Dinah Shelton distinguishes three ways in which the rights and environment contexts can come together. First, the objective of environmental protection might be pursued using existing human rights, 'such as the rights to life, personal security, health, and food ... [I]n this regard, a safe and healthy environment may be viewed either as a pre-condition to the exercise of existing rights or as inextricably entwined with the enjoyment of these rights' (Shelton 1991: 105). [...] Second, the list of human rights might be extended to include the right to a liveable and sustainable environment, and third, a right *of* the environment itself might be established (Ibid.; see also Turner 1986: 9; Waks 1996: 143). [...] Ralf Dahrendorf wonders whether the idea of environmental rights (in Shelton's second usage above) makes sense at all: 'I am not sure whether one can stipulate an entitlement for all of us as world citizens to a liveable habitat, and thus to actions which sustain it' (Dahrendorf 1994: 18; see also Hayward 2000: 560–3). [...] One key context for the idea of environmental rights is national constitutions, and Tim Hayward points out that, 'more than 70 countries have constitutional environmental provisions of some kind, and in at least 30 cases these take the form of environmental rights ... No recently promulgated constitution has omitted reference to environmental principles, and many older constitutions are being amended to include them' (Hayward 2000: 558). Constitutions might be regarded as standards by which behaviour and performance are judged, and the political importance of the presence of environmental statutes in constitutions should not be underestimated. [...] Even when not enshrined in constitutions, the vocabulary of rights has tremendous discursive and political potential. The important 'environmental justice' movement in the United States, for example, has tapped very successfully into the civil rights language of US political culture (Hofrichter 1994; Szasz 1994; Dowie 1995; Taylor 1995; Pulido 1996; Schlosberg 1999). Environmental justice activists might plausibly be regarded as 'environmental citizens', understood as claimers of the right referred to by Christopher Miller: 'All human beings have the fundamental right to an environment adequate for their health and well-being.' Reid and Taylor graphically and explicitly refer to such activists as 'ecological citizens' whose 'lives were fairly well contained within the dominant narratives until they became aware of environmental damage in their home, neighborhood, or beloved commons or wilds, thus rupturing the logic of their American Dream' (2000: 458). [I would] quibble with their vocabulary – I regard environmental justice activists as 'environmental' rather than 'ecological' citizens [...]

Ecological non-territoriality

If ecological citizenship is to make any sense, then, it has to do so outside the realm of activity most normally associated with contemporary citizenship: the nation-state. As Peter Christoff points out, 'because of the nation-state's territorial boundedness, ecological citizens ... increasingly work "beyond" and "around" as well as "in and against" the state' (1996: 160). This might appear to be a statement of fact, but it presupposes [...] that the political activity to which Christoff refers can be regarded as *citizenly* activity. It is crucial to see that as well as taking us beyond the nation-state, ecological citizenship also takes us beyond both a simple internationalism and a more complex cosmopolitanism. Ecological citizenship works with a novel conception of political space that builds in a concrete and material way on the 'historical' reasons for obligation [...]

'Lichtenberg distinguishes between what she calls "historical" and "moral" arguments. The moral view has it that "A owes something positive to B ... not in virtue of any causal role he has had in B's situation or any prior relationship or agreement, but just because, for example, he is able to benefit B or alleviate his plight" (Lichtenberg 1981: 80). In contrast, the historical view suggests that, "what A owes to B he owes in virtue of some antecedent action, undertaking, agreement, relationship, or the like"' (Ibid.: 81).

I characterized the 'moral' view of obligation as that of the Good Samaritan, and the 'historical' view as that of the Good Citizen. What I want to show here is that there is a specifically ecological conception of political space, and that this gives rise to the kinds of obligations that lead to citizenship rather than Samaritanism. [...] Ecological citizens, then, are not merely 'international' or even 'global' – but nor are they cosmopolitan, if by this we mean that they inhabit the space created in and by the unreal conditions of the ideal-speech situation, or in virtue of their being part of a 'common humanity'. [...] The principal difference between cosmopolitan and post-cosmopolitan citizenship is that between the 'thin' community of common humanity and the 'thick' community of 'historical obligation'. [...] Globalizing countries, and some of their citizens, have an 'always already' impact on other countries and their citizens. As a particular instantiation of post-cosmopolitan citizenship, ecological citizenship brings out this cosmopolitan/post-cosmopolitan contrast very clearly. Ecological citizenship's version of the community of historical, or always-already, obligation is best expressed via the earthy notion of the 'ecological footprint'. This, in considerable contrast to the nation-state, the international community, the globe, the world, or the metaphorical table around which cosmopolitanism's ideal speakers are sat, is ecological citizenship's version of political space. Let me say something more, then, about the ecological footprint. Nicky Chambers, Craig Simmons, and Mathis Wackernagel point out that, 'Every organism, be it a bacterium, whale or person, has an impact on the earth. We all rely upon the products and services of nature, both to supply us with raw materials and to assimilate our wastes. The impact we have on our environment is related to the "quantity" of nature that we use or "appropriate" to sustain our consumption patterns' (2000: xiii). Wackernagel then defines the ecological footprint as 'the land (and water) area that would be required to support a defined human population and material standard indefinitely' (Wackernagel and Rees 1996: 158). It will be immediately apparent that difficulties of measurement dog the idea of the ecological footprint but without [...] undermining the basic

Andrew Dobson

idea it conveys. To eliminate unnecessary complications, though, allow me to adapt Wackernagel's definition by leaving out the 'indefinitely' condition. The ecological footprint then becomes a time-slice indicator of a human community's metabolistic relationship with the goods and services provided by its natural environment:

Ecological footprint analysis is an accounting tool that enables us to estimate the resource consumption and waste assimilation requirements of a defined human population or economy in terms of a corresponding productive land area. Typical questions we can ask with this tool include: how dependent is our study population on resource imports from 'else-where' and on the waste assimilation capacity of the global commons? (Ibid. 1996: 9)

Chambers and her co-authors offer us a representative example of the kinds of factors that combine in calculating the size of an ecological footprint:

Consider a cooked meal of lamb and rice. The lamb requires a certain amount of grazing land, road space for transportation, and energy for processing, transportation and cooking. Similarly, the rice requires arable land for production, road space for transportation and energy for processing, transportation and cooking. A detailed ecological footprint analysis would consider all of these environmental impacts, and possibly more, when calculating a total footprint. (Chambers *et al.* 2000: 60)

The potentially asymmetric relationship between the space actually inhabited by a given human population and the ecological space required to sustain it is graphically illustrated by Wackernagel:

[I]magine what would happen to any modern city or urban region – Vancouver, Philadelphia or London – as defined by its political boundaries, the area of built-up land, or the concentration of socioeconomic activities, if it were enclosed in a glass or plastic hemisphere that let in light but prevented material things of any kind from entering or leaving ... The health and integrity of the entire human system so contained would depend entirely on whatever was initially trapped within the hemisphere. It is obvious to most people that such a city would cease to function and its inhabitants would perish within a few days. (Wackernagel and Rees 1996: 9)

In effect, Wackernagel's city borrows ecological space from somewhere else to enable it to survive. As long as ecological space is regarded as unlimited, this is an unremarkable fact. The 'ecological space debt' incurred by the city can be redeemed by drawing on the limitless fund of natural resources elsewhere in the world. But if we start thinking in terms of limits or thresholds, locally, regionally, or globally, we encounter the possibility of unredeemable ecological space debt – unredeemable because the fund on which to draw is exhausted or degraded. [...] Now there are various ways of disaggregating the human community so as to determine to whom or what ecological space quotas should be applied. We might think of states, regions, cities, or towns, for example. We might also think of individuals, and two issues count in favour of doing so here. First, while it may be interesting to see that 'the average Briton's' occupation of ecological space is five times larger than the sustainability objective says it ought to be, this says nothing about the distribution of ecological space among individuals *within* Britain. Second, the context of our discussion is citizenship, and if ecological citizenship is to be related to the responsibilities incurred by the over-occupation of ecological space, then these responsibilities must at some point relate to individual citizens. [...]

The idea of the ecological footprint converts relationships we had thought to be 'Samaritan' into relationships of citizenship. And it does so not by some sleight of hand, but by pointing to 'antecedent actions and relationships' (in Lichtenberg's terms) where we had thought they did not exist. [...] The 'space' of ecological citizenship is therefore not something *given* by the boundaries of nation-states or of supranational organizations such as the European Union, or even by the imagined territory of the cosmopolis. It is, rather, *produced* by the metabolistic and material relationship of individual people with their environment. This relationship gives rise to an ecological footprint which gives rise, in turn, to relationships with those on whom it impacts. We are unlikely to have met, or be ever likely to meet, those with whom we have these relationships. They may live near by or be far away, and they may be of this generation or of generations yet to be born. It is important to recognize too, of course, that they may live in our own nation-state. In this last case, though, I do not have ecological citizenly relations with them because they are fellow citizens in the traditional nation-state sense, but because they (may) inhabit the territory created by my ecological footprint. By definition, then, ecological citizenship is a citizenship of strangers – as is, in a sense, all citizenship: 'citizens accept that in principle and in fact they are and will remain strangers to each other: there are more citizens in any nation-state than any individual could meet, let alone get to know well, in a lifetime' (Roche 1987: 376). [...]

This may be the best place to put down another marker: I regard ecological citizenship as a fundamentally anthropocentric notion. This

263

is to say that while ecological citizenship obviously has to do with the relationship between human beings and the non-human natural world, as well as between human beings themselves, there is no need – either politically or intellectually – to express this relationship in ecocentric terms. Let me try to make this clearer by commenting on a remark made by Fred Steward. He writes as follows:

> The politics of citizenship runs into a second major problem in its encounter with environmentalism. The concept is formulated to deal with the relationship between the individual and the community within human society, but the fundamental issue addressed by green politics is the status of nature as separate and distinct from human society. Does nature have *rights* and if so, then how are they to be articulated and represented in a discourse of social citizenship? (Steward 1991: 73)

The implicit attempt to generate a notion of environmental or ecological citizenship by referring to the 'rights of nature' obviously runs into the 'nonsense on stilts'. [...] One argument for making ecological citizenship an anthropocentric idea, then, is expedience. But there is another more principled argument, one drawn from what we might call 'future generationism'. Its most articulate exponent, Bryan Norton, has written that:

> introducing the idea that other species have intrinsic value, that humans should be 'fair' to all other species, provides no operationally recognizable constraints on human behaviour that are not already implicit in the generalized, cross-temporal obligations to protect a healthy, complex, and autonomously functioning system for the benefit of future generations of humans. (Norton 1991: 239)

Norton's basic idea is that the vast majority of environmentalists' demands regarding the protection of non-human nature can be met through attending to our obligations to future generations of human beings. These obligations, he says, amount to passing on a 'healthy, complex and autonomously functioning system', and so the sustaining of such a system is a by-product, as it were, of doing the right thing by future human beings. From this point of view there is no need for arcane, contentious, and politically unpopular debates regarding either 'the rights of nature' or the 'ontological shift' favoured by deep ecologists. It is enough to recognize that we have obligations to future humans, and that these obligations include that of providing them with the means to life (broadly understood – I shall be more precise shortly). [...] The ecological footprint extends into the future as well as across territories in the present, so the obligations of which Norton speaks can properly be thought of in terms of citizenship. So I regard ecological citizenship as anthropocentric, but anthropocentric in a 'long-sighted' way (Barry 1999: 223). John Barry rightly points out that,

> ecological stewardship [which Barry equates with ecological citizenship; see 2002: 146] 'taps into' and incorporates the idea that one of the most politically and ethically robust grounds upon which to defend the preservation of nature, and many other policy objectives of environmental politics, is an appeal to the obligations we owe to future generations ... this idea of obligations to future generations is integral to the stewardship ethic. (Barry 2002: 142)

A familiar injunction in this regard is offered by Mark Smith: 'present generations should not act in ways which jeopardize the existence of future generations and their ability to live in dignity, and, if we do act in ways which contain the possibility of adverse future consequences, we should minimize such risks' (1998: 97). For all its superficial radical attractions, then, I do not endorse explicitly ecocentric accounts of ecological citizenship. The most fundamental reason I have for rejecting ecocentric ecological citizenship is that I regard the principal virtue of ecological citizenship to be that of justice, and I believe that justice can only very arguably be predicated of non-human natural beings. Put differently, the community of justice is, for me, a human community, so if the community of ecological citizens is primarily a community of justice, the community must be a human one. While there is considerable metaphorical mileage in the idea that, 'Citizenship, in its fullest expression, must be understood as encompassing the more-than-human community' (Curtin 2002: 302), my view is that we can only have moral as opposed to citizenly relations with non-human beings. [...] I believe that the moral community can be usefully regarded in an ecocentric way, but the community of citizens cannot. In this connection, I think that Mark Smith gets the two communities mixed up in the following reflection: 'Ecological citizenship ... transforms the nature of the moral community itself, by displacing the human species from the central ethical position it has always held' (1998: 99). To my mind it is not ecological *citizenship* that transforms the moral community, but environmental *philosophy*, and particularly environmental *ethics*. Ecological citizenship transforms the community of citizenship, not the moral community. In sum I endorse Robin Attfield's view that, 'the boundaries of moral concern, including the concern of global citizens, do not and should not exclude non-human interests, even though global citizenship is almost entirely confined to human beings' (Attfield 2002: 197).

I similarly endorse Andrew Light's definition of ecological citizenship as 'the description of some set of moral and political rights and responsibilities of agents in a democratic community, defined in terms of their obligations to other humans taking into account those forms of human engagement and interaction that best preserve the long-term sustainability of nature' (2002: 159). As Light correctly points out, in echo of Attfield, 'Such a view need not consider nature as a direct object of moral concern or as a moral subject in its own right' (Ibid.). [...] If entitlements are due only to citizens, then the criteria for citizenship are clearly of crucial importance. Both ecological and cosmopolitan citizenship swim against the tide here, though, and there are two reasons for this. First, the importance of the membership issue for traditional notions of citizenship is due to the tight relationship between membership and entitlement: no membership, no entitlement. Ecological citizenship's focus on duties rather than entitlements, on the other hand, makes for a much less specific relationship between the citizen and what s/he ought to do *as* a citizen. The duties of ecological citizenship are owed non-specifically. [...] Second, the *relations* of citizenship according to the ecological conception differ from those envisaged in the traditional entitlements model. According to this latter model, the principal relationship is that between the individual citizen and the constituted political authority: the individual citizen claims entitlements from and against the constituted political authority. Ecological citizenship, in contrast, is about the horizontal relationship between citizens rather than the vertical (even if reciprocal) relationship between citizen and state. [...]

Duty and responsibility in ecological citizenship

I endorse Bart van Steenbergen's view that, 'There is one important difference between the environmental movement and other emancipation movements. This difference has to do with the notion of *responsibility* ... citizenship not only concerns rights and entitlements, but also duties, obligations and responsibilities' (1994: 146). A number of commentators on ecological citizenship agree with this (see e.g. Smith 1998: 99–100; Barry 1999: 126), but such a bare statement prompts two obvious yet important questions: just what are these duties, obligations, and responsibilities, and to whom or what are they owed? It also prompts a third, rather less obvious question, but one that is important as far as 'citizenship' as an idea is concerned. Whatever these duties, obligations, and responsibilities are, and to whomever or whatever they are owed, can they be regarded as obligations of citizenship? [...]

First, then, *what are the obligations of ecological citizenship?* These follow very obviously from the discussion of ecological non-territoriality. [...] The 'space' of ecological citizenship is the ecological footprint, and [...] the ecological footprints of some members of some countries have a damaging impact on the life chances of some members of other countries, as well as members of their own country. Simply put, then, the principal ecological citizenship obligation is to ensure that ecological footprints make a sustainable, rather than an unsustainable, impact. [...] This formulation also offers an answer to the second question: *to whom or to what are the obligations of ecological citizenship owed?* Once again the answer flows from the 'ecological non-territoriality' of the previous section. Ecological footprints are an expression of the impact of the production and reproduction of individuals' and collectives' daily lives on strangers near and far. It is these strangers to whom the obligations of ecological citizenship are owed. [Also, *are these responsibilities obligations of citizenship?*] Obligations might be owed either to fellow-citizens or to the state itself, but even in the former case the obligations of citizenship extend no further than those who are defined as citizens by the constituted political authority in question. Obligations of ecological citizenship, on the other hand, are due to anyone who is owed ecological space. [...] A critical implication of these types of obligation and to whom they are owed is that they contain no explicit expectations of reciprocity. If my ecological footprint is an unsustainable size then my obligation is to reduce it. It would be absurd to ask someone in ecological space deficit reciprocally to reduce theirs. The duty to reduce the size of an overlarge footprint is, however, driven by the correlative right to sufficient ecological space.

My current formulation should make it clear that while the obligations of ecological citizens have a non-reciprocal and asymmetrical character, they are not unlimited. They are owed because of an unjust distribution of ecological space, and they end when that imbalance has been addressed. [...]

In the post-cosmopolitan context it is not so much a question of which virtues are citizenship virtues, as of which kinds of relationships give rise to citizenship obligations. The virtues of post-cosmopolitan citizenship are then those virtues that enable these obligations to be met [and the] first virtue of ecological citizenship is justice. More specifically, ecological citizenship virtue aims at ensuring a just distribution of ecological space. In contrast, John Barry has argued that, 'It is relations of harm and vulnerability that underpin the community or network within which ecological stewardship and citizenship operate' (2002: 146). My view is that it is relations of systematic ecological injustice that give rise to the obligations of ecological citizenship. Vulnerability is a symptom of injustice rather than that which, in the first instance, generates networks of citizenship, and not all relations of vulnerability can be regarded as relations of citizenship.

So my reference to a 'first' virtue of ecological citizenship is important and deliberate. With it, I intend to distinguish both between the foundational virtue of ecological citizenship and other virtues that may be instrumentally required by it, and also between virtue as Aristotelian 'dispositions of character' and *political* virtue. It is very common to see accounts of ecological virtue expressed in the Aristotelian idiom, but while this may be appropriate in broader contexts, I do not think it works in the specifically political context of citizenship. [...] I agree that 'virtues are central' to green politics – and to ecological citizenship – but I do not think that the 'dispositions of character' [...] are the central virtues of ecological citizenship. The key virtue is, rather, justice – although I entirely agree that certain dispositions of character may be required to meet its demands. [...] For example, Barry's 'sympathy' is a virtue appropriate to the Good Samaritan rather than to the Good Citizen. Importantly, though, this leaves the possibility that sympathy, or other candidates such as care and compassion, might be regarded as ecological citizenship virtues *in the second instance*. [...] Hartley Dean, for example, writes that, 'An ethic of care – whether it is defined as a feminist or an ecological ethic – provides the crucial link between an abstract principle of co-responsibility and the substantive practice by which we continually negotiate our rights and duties' (2001: 502). [...]

The private realm is a crucial site of citizenship activity for post-cosmopolitan citizenship. This is so for two reasons. First, private acts can have public implications in ways that can be related to the category of citizenship. And second, some of the virtues [...] – care and compassion in particular, with their unconditional and non-reciprocal character – are characteristic of ideal-typical versions of private realm relationships. [...] The private realm is important to ecological citizenship because it is a site of citizenship activity, and because the kinds of obligations it generates and the virtues necessary to meeting those obligations are analogously and actually present in the types of relationship we normally designate as 'private'. Although this is counter-intuitive in respect of the vast bulk of work done on citizenship in general, it is absolutely consistent with what political ecologists take citizenship to be about. [...] For liberals, this politicization of the private sphere will sound an alarm. Mark Smith is surely right to point out that, 'Many basic personal choices which were previously considered inviolable will be subject to challenge' (1998: 99).

[...] And if so, how can liberal states pursue it, given the ground rule of neutrality as far as the good life is concerned?

References

Attfield, R. (2002), 'Global Citizenship and the Global Environment', in N. Dower and J. Williams (eds), *Global Citizenship: A Critical Reader*, Edinburgh: Edinburgh University Press.

Barry, J. (1999), *Rethinking Green Politics*, London, New Delhi: Sage.

— (2002), 'Vulnerability and Virtue: Democracy, Dependency, and Ecological Stewardship', in B. Minteer and Pepperman B. Taylor (eds), *Democracy and the Claims of Nature*, Lanham, Boulder, New York, Oxford: Rowan & Littlefield.

Chambers, N., Simmons, C., and Wackernagel, M. (2000), *Sharing Nature's Interest: Ecological Footprints as an Indicator of Sustainability*, London: Earthscan.

Christoff, P. (1996), 'Ecological Citizens and Ecologically Guided Democracy', in B. Doherty and M. de Geus (eds), *Democracy and Green Political Thought: Sustainability, Rights and Citizenship*, London, New York: Routledge.

Curtin, D. (2002), 'Ecological Citizenship', in I. Isin and B. Turner (eds), *Handbook of Citizenship Studies*, London: Sage.

Dahrendorf, R. (1994), 'The Changing Quality of Citizenship', in B. van Steenbergen (ed.), *The Condition of Citizenship*, London: Sage.

Dean, H. (2001), 'Green Citizenship', *Social Policy and Administration*, 35/5, 490–505.

Dobson, A. (1998), *Justice and the Environment: Conceptions of Environmental Sustainability and Dimensions of Social Justice*, Oxford: Oxford University Press.

— (2003) *Citizenship and the Environment*, Oxford: Oxford University Press.

Dowie, M. (1995), *Losing Ground: American Environmentalism at the Close of the Twentieth Century*, Cambridge: MIT Press.

Hayward T. (2000), 'Constitutional Environmental Rights: A Case for Political Analysis', *Political Studies*, 48/3, 558–72.

Hofrichter, R. (ed.) (1994), *Toxic Struggles: The Theory and Practice of Environmental Justice*, Philadelphia: New Society Publishers.

Lichtenberg, J. (1981) 'National Boundaries and Moral Boundaries: A Cosmopolitan View', in P. Brown and H. Shue (eds), *Boundaries: National Autonomy and Its Limits*, New Jersey: Rowan and Littlefield.

Light, A. (2002) 'Restoring Ecological Citizenship', in B. Minteer and Pepperman B. Taylor (eds), *Democracy and the Claims of Nature*, Lanham, Boulder, New York, Oxford: Rowan & Littlefield.

Norton, B. (1991), *Toward Unity Among Environmentalists*, New York, Oxford: Oxford University Press.

Pulido, L. (1996), *Environmentalism and Economic Justice*, Tucson: University of Arizona Press.

Reid, B. and Taylor, B. (2000), 'Embodying Ecological Citizenship: Rethinking the Politics of Grassroots Globalization in the United States', *Alternatives*, 25/4, 439–66.

Roche, M. (1987), 'Citizenship, Social Theory and Social Change', *Theory and Society*, 16/3, 363–99.

Andrew Dobson

Schlosberg, D. (1999), *Environmental Justice and the New Pluralism*, Oxford: Oxford University Press.

Shelton, D. (1991), 'Human Rights, Environmental Rights, and the Right to the Environment', *Stanford Journal of International Law*, 28, 103–38.

Smith, M. J. (1998), *Ecologism: Towards Ecological Citizenship*, Buckingham: Open University Press.

Steward, F. (1991), 'Citizens of Planet Earth', in G. Andrews (ed.), *Citizenship*, London: Lawrence and Wishart.

Szasz, A. (1994), *Ecopopulism: Toxic Waste and the Movement for Environmental Justice*, Minneapolis: University of Minnesota Press.

Taylor, B. (ed.) (1995), *Ecological Resistance Movements: The Global Emergence of Radical and Popular Environmentalism*, New York: SUNY Press.

Turner, B. (1986), 'Personhood and Citizenship', *Theory, Culture and Society*, 3/1, 1–16.

Valencia, A. (2002), 'Ciudadanía y teoría política verde: hacia una arquitectura conceptual propia', in M. Alcántara Sáez (ed.), *Política en América Latina*, Salamanca: Ediciones Universidad de Salamanca.

Van Steenbergen, B. (ed.) (1994), 'Towards a Global Ecological Citizen', *The Condition of Citizenship*, London: Sage.

Wackernagel, M. and Rees, W. (1996) *Our Ecological Footprint: Reducing Human Impact on the Earth*, British Columbia: New Society Publishers.

Waks, L. (1996), 'Environmental Claims and Citizen Rights', *Environmental Ethics*, 18/2, 133–48.

25 | Just sustainability in practice

JULIAN AGYEMAN

Julian Agyeman's research on urban environmental planning is influential in developing the idea of 'Just Sustainability' in both local environmental studies and the environmental justice movement (the focus of this reading). This reading outlines a 'Just Sustainability Index' for assessing the commitment to social and environmental responsibility by environmental organizations. In addition, it provides concrete illustrations of how local organizations find solutions to both social and environmental injustice. A founder and chair of the first environmental justice organization in the UK, the Black Environment Network, as well as an environmental consultant for sustainability projects for local governments, Agyeman explores the links between practical environmental policies and environmental theory that takes account of an increasingly urbanized world.

§ First, I develop a Just Sustainability Index; through which I assess the commitment of a range of national environmental and sustainability organizations to the JSP [Just Sustainability Paradigm] to provide [...] a rule of thumb as to where well-known national organizations stand in relation to justice and equity issues. I then present three representative programs or projects in each of five sustainability issue categories (land-use planning, solid waste, toxic chemical use, residential energy use, and transportation) that are demonstrating just sustainability in practice in U.S. cities.

The Just Sustainability Index

In order to chart the current status of the just sustainability discourse and of the JSP among national environmental and sustainability membership organizations in the United States, a selection of international organizations, and programs and projects in U.S. cities, I developed a Just Sustainability Index (JSI) as a hybrid of discourse analysis, content/relational analysis, and interpretive analysis. The JSI uses the categories listed in Table 1. Using organizational websites and the search terms 'equity,' 'justice,' and 'sustainability,' I looked at both organizational mission statements and prominent contemporary textual or programmatic material. [...] In addition, to fully ensure that no organization was potentially excluded, sentiments such as 'the fundamental right of all people to have a voice in decisions,' 'disproportionate environmental burdens,' and mention of 'environment' instead of 'sustainability' (only if associated with 'justice' or 'just') were counted as having fulfilled the search terms. [...]

TABLE 1 The Just Sustainability Index

No mention of equity or justice in core mission statement or in prominent contemporary textual or programmatic material.

No mention of equity or justice in core mission statement. Limited mention (once or twice) in prominent contemporary textual or programmatic material.

Equity and justice mentioned, bur focused on intergenerational equity in core mission statement. Limited mention (once or twice) in prominent contemporary textual or programmatic material.

Core mission statement relates intra- and intergenerational equity and justice and/or justice and equity occur in same sentence in prominent contemporary textual or programmatic material.

The JSI comes with some caveats and limitations. If I only looked at organizations' statement of their mission, I could be accused of not actually getting at behavior, merely textual representations of reality and symbolic declarations. That is why I look at both 'mission' and 'program' issues, since most organizational websites, certainly those of the organizations I dealt with, have a wealth of up-to-date programmatic information. [...] The choice of which organizations to survey, it could be argued, is somewhat arbitrary. No official list of national environmental and sustainability organizations exists. Many of the organizations that I surveyed (see Table 2) were derived from SaveOurEnvironment.org, a collaborative effort of the nation's most influential environmental advocacy organizations including all the Big Ten groups. From these groups, a 'snowball' technique was applied in order to find more organizations. Three conclusions can be drawn from the results of my survey. First, among the thirty national environmental and sustainability membership organizations selected in my survey, more than 30 percent had a JSI of 0. This means that in such organizations there is no mention of equity or justice in their core mission statement or in prominent contemporary

TABLE 2 Just Sustainability Indices for National Environmental/
Sustainability Organizations Requiring Membership

Organizations[1]	Just Sustainability Index
American Rivers	0
American Solar Energy Society	0
Center for Health, Environment and Justice	3
Center for a New American Dream	3
Defenders of Wildlife	0
Earth Island Institute	2
Earthjustice	2
Environmental Defense	3
Environmental Law Institute	1
Friends of the Earth	2
Greenpeace	1
Izaak Walton League	1
League of Conservation Voters	0
National Audubon Society	0
National Environmental Trust	0
National Parks Conservation Association	1
National Wildlife Federation	0
Natural Resources Defense Council	2
Nature Conservancy	0
North American Association for Environmental Education	2
Ocean Conservancy	0
Physicians for Social Responsibility/EnviroHealth Action	1
Redefining Progress	3
Resources for the Future	0
Sierra Club	2
State PIRGs	0
Union of Concerned Scientists	0
Wilderness Society	1
Wildlife Society	1
WWF	1

Note: 1. All websites for organizations were initially assessed on March 20,
2004. Coding was done at a later date

textual or programmatic material. Second, the average JSI was 1.06.
While not statistically significant, this suggests that the majority of U.S.
national environmental and sustainability membership organizations
make no mention of equity or justice in their core mission statements
and limited mention (once or twice) in prominent contemporary textual

or programmatic material. [...] Third, only organizations with a JSI of 3 could be considered to have more than a passing concern for just sustainability and be operating within the JSP. In other words, their core mission statement relates to intra- and intergenerational equity and justice and/or justice and equity occur in the same sentence in prominent, contemporary textual or programmatic material. [...]

Just sustainability in practice in U.S. cities

I want to turn now to a set of examples. These are *not* specifically programs or projects of the national membership organizations in my JSI survey, although they may have had some influence. Neither are they full case studies; rather, they are short, focused vignettes. I have simply put together a collection of five sustainability issue categories – land-use planning, solid waste, toxic chemical use, residential energy use, and transportation, and representative programs or projects [of which two are included below] that are providing proactive, balanced efforts to create a just sustainability in practice in U.S. cities. [...] Many are based on multistakeholder partnerships between community non-profits, national non-profits, local or federal governments, and/or private industries. The avenues of implementation used at the community level are varied, involving tools and techniques ranging from the simplest and most reactive – street activism – through more deliberative processes and procedures typical of the JSP, to the most complex and proactive-building – local economic security through private enterprise. [...]

Issue category: solid waste management Solid waste reduction is one of the keys to the issues of the NEP [New Environmental Paradigm] and the traditional environmental movement. The most widely practiced strategy, however, is recycling, although the hierarchy of actions should be 'Refuse, Reuse, Recycle.' Recycling is promoted as a municipal effort to reduce urban ecological footprints, partly because the public has seen it as 'doing their bit,' partly because it is heavily promoted by industry associations that do not want the public to move up the waste hierarchy by refusing or reusing their products, and partly because it is relatively easy to do if your municipality has a collection scheme. At the same time, waste facility siting is one of the major issues confronted frequently by environmental justice groups (Cole and Foster 2001). [...] Sustainability advocates must use caution when proposing recycling-industry facilities as community economic-development opportunities for low-income areas. Waste facilities can be an *asset* in local economic development, contributing to work opportunities such as Garbage Reincarnation of

Santa Rosa, California, but some waste facilities, primarily those for toxic waste [...] can be an *assault* on such communities (Ackerman and Mirza 2001). [...]

Representative Program 1: The Green Institute, Minneapolis, Minnesota
The Phillips community is one of the most diverse neighborhoods in Minneapolis, and it has a long history of community activism. [...] In the 1980s, the residents of Phillips organized an environmental justice campaign to resist the construction of a garbage transfer station in their community. The city cleared twenty-eight homes for the ten-acre site, but the construction of the project was eventually halted by the residents of the Phillips neighborhood [who] created the Green Institute to create sustainable business enterprises on the now-vacant site. The Green Institute is an entrepreneurial environmental organization creating jobs, improving the quality of life, and enhancing the urban environment in inner-city Minneapolis. It now operates three revenue-generating ventures designed to combine green industry with local economic development. First, in 1995, the ReUse Center was developed to sell scavenged building and construction materials. The retail store reclaims materials from the local waste stream and sells them at low cost. The center offers living wages for employees and offers community classes on home improvement. Second, in 1997 the Green Institute began a 'DeConstruction' service to remove salvage materials from building or demolition sites. Through DeConstruction, up to 75 percent of an old structure can be reclaimed rather than demolished, with the materials sold at the ReUse Center. Third, the Phillips Eco-Enterprise Center, an award-winning business center built with green building technologies, was completed in 1999 on the site originally intended for the garbage transfer station. The Green Institute and its Phillips Eco-Enterprise Center are working to attract other environmentally conscious organizations and companies to continue their pursuit of sustainable economic development within the Phillips community. [...]

JSI – 3. Main JSP points of contact: combining green industry with local economic development in a diverse neighborhood.

Representative Program 2: The New York City Environmental Justice Alliance, New York City NYCEJA is a city-wide network that links community organizations, low-income communities, and communities of color in their struggles for justice. It was founded in 1991 to support community-based projects through a network of professional environmental advocates, attorneys, scientists, and health specialists. NYCEJA

275

Julian Agyeman

allocates resources to enable its members to be effective advocates for communities that are disproportionately and unjustly affected by the environmental and health impacts of public and private actions, policies, and plans. In terms of solid waste activism, several communities are surrounded by heavy industrial areas, especially on their waterfronts. These areas have attracted private garbage transfer stations handling commercial waste from hotels, offices, and restaurants. These transfer stations bring in thousands of heavy diesel trucks each day. However, Fresh Kills landfill on Staten Island, the local destination for New York's garbage, was permanently closed in 2001, so the city has started sending some of its eleven thousand tons per day of residential garbage to these private facilities. This has nearly doubled the amount of garbage processed in EJ [Environmental Justice] communities. The Organization of Waterfront Neighborhoods (OWN), a city-wide coalition of groups fighting for just sustainability through their solid waste plan for New York City, was founded by NYCEJA in 1996. In 'Taking Out the Trash: A New Direction for New York City's Waste' (Warren 2000), the aim is to maximize the sustainability – environmental, economic, and social – of the waste system by minimizing the export of waste and maximizing waste prevention and recycling. These options are cheaper, more environmentally sound, and can result in social benefits for low- and middle-income neighborhoods (cf. Ackerman and Mirza 2001). Together, these groups have been successful in raising the profile of sustainability and have won significant legal battles to enforce NYC transfer-station siting regulations. At the same time, NYCEJA has helped organize Community Solid Waste Watch programs and developed a manual for local volunteers about the laws governing transfer stations and how to document violations. NYCEJA is also working on transportation justice issues at Melrose station with the Bronx Center and Nos Quedamos/We Stay.

JSI = 3. Main JSP points of contact: proactive policy development: 'Taking Out the Trash: A New Direction for New York City's Waste.'

Representative Program 3: Reuse Development Organization, Baltimore, Maryland The mission of ReDO is to promote reuse as an environmentally sound, socially beneficial, and economical means for managing surplus and discarded materials. Developed out of a conference in 1995 to fill a perceived information gap, reuse is the second priority in the solid waste management hierarchy after 'refuse.' Reuse means finding a use for something that someone thinks they no longer need. Although refusing something is preferable, reuse is better than recycling, the third priority, because it conserves valuable natural resources, reduces the amount of water and air pollution, and reduces greenhouse gases, and it is a means for getting materials to disadvantaged people and organizations. Recycling actually uses a lot of energy. ReDO provides education, training, and technical assistance to start up and operate reuse programs. As part of their Donations Program, ReDO has responded to many requests from nonprofit organizations and businesses that want an efficient, cost-effective way to give items that they no longer use to those who can use them. The program takes items that cost money to warehouse, transport, manage, and dispose of and provides a way of getting the materials to nonprofits that focus on people with low incomes, the ill, those assisting children, or the needy or disadvantaged. This gives businesses tax benefits (Internal Revenue Code Section 170e3, 'enhanced deduction') while building social capital in local communities. It also ensures that the donated materials stay out of the new-products marketplace.

JSI = 3. Main JSP points of contact: focusing profits from environmental industry on low-income and underprivileged people.

Issue category: residential energy use Energy conservation in general is a win-win opportunity within the just sustainability agenda, as ACE is investigating with regard to energy-efficient affordable housing in Roxbury and as the Green Institute in Minneapolis is doing with regard to its proposed urban energy cooperative and renewable biomass cogeneration facility. Cutting energy costs can provide economic assistance to low-income residents, particularly in northern regions. Demand management with regard to energy resources has a long-distance benefit to communities affected by their proximity to mining operations, power plants, and hazardous waste disposal facilities.

However, the investment necessary to increase the environmental efficiency of existing homes and reduce the ecological impact of new home construction is often seen as incompatible with affordability goals. The result is that cities often rely on the 'filtering principle' to generate affordable housing stock: namely, older, less energy-efficient houses become occupied by lower-income residents while wealthier residents purchase new houses. Older rental housing units create a particularly difficult problem in energy-efficiency policy, as the benefactor of home infrastructure improvements is not always the owner. Even as new green building technology improves household energy efficiency, the challenge to broad energy use reduction will be creating the economic opportunity for technology investment and retrofitting old infrastructure.

Representative Program 1: National Center for Appropriate Technology,

Butte, Montana NCAT, established as a non-profit corporation in 1976, works to find just solutions to environmental or economic challenges, solutions that use local resources and assist society's most disadvantaged citizens. It has developed multiple programs to address energy use for low-income communities. There are three noteworthy programs under its Sustainable Energy Program; the first two are current, and while the third has now ceased, it is mentioned because of the topicality of the issue. First, the National Energy Affordability and Accessibility Project (NEAAP) is researching the impacts of energy-market restructuring and market changes on low- to moderate-income households. The project has a website and newsletter, and through the NEAAP Residential Energy Efficiency Database, domestic electric and natural gas customers can search for incentive programs offered by their local utility, such as home energy audits, energy-efficient appliance rebates, and loans at zero or low interest to upgrade insulation or replace old heating and cooling equipment. Second, NCAT operates the Low-Income Home Energy Assistance Program (LIHEAP) as an information clearing house on residential energy conservation for those with the greatest energy cost burden and/or highest need. The program targets community groups, housing officials, energy providers, and low-income residents, providing information on conservation, energy self-sufficiency, and cooperative utility programs. The LIHEAP administers grants to help implement the goals of reducing the energy burden of households. Third is the Affordable Sustainability Technical Assistance (ASTA) program that worked with Housing and Urban Development (HUD) grant programs. [...]

JSI = 3. Main points of contact with JSP: multiple programs to address energy use for low-income communities.

Representative Program 2: Massachusetts Energy Consumer's Alliance, Boston, Massachusetts Mass Energy, under its previous name – the Boston Oil Consumers' Alliance (BOCA) – was formed in 1982 to provide lower home oil heating cost through the buying power of bulk purchasing. With more than 7,000 residential members and 150 nonresidential members, Mass Energy collectively purchases more than five million gallons of oil per year, and with this enhanced buying power charges fifteen to thirty cents per gallon less than the average retail price, saving $150 to $300 per year per household.

Mass Energy's two-pronged approach is to increase both energy affordability and environmental sustainability. It does this through two community assistance programs: the Clean Energy for Communities Fund and the Oil Bank. The Clean Energy for Communities Fund is a new program aimed at supporting the installation of clean energy technologies at community-based nonprofits within its service territory. The Oil Bank program works each year through member donations that enable Mass Energy to help a small number of people who are put in the invidious position of choosing between food and heat. In 2003, it gave out more than $12,000 worth of heating oil to the neediest people.

In 2000, Mass Energy spearheaded the Solar Boston Initiative with a number of area nonprofits such as Episcopal Power and Light, DSNI, the Fenway Community Development Corporation, and the Tufts Climate Initiative, along with members of the solar energy industry. In partnership with the U.S. Department of Energy's Million Solar Roofs Program, the goal of Solar Boston is to serve as a link between the solar industry and consumers in order to reduce transaction costs of solar design and installations. Through consumer education, demonstration projects, and member consultations, Mass Energy has helped facilitate placing solar arrays on ten thousand homes in the Boston area.

Following the state's recent deregulation, Mass Energy has also been developing a green electricity product, New England GreenStart, with options for members to purchase renewable electricity. The catch is that it is currently being offered only to Massachusetts Electric's (National Grid) 1.2 million customers in 168 Massachusetts communities. The state's major provider, NSTAR, does not yet allow its customers to purchase New England GreenStart.

JSl = 3. Main points of contact with JSP: Oil Bank and Clean Energy for Communities programs.

Representative Program 3: Communities for a Better Environment, Oakland, California CBE currently runs Toxics, Oil Refineries, and Community Monitor campaigns. In addition, through its Power Plants Campaign, it has helped Californians learn about the state's highly publicized energy issues and organize against the Mirant Corporation-owned Potrero Plant. Mirant proposed expanding its plant in an already overburdened neighborhood of southeast San Francisco, which has two freeways and two major roads that carry a lot of trucks, resulting in poor air quality, high pollution levels, and health problems. CBE argued that Potrero would produce an additional 62.5 tons of airborne pollutants per year for forty years, the life of the power plant. [...] The December 2002 'Electricity Resource Plan' by San Francisco's Environment Department and Public Utilities Commission supported CBE's conclusion about Potrero and marked the first government-proposed alternative to the Mirant Corporation's plan. The plan, argued CBE, would reduce local health risks

Julian Agyeman

279

because it would put 150 megawatts of mid-sized power plants in the city by 2004 while ramping up about 480 MW of electricity efficiency, solar, windpower, cogeneration, fuel cell, and other alternative technologies at many locations in and around the city by 2012. It seeks to phase out fossil fuel burning for the city's electricity over 20 to 30 years (www.cbecal.org/alerts/power/pP 0902.shtml).

JSI = 3. Main points of contact with JSP: low-income conservation vouchers.

'Just sustainability': from theory to practice

The JSI shows that there are a minority of national environmental and sustainability membership-based organizations in the United States that show a stated concern for equity and justice within the context of their work in environmental or sustainability issues. [...] The more positive story is that all of the three representative programs or projects from each of the sustainability issue categories [...] represent a small sample of local, practical initiatives. They are demonstrating the implementation of the JSP in urban America. Perhaps it is because they are smaller organizations, not large national membership-based organizations, that they can be more locally responsive to the needs of diverse communities. Whatever the reason, these leading-edge projects show how inner urban communities can use asset-based approaches to develop their local economy in both a socially just and a sustainable manner.

References

Ackerman, F., and Mirza, S. (2001) 'Waste in the Inner City: Asset or Assault?' *Local Environment*. Vol. 6, No. 2, pp. 113–20.

Cole, L., and Foster, S. (2001) *From the Ground Up: Environmental Racism and the Rise of the Environmental Justice Movement*. New York: NYU Press.

Warren, B. (2000) 'Taking Out the Trash: A New Direction for New York City's Waste', OWN and Consumer Policy Institute/ Consumers Union, available at www.consumersunion.org/ other/trash/trashI.htm (accessed February 6, 2004).

26 | Justice, governance and sustainability: some perspectives on environmental citizenship from North America and Europe

JULIAN AGYEMAN AND BOB EVANS

Julian Agyeman and Bob Evans have been concerned with civic environmentalism, particularly in urban planning. They founded one of the key academic journals linking academic research to policy networks, *Local Environment*. This reading compares the US experience of civic engagement strategies on the environment with new developments in the European Union. It also provides insights into the relevance of equity, justice, governance and democracy for understanding these developments while posing challenges for some understandings of environmental citizenship. This reading is informed by their broader research on 'just sustainability', civic environmentalism (the focus of this reading) and environmental leadership or advocacy.

Introduction

If citizenship is to be a core theme of environmental discourses, politics and policy, then it must be more broadly linked to environmental justice and set within the wider context of firstly the sustainability discourse and secondly the current debates on governance. We recognise that the contemporary debate around environmental citizenship is both vigorous and erudite (see, for example, Barry, 1999). Dobson (2003) for example offers a conception of *ecological* citizenship which is more theoretically robust than the rather naïve conceptions of *environmental* citizenship typified by the Environment Canada approach discussed later (Environment Canada, 2001). We are interested in the political and policy implications and opportunities of the concept of environmental citizenship, and whilst we recognise the importance of Dobson's distinction between environmental and ecological citizenships, for the purposes of our argument, we will conflate the two. In pursuit of this, we would therefore wish to address three themes:

- Environmental citizenship is not, in our view, a particularly useful term upon which to base political action. It is important to recognise the need to encourage changes in human behaviour in relation to the environment, and that individuals should have both rights and responsibilities with respect to this. It may also be useful to regard environmental citizenship as part of the educational agenda [but it] underplays the broader social and political dimensions implicit in the concept of sustainability or sustainable development. [...]

• Following from this, any conception of citizenship must be more broadly and centrally linked to both justice and equity. In the case of environmental citizenship, we wish to argue that the emergence of environmental justice as both a *vocabulary for political mobilization and action* and as a *policy principle* (Agyeman and Evans, 2004) gives cause to see this as a more powerful tool for securing change than the concept of environmental citizenship.

• Finally, citizenship is integrally connected to questions of governance, and in turn to sustainability. Citizenship for sustainability can only be understood as part of a reconstituted commitment to the processes of governance and justice. [...]

The US experience

While the Canadian government has a primer on environmental citizenship on its Environment Canada website, a search on the US Environmental Protection Agency's (EPA) website brings up 'Community Based Environmental Protection' (CBEP), a manifestation of the US-based equivalent of environmental citizenship: *civic environmentalism*. [...] The Washington DC-based not-for-profit 'Center for Environmental Citizenship' has as its strap-line 'networking young leaders to protect the environment', an indication that the dominant orientation of 'citizenship' is about getting young people involved in environmental action [...] whereas civic environmentalism is seen as the more adult version. [This] is complicated in the US by two concepts that have evolved over the past two decades that provide new directions for public policy, namely *environmental justice* and *sustainability*. [...] The environmental justice movement is typically a grassroots, or 'bottom-up', political response to external threats whereas the sustainability agenda emerged largely from international processes and committees, governmental structures, think tanks and international NGO networks. Despite their historically different origins, there is an area of theoretical compatibility between them, which is increasingly evidenced in practice (Schlosberg, 1999, Cole and Foster, 2001, Agyeman and Evans, 2003). This conceptual and increasingly practical overlap [...] represents a critical nexus for a broad social movement to create livable, sustainable communities for all people in the future (Agyeman, Bullard and Evans, 2003). Straddling this nexus is the concept of civic environmentalism.

Civic environmentalism has emerged over the past ten years as the dominant US discourse on environmental policy making at the sub-national level. The first person to articulate and name civic environmentalism as an emergent policy framework that recognized the limits of top-down, command and control environmental regulation was a former employee of the US National Academy of Public Administration, DeWitt John. Its approach, and that of its practical, EPA-inspired cousin, CBEP, stems from an increasing awareness that centrally imposed, media-specific environmental policy found in legislation like the Clean Air Act or Clean Water Act is not sufficient for dealing with contemporary environmental problems and that more flexible and collaborative solutions should be found. John (1994: 7) sees civic environmentalism in a *narrow* sense. To him it 'is *fundamentally* a bottom up approach to *environmental* protection' (our emphasis). Since John's (1994) work, there have been a variety of interpretations of the concept of civic environmentalism. [...] Shutkin (2000) [and] Roseland (1998), Hempel (1999) and Mazmanian and Kraft (1999) see civic environmentalism as a much more *broadly* based concept than John and their contemporaries. To them, it is the idea that members of a particular geographic and political community 'should engage in planning and organizing activities to ensure a future that is *environmentally healthy and economically and socially vibrant* at the local and regional levels. It is based on the notion that environmental quality and economic and social health are mutually constitutive' (Shutkin, 2000: 14; emphasis added). While John (1994) did not problematise the concept of civic environmentalism, a survey of the range of scholarship on the concept has indicated that there are (at least) two major orientations. Table 1 makes the distinction between these different *orientations*, which Agyeman and Angus (2003) call '*narrow focus*' and '*broad focus*' civic environmentalism. Some may argue that there are two types of 'narrowness'; one based on '*environment*', to the exclusion of justice, and the other on '*justice*' to the exclusion of environment. The former is our interpretation of '*narrow focus*' civic environmentalism. In this orientation, justice or equity are not mentioned in the survey literature. The latter position does not appear to exist in the literature surveyed. '*Broad focus*' civic environmentalism is explicit and clear: environment, economy and social justice issues are 'mutually constitutive' (Shutkin (2000: 14).

An example of narrow focus civic environmentalism is the Chesa-peake Bay Program (CBP), a collaborative approach to restore a severely

TABLE 1 'Narrow focus' and 'broad focus' civic environmentalism (Agyeman and Angus 2003)

	'Narrow focus' civic environmentalism	'Broad focus' civic environmentalism
Main contributors	John (1994), EPA (1997), Sabel et al. (1999), Friedland & Sirianni (1995), Landy et al. (1999)	Shutkin (2000), Roseland (1998), Hempel (1999), Mazmanian and Kraft (1999)
Central premise	Stresses limits of top-down command and control environmental regulation. Civic environmentalist policies are best suited to dealing with the local nature of contemporary environmental problems.	Stresses interdependent nature of environmental, social, political, and economic problems. Civic is fundamentally about environmentalism ensuring the quality and sustainability of communities.
Central focus	The focus is on the interconnected nature of environmental problems. Using an ecosystem focus, the argument is that environmental problems do not correspond to political boundaries.	The focus on the connections between environmental, economic and social issues such as urban disinvestment, racial segregation, unemployment, and civic disengagement.
Contribution to sustainable communities	Can only help achieve the environmental goals of a sustainable community, namely to protect and enhance the environment, e.g: pollution control, protection of bio-diversity etc.	Can help to protect and enhance the environment, while meeting social needs and promoting economic success, i.e. meets all the goals of a sustainable community.
Nature of change	Technical, reformist. Policy change to incorporate community perspectives.	Political, transformative. Change requires paradigm shift.
On the role of the citizen	Passive citizenship, focus on rights of citizen access to legislative and judicial procedures, community right-to-know laws.	Active citizenship, focus on responsibilities of the citizen to the environmental, social and economic health of the community.
Role of social capital	Builds social capital as citizens gain access to the regulatory and public interest arena. But 'narrow focus' precludes broader conception of and growth of social capital because of unrepresentative nature of local environmental action.	Environmental, economic and social decline mirrors decline of social capital. Increasing social capital and networks of social capital is essential for developing sustainable communities.
Stance on environmental justice	Environmental injustice is mostly related to lack of access to, and protection from, public policy. The primary focus is on procedural justice.	Environmental injustice is a result and cause of social, economic and racial inequity. The focus is on both procedural and substantive justice.

damaged watershed. The EPA, the states of Maryland, Virginia, Pennsylvania, Virginia, and Washington DC, together with the Chesapeake Bay Commission, use voluntary measures such as education and technical assistance to achieve their goals. Since its inception in 1983, the highest priority has been the restoration of its living resources – finfish, shellfish, Bay grasses, and other aquatic life and wildlife. Improvements include the restoration of fisheries and habitat, the recovery of Bay grasses and decreases in nutrient and toxic loads.

An example of broad focus civic environmentalism is one of the classic US cases of community revitalization: Boston's Dudley Street, by the Dudley Street Neighborhood Initiative (DSNI) (Medoff and Sklar, 1994). DSNI was formed in 1984 when residents of the area became increasingly frustrated and wanted to revive their neighbourhood which was under siege from arson, disinvestment, neglect and redlining practices, and to protect it from outside speculators. DSNI is the only community-based non-profit in the US that has been granted eminent domain authority over abandoned land within its boundaries. DSNI works to implement resident-driven plans through partnerships with Community Development Corporations (CDCs), various nonprofit and religious organizations which serve the neighbourhood, and others such as banks, government agencies, businesses and foundations. Unlike the narrow focus of the CBP, DSNI's approach is broad focus and comprehensive.

[This] does not imply that narrow focus environmental action is *devoid* of meaningful participation [but] it will be far more difficult to achieve what Hempel (1999: 48) describes as the 'economic vitality, ecological integrity, civic democracy, and social well-being' that are necessary for the development of sustainable communities, without a more broadly based, social, economic and political analysis. [...] Within the discourse of broad focus civic environmentalism, with its attention to urban disinvestment, racial segregation, unemployment and civic engagement, together with a vision of political transformation and paradigm shift, lies the hope for a deeper US discourse on sustainability than the dominant discourse of *'environmental sustainability'*, which equates to narrow focus civic environmentalism. [...]

The European experience

During the last decade, the European Union (EU) has approved a range of initiatives that are collectively creating a policy framework which it wishes to see adopted by all member States, although there are clearly considerable variations across the EU in terms of levels of compliance. The EU has adopted a *Strategy for Sustainable Development* (European

Commission, 2002) that seeks to embed the principle of sustainability into all areas of policy development and implementation. All policies must have sustainable development as their core concern. [...] Sustainable development is clearly defined by the EU as being more than *environmental* sustainability, important though that is. The Presidency Conclusions of the Gothenburg Summit stated: 'The Union's Sustainable Development Strategy is based on the principle that the economic, social and environmental effects of all policies should be examined in a co-ordinated way and taken into account in decision making' (European Commission, 2002: para. 22).

This commitment to a broadly based sustainable development is closely linked to an emerging European policy on governance as presented in *European Governance – A White Paper* (European Commission, 2001). In this paper, a modernisation of European governance is seen as a necessary precondition for European integration through a process of decentralisation, combating the impact of globalisation, and a restoration of faith in democracy through wider involvement in decision-making. The White Paper identifies five principles that underpin good governance – *openness, participation, accountability, effectiveness and coherence* – which should apply to all levels of government from local to global. [...] The sustainable development discourse places heavy emphasis upon the need to develop more democratic mechanisms for decision-making and -taking – for instance in policy guidance at the international level, 'good governance' is seen to be evidenced in a strong and dynamic organisation of local government and a culture of 'institutional learning'. According to this perspective, there needs to be creative intervention by political actors to change structures, but in turn citizens' concerns are well informed and they are seeking better 'performance' from public agencies.

The emphasis on improving democratic mechanisms for decision-making leads to calls for human equity and environmental justice, more effective environmental governance, and greater environmental democracy [...]:

• *Equity*: Moves towards greater sustainability imply a series of difficult decisions which will need to be faced, and the consequences of not taking these decisions (for example about resource use, consumption and pollution) will seriously compromise the quality of life of both current and future generations. Those societies which exhibit a more equal income distribution, greater civil liberties and political rights and higher literacy levels tend to have higher environmental quality (Torras and Boyce, 1998). The sharing of common futures and fates (and the difficult decisions involved in this) is more likely when there is a higher level of social, economic and political equality. This principle applies both within and between nations.

- *Justice*: Environmental problems bear down disproportionately upon the poor, although it is the rich nations and the prosperous within those nations who are the greatest consumers and consequently polluters (Agyeman, Bullard and Evans, 2003). The principles of environmental justice demand that environmental decision-making does not disproportionately disadvantage any particular social group, society or nation.

- *Governance*: The changes implied in a move towards more sustainable societies are so immense that they cannot be imposed by governments alone. This central fact was a major impetus behind the agreement to Local Agenda 21 at the 1992 Earth Summit which recognised that change of the magnitude envisaged by Agenda 21 can only be achieved by mobilising the energy, creativity, knowledge and support of local communities, stakeholders, interest organisations and citizens worldwide. More open, deliberative processes, which facilitate the participation of civil society in taking decisions, will be required to secure this involvement.

- *Democracy*: The right to information, to freedom of speech, association and dissent, to meaningful participation in decision-making – these and other rights underpin most conceptions of modern liberal democracy. Democracy is vital for sustainability in that it facilitates involvement, but through this it also nurtures understanding and education. Moreover, to encourage the involvement of citizens is to develop ownership and to combat the alienation and civic disengagement that must undermine the drive to more sustainable societies.

Christie and Warburton (2001) argue that good governance is central to sustainability. 'The fundamental driver of sustainable development must be democratic debate – decisions reached through open discussion, consensus based on shared goals and trust. Sustainable development needs representative democracy that is trusted and vibrant, and new forms of participatory democracy to complement it that can inspire greater engagement by citizens in creating a better world' (Christie and Warburton, 2001: 154). They maintain that a renewal of trust in public institutions, and of local democracy, will be required if the sustainability agenda is to be delivered. [...]

The final component of the emerging European policy 'architecture' is related to rights and citizen participation. The UN Economic Commission for Europe (UNECE) *Convention on Access to Information, Public Participation in Decision-Making and Access to Justice in Environmental Matters*, also known simply as the *Aarhus Declaration*, was adopted on 25 June 1998 in the Danish city of Aarhus at the Fourth Ministerial Conference in the 'Environment for Europe' process. The Aarhus Convention lays down the basic rules to promote citizens' involvement in environmental matters and enforcement of environmental law. The Aarhus Convention consists of three 'pillars', each of which grants different rights:

- the first pillar gives the public the *right of access to environmental information*;
- the second pillar gives the public the *right to participate in decision-making processes*; and
- the third pillar ensures *access to justice for the public*.

These three elements of European policy relating to sustainable development, to governance and to environmental rights, collectively provide a Europe-wide policy framework which, it is anticipated, will eventually determine and condition the policies and practices of European national governments. As might be expected, the actual implementation of these policies across Europe is patchy, and until the European Commission constructs and applies Directives with which national governments have to comply, progress is likely to be slow. Moreover, it might be objected that these approaches are 'procedural' rather than 'substantive', in that they do not necessarily imply any real changes in levels of social inclusion or social justice, but an optimistic position would be that such 'top-down' intitiatives, however limited, are steps in the right direction. [...]

Conclusions

First, in our view, the concept of environmental citizenship as popularly defined (for example, by Environment Canada) has limited utility as an analytical tool or a vehicle for securing change. It may have potential as a mechanism for inculcating responsibilities through the educational process [...]. The narrow emphasis upon 'environment' rather than a broader emphasis on 'sustainability' is important, but probably not crucial. In contrast, the unproblematic assumption that rational argument, more information and examples of good practice will somehow change individual behaviour is unnecessarily naïve (Kollmuss and Agyeman, 2002). Sustainable development (and for that matter *environmental* sustainability) is a contested approach that will be resisted by powerful lobby interests and by the bulk of the privileged consuming classes. [...]

Second, in contrast, we are more optimistic about the potential within environmental justice. Environmental justice offers (at least) two different but complementary paths towards transformation. Firstly, it is a *vocabulary for political mobilization and action*, predominantly at the local level. [...] It facilitates political organisation and, when the environmental justice 'frame' is aligned with other powerful frames, such as that of the Civil Rights Movement (US) or the unions (South Africa), it offers a wider perspective, a *'just sustainability'* which confronts the potential for more powerful interests to displace their problems on to localities and people with less power. Secondly, it is a *policy principle*, that no public action should disproportionately disadvantage any particular social group. [...] Combined with other principles, such as the proximity and precautionary principles, environmental justice could become a very powerful tool for both the sustainability movement and for the quality of life of some excluded groups.

Third, we cannot see how a discussion of environmental citizenship can be divorced from wider questions of equity and governance. The linkages between sustainability and equity are well rehearsed, and similarly, the move to more deliberative and open processes of governance, with greater levels of civic engagement and participation, are equally wedded to sustainability, not least through the worldwide Local Agenda 21 initiative (Evans and Theobald, 2003). The European Union commitment to more open and inclusive approaches to governance is not replicated in the United States, and will inevitably progress slowly in Europe. [...]

Finally, the ideas of sustainability and justice are also being linked, and used to influence policy at the global level. The Earth Charter (2000) represents an initiative to form a global partnership that hopes to recognise the common destiny of all cultures and life forms on earth and to foster a sense of universal responsibility for the present and future wellbeing of the living world. [...] It is these linkages between the challenges of sustainability, justice, equity, the awareness of global responsibilities and the processes of governance that might help to deliver the individual behaviour implied in the concept of environmental citizenship. Until these elements are blended together the concept will remain fragile and elusive.

References

Agyeman, J. and B. Angus, 2003. 'The Role of Civic Environmentalism in the Pursuit of Sustainable Communities'. *Journal of Environmental Planning and Management* 46, no. 3: 345–63.

Agyeman, J., R. D. Bullard, and B. Evans, 2003. *Just Sustainabilities: Development in an Unequal World*. London: Earthscan/MIT Press.

Agyeman, J. and T. Evans, 2003.

'Towards Just Sustainability in Urban Communities: Building Equity Rights with Sustainable Solutions'. *Annals of American Academy of Political and Social Science* 590: 35–53.

Agyeman, J. and B. Evans, 2004. '"Just Sustainability": The Emerging Discourse of Environmental Justice in Britain?' *Geographical Journal* 170, no. 2: 155–64.

Barry, J., 1999. *Rethinking Green Politics*. London: Sage.

Christie, I. and D. Warburton, 2001. *From Here to Sustainability*. London: Earthscan.

Cole, L. and S. Foster, 2001. *From the Ground Up. Environmental Racism and the Rise of the Environmental Justice Movement*. New York: NYU Press.

Dobson, A., 1998. *Justice and the Environment: Conceptions of Environmental Sustainability and Dimensions of Social Justice*. Oxford: Oxford University Press.

Dobson, A., 2003. *Citizenship and the Environment*. Oxford: Oxford University Press.

Environment Canada, 2001. Available at www.ns.ec.gc.ca/msc/as/primer. html.

Environmental Protection Agency, 1997. *Community-Based Environmental Protection: A Resource Book for Protecting Ecosystems and Communities*. Washington DC: Environmental Protection Agency.

European Commission, 2001. *European Governance – A White Paper*. Brussels: European Commission.

European Commission, 2002. *A European Union Strategy for Sustainable Development*. Luxembourg: European Commission.

Evans, B. and K. Theobald, 2003. LASALA: Evaluating Local Agenda 21 in Europe. *Journal of Environmental Planning and Management* 46, no. 5: 781–94.

Friedland, L. and C. Sirianni, 1995. *Civic Environmentalism*. Civic Practices Network. Available at www.cpn.org/imagemaps/topicon. map?333,242.

Hempel, L. C., 1999. 'Conceptual and Analytical Challenges in Building Sustainable Communities'. In *Towards Sustainable Communities: Transition and Transformations in Environmental Policy*, ed. D. A. Mazmanian and M. E. Kraft, 43–74. Cambridge: MIT Press.

John, D., 1994. *Civic Environmentalism*. Washington DC: Congressional Quarterly Press.

Kollmuss, A. and J. Agyeman, 2002. 'Mind the Gap: Why Do People Act Environmentally and What are the Barriers to Pro-environmental Behavior?' *Environmental Education Research* 8: 239–60.

Landy, M. K., M. M. Susman, and D. S. Knopman, 1999. *Civic Environmentalism in Action: A Field Guide to Regional and Local Initiatives*. Washington DC: Progressive Policy Institute, Center for Innovation and the Environment. Available at www. dlcppi.org.

Mazmanian, D. A. and M. E. Kraft, eds, 1999. *Towards Sustainable Communities: Transition and Transformations in Environmental Policy*. Cambridge: MIT Press.

Medoff, P. and H. Sklar, 1994. *Streets of Hope: The Fall and Rise of an Urban Neighborhood*. Boston, MA: South End Press.

Roseland, M., 1998. *Toward Sustainable Communities: Resources for Citizens and Their Governments*. Gabriola Island, BC: New Society Publishers.

Sabel, C., A. Fung, and B. Karkkainen, 1999. 'Beyond Backyard Environmentalism: How Communities are Quietly Refashioning Environmental Regulation'. *Boston Review* 1, no. 12. Available at www.bostonreview.mit.edu/BR24.5/sabel.html.

Schlosberg, D., 1999. *Environmental Justice and the New Pluralism: The Challenge of Difference for Environmentalism*. Oxford: Oxford University Press.

Shutkin, W. A., 2000. *The Land that Could Be: Environmentalism and Democracy in the Twenty-First Century*. Cambridge, MA: MIT Press.

Torras, M. and J. K. Boyce, 1998. 'Income, Inequality and Pollution: a Reassessment of the Environmental Kuznets Curve'. *Ecological Economics* 25: 147–60.

27 | The project of feminist ecological citizenship

SHERILYN MACGREGOR

Sherilyn MacGregor's research on women's environmental activism forms the basis for immanent critiques of both ecofeminism and green political thought, and provides substantive empirical support for the development of feminist ecological citizenship (the focus of this reading). MacGregor draws on anti-essentialist feminist theory to question some of the key distinctions in liberal and green thinking, including the distinction between the public and private spheres. In this reading, she focuses on how citizenship discourses help us to rethink the relationship between environment, gender and justice and, in so doing, move beyond the idea that care – for people and the planet – should be a solely private matter.

§ [...] Although women may make meaningful connections between their mothering roles and their engagement in ecopolitical and grassroots activism, ecofeminists who translate these connections into narratives that reify their 'lived experiences' and reduce them to care tread perilously close to undermining the democratic potential of ecofeminist politics. Recognizing that maternalist strategies are dangerous opens up new and hopefully more fruitful conversations. [...] It is not my intention to offer a definition of feminist ecological citizenship but to propose it as a project that entails ongoing thought, practice and debate. [...]

Perhaps it is unavoidable that when 'abstract theorizing' and 'real life' collide, the insights that emerge from the latter always sound more sensible than the former. This observation makes empirical research both necessary to the development of theoretical ideas and frustrating for the desire to arrive at pat conclusions. I [choose] to include the first-hand accounts [...] of women activists in my research because of a dissatisfaction with the absence of 'the empirical' in the writings of green theorists of citizenship and the over-reliance on women's experiences (as incontestable truth) in ecofeminist scholarship. While my effort to synthesize theory and practice makes for a much messier narrative than the ones now on offer, it is my hope that it will also provide a much more useful one. There are five interconnected points of tension and contradiction. [...] Expressed as questions, these tensions are:

1 What is the balance between feminist and ecological political goals?
2 Should the aim be an instrumental or performative approach to politics?
3 Should it be a local and particular or global and universal sense of citizenship?
4 Should there be public or private means of redistributing care?
5 Should feminists demand that men change or ... is the future female?

[...] Citizenship discourse [...] has the potential to politicize women's environmental concerns, to assert that they are not mere 'motherhood issues' but deeply political ones that should become relevant to all citizens regardless of their private identities if a sustainable, democratic, and egalitarian society is to be possible. Significantly, the notion of feminist ecological citizenship [...] offers a direct challenge to left-green conceptions of citizenship. I have shown that in so far as they are blind to the specificities of gender, most ecopolitical theorists make proposals for recasting citizenship that will not contribute to gender equality. For example, without an analysis of the gendered division of necessary labour, green notions of self-reliance, sustainable community, and 'doing one's bit' at home and in the public domain threaten to intensify women's already unsustainable burden of responsibility for care. [...]

Caring responsibilities can also interfere with the practice of citizenship. This is not surprising, since – as feminists have been pointing out for decades – the public practice of citizenship has been kept separate from private life, even though private acts are a precondition for citizenship. [...] A feminist approach to ecological citizenship calls into question the public–private divide that is taken for granted in both green political theories and in ecofeminist narratives that celebrate care. The very fact of its redrawing by those on the left and the right shows that the boundary between public and private spheres is not fixed but, rather, is a social and political construction that is fluid and changeable. What makes feminist ecological citizenship distinct from other approaches is that it refuses the privatization and feminization of care and calls for public debate and action on how foundational acts of labour (e.g., care) can be reorganized to allow for women's equal participation as citizens. Care is thereby *politicized* as a necessary part of citizenship. While green politics questions the boundary between public and private in terms of the obligations and duties of citizens, there is scant recognition that what takes place in the private sphere is much more than consumption and

Sherilyn MacGregor

reproduction. Ecopolitical thinkers must begin to see care not only as an ethic or virtue that can inform citizenship but also as a set of time-consuming practices that make citizenship possible. [...]

Tension 1: Balancing feminist and ecological political goals

How does citizenship address the ecopolitical goal of redefining human–nature relationships in a more 'sustainable' way? [...] Against some greens who would dismiss a focus on citizenship as anthropo-centric, other ecopolitical theorists [...] argue that, in conditions of un-certainty, the best way to deal with decisions about how to sustain human life into the future is through the expansion of democracy so that the interests of 'nature' can be taken into account (even perhaps represented). Although there is a range of approaches to ecological citizenship, they share a common element: by recasting the ethico-political boundaries between public and private, human and non-human, and present and future generations, ecological citizenship aims to redress the neglect of nature by changing the attitudes and behaviours of institutions and individual citizens. [...]

What is the link between ecofeminism and citizenship? Val Plumwood (1995, 155) captures in one sentence the basic link between feminist and ecological politics: 'The demarcation of the household and the economy as private removes from political contest and democratic res-ponsibility the major areas of material need satisfaction, production and consumption, and ecological impact.' It is a unique analytical insight of ecofeminism that it is this very (hierarchical) dualism of public and private that underpins the devaluation of nature and women. The link to citizenship lies in Plumwood's endorsement of the virtue of 'political contest' and 'democratic responsibility': it is through the action of citi-zens that questions about the private–public split may become subjects of political debate. By demanding the valuation of hitherto invisible and externalized services (performed by non-citizens, colonized peoples, women, animals), moreover, ecofeminist politics presents a fundamental challenge to liberalism's denial of the inevitable interdependence of human beings. To the extent that scraps of the liberal gender blindfold exist in ecopolitical approaches to citizenship, ecofeminism offers the insight that the gendered politics of care must be addressed if the concept of ecological citizenship is to be effective.

[...] The women in my study noted clashes between their green and social justice values and their responsibilities to family and paid work. A woman activist may be committed to green household practices, advocate green values in her community work, and then resort to wasteful consumer practices in order to save time. [...] Feminist ecological citizenship [...] recognizes the importance of ecological principles but speaks up to say it is not fair that women should do it all, that overburdened women will not be able to live green without incurring significant personal costs. Instead, what is needed is the extension of democratic and feminist principles into ecologically important aspects of daily life, especially in the private sphere of the household. The women activists' approach to 'environmental' quality-of-life issues also complicates the neat distinction between 'the environment' and 'the social' that is often found in ecopolitical and ecofeminist scholarship. For example, few women talked about 'nature' in the reified sense used in ecopolitical discussions. And in contrast to the rhetoric of ecofeminism, none spoke of 'caring for nature'; the women's caring practices and feelings were largely limited to care for people. This observation would no doubt trouble deep ecologists and others who want to move away from anthropocentrism. It was also interesting that the women's definition of 'environment' was varied: some accept a conventional definition and do work to improve the quality of the 'natural' environment (water, soil, air), while others do not distinguish the quality of natural from the quality of social and economic 'environment'. For the latter, not unlike those in the environmental justice movement, economic security and access to public services such as education and housing were included in their list of environmental concerns. [...] If ecofeminist politics is about a redrawing of these boundaries and politicizing what has hitherto been regarded as private, then the language of citizenship, rather than the language of care, is a better language for communicating this message.

Tension 2: Instrumental or performative politics?

There is a contradiction [...] between instrumentalist and [performative] views of politics. [...] Citizenship can contribute to the realization of feminist and ecological goals. Yet [for civic republicans and advocates of performative politics] citizenship [can also be] a form of self-expression important for its own sake.

[...] It is important to ask, who gets to 'do politics' as anything other than an instrumental goal? One of the most significant contributions of feminist theories of citizenship is the point that time is a necessary resource for the practice of citizenship, whose distribution is in large part determined by the gendered division of labour. Lister (1997, 201) writes that 'citizenship politics is ... in part a politics of time'. [...] An important aspect of any vision of a sustainable society should be increased time for non-productive and non-consumptive pursuits such as leisure, education, and civic participation. But is having time for citizenship enough to compel people to engage actively in its practice? While [...] citizen participation will always be in some measure instrumental [...] feminist ecological citizenship should be more than a means to achieving a particular end [...] Feminists must not focus on material conditions necessary for citizenship to the exclusion of the specific value of citizenship as active participation in public life. Part of the project, therefore, is a discussion of how a democratic public culture may be cultivated [...]

Tension 3: Local-particular or global-universal citizenship?

By recasting citizenship as a distinct political activity valuable in its own right, one cannot avoid the question about what is the most appropriate site for citizenship: is it in community, a nation-state, the planet, or some nebulously inclusive, perhaps virtual, public sphere? Or perhaps it is more useful theoretically to eschew either-or dichotomies in favour of a more complex and 'nested' picture of social, political, and ecological space(s). In any case, given that citizenship has been about membership and exclusion, any feminist attempt to reclaim and re-create citizenship must be founded on a principled stance in favour of inclusivity. Some feminists seek inclusion into an exclusionary definition of citizenship by deploying a strategy of reversal (i.e., rehabilitating masculine citizenship with feminine and maternal values), but they generally leave its territoriality – its connections to particular places – unquestioned. Against this approach, I am in agreement with feminist theorists who consider the concept of universal citizenship to be central to a non-essentialist feminist political project for social justice. [...]

A cosmopolitan approach to ecological citizenship, with its emphasis on universal rights, responsibilities, and risks, is more in line with a feminist desire for a politicized and generalized ethics of care than eco-communitarian or individualist approaches to green virtue. A post-cosmopolitan approach, as suggested by Dobson (2003), is even more compatible because it allows us to envision a global civil society that transcends the particular concerns of private life, the local community, and the nation-state (thereby holding the possibility for inclusivity and 'solidarity in difference') while also addressing issues of international social and environmental injustice (e.g., the global asymmetries produced by the North's economic exploitation and pollution of the South's natural resources). A post-cosmopolitan approach to citizenship offers an alternative to the view that powerless people in specific places (i.e., countries in the South) are to blame for the purportedly interrelated problems of environmental degradation and global insecurity because they are exhausting scarce resources to sustain unchecked population growth (see, for example, Kaplan 1994; Homer-Dixon 1999) – a view that may be used to justify the violation of their human rights. It instead turns the blame back on the powerful and persuades us that with affluence and power come the *responsibility* for global unsustainability and, by extension, the obligation to work – ideally as an ecological citizen – towards a just and sustainable society. [...]

The feminist approach to citizenship that I favour, because of its principled stance against exclusion, also embraces a notion of global citizenship so that it includes all those who are non-citizens in current conceptions of place-based citizenship (e.g., refugees, temporary guest workers, nannies, etc.). [...] My vision of feminist ecological citizenship provisionally entails a commitment to inclusivity, the protection of universal human rights, a view of environmental problems as globally complex and interrelated (yet asymmetrically caused and experienced), and [...] multiple public spheres not tied to place or territory. [...]

There is a tension, however, between [...] citizenship that is universal in scope and transcendent of local and national (and perhaps temporal and species) boundaries and the women activists' rootedness in their own communities and their particular interests as mothers and carers. [...] For them the local as a site for the expression of citizenship makes more sense as it is at the local level that they can get things done [...] Like 'grassroots' environmental justice activists who define the environment as the place where they 'live, work and play', the women in my study derive meaning and satisfaction from improving the quality of life in their own locality, not from working to save a distant rain forest or from some abstract concept of Gaia. [...] [They] are a long way from resembling global feminist ecocitizens. [...] What is to stop grassroots campaigns from becoming parochial and exclusionary? As Catriona Sandilands (1999, 123) points out, 'it remains important to distinguish acts of community defence and empowerment from the acts of political reflection and imagination that cultivate a common world.' [...] I would argue that what distinguishes Not In Anybody's Back Yard (NIABY) movements (to protect the quality of life everywhere, now and in the future) from NIMBY struggles (to protect one's own child's health) is a cosmopolitan consciousness that transcends local and private interests. [...]

Tension 4: Public or private means of redistributing care?

People cannot be expected to engage in politics for its own sake unless sufficient conditions for citizenship practice are in place. [...] Civic republican and communitarian theorists of citizenship believe it is 'natural' for human beings to join together in pursuit of the common good, while liberals are concerned about the equal rights of citizens (which includes a just distribution of basic needs) to pursue their own individual notion of the good. [...] Here it becomes important to incorporate a modified version of Chantal Mouffe's (1992a) radical democracy into my project of feminist ecological citizenship. In proposing a radical democratic synthesis, Mouffe's concern is to (1) embrace a republican vision of citizenship as a common political identity that centres on active participation in the public sphere while (2) rejecting the imposition of a notion of a substantive common good on the liberal grounds that this interferes with individual liberty. I [...] would modify it by adding to the second action in a rejection of the assumption, on feminist grounds, that citizens will naturally cooperate in their pursuit of the common good. [...] It is central to a feminist vision of an egalitarian society that care be organized socially and institutionally rather than privately and voluntarily.

[...] A key task in my project of feminist ecological citizenship is to join green political arguments about public ecological ethics (which are in many ways connected to communitarianism) to feminists' arguments about social citizenship rights (which have a history in liberalism and social democracy). Feminists have proposed a range of ways to destabilize the public–private divide and to redistribute the division of care so that more women have more time to participate. [...] I am not suggesting the replacement of all private caring with state or institutional care. In less extreme terms, like feminist proponents of social democracy, I see the provision of welfare state-type policies as necessary in order to overcome some of the historical, gender-related obstacles to women's participation as citizens and therefore as an obvious, although not uncontroversial, part of this project (e.g., Savarsy 1992). Many care-friendly social policies have been proposed by feminist theorists of citizenship, such as extended paid maternity and paternity leaves; universal provision of services such as health care, child care, and elder care; and a guaranteed annual income that supports carers who do not participate in paid employment (Lister 1997). [...]

Tension 5: Can men change or is the future female?

[...] There is no avoiding one crucial question: how to get men to equally participate in caring labour, to take equal responsibility for caring for and about other people and their environments. This is an endpoint to which feminist discussions about changing the gendered division of labour seem inevitably to lead. Feminist research shows that, even when policies and programmes are implemented that give men and women more time to devote to necessary, unpaid labour, women in general still end up doing more of it than men in general (of course we all know exceptions). [...]

Many of the women I interviewed gave what I would call maternalist explanations for the high rates of women's participation in quality-of-life activism. Echoing prominent ecofeminists, they said that women, because they perform the work of mothering, just *care more*. Several were reluctant to problematize women's sense of responsibility, suggesting that women were the planet's best hope for survival. One woman said: 'I see women as "guiding lights" of the world. I feel women are capable to make the changes.' [...] When I asked them 'where are the men?' [...] they noted men's lack of interest in unglamorous issues (e.g., chemical-free house cleaning, lice infestations at school, and food banks in the community) that are perceived to be women's concerns, women's work. [...] Significantly, several women made connections between men's lack of involvement in local quality-of-life campaigns and their lack of responsibility for caring for children:

> Men are not as connected to the concept of their children's future world. It seems like men are more black and white about it and it doesn't pain them in the way that it pains women. I can't speak for men; I can only speak from my personal observations of men ... Personally I know there is a connection between my feelings about my children and my family and my role in the world

[...] Also concerned about men's lack of participation in caring activities, maternalist feminists see 'shared parenting' as a solution to myriad social problems [...] In much the same vein [...] Maria Mies (1993, 321) says that men 'must give up their involvement in destructive commodity production for the sake of accumulation and begin to share women's work for the preservation of life. In practical terms, this means they have to share unpaid subsistence work: in the household, with children, with the old and sick, in ecological work to heal the earth.' Is the aim to make men take on the work of women (i.e., mothering) so that they act and think more like women? If so, then the added bonus, of course, might be that women will have to do less. [...] [But] in an age when intentional childlessness, lone parenting, and non-nuclear and non-heterosexual family forms are commonplace, 'shared parenting' seems an anachronistic, even conservative, solution. Perhaps more significantly, it does nothing to challenge the ideology that caring is largely a private responsibility. [...]

A key part of the project of feminist ecological citizenship is to call for the democratization of the household so that household and caring tasks are divided fairly between men and women. [...] The other side of the coin is that caring work needs to be supported institutionally – by the state and by the market and in the workplace. [...] But I also think that another key part of the project should be principled feminist resistance to gender codes through the language and practice of citizenship. The project may thus involve the renewal of feminist consciousness-raising that inspires women to [...] claim the political identity of 'citizen'. As citizens, women activists in volunteer organizations might refuse being exploited and demand recognition through state support either direct funding or tax breaks. As citizens, when the tasks are being divided among members of a social movement organization women might challenge gendered assumptions about appropriate tasks for men and women. As citizens, women might resist social expectations that they should 'naturally' be able to take on ever-expanding loads of care [...]

And what about the men who write about ecological citizenship? Mouffe's (1992b) idea that citizenship can be an articulating principle for many social movements never deals with what feminists know through decades of social movement experience: even when the ideals of liberty, equality, and solidarity (formerly known as fraternity) are held in common, the masculinism of men persists. Lynne Segal's (1987) analysis, on the other hand, leads her to conclude that a coalition of feminists and left men, while necessary, will not work as long as the latter remain stuck in their patriarchal ways. She then argues that feminists should engage politically 'with' and 'against' men in left-wing social movements, that they should be neither their 'foes nor loving friends'. The same might be said about the pervasive (subtle and often denied) masculinism of many of the men who are the intellectual leaders of the green movement. Some have taken ecofeminists and feminist ideas on board (e.g., Barry 1999; Dobson 2003), and it would be counter-productive not to give credit where it is due. But fruitful conversations between the green men and ecofeminists' theorists [...] have thus far been lacking. [...] The way to challenge the fact that care is 'irrelevant to the moral life of the powerful' (Tronto 1993, 89) is not to claim it is as women's special gift but, rather, to assert it as a political ideal that no democratic and sustainable society can do without. If we accept Mouffe's (1992a, 225) suggestion that 'the way we define citizenship is intimately linked to the kind of society and political community we want', then gender-blind green men must be called to account for why an analysis of masculinist privilege has thus far been absent in their definitions.

References

Barry, J. (1999) *Rethinking Green Politics*, London: Sage.

Dobson, A. (2003) *Citizenship and the Environment*, Oxford: Oxford University Press.

Homer-Dixon, T. F. (1999) *Environment, Scarcity and Violence*, Princeton, NJ: Princeton University Press .

Kaplan, R. (1994) 'The coming anarchy', *Atlantic Monthly*, 274(2): 44–76.

Lister, R. (1997) *Citizenship: Feminist Perspectives*, New York: New York University Press.

Mies, M. and Shiva, V. (1993) *Ecofeminism*, London: Zed Books.

Mouffe, C. (1992a) 'Democratic citizenship and the political community', in *Dimensions of Radical Democracy: Pluralism, Citizenship, Community*, ed. C. Mouffe, 225–39. London: Verso

Mouffe, C. (1992b) 'Feminism, citizenship and radical democratic politics', in *Feminists Theorize the Political*, ed. J. Butler and J. W. Scott, 369–84. New York: Routledge.

Plumwood, V. (1995) 'Has democracy failed ecology? An ecofeminist perspective', *Environmental Politics* 4(4): 136–69.

Sandilands, Catriona (1999). *The Good-Natured Feminist: Ecofeminism and the Quest for Democracy*, Minneapolis: University of Minnesota Press.

Savarsy, W. (1992) 'Beyond the difference versus equality debate: Postsuffrage feminism, citizenship and the quest for a feminist welfare state', *Signs* 17(2): 329–63.

Segal, L. (1987) *Is the Future Female? Troubled Thoughts on Contemporary Feminism*, London: Virago Press.

Tronto, J. (1993) *Moral Boundaries: A Political Argument for an Ethic of Care*, New York: Routledge.

Sherilyn MacGregor

28 | Shopping for sustainability: can sustainable consumption promote ecological citizenship?

GILL SEYFANG

Gill Seyfang has conducted extensive work on sustainable consumption (the focus of this reading) covering issues as diverse as community currencies, Local Exchange Trading Schemes (LETS), personal carbon trading, fair trade, alternative indicators and evaluation methodologies. In this reading, Seyfang assesses whether 'shopping for sustainability' can provide practical insights for constructing *ecological citizenship* by emphasizing the 'responsibilities that citizens of the environment must bear'. By focusing on grassroots or citizen-led initiatives as well as on ethical trade and labour standards, Seyfang examines the dilemmas facing sustainable lifestyle projects and their resilience in the face of mainstream economic priorities, which remain oriented towards the goal of economic growth. This reading argues that ecological citizenship involves reducing unsustainable impacts by promoting reflection on environmental responsibility on the part of consumers and political decision-makers.

Introduction: citizenship in the supermarket

[...] Shopping and consumption behaviour are increasingly seen as a public arena of activism and the expression of citizenship, and environmentalists are encouraged to put their money where their mouth is and 'do their bit' by buying 'green' or 'ethical' goods – also known as sustainable consumption [...] This article critically examines sustainable consumption policy and practice in the UK in order to assess its effectiveness as a tool to allow people to make political decisions and put their environmental and social concerns into practice. In its traditional guises within liberalism and civic republicanism, citizenship is a public matter concerning the relationship between individual and state. While the environment can be incorporated into liberalism with a new language of environmental rights [...], other complementary discourses of environmentalism emphasise the duties and responsibilities that citizens of the environment must bear, and new political developments resulting from globalisation and feminism have forced citizenship to break free of the traditional boundaries, embracing the private sphere ('the personal is political!') and including action extraneous to government. This new 'postcosmopolitanism' incorporates what Dobson (2003) terms 'ecological citizenship' – a justice-based account of how we should live, based upon private and public action to reduce the environmental impacts of our everyday lives on others.

Dobson's ecological citizenship uses the 'ecological footprint' metaphor (Wackernagel and Rees, 1996) as a touchstone. Everyone takes up a certain amount of ecological 'space' in the sense of resource use and carrying capacity burden, and this space is expressed as a footprint on the earth. The ecological footprint of a Western consumer includes areas spread across the globe, and impacts upon people distant in space and time. The footprints of people within industrialised nations are generally much larger than those of, and indeed have negative impacts upon the life chances of, the inhabitants of developing countries. The burning of fossil fuels, for example, has multiplied almost fivefold since 1950, threatening the pollution-absorbing capacities of the environment, and the consumption differentials between developed and developing nations are extreme (UNDP, 1998). In this way environmental and social inequity and injustice are visualised. An ecological citizen's duties are therefore to minimise the size and unsustainable impacts of one's ecological footprint – though what is sustainable is of course a normative rather than technical question (Dobson, 2003). Dobson's ecological citizenship is non-territorial and non-contractual and is concerned with responsibilities and the implications of one's actions on the environment and on other, distant people – a similar model, called 'planetary citizenship', is put forward by Henderson and Ikeda (2004). Developing this idea into a practical network application, Alexander (2004) explains that 'Planetary Citizenship is about identifying with the Earth as a whole and the whole of humanity, about working towards a collaborative instead of a competitive world, with a re-shaped economy driven by social and environmental need rather than financial pressures'. In both these cases, the challenge is to find mechanisms and initiatives which enable and encourage people to act as ecological citizens, in other words, to reduce their ecological footprints. 'Sustainable consumption' appears to meet that need.

This article examines [...] the choices and actions which individuals and households make on a daily basis, in the supermarket and on the high street. It deals with changing consumption patterns, consumer behaviour and lifestyles, and how these relate to environmental and social demands for sustainability. 'Sustainable consumption' has become a core policy objective of the new millennium in national and international

Gill Seyfang

arenas, despite the fact that its precise definition is as elusive as that of its companion on the environmental agenda, sustainable development. Current patterns of consumption are, quite clearly, unjust and unsustainable; the extent and nature of the transformation required are hotly debated, reflecting as they do competing deep-rooted beliefs about society and nature (Seyfang, 2003, 2004a). For some, it is sufficient to 'clean up' polluting production processes and thereby produce 'greener' products (OECD, 2002; DEFRA, 2003); for others, a wholesale rethinking of affluent lifestyles and material consumption per se is required (Douthwaite, 1992; Schumacher, 1993). In both these conceptions of sustainable consumption, one of the principal actors for change is the individual consumer, regularly exhorted to 'do their bit' to 'save the planet' by purchasing recycled goods and demanding ethically produced products, for example (DETR, 1999). In this way, sustainable consumption is clearly identified as a tool for practising ecological citizenship – requiring individuals to make political and environmental choices in their private consumption decisions. Now that consumers, corporations, non-governmental organisations (NGOs) and policymakers are all accorded with the duties of citizenly behaviour, does this new age of responsibility result in more effective environmental stewardship? [...]

Sustainable consumption: shopping to save the planet?

The term 'sustainable consumption' entered the international policy arena in Agenda 21, the action plan for sustainable development adopted by 179 heads of state at the 1992 Rio Earth Summit. This was the first time in international environmental discourse that over-consumption in the developed world was implicated as a direct cause of unsustainability. The proposed solutions included promoting eco-efficiency and using market instruments for shifting consumption patterns, but it was also recommended that governments should develop 'new concepts of wealth and prosperity which allow higher standards of living through changed lifestyles and are less dependent on the Earth's finite resources and more in harmony with the Earth's carrying capacity' (UNCED, 1992: section 4.11). These two proposals – the former suggesting reform and the latter a radical realignment of social and economic institutions – represent competing perspectives of the nature of the problem and its solution, and illustrate some of the tensions inherent in a pluralistic concept like sustainable consumption. For present purposes, this article will refer to them as 'mainstream' and 'alternative' perspectives on sustainable consumption – see also Jackson and Michaelis (2003), Jackson (2004b) and Seyfang (2004a) for other reviews of sustainable consumption discourses.

Each approach holds promise as a tool for ecological citizenship, for enabling individuals to make political decisions with their consumption behaviour to reduce their ecological footprints and unsustainable impacts of their behaviour. This section of the study will discuss the mainstream policy approach to sustainable consumption as embodied in UK strategy, and critically assess its potential as a tool for ecological citizenship.

Mainstream policy frameworks for sustainable consumption

From its auspicious beginnings at Rio, the term 'sustainable consumption' evolved through a range of international policy arenas, and its definition narrowed as it became more widely accepted as a policy goal. The more challenging ideas became marginalised as governments instead focused on politically and socially acceptable, and economically rational, tools for changing consumption patterns such as cleaning up production processes and marketing green products. [...] The agenda has narrowed from initial possibilities of redefining prosperity and wealth and radically transforming lifestyles, to a focus on improving resource productivity and marketing 'green' or 'ethical' products such as fairly traded coffee, low-energy light bulbs, more fuel-efficient vehicles, biodegradable washing powder, and so forth. Hence sustainable consumption is implicitly defined as the consumption of more efficiently produced goods, and the 'green' and 'ethical' consumer is the driving force of market transformation, incorporating both social and environmental concerns when making purchasing decisions. This policy relies upon 'sustainable consumers' to demand sustainably produced goods and exercise consumer choice to send market signals, for example using consumer fora such as Green Choices (www.greenchoices.org), which promises 'a guide to greener living', Green Home (www.greenhome.com), an online store for environmentally friendly goods, and Ethical Consumer, the UK's alternative consumer organisation, which publishes investigations into firms' social and environmental records (www.ethicalconsumer.org). Ethical consumerism is a growing trend. The 2003 Ethical Purchasing Index reported that total sales of ethical products rose by 44% between 1999 and 2002 to £6.9bn, while the market share this represented grew by 30%. Boycotting and ethical non-consumerism was a major force among consumers too: 52% of consumers reported boycotting a product during the previous year, and two-thirds said they would refuse to buy a firm's products if it was associated with unethical practices (Demetriou, 2003) [...]

Market failures Given that mainstream sustainable consumption is a market-based tool for change, the effectiveness of this mechanism is the first thing to examine, and there are failures of pricing, measurement and information to consider. The present economic system externalises the environmental and social costs of economic activity, and so sends producers and consumers the wrong signals. For example, fuel prices do not account for the costs of climate change, and aviation fuel is subsidised further as it is not taxed. This unwitting subsidy that the environment makes to the economy ensures that particular activities, such as transporting food around the world by air freight, or maintaining a transport infrastructure geared for private motor cars, appear economically rational (Pretty, 2001). The UK strategy for sustainable consumption and production recognises this problem and indicates some areas where full-cost pricing is being introduced, for example through the landfill tax or climate change levy on energy (DEFRA, 2003). [...] Second, it is a truism that what gets measured, counts, and the key indicator of wealth (and proxy of well-being) is gross domestic product (GDP) which makes no distinction between those activities which enhance quality of life, and those which do not (expenditure on pollution clean-up technology, for instance). [...] Third, ecological citizens seeking to make their preferences known in the marketplace face several information barriers, for example a lack of information about environmental and social implications of consumption decisions, or issues of credibility and consistency of marketing information relating to sustainable products. Some of these are the targets of government action to improve market efficiency, such as public awareness campaigns and independent labelling schemes which seek to overcome these obstacles (Holdsworth, 2003).

Failing to make an impact A second set of problems which reduce the effectiveness of the mainstream sustainable consumption policy model as a tool for ecological citizenship is that even assuming an efficient market mechanism, the desired transformations can be elusive. The vulnerability of voluntary changes is a key problem. In the case of both green and ethical consumption, most corporations only responded to public pressure when their reputations or sales were at stake, thanks to activist groups such as Corporate Watch and Ethical Consumer. While consumer demand may be the carrot, it is high-profile and potentially damaging media reports into the less palatable aspects of firms' activities which provide the very necessary stick to prompt changes in corporate behaviour (Pearson and Seyfang, 2001). Even these voluntary changes are vulnerable to erosion and shifting trends. In the UK, Littlewoods clothing stores were a major participant in the Ethical Trading Initiative (ETI), but a change of management led to their withdrawal from the ETI and their ethical trading team being closed down, as corporate responsibility was not seen as an important issue to consumers (ETI, 2003). Green consumerism was a trend during the early 1990s, but as a result of changes in consumer preference during the 1990s, sales of 'green' ranges of products fell and many supermarket own-brand ranges of 'green' cleaning products, for example, were discontinued (Childs and Whiting, 1998). These examples suggest that the social or environmental improvements made as a response to consumer pressure have been rescinded as attention shifted, rather than taken up as new minimum standards, and that 'left to their own devices, [transnational corporations] are likely to fulfil their responsibilities in a minimalist and fragmentary fashion ... they still need strong and effective regulation and a coherent response from civil society' (UNRISD, 2000: 90).

A major criticism of the mainstream model of sustainable consumption through market transformation, from an ecological citizenship perspective, is that it is a citizenship of the market, and purchases are the only votes that count. Individuals may not be able to act on their ecological citizenship preferences for a variety of reasons, and therefore are unable to influence the market. These barriers include the affordability, availability and convenience of sustainable products, as well as feelings of powerlessness generated by the thought that individual action will not make any difference, disenchantment with corporate green marketing and preference for products that are not available, such as an efficient, clean and safe public transport system (Holdsworth, 2003; Bibbings, 2004). [...] Patterns of material consumption exercised through the marketplace embody multi-layered meanings above simple provisioning, for example aspirational consumption, retail therapy, self-expression, a need for belongingness, self-esteem, self-validation, a political statement, an ethical choice, status display, loyalty to social groups, identity, and so forth (Burgess *et al.*, 2003; Jackson, 2004b). Accordingly, these motivations may be incompatible with ecological citizenship desires for sustainable consumption.

Ecological citizenship entails reducing one's unsustainable impacts upon the environment and other people, and may therefore require an absolute reduction in consumption to reduce the size of ecological footprints, and quite different social institutions to facilitate those choices. How does the mainstream sustainable consumption model meet this need? One barrier to effectiveness is that 'institutional consumption' decisions are made on a societal level, rather than by individuals, and only products and brands with which consumers are familiar are subject to transformative consumer pressure. Institutional consumption, which

Gill Seyfang

includes producer goods, public procurement (purchasing by the state for building and maintaining roads, hospitals, schools, the military, and so forth, accounts for half of all consumption throughout western Europe) and most investment products, is extraneous to the hands of individual domestic consumers, according to Lodziak (2002). Levett et al. (2003) argue that while the market defines an ever-expanding range of goods and services to choose from, it cannot, by definition, offer choices external to itself. For example, a person might choose one brand of washing-machine over another because of its greater energy-efficiency, but what they cannot easily choose is to purchase collectively and share common laundry facilities among a local group of residents. Consumers are effectively locked in to particular consumption patterns by the overarching social structures of market, business, working patterns, urban planning and development (Sanne, 2002; Bibbings, 2004). Hence while ecological citizens struggle to use their limited influence to transform the market through mainstream channels, the constraining institutional factors which delimit the choices available are being reproduced societally, and the major consumption decisions are being made out of the public eye, away from market pressures.

An alternative strategy for sustainable consumption

Despite the direction the mainstream policy framework and the UK strategy for sustainable consumption have taken, the challenge laid down at Rio not only to promote greater efficiency in resource use, but also to realign development goals according to wider social and environmental priorities rather than narrow economic criteria, and to consider the possibilities of lifestyles founded upon values other than material consumption, has not fallen on deaf ears. These ideas are common among the 'new economics' or 'deep green' environmentalist literature, and include radical reorganising of economies to be more localised, decentralised, smaller-scale, and oriented towards human well-being and environmental protection (Robertson, 1990; Douthwaite, 1992; Ekins and Max-Neef, 1993; Schumacher, 1993). The central point of departure for the alternative approach to sustainable consumption is the question of economic growth. Mainstream strategies for sustainable consumption assume this is a necessary prerequisite, despite the failings of indicators such as GDP, as the discussion above has shown. These alternative sustainable consumption proposals entail cutting absolute levels of consumption in order to reduce the ecological footprints of modern industrialised societies – ideas which resonate strongly with ecological citizenship. [...] This alternative perspective on sustainable consumption currently exists largely outside the policy framework – its radical messages are not welcomed by policymakers, and with the exception of Agenda 21, no international strategies have embraced these ideas. Nevertheless they are strongly represented by networks of grassroots initiatives and community activists, many of them inspired by the Rio Summit itself, working to challenge existing practices, and create new social and economic institutions which allow people to enact these values in their daily lives (Shell Better Britain Campaign, 2002). [...]

The first example of new tools and instruments used by proponents of this perspective is indicators which redefine 'progress' and 'wealth' and create new national accounting mechanisms to reflect well-being, for example the Measure of Domestic Progress or MDP. This index finds that while GDP has increased rapidly since 1950, MDP has barely grown at all. The divergence is more noticeable in the last 30 years, as GDP has grown by 80% but MDP has fallen during the 1980s mainly due to environmental degradation, growing inequality and associated social costs, and has still not regained the peak achieved in 1976 (Jackson, 2004a). As this report states: 'every society clings to a myth by which it lives; ours is the myth of economic progress' (Jackson, 2004a: 1).

A second example of tools for alternative sustainable consumption is that of localised food supply chains. These aim to strengthen local economies against dependence upon external forces, avoid unnecessary global food transportation (cutting 'food miles') and reconnect local communities with farmers and the landscape. In the case of local organic production, there is the added environmental benefit of improved land management, and consumers identify organic food strongly with better health, nutrition, and food safety (Jones, 2001; Pretty, 2001; Saltmarsh, 2004). In these cases, consumers are overcoming the limitations of market pricing regimes by voluntarily internalising the normally externalised environmental and social costs and benefits of local organic food production, and are making consumption choices according to these new relative values rather than market signals. They are giving a positive value to local economic and social connectivity, environmental conservation, and known provenance and quality – in other words authenticity – and considering the negative costs of global food transportation, pesticide use and industrial agriculture. These consumers are clearly behaving as ecological citizens, seeking to reduce the size of their footprints, in the face of pricing patterns which encourage them otherwise. [...]

A third example of a tool to put the alternative perspective on sustainable consumption into practice is that of non-market exchange mechanisms, such as community currencies. Despite claims that commodification is

309

inevitably spreading and eliminating non-commodified exchange, there is evidence that non-market exchange (informal exchange networks and community currencies, recycling, second-hand goods, and so forth) is still a powerful force in industrialised economies (Williams, 2004). Furthermore, consumers choose these alternative exchange networks for a variety of reasons, not only affordability, but also to experience and strengthen the anti-materialist values that such consumption embodies (Seyfang, 2001, 2004c; Manno, 2002; Leyshon et al., 2003).

Collective currency initiatives to promote alternative models of economic exchange, needs-satisfaction and socially embedded development are plentiful. For example, time banks use time as a currency to build social capital and cohesion while nurturing reciprocity and mutual aid, and everyone's time is worth the same – a key attraction for socially excluded participants. They have grown rapidly in the UK in the last five years, and in 2002 there were 36 active time banks, with an average of 61 participants each, who had exchanged (given or received) a mean of 29 hours each. This equates to 2,196 participants in total, and nearly 64,000 hours exchanged (Seyfang and Smith, 2002). By 2004, there were 68 time banks up and running, according to Time Banks UK (www.timebanks. co.uk). Time banks promote engagement in community activities, and have great potential as enablers of civic engagement in public services provision and local decision-making. Local Exchange Trading Schemes (LETS) aim to build communities and strengthen local economies through a system of multilateral barter; they are usually community-run initiatives, whose members exchange goods and services for a virtual local currency. LETS has grown to about 300 schemes in operation at present, with an estimated 22,000 people involved and an annual turnover equivalent to £1.4m (Williams, 2000). [...] Nonmarket exchange is therefore a space for expressing political vision about economic, social and environmental governance – in other words, for ecological citizenship. Time banks and LETS have so far been small-scale initiatives, but both display great potential for achieving significant impacts in terms of enabling sustainable consumption and greater active citizenship if adopted on a wider scale. The main policy obstacles include interfaces with the tax and benefits systems, which penalise some participants who earn community currency, and a need for sustainable long-term funding to develop effective community social economies, as well as a need for government to recognise the shift in behaviour, consumption and attitudes that could emerge through utilising alternative exchange mechanisms. [...]

Conclusions

[...] Sustainable consumption has been proposed as a tool for encouraging ecological citizenship, which entails shrinking ecological footprints. The UK's sustainable consumption and production strategy embodies what is termed here a mainstream policy strategy reliant upon motivated consumers. A critical analysis of this approach has identified that the mainstream policy approach to sustainable consumption is an ineffective tool for ecological citizenship. However, it may be a useful first step along the path to greater reflection and awareness of sustainability issues and their relationship to individual behaviour, and is arguably a necessary complement to the alternative approach, and there is much that governments can do to improve its effectiveness. They can get prices right, improve information flows, measure appropriate indicators of progress, and introduce 'ratcheting up' regulation to prevent backsliding in social and environmental performance. Nevertheless, there are significant problems with an approach which burdens individuals with the responsibility for achieving sustainable consumption. [...] Therefore, to build a social context consistent with an enabled ecological citizenry, governments must look to the alternative perspective to sustainable consumption which aims to provide this context through radical changes to lifestyles, infrastructure and social and economic governance institutions, in order to redirect development goals and reduce absolute consumption levels – thereby reducing ecological footprints. [...] Ecological citizenship offers a practical, everyday framework for understanding and expressing action which reflects a sense of justice about environmental and social matters through collective efforts to change the institutions which reproduce unsustainable consumption. By combining improvements to the mainstream policy strategy with explicit support for a diversity of alternative approaches which build new social and economic institutions for consumption, governments could harness the energies of ecological citizens to make significant strides along the road to sustainability.

References

Alexander, G. (2004) 'Welcome to the Planetary Citizenship stream of T171 on the PlaNet weblog!', posted 18 February 2004, PlaNet. Available at: www.planetarycitizen.open.ac.uk (accessed 4 June 2004).

Bibbings, J. (2004) *High Price to Pay: Consumer Attitudes to Sustainable Consumption in Wales* (Cardiff: Welsh Consumer Council).

Burgess, J., Bedford, T., Hobson, K., Davies, G. and Harrison, C. (2003) '(Un)sustainable consumption', in F. Berkhout, M. Leach and I. Scoones (eds) *Negotiating Environmental Change: New Perspectives from Social Science*

Gill Seyfang

(Cheltenham: Edward Elgar), pp. 261–91.

Childs, C. and Whiting, S. (1998) 'Eco-Labelling and the Green Consumer', Sustainable Business Publications Working Paper, Bradford: University of Bradford.

DEFRA (Department for Environment, Food and Rural Affairs) (2003) *Changing Patterns: UK Government Framework for Sustainable Consumption and Production* (London: DEFRA).

Demetriou, D. (2003) 'Consumers embrace ethical sales, costing firms 2.6bn a year', *Independent*, 9 December, p. 6.

DETR (Department of the Environment, Transport and the Regions) (1999) 'Every Little Bit Helps: Are You Doing Your Bit?' (London: DETR). Available at: www.air quality.co.uk/archive/yourbit.pdf (accessed 11 December 2003).

Dobson, A. (2003) *Citizenship and the Environment* (Oxford: Oxford University Press).

Douthwaite, R. (1992) *The Growth Illusion* (Bideford: Green Books).

Ekins, P. and Max-Neef, M. (eds) (1993) *Real-Life Economics: Understanding Wealth Creation* (London: Routledge).

ETI (Ethical Trade Initiative) (2003) ETI Statement on Littlewoods and Ethical Trading Initiative Membership, press release, 24 January. Available at: www.ethicaltrade. org/pub/publications/2003/ 01–stmt-ltlwds/index.shtml.

Henderson, H. and Ikeda, D. (2004) *Planetary Citizenship: Your Values, Beliefs and Actions Can Shape a Sustainable World!* (Santa Monica, CA: Middleway Press).

Holdsworth, M. (2003) *Green Choice: What Choice?* (London: National Consumer Council).

Jackson, T. (2004a) *Chasing Progress: Beyond Measuring Economic Growth* (London: New Economics Foundation).

Jackson, T. (2004b) 'Models of Mammon: A Cross-Disciplinary Survey in Pursuit of the "Sustainable Consumer"', ESRC Sustainable Technologies Programme Working Paper Number 2004/1, Centre for Environmental Strategy, University of Surrey.

Jackson, T. and Michaelis, L. (2003) *Policies for Sustainable Consumption* (Oxford: Sustainable Development Commission).

Jones, A. (2001) *Eating Oil: Food Supply in a Changing Climate* (London: Sustain and Newbury: Elm Farm Research Centre).

Levett, R., with Christie, I., Jacobs, M. and Therivel, R. (2003) *A Better Choice of Choice: Quality of Life, Consumption and Economic Growth* (London: Fabian Society).

Leyshon, A., Lee, R. and Williams, C. (eds) (2003) *Alternative Economic Spaces* (London: Sage).

Lodziak, C. (2002) *The Myth of Consumerism* (London: Pluto Press).

Manno, J. (2002) 'Commoditization: consumption efficiency and an economy of care and connection', in T. Princen, M. Maniates and K. Konca (eds) *Confronting Consumption* (London: MIT Press), pp. 67–99.

OECD (Organization for Economic Co-operation and Development) (2002) 'Policies to Promote Sustainable Consumption: An Overview', ENV/EPOC/WPNEP (2001)18/FINAL (Paris: OECD).

Pearson, R. and Seyfang, G. (2001) 'New dawn or false hope? Codes of conduct and social policy in a globalising world', *Global Social Policy* 1(1): pp. 49–79.

Pretty, J. (2001) 'Some Benefits and Drawbacks of Local Food Systems', briefing note for Thames Valley University/Sustain AgriFood Network Inaugural Seminar and Meeting, 2 November.

Robertson, J. (1990) *Future Wealth: A New Economics for the 21st Century* (London: Cassell).

Saltmarsh, N. (2004) *Mapping the Food Supply Chain in the Broads and Rivers Area* (Watton: East Anglia Food Link).

Sanne, C. (2002) 'Willing consumers – or locked-in? Policies for a sustainable consumption', *Ecological Economics* 42: pp. 273–87.

Schumacher, E. F. (1993 [1973]) *Small is Beautiful: A Study of Economics as if People Mattered* (London: Vintage).

Seyfang, G. (2001) 'Community currencies: small change for a green economy', *Environment and Planning* A 33(6): pp. 975–96.

Seyfang, G. (2003) 'From Frankenstein Foods to Veggie Box Schemes: Sustainable Consumption in Cultural Perspective', Centre for Social and Economic Research on the Global Environment Working Paper, EDM 03–13, CSERGE, University of East Anglia, Norwich.

Seyfang, G. (2004a) 'Consuming values and contested cultures: a critical analysis of the UK strategy for sustainable consumption and production', *Review of Social Economy* 62(3): pp. 323–38.

Seyfang, G. (2004b) 'Local Organic Food: The Social Implications of Sustainable Consumption', Centre for Social and Economic Research on the Global Environment Working Paper, EDM 2004–09, University of East Anglia, CSERGE, Norwich.

Seyfang, G. (2004c) 'Bartering for a Better Future? Community Currencies and Sustainable Consumption', Centre for Social and Economic Research on the Global Environment Working Paper, EDM 2004–10, University of East Anglia, CSERGE, Norwich.

Seyfang, G. and Smith, K. (2002) *The Time of Our Lives: Using Time Banking for Neighbourhood Renewal and Community Capacity Building* (London: New Economics Foundation).

Shell Better Britain Campaign (2002) *The Quiet Revolution* (Birmingham: Shell Better Britain Campaign).

UNCED (United Nations Conference on Environment and Development) (1992) Agenda 21: The United Nations Program of Action from Rio (New York: UN Publications). Available at: www.un.org/esa/sustdev/agenda21.htm (accessed 16 January 2003).

UNDP (United Nations Development Programme) (1998) *Human Development Report* (Geneva: UNDP).

UNRISD (United Nations Research Institute for Social Development) (2000) *Visible Hands: Taking Responsibility for Social Development* (Geneva: UNRISD).

Wackernagel, M. and Rees, W. (1996) *Our Ecological Footprint: Reducing Human Impact on the Earth* (Philadelphia, PA: New Society Publishers).

Williams, C. C. (2000) 'Are local currencies an effective tool for tackling social exclusion?', *Town and Country Planning* 69(11): pp. 323–5.

Williams, C. (2004) *A Commodified World?* (London: Zed Books).

29 | Buddhist virtues and environmental responsibility in Thailand

MARK J. SMITH AND PIYA PANGSAPA

Mark J. Smith and Piya Pangsapa have used ethnographic research techniques to explore how culturally specific assumptions have effects on the meaning of ecological citizenship depending on when and where it is constructed. This reading highlights how a specific meaning of environmental responsibility depends on its inflection through cultures, in this case through Buddhist values in the Southeast Asian mainland. Theravada Buddhist religious values place a special emphasis on living a *good life*, and this reading highlights how Buddhist virtues such as *forgiveness* and *wisdom*, as part of Thai cultural values, can help us understand how environmental problems have been addressed in a non-Western context. This reading also highlights the conflicts that occur between development, community livelihoods and environmental sustainability.

§ Many of the environmental movements in Thailand have been defensive reactions against the effects of development, whether this has been the effects of dam construction and power plants to provide the energy supply for the Thai modernization project or the increased reach of transnational agribusiness and biotechnology companies into the rural areas. The context is shaped by a distinctively Thai form of politics and notion of development that takes environmental responsibility seriously (expressed in the idea of the *Sufficiency Economy*) and reinforced by the predominant Theravada Buddhist religious belief system that emphasizes well-being over materialist growth. Jim Taylor (1997) argues that the Buddhist concept of *Kamma*, intentional action with many consequences in the context of Buddhism, is a key part of understanding environmental issues. The everyday meaning of *Kamma* often focuses on the negative consequences of actions, although in Buddhist teachings it often emphasizes learning from mistakes within the context of action, speech and thought. Buddhism also stresses the interdependency of society and nature, the importance of a range of environmental virtues (such as restraint, generosity and kindness), and the need for developing a respectful approach to nature in communal life. In addition, powerful and wealthy individuals in the corporate and political sectors may also engage in merit-making behaviour.

For Swearer, whose work focuses on the relationship between Buddhism and environmental problems, the problems created by the asymmetries between globalizers and globalized demand not simply a quantitative answer but a qualitative one based on asking how it is possible to live a *good life*. In addition, the Buddhist belief system emphasizes the virtues of simplicity, compassion, loving kindness, empathy, and an awareness of suffering of all living things as well as of the land. In the context of Southeast Asia, notwithstanding the increase in materialism, Theravada Buddhism remains a key part of everyday discourse, in particular the importance of refraining from doing evil and seeking to do good. Underpinning these virtues and maxims is a belief in the need to maintain a cooperative relationship between society and nature where human beings are displaced from top of the ethical hierarchy (Swearer et al. 2004: 1–2). In many ways this is analogous to some conceptions of ecological citizenship (for example, Smith 1998: 96–100).

For David Engel, in his study of 'injury narratives' in Northern Thailand, Buddhist values led to distinctive ways of settling environmental disputes and remedying harms where locally sanctioned remediation processes existed without rights. The emphasis on duty and obligation applied to the victim as well as the injurer, and where compensation was judged to be appropriate it could sometimes be notional or less than the value of the harm inflicted. Victims would often accept such settlements as just because balance had been restored, in part through their acts of forgiveness and selflessness. However, as Engel concludes, one key problem that exists is the undermining of customary justice without its replacement by effective replacement in the Thai legal system (Engel 2007). In order to address the needs of rural communities, address environmental problems arising from development in the provinces and ensure that the benefits of economic growth were more fairly distributed, rural monks have become involved in community-based projects. These 'development monks' sought to preserve Thai culture by linking Buddhist values to development projects but also sought to provide a space to defend cultural identity and community rights. Anan Ganjanapan highlights how some ceremonies involving donations also have a redistributive function within communities (Ganjanapan 2000: 6–7).

NGOs engaged in advocacy work, project development and activism in Thailand, such as the long-established Thailand Rural Reconstruction Movement, Wildlife Fund Thailand and initially Greenpeace Southeast

Asia, have been primarily concerned with the effects of economic development on rural livelihoods and the step-by-step encroachment of environmental resources that have hitherto been treated with respect by the communities sustained by them. The attitude of local Thais to forests in many areas of the North is to view them as sacred places. In line with Buddhist beliefs, those that draw on the forests and land are inhabited by spirits or guardians, requiring the performance of rituals to request permission before they engage in foraging, collecting wood, tree-felling, constructing buildings and even for pilgrimage, believing that the forest and land have spiritual value. This encourages respect for the environment but also helps to create a sense of responsibility to ensure the same resources will be available for the future.

Sophon Suphaphong, along with other leading political and business figures, sponsored the Thailand Environment Institute (established in 1993), a think-tank devoted to linking grassroots activism to scientific and policy work in order to provide environmental training and aware-ness. It also has close connections within the urban elite, including the President of TEI, Phaichitr Uathavikul, former Minister of the Ministry of Science, Technology and Environment. More recently, the TEI has become an important advocate of public–private partnerships and the participatory approach to environmental responsibility while at the same time focusing on poverty alleviation. An interesting feature of TEI work is to link up to transnational initiatives on political participation and stakeholding. Like the Thailand Development Institute, the TEI has a technocratic orientation that ensures that many of their policy proposals are geared towards general rules for environmental management and information systems rather than working with the plural groups and localized information.

The traditional approach of environmental management has been oriented towards state control of resources although many commun-ities living in designated conservation areas have often discovered that environmental policy has ignored or had adverse effects on their needs. There have been conflicts over forest, land and water resources – the development of hydroelectric dams on Thai rivers led to ongoing protests, especially in times of drought, while the 1989 logging ban supported by conservationist environmental discourses (as part of a strategy for refores-tation) ignored considerable encroachment by established interests that are linked to the main political parties but still severely restricted the ability of rural communities to use forest resources. Where the ban was enforced it had a disproportionate effect on the rural poor and the hill tribes in the border regions. Similar problems emerged in actions by state officials and the military in the Kho Cho Ko programme to resettle village communities in areas severely affected by deforestation. Some relocations took the form of forced displacement (including burning down villages and temples to ensure that the villages could not be easily re-established), producing large-scale protests in Bangkok. Their inventive demonstration tactics included lying flat out in rows on the pavement to imitate corpses, raising detailed placards explaining their situation, placing life-size papier mâché figures of monitor lizards symbolizing human vileness and misfortune in their march against relocation schemes and irrigation projects that degrade the land and marine environment.

According to Pinkaew Laungaramsri (2002), movements against the Nam Songkram dam developed a broad base of support by mobilizing cultural identity. She highlights the sentimental form of identification, *Watthanatham Pladaek*, or the culture of fermented fish, *pladaek*, which highlights how culture is understood as a practice of doing rather than an ossified set of beliefs, and stresses the vital role of river resources in daily life in Isaan culture (although the urban classes call fermented fish *plalah* instead of *pladaek*, which is used primarily by provincial peoples or rural farmers referred to as *chao baan, chao na*). In the protests covered by Manit Sriwanichpoon, Assembly of the Poor members repeatedly stressed the importance of fermented fish culture as part of their livelihood and would hold up jars of the strong-smelling fish (comparable to fermented cheese) as they marched in front of the House against the decision that would allow the Pak Mun Dam sluice gates to be open for only four months a year. One woman farmer held up a placard that was a symbolic expression of their plight. The placard read 'Don't destroy Fermented Fish Culture' and displayed a picture of 'a natural rock pool that re-emerged from under the dam lake after the sluice gates were open, allowing villagers to go fishing there as they used to' (Sriwanichpoom 2003: 142). Villagers also acted out plays in front of the Government House in an attempt to give those in power 'some understanding of their traditional fishing life' (ibid.: 143). Deane Curtin (1999) has highlighted similar examples in South Asia where wildlife conservation measures often deprive local communities of the customary rights to livelihood. This highlights the crucial role played by NGOs as potential mediators between grassroots activism and more generalized political structures, environmental research institutes, and the mass media.

We should also bear in mind that many NGOs that play a stakeholding role are unrepresentative of the groups that they seek to protect. Many NGOs were founded externally to Thailand, such as WWF and Greenpeace. While they often provide movements with valuable social capital, their social composition and the backgrounds of key workers and volunteers are often quite different from the interests and communities with which they engage and seek to represent. Nevertheless, they often provide an important link between grassroots movements and political authorities as well as corporations, as well as providing skills that local movements lack such as report writing, lobbying and coordination (Pfirrman and Kron 1992; Hirsch 1998). In terms of issue focus, environmental NGOs have also found that campaign allies are likely to be preoccupied with community and livelihood issues. For NGOs heavily influenced by Western environmental issues there is also the problem of discursive dissonance between their stated objectives of environmental protection (sometimes regarding the environment as a pristine space that should not be interfered with rather than an evolving ecosystem inhabited by existing stakeholders) and the concerns of local communities, peasant farmers and local NGOs run by local leaders and often by monks. In turn, local campaigners concerned with social justice issues have at times viewed environmental NGOs as having views that are too distanced from conditions on the ground.

Some of the early environmental campaigners were social entrepreneurs from some of the wealthiest families. Khunying Chodchoy Sophonpanich's (daughter of the founder of Bangkok Bank) campaign emerged when Bangkok was classed as one of the five dirtiest cities in the world. The *Ta Viset*, 'Magic Eyes', anti-litter campaign initially campaigned for children to police their parents' and community's behaviour then later diversified into recycling projects. The Magic Eye campaigns established links between children, school teachers, families and communities to promote awarenesss of the need for recycling when there were few opportunities and no requirements for recycling – Magic Eye's glass bottles campaigns aimed to reduce landfill by 8%. The campaign was formally instituted as an NGO, the Thai Environmental and Community Development Association, in 1986. TECDA has a capacity-building focus, initially working in Bangkok and later in the province's schools, but now only becomes directly involved when new schools join. The campaigns have also diversified into environmental education such as the Prem Tinsulanonda Centre's 'MagicEyes' barge programme, which creates outdoor opportunities for children to study wildlife and the ecosystem of the Chao Phraya river. The campaign now works on environmental awareness of water pollution and deforestation as well as project consultancy, such as advising on integrated waste management systems in Phuket. The success of the programme in promoting personal and community responsibility has, in part, been the result of the campaign, tapping into Thai culture

– in particular, the shame of losing face (*seayah naah*), whereby citizens were embarrassed if they were seen dropping litter, thus linking Buddhist values to action through citizens coming to understand the reasons for it, but also being able to ensure compliance through moral coercion.

These distinctive kinds of environmental action draw on Buddhist understandings of wisdom in the context of environmental responsibility and demonstrate the culturally specific possibilities of virtues tied to 'right behaviour' in a non-Western context. Buddhism provides a template for wise action rather than suggesting that a specific outcome is of itself wise or not. In addition, being wise is seen in Buddhist thinking as a combination of *vijja* (awareness) and *panna* (wisdom) – that wisdom is the deliberative outcome of a deeper knowledge of a specific environmental problem in a particular context. Wisdom (*panna*) in this tradition is also associated with a specific understanding of the idea of 'suffering'. In some ways, wisdom in Buddhism is analogous to the Western conception of prudence or practical wisdom and the cultivation of virtues that enhance both collective and individual improvement and development. However, rather than being fearful of change, the Buddhist conception embraces it as part of nature, humanity and the interdependent relations between them. Thus we can see that the meaning of wisdom as a virtue is context-dependent, based on distinctive philosophical traditions in different cultural contexts, often compounded by deeper religious differences.

References

Curtin, D. (1999) *Chinnagounder's Challenge: The Question of Ecological Citizenship*, Bloomington: Indiana University Press.

Engel, D. M. (2007) 'Globalization and the decline of legal consciousness: torts, ghosts, and karma in Thailand', *Thailand Law Journal*, (10)1.

Ganjanapan, A. (2000) *Local Control of Land and Forest: Cultural Dimensions of Resource Management in Northern Thailand*, Regional Centre for Social Science and Sustainable Development, Chiang Mai: Chiang Mai University.

Hirsch, P. (1998) 'Community forestry revisited: messages from the periphery', in M. Victor, C. Lang and J. Bornemeier (eds), *Community Forestry at a Crossroads: Reflections and Future Directions in the Development of Community Forestry*, Bangkok: RECOFTC.

Laungaramsri, P. (2002) 'Competing discourses and practices of "Civil Society": a reflection on the environmental movement in Thailand and some implications for the Mekong Region', Mekong Dialogue Workshop International, transfer of river basin development experience: Australia and the Mekong Region, 2 September, Regional Centre for Sustainable Development and Social Science, Faculty of Social Sciences, Chiang Mai: Chiang Mai University.

Pfirrman, C. and D. Kron (1992) *Environment and NGOs in Thailand*,

Bangkok: Thai NGO Support Project and Friedrich Naumann Stiftung.

Smith, M. J. (1998) *Ecologism: Towards Ecological Citizenship*, Buckingham: Open University Press.

Sriwanichpoom, M. (2003) *Protest*, Bangkok: Manit Sriwanichpoom.

Swearer, D. K., S. Premchit and P. Dokbuakaew (2004) *Sacred Mountains of Northern Thailand and Their Legends*, Chiang Mai: Silkworm Books.

Taylor, J. (1997) 'Thamma-chat: activist monks and competing discourses of nature and nation in northeastern Thailand', in P. Hirsch (ed.), *Seeing Forests for Trees: Environment and Environmentalism in Thailand*, Chiang Mai: Silkworm Books.

30 | Corporate environmental responsibility and citizenship

MARK J. SMITH AND PIYA PANGSAPA

With the decline of state regulation and the emergence of
self-regulation in the corporate sector (endorsed by the United
Nations Global Compact), environmental responsibility has
become a major concern, especially for companies engaged in
outsourcing production in distant parts of the world. Here, Mark
J. Smith and Piya Pangsapa outline the potential for transforming
corporate social and environmental responsibility into corporate
citizenship, part of their ongoing project to develop new forms of
responsible politics. The focus is on developing effective mechanisms for holding companies accountable for their decisions
and activities in the global supply chain. Decisions in Western
company boardrooms can have significant effects on distant
communities in developing countries as well as in the developed
world. In particular, this reading highlights how the affected 'constituencies' should be incorporated as stakeholders in the internal
structures of transnational private corporations.

§ Here we consider how private corporations have responded to the
challenge of constructing, implementing and monitoring codes of responsible conduct in relation to the environment. The development
of corporate responsibility and more recently corporate citizenship is
central to effective action for environmental sustainability. Corporate
environmental responsibility statements are increasingly linked in the
marketing of specific brands, with companies being prompted to rethink
the sourcing of products and packaging in terms of environmental sustainability, fair trade and the protection of human rights and labour
standards. The idea that corporations should have obligations towards
those affected by their decisions is not new – it was embedded in state
regulation before globalization became such a burning issue. However,
as Korten (1995) and Richter (2001) demonstrate, the classification of
companies as 'natural persons' entitled to protection within the terms
of the US Bill of Rights already created scope for corporations to take

advantage of the entitlements of citizenship without necessarily having the responsibilities possessed by individual citizens.

The internationalization of capital and the emergence of neo-liberal policies that reined in the ability of states to legitimately regulate their actions led to a dramatic depoliticization of many areas that had hitherto been subject to state intervention. From 'the environment' and labour relations to welfare, housing and education, the rationale for state regulation was weakened so that unemployment, industrial relocation, poverty, homelessness and so on were portrayed as personal difficulties and not social problems, never mind global ones. States resorted to offering to reduce the burdens of regulatory practices and offering subsidies to attract increasingly mobile capital investment projects (including developing societies which did not want to inhibit industrial growth). Subsequently, 'the impetus for industry regulation shifted from the UN to the business and NGO community' (Richter 2001: 8). As confirmation of this trend, the final attempt to develop more comprehensive international regulations on the environment (drafted by UNCTC) as part of UNCED in Rio in 1992, with the aim of embedding these in Agenda 21, met effective opposition from key UN members and private corporations. In its place, the World Business Council for Sustainable Development provided some non-binding guidelines or recommendations on the environmental responsibilities of corporations. International regulation has been off the agenda, replaced by self-regulation within corporations or co-regulation with other civil society bodies. The tentacular character of global supply chains and the bargaining power of Western brand companies in relation to production, while making it notionally difficult to regulate and mobilize against, also present a unique opportunity if these corporations internalize a culture of obligation. This would ensure that they can respond to criticisms that corporate responsibility is no more than window dressing.

In many areas, companies see a strategic market advantage in adopting ethical standards, that the investment can be recouped by encouraging regulative regimes in national states that drive out competition from other companies that have not adopted initiatives couched in terms of responsibility. For example, in 2006 Vodafone, Unilever, BAA, the John Lewis Partnership, Tesco, Shell and eight other leading companies lobbied the UK government to adopt stricter regulations on climate change through the adoption of low-carbon technologies. These companies see themselves as 'first-movers' and wish to take advantage of market share growth. The method of reducing environmental impact throughout the product life cycle has become increasingly popular among companies with an expressed commitment to environmental responsibility. Clean Production Action is an NGO that works with environmental and public health advocates, trade unions, progressive companies and governments to promote the use of safer and cleaner products across their life cycle. Market-driven Extended Producer Responsibility (EPR) mechanisms, whereby a company finds it profitable to retain ownership and responsibility for a product throughout its life cycle through leasing it to consumers, not only produce customer loyalty but also secure environmental objectives. Avoiding the reputation of being an unsafe company is a key issue for many corporations.

Holding companies accountable

The transformation of the global supply chain has created new problems for holding companies accountable but has also generated a new awareness of the environmental issues and prompted the formation of a variety of NGOs and transnational activist networks specifically concerned to monitor the broad and narrow scope effects on the environment. At the intergovernmental level, the OECD, World Bank and United Nations (including the Global Compact initiative) have sought to bring together private corporations, environmental and other NGOs with national governments to encourage self-regulating corporate responsibility and better environmental performance (through environmental management systems, auditing tools, performance indicators and environmental reports). This has been more effective where the reputations (as an intangible asset) and efficiency of companies are at stake. Companies such as Nike have been increasingly derogated for being irresponsible (so much so, that many marketing departments in corporations use the buzzword 'NIKE-mare' as a worst-case scenario). There is also evidence that corporations are beginning to use the guidelines to connect environmental protection to social issues such as human rights. Current concerns include the effectiveness of top-down initiatives generating problems farther down the organizational hierarchy, as well as difficulties in coordination across different corporate sectors, between corporations and the role of small or medium-sized enterprises (where proximity to environmental problems is an important factor for success). The emergence of corporate citizenship has also led some companies to include affected constituencies in stakeholder deliberation with company structures becoming arenas for conflicts and negotiation, providing strategic opportunities for NGOs and environmental movements.

In the European Union, environmental responsibility is also promoted through political regulation. One of the most challenging regulatory ideas for the corporate sector is the 'polluter pays principle', which states that the costs of measures necessary to address the impact of a company on the environment should be borne by the company – that they should be reflected in the price of the goods and services. For some environmentalists, this involves passing on the costs of environmental protection to the consumers, but in a global market there are additional incentives for companies to change their manufacturing and packaging processes to maintain price competitiveness and reduce impacts. While the polluter pays principle internalizes environmental externalities in the production process or can be addressed through environmental taxes, addressing the precautionary principle demands a more robust response from corporations. This idea highlights the importance of forward thinking when production processes are being planned by seeking to avoid pollution, searching for alternatives and less degrading forms of activity and considering whether a particular production process is actually needed when the impacts will be substantive.

In England and Wales, the duty-of-care principle was incorporated into the 1990 Environmental Protection Act concerned with the transfer, treatment and disposal of controlled waste materials, including the requirement that waste can be handled only by a legal entity that possesses a waste management agreement licence. In addition, documentation must be provided to the Waste Regulation Authority, and the business or other institutions such as hospitals have a corresponding duty to identify where the waste is taken by registered carriers and visit the disposal sites to ensure compliance. In response to problems generated by illegal tipping (fly-tipping), under the 2005 Waste (Household Waste) Duty of Care regulations in England and Wales, householders have a duty to take all reasonable steps to ensure that their waste is passed to an authorized person. In addition, in 2006 the EU established new chemicals regulations (Registration, Evaluation and Authorisation of Chemicals – REACH) for 30,000 substances which came into effect in June 2007, whereby companies transporting controlled waste in excess of one tonne are required to register the process with a new body, the Chemicals Agency. In the case of the 3,000 hazardous materials where no alternatives exist, producers have to submit a research plan indicating their search for less hazardous alternatives. This points not only to the extension of the duty of care to individual citizens but also points to a convergence between the duty of care and the precautionary principle. In other words, what was once a matter of obligation is increasingly becoming a matter of duty.

From constituencies to stakeholders in the global corporate sector

Corporate responsibility is a stepping stone towards a more accountable corporate sector.

While corporate marketers promote brands through speaking the language of desire, the agents of justice seek to ensure that this includes an internalized set of obligations – that a politics of obligation can exist where corporate decision-makers understand the reasons for acting responsibly (as the right, good or virtuous thing to do). Zadek (2001) suggests that these NGOs, as 'not-for-profit' private organizations, create the possibility for civil regulation of 'for-profit' private organizations by developing intimacy and knowledge of the production process, seeking to influence corporate and state decisions through audits and management systems as well as through personal relations and media-savvy campaigns. He also highlights the fact that there are limits to corporate responsibility in terms of events and states of affairs beyond the control of corporate executives, and that companies cannot be blamed for only seeking to take on board social and environmental responsibility when it is commercially advantageous and/or viable. Corporate responsibility as a form of self-regulation provides the basis for setting standards for private corporations so that their conduct meets ethical and political standards.

Transnational private corporations have increasingly sought an appropriate balance between the interests of investment and market share strategy, shareholders and market value alongside environmental concerns and social obligations. In short, corporations have sought growth strategies that depend on securing the increased value of *intangible assets* such as reputations, confidence of stakeholders (investors, customers, regulators and employees), brand identities, talent, capacity for innovation, intellectual property, networks and relationships with clients. Company structures are thus arenas for conflicts and tensions between competing imperatives – and, as such, we should regard these as strategic domains in which there are advantages to be gained for the workforce and the demands of environmental movements (that is, if they develop stronger links and coordinate their activities). It is also useful to consider what constitutes a sound basis for environmental responsibility in a corporate context:

1 the construction of corporate policy on the environment that coordinates all the activities of the company, with measurable benchmarks or targets against which success can be identified;

2 coordinated responsiveness to the task throughout the company,

including adequate environmental leadership, open deliberative and integrative mechanisms within all parts of the company and transparent dissemination when a policy is achieved;

3 flexibility to allow for innovation in all parts of the company and adequate resources to aid implementation (a key indicator that the company board and CEO are taking the issue seriously);

4 understanding of the implementation of policy as a process rather than a static plan to accommodate improvements in internal corporate and external market and environmental knowledge.

One of the difficulties arises from different ways of thinking about 'ethical' and 'social' – for some, ethics covers both the organizational system and individual behaviour whereas, for others, ethics solely concerns the behaviour of members of the organization and is not relevant to the total impact of the organization's activities, impacts on stakeholders, and relevant constituencies. The latter provides a weaker basis for generating cultures of obligation. A key factor in ensuring accountability is the selection of appropriate performance indicators that match the objectives of the organization (i.e. in terms of its legally defined status and objectives) and the collection and analysis of relevant information while at the same time incorporating the aspirations of stakeholders (in part to ensure opportunities for revising both objectives and targets) by making sure that the methods are transparent, by measuring the scope of the audit, by providing quality assurance through specific auditors, and by communicating this information to all relevant parties. The AA1000 audit process involves the delivery of a social and ethical report that speaks to the objectives and targets while at the same time ensuring transparency to and seeking feedback from all stakeholders. The responsibility for this process is held by the governing body or committee of the organization in question, which may or may not include the stakeholders. In addition, stakeholders (including owners, trustees, employees, suppliers, partners or even customers, NGOs and public bodies) may have formal representation on the publicly recognized audit panel and/or be actually involved in the auditing process itself.

The ideological character of the debate on corporate responsibility and citizenship tends to polarize the two options of the corporate sector regulating itself voluntarily and the need for the state to regulate in a mandatory way. Each has positive and negative qualities. Self-regulation will work when it is genuine in both the operational and participatory sense but suffers from flaws when the company objectives produce decisions that bypass responsible actions. State regulation would work in situations where the political authorities have leverage over a company's decision-making processes but, in a global economy, if companies decide that regulations are onerous then capital flight leads to the redeployment of problems in other political as well as social and environmental spaces. Initiatives such as SA8000 and AA1000 are interesting developments for they offer practical ways to address these difficulties in the global supply chain and the externalities that result from the production, distribution and exchange of commodities. As a result, future research should focus on the intersections between intergovernmental, state and civil society initiatives as well as highlighting the potentialities for effective verification and more inclusive stakeholder consultations.

References

Korten, D. C. (1995) *When Corporations Rule the World*, West Hartford, CT: Kumarian Press.

Richter, J. (2001) *Holding Corporations Accountable: Corporate Conduct, International Codes, and Citizen Action*, London and Sterling, VA: Zed Books.

Thompson, G. F. (2005) 'Global corporate citizenship: what does it mean?', Paper presented at The Open University, Milton Keynes.

Zadek, S. (2001) *The Civil Corporation: The New Economy of Corporate Citizenship*, London: Earthscan.

31 | Strategic thinking and the practices of ecological citizenship: bringing together the ties that bind and bond

MARK J. SMITH AND PIYA PANGSAPA

In this reading, Mark J. Smith and Piya Pangsapa respond directly to the arguments of Andrew Dobson (see Reading 24) on the meaning of ecological citizenship and whether it is feasible and sensible to separate morality and politics. Like Sherilyn MacGregor (see Reading 27), they argue that, when considering the concrete strategic situations faced by environmental activists, NGOs and individual citizens, it is more useful to consider their *ethico-political* responses. Unlike academic theorists, these environmental actors often draw upon a variety of ethical traditions and standpoints as well as inventing their own. In the process, they link these ethical assumptions to political activity in hybrid and innovative ways, often very effectively as part of their campaigns. In addition, Smith and Pangsapa's work explores how activist networks constructed between NGOs, policy-making communities, state authorities, community groups, and local and regional campaigns on gender, labour and environmental issues explicitly link social and environment justice. Rather than start with philosophical or theoretical assumptions, they argue (based on the postulate of adequacy) that the second-order constructs of researchers should draw on the first-order constructs of everyday life and that our outputs as researchers should be intelligible to the people they study.

§ The debate on environmental and ecological citizenship provides an important opportunity for us to explore the relations between ethical and political discourses and to consider how the ideas of moral community and political community are articulated. Two options for exploring the relations and ideas have emerged. First, privileging philosophy, particularly environmental ethics, as a guide to the normative conduct of politics, alongside suggestions for expanding the moral community so that future generations (Kavka and Warren 1983), non-human animals (Regan 1984), living things (Goodpaster 1983) or varying conceptions of broader ecosystems (Leopold 1949; Naess 1973; Devall and Sessions 1985) receive moral consideration. Grounding ecological citizenship in the application of a specific tradition of environmental ethics, such as utilitarianism or deep ecology, however, often assumes that there are universal principles that can be applied to all cases. The second option draws from political theory and develops conceptions of the political community to establish realistic objectives through which environmental or ecological citizenship can be achieved while also squeezing the gap between 'law and justice' (Dobson 2003; Bell 2005) and pushes us towards a strategic concern with the gap between values and action. Here we argue that ethical concerns are also better understood in the context of application. The actors involved in environmental action may subscribe to a heady mix of religious values, utilitarian logic, a Kantian sense of injustice (i.e. 'why should I not be treated like everyone else?'), ecological consciousness, and even endorse a range of virtues from prudence to temperance. The ways in which these are manifest are often hybrid and analytically inconsistent. Nevertheless, the hybrid expressions of ethical judgements can be just as effective as a basis for action and as a basis for achieving change in environmental policy.

Academic researchers often impose rationalist conceptions of actual or ideal political or moral communities, where everyone has the same opportunity to initiate speech acts, interrogate, open debate, or make judgements in the 'original position'. These approaches, however, relegate concern for the environment in terms of 'content' rather than form, and neglect the actual processes of civic engagement in the concrete strategic situation. In addition, they rest their case on a conception of the citizen as a rational 'minimaxing' actor who makes decisions according to rational calculations and who assumes that other actors will do likewise. This simplification of human action to one ideal type, rational action, is a simplistic exaggeration of one human trait. Certainly, the application of incentives has led to greater compliance with certain environmental policy measures, but it has not always generated a sense of responsibility that leads to changes in other aspects in the lives of citizens. The assumptions behind these measures not only present us with an unrealistic account of how citizens behave, but also neglect a range of so-called 'non-rational' motivations that can have environmentally beneficial effects. Many environmental actions are seen as being in the self-interest of citizens, such as installing energy-efficient light bulbs and solar panels in households or utilizing other energy conservation measures. The adoption of similar measures by companies, and applied to the whole life cycle of their products and services, is part and parcel

329

of ecological modernization. Yet many of these actions do not lead to changes in understanding. Citizens may adopt energy conservation techniques simply as a way of reducing their fuel bills rather than out of a concern for the environment, and may not even be aware of the causes and far-flung effects of climate change. Likewise businesses may adopt life-cycle analysis and promote recycling of their products but do so to cut costs and improve profitability. Moreover, these measures do not necessarily affect other activities by citizens or corporations unless immediate interests are at stake. Environmental action seeks to use levers that discourage particular actions while encouraging others, but less attention is paid to whether citizens understand the reasons for acting responsibly. We need to challenge both philosophy-centred and politics-centred approaches in favour of a strategic orientation that focuses on how ethical and political *elements* are articulated in 'modes of citizenship', whether these are civil, political, social or ecological (Roche 1992; Christoff 1996; Smith 1998), and transformed into *moments* where these conceptions have the temporary appearance of permanence, generating 'subject positions' in which individuals can invest their identities. Rather than treating *citizenship* as an abstract conceptual device, we argue that it is better understood as an *ethico-political space* where the right, the good and the virtuous are acknowledged as provisional, open to contestation and subject to deliberation.

Opinion research has often indicated that individuals have broad commitments to addressing climate change, the safe storage and disposal of hazardous wastes, to promoting renewable energy sources, and to reducing pollution levels. At the same time, studies of behaviour often do not demonstrate how attitudes generate activities that lead to environmentally responsible actions, especially when the means of resolving a problem (waste incinerators, wind farms, nuclear waste storage facilities, highway construction projects to reroute traffic from population centres, or indirect impacts such as the fall in employment opportunities) are perceived as having an adverse effect on a particular community generating localized NIMBY ('not in my backyard') responses. Also, they do not account for the gaps between knowledge and understanding of the processes of climate change and personal decisions to invest in motor vehicle transportation over long distances between home and work or in holiday travel that requires long-haul flights to different parts of the world. Indeed, environmental awareness is often associated with the desire to be closer to nature, to have access to green spaces and experience environments that are in many cases unlike the ones with which we are familiar. Parents move their families from urban areas to suburban or rural ones in the desire to have a better environment for their children to grow up in, consequently having to commute long distances to work in order to maintain their 'nouveau-environmental' lifestyles.

In many developed societies, researchers and governments often equate the problem of a lack of civic engagement on environmental issues simply with a lack of awareness of environmental issues (Barr 2003), and point out that knowing the facts often leads to attitudinal change and, in turn, in a linear way, to more responsible behaviour. Certainly, the possession of practical knowledge (such as 'knowledge of' vegetable gardening and animal husbandry in the slow food movement) provides a basis for responsible action, and this can be a significant factor, as opposed to 'knowledge about' (James 1890), i.e. general abstract knowledge of climate change or the effects of toxic chemicals. This ignores two important issues, however: that a range of other factors may be involved; and that citizens accept, modify and reinterpret the information provided by scientists, governments, NGOs and other sources, in the everyday discourses through which they make sense of the world (Burningham and O'Brien 1994). Rather than just focus on the search for empirical regularities between attitudes and behaviour, it is crucial to examine the intentions of actors and the tacit knowledge or the taken-for-granted assumptions of citizens. In addition, psychological approaches tend to consider actors in individualistic terms rather than as citizens that may be individuals, corporations, NGOs, unions or movements. All of these 'citizens' should not be viewed as solely operating in the private sphere but also seen as making interventions in the public sphere, participating in partnerships with political authorities while also simultaneously engaging in self-regulation. The construction of ecological citizens is better seen as involving new ways of producing the meaning of entitlements and obligations, whereby values and action inform one another in culturally specific ways but are also shaped by open and tolerant discussion that does not ignore the passions and commitments involved in environmental activism. In more concrete terms, the precise configuration of entitlements and obligations (and whether these should be reciprocal) will be subject to negotiation. And in the strategic context of ethico-political discourses, subject positions provide the means through which politics is lived. The *return to virtues* in ethical and political discussions on the environment (Barry 1999; Dobson 2003) offers interesting ways of rethinking the meaning of obligation, where the cultivation of the character of the self acts as a route for the regard of others. This chapter argues, however, that we should not treat one kind of virtue – compassion, courage, practical wisdom or justice – as

331

the basis of all other virtues. There are plenty to choose from that are directly relevant to environmental problems.

Andrew Dobson (2003) draws on Vandana Shiva (1992) to argue that the constitutional asymmetries should be factored into globalization processes at the start, and not added to a picture of a more interconnected world developed by theorists of cosmopolitanism. The effects of social and economic changes in advanced countries are global, but this does not necessarily mean that the processes work both ways. In addition, the focus on networks and flows tends to ignore the differential power of the actors in negotiations and bargaining at the international level – the experience of time–space compression is enjoyed by those who have the privilege of belonging to the gated communities of industrial societies (the globalizers) rather than those on the outside (the globalized). These asymmetries within current generations and the lack of reciprocity are analogous to those identified in debates on obligations to future generations (Barry 1978).

Dobson suggests that some kinds of cosmopolitanism offer the hope of resistance to the asymmetrical tendencies of actual globalization and heralds the possibility of constructing political communities beyond the nation-state that can be achieved through social bonding through a commitment to open dialogue (with the creation of institutional conditions for realizing this), so that all participants are recognized and can voice their concerns. This approach focuses on the human community, assumes that impartiality is the modus operandi, and posits that greater or more intense dialogue is the democratic objective. Bonding develops the sense of belonging to the human community and the duties this entails. We are obliged to act with regard to the needs of strangers out of *compassion* and charity – the 'good Samaritan' principle of global citizenship. For Dobson, this not only leaves obligations hanging (as charity can be withdrawn or even reproduce the vulnerability of the recipient), but it lacks a specific mechanism for addressing environmental harms, even if transnational dialogue can help crystallize the duty of protecting the vulnerable. What Dobson has in mind is a focus on specific communities of obligation, in other words obligation spaces with their own injustices and coerced dialogues. He argues that partiality is crucial for effective strategies to achieve more justice, so the objective should be to change the reasons for acting.

Other forms of cosmopolitanism have influenced Dobson's approach, such as the stress on the first virtue of more justice in response to harm (in addition to the commitment to open and uncoerced dialogue). Drawing on Simon Caney (2001), Dobson highlights how a theory of distribution can be defended by reference to a theory of moral personality, whereby entitlements to an equal share can be established *prior to* inhabiting culture, national identity or ethnicity. Such entitlements are viewed as being grounded in human autonomy or the possession of rights, the selection of which lends plausibility to his contention that this is 'a specifically political type of obligation as opposed to a more broadly moral type' (Dobson 2003: 29). This reasoning is portrayed as a more convincing basis for thinking through citizenship beyond the state, dealing in the *currency of justice rather than compassion*, but this approach also still lacks a clear idea of the reasons *why* we should act. He also argues that being obliged to do justice, to act in a way because it is *binding* rather than just bonding, is, for Dobson, a political rather than a moral obligation. Justice is thus portrayed as a *binding* relationship between equals rather than the one-way and revocable consequence of humanitarian obligations. Recognizing that morals and politics operate together in environmental activism does not mean, however, that this is mixing them up. Different values operate in different contexts and environmental movements and NGO activism can provide convincing explanations of environmental responsibility through appeals to ties that bond as well as bind. Bonding operates in many ways. It includes recognizing that human strangers deserve environmental quality and social justice combined as well as recognizing that we have the capacity to bond with other species and the physical environment they experience.

Dobson makes a distinction between moral obligations as a non-reciprocal commitment to others and political obligations as grounded in binding relationships based on some degree of parity, as well as between *specifically* political obligations and *general* moral obligations, with politics and morality also distinct in terms of scope. By grounding entitlements in autonomy and the possession of rights, this already assumes some understanding of rationality or species membership. The line drawn between politics and morality is asserted but not substantiated, suggesting that politics is ethics-free. Analytic distinctions clarify the precise kinds of ethical and political judgements, but assuming that they can be separated in substantive terms within everyday life is misleading. Passions and emotional attachment have always been and will always remain a key feature of environmental action. It is through passion that movements mobilize, it is through compassion that activists support each other even before they become friends, it is through culturally specific virtues that vary from place to place and it is because they care that they endure the defeats and celebrate the successes. Trust and commitment are also central to environmental action and processes

333

of accountability. That's why we say 'our word is our bond' and not 'our bind'. We agree that the ties that bind are an important corollary and essential in forming obligations into more established duties, but we should not exclude human bonding.

This also leads us back to the importance of the cultivation of characteristics that are virtuous. When we live in a 'community', we are simultaneously human and a citizen – what matters then is how these are defined and how they are articulated in the concrete situations of 'ineradicable antagonism' (Mouffe 2000, 2005; Smith 2005). Citizenly 'subject positions' are temporary respites in ongoing confrontations over the meaning of citizenship, and the virtues each subject position mobilizes are provisional. In agonistic democracy, struggles are staged around diverse conceptions of citizenship with each proposing its interpretation of the common good, right courses of action and virtues that should be cultivated. Ecological citizenship is just one way of engaging in 'the political'. The key task is to identify the potential and limits of subject positions that feature in environmental discourses following the *postulate of adequacy* (that the second-order constructs of social and natural scientists should draw from the first-order constructs of lived experience, and that the knowledge produced should be intelligible to those people in the context of the environments studied).

Artificially separating morals and politics smacks of the *attachment to detachment*, a key feature of disciplinary knowledge in Western societies (Smith 2000) that ignores the historical and social rootedness of environmental knowledge. To separate the community of citizens from the community of humanity (Dobson 2003: 27), or alternatively separating the currencies of justice and compassion, also potentially drives a wedge between values and action as well as obscuring the connections between environmental and social justice.

This treatment of the virtue of justice is comparable to the unification of virtues developed in Christian accounts privileging compassion or charity (along with faith and hope) over the classical virtues of courage, practical wisdom (prudence), justice and temperance. This kind of unification process is questionable. Instead, we need a more flexible framework that recognizes the codependence of and overlaps between virtues. Being compassionate depends on having courage, while being *just* depends on temperance – restraining materialistic appetites – as implied in Dobson's endorsement of ecological footprint analysis. In place of these thin and non-material cosmopolitan accounts of 'the ties that bind', he proposes post-cosmopolitanism, whereby the ties are materially (re-) produced in daily life within an unequal and asymmetrically globalizing context. As a consequence of globalization, relations once considered a matter of compassion are increasingly citizen relations. The provision of 'aid' in response to natural hazards should be seen not as benevolent acts of charity but compensatory justice, for the harm inflicted by industrial societies on others is a result of human-induced climate change, altering the nature and the source of obligation.

The arguments above alert us to the difference between obligations and duties as well as identifying the informal kinds of binding and bonding through which obligations are sustained. This approach avoids privileging one virtue, such as justice or compassion, over the range of different virtues (often combined) which may be relevant in each manifestation of citizenship (including environmental and ecological varieties). Practical wisdom (or prudence) is more compatible with the precautionary principle and notions of environmental stewardship than justice. Potential exists in using the virtues of temperance, kindness, generosity, humility, simplicity, gentleness, tolerance, forgiveness, self-sacrifice and even sadness (being resigned to one's fate). The list could be longer, but a brief scan of these should immediately demonstrate that they may or may not be articulated in terms of Dobson's case for justice as fair shares of ecological space. The key point is that notions of virtue are not simply imposed, they are cultivated as deliberate attempts to live up to regard for others (whether they are our adversaries or our friends). Fulfilling obligations is also an honourable act of self-regard, completing one's side of an agreement, living up to a mission, feeling good about one's reputation, being a 'good human being' or leading a flourishing life. There will be dilemmas when adjudicating upon the relative importance of one species compared to another (including the human species), but then ethical dilemmas are not absent from other approaches and we should not anticipate their absence here. We started out by stressing that citizens often articulate ethical and political ideas in hybridized and analytically inconsistent ways, so by focusing on concrete manifestations of 'the virtuous', 'the good' or 'the right' – along with the use of epistemological and aesthetic judgements – we can begin to understand how culturally specific antagonisms affect environmental debate and encourage us to treat other political subjects as adversaries we can respect rather than as enemies to confront.

Once we acknowledge that moral traditions, such as utilitarianism and Kantian contractarianism, simply offer guidance on particular problems in specific circumstances, rather than absolute solutions, then ethical standpoints can be understood as being relevant to definite spheres of existence, rather than suggesting that one form of morality is applicable across all forms of existence. As Christopher D. Stone suggests, the ethical act of becoming a vegetarian or preserving an acre of wilderness does not follow from the application of a single principle but makes sense only when it becomes part of an integrated 'network of mutually supportive principles, theories, and attitudes toward consequences' (Stone 1987: 242). The environmental priorities of each situation vary. Different ecological and cultural conditions prevail within a particular biome, so we should be suspicious of universal solutions and perfect answers; they are unlikely to be effective. We do not require a 'blueprint' – an ideal 'ecotopia' – worked out to the last detail, but we need to work towards a 'greenprint' – that is, a set of working principles that acknowledge the complexity, uncertainty and interdependency between society and nature in order to develop flexible strategies for change.

References

Barr, S. (2003) 'Strategies for sustainability: citizens and responsible environmental behaviour', *Area*, 35(3): 227–40.

Barry, B. (1978) 'Justice between generations', in P. Hacker and J. Raz (eds), *Law, Morality and Society*, Oxford: Clarendon Press.

Barry, J. (1999) *Rethinking Green Theory*, London: Sage.

Bell, D. (2005) 'Liberal environmental citizenship', *Environmental Politics*, 14(2): 179–94.

Burningham, K. and M. O'Brien (1994) 'Global environmental values and local contexts of action', *Sociology*, 28: 913–32.

Caney, S. (2001) 'International distributive justice', *Political Studies*, 49(5): 974–7.

Christoff, P. (1996) 'Ecological citizens and ecologically guided democracy', in B. Doherty and M. de Geus (eds), *Democracy and Green Political Thought: Sustainability, Rights and Citizenship*, London: Routledge.

Devall, B. and G. Sessions (1985) *Deep Ecology*, Utah: Peregrine Smith Books.

Dobson, A. (2003) *Citizenship and the Environment*, Oxford: Oxford University Press.

Goodpaster, K. (1983) 'On being morally considerable', in D. Scherer and T. Attig (eds), *Ethics and the Environment*, Englewood Cliffs, NJ: Prentice Hall.

James, W. (1890) *The Principles of Psychology*, vol. II, New York: Holt.

Kavka, G. and V. Warren (1983) 'Political representation for future generations', in R. Elliot and A. Gare (eds), *Environmental Philosophy*, Milton Keynes: Open University Press.

Leopold, A. (1949) *A Sand County Almanac – and Sketches Here and There*, Oxford: Oxford University Press.

Mouffe, C. (2000) *The Democratic Paradox*, London: Verso.

— (2005) *On the Political*, London: Routledge.

Naess, A. (1973) 'The shallow and the deep, long-range ecology movement', *Inquiry*, 16: 95–100.

Regan, T. (1984) 'The case for animal rights', in P. Singer (ed.), *Applied*

Ethics, Oxford: Oxford University Press.

Roche, M. (1992) *Rethinking Citizenship: Welfare, Ideology and Change in Modern Society*, Cambridge: Polity Press.

Shiva, V. (1992) 'The greening of global reach', *Ecologist*, 22(6): 258–9.

Smith, M. J. (1998) *Ecologism: Towards Ecological Citizenship*, Buckingham: Open University Press.

— (2000) *Culture: Reinventing the Social Sciences*, Buckingham: Open University Press.

— (2005) 'Obligation and ecological citizenship', *Environments*, 33(4): 9–23.

Stone, C. D. (1987) *Earth and Other Ethics: A Practical Politics of the Environment*, London: Routledge.

Summary of part four

MARK J. SMITH

The introduction and readings in this part highlight the increased focus on developing as well as developed societies and show that political change has to take place in the everyday lives of citizens, the organizations of companies and NGOs, the networks formed by environmental and social movements, and the institutions of governance, from the most local to those with (potentially) a global scope. Recognition of these developments comes from a shift in environmental action, the result of initiatives such as Local Agenda 21 and, more recently, Local Action 21. This also highlights the increased importance of political participation and civic engagement in the development of environmental policy and responsible actions at local, national and regional levels. In recent years these changes have been captured in the debate on environmental and ecological citizenship, where citizens appreciate their responsibilities – understanding the reasons for their duties and obligations as well as their rights and entitlements to, for example, environmental quality.

Of course, in many parts of the world, civic engagement is circumscribed and even risky, especially in less democratic societies. Yet even here, activism to link justice with responsibility has been achieved through transnational networks. Examples of local activist groups joining with transnational NGOs to apply pressure on national governments and transnational private corporations are myriad and growing. To provide a storyline or narrative for these changes, the readings in this part of the book demonstrate that our increased awareness of social and environmental injustices leads to new forms of environmental responsibility through civic engagement and the practices of citizenship. In short, for contemporary environmental issues to be addressed we need to integrate our understandings of ethics, policy and action.

Epilogue

MARTIN REYNOLDS, CHRIS BLACKMORE
AND MARK J. SMITH

Imagine a world where all waste is sorted and recycled so that there is no need for landfill sites, where all energy is produced from renewable sources and generates minimal or zero pollution, where biodiversity is increasing rather than decreasing, where all holidays enhance the ecological systems they affect. All this sounds a little idealistic and perhaps utopian, even fanciful; but this is the kind of world that environmentally responsible behaviour would create. If only it was that easy. In practice there are different environmental issues that demand different responses, there are other needs that conflict with the objectives of environmentalists, there are other motives that are arguably just as legitimate which do not promote environmental responsibility.

The readings making up this collection are selected from a vast and growing body of literature addressing issues of environmental responsibility in our changing world. We have brought together some quite different perspectives concerning ethics, policy and action associated with caring for our environment and bearing accountability for harm and wrongdoing. Our endeavour has necessarily been partial, but our purpose in providing this text is to signpost a path towards an improved constructive engagement with environmental issues from a standpoint of environmental responsibility. Throughout this collection we have sought to provide a narrative that might be used as a learning framework for thinking responsibly and creatively about the challenges of sustainable development in the twenty-first century.

In its most simplistic formulation, our framework is structured around three questions of environmental responsibility: first, the issues of what matters, as expressed in Part Two of this reader; second, the agency of responsibility, or who matters and in what sense, as discussed in Part Three; and last, the justification for responsibility, or why some issues matter more than others and why some stakeholder roles matter more than others, as reflected in the readings in Part Four. Raising these questions can help begin to counter often-expressed concerns about (i) complexity associated with many issues at stake; (ii) a need for engagement, through recognizing agency and building personal and collective stakeholding associated with such issues; and (iii) constructing the overall rationale and political space for actively and fairly addressing them – the justification for environmental responsibility.

For guidance on how these questions of what, who and why might be addressed, and, moreover, in an integral manner, we can draw on insights offered by traditions of philosophical ethics on how we ought to live, as applied to environmental issues. Three ethical traditions – consequentialist, deontological and virtue-based ethics – are identified in Part One of this reader (see the readings from Holbrook, Elliot and Connelly respectively). In turn, these traditions suggest three moral imperatives – doing good, doing the right thing and being virtuous. One message arising from the Part One readings, however, is that a focus on any one dimension of moral concern – the good outcome, the right course of action or the virtuous activity – can be pursued separately or in combination. For some these are separate pathways to environmental responsibility, but for others they may be compatible. A similar message comes from other parts of the reader. Reducing what is in focus to just one dimension risks losing sight of the bigger picture that is needed in order for us to contextualize our environmental actions and judge whether we are acting responsibly. The framework for responsibility suggested in Figure 1 is one way of trying to ensure that questions of environmental responsibility are addressed in an integral manner. It can be regarded as a device for synthesizing the questions and moral imperatives of environmental responsibility so as to bring out their respective interdependencies.

The framework provides one way of locating or situating particular ethically informed endeavours on issues of environmental concern and how those endeavours might relate to each other. If, for example, air quality is deemed an issue of concern (what matters and doing what's good), then we might anticipate that concern will follow around the agents of pollution, such as the individual and collective users and developers of industry and transport (who matters and doing what's right). Furthermore, concern around these issues and agents might be justifiable on the basis of a general virtue of environmental responsibility (why it matters and doing what's virtuous) – for example, it might be argued that they are of concern because we care for and bear accountability towards human and non-human flourishing. In actually addressing the issue of poor air quality, a utilitarian in a consequentialist tradition may focus on calculating the costs and benefits associated with different policy initiatives, a deontologist may be concerned more with setting a standard of air quality that applies to all (perhaps regardless of the benefits of some air

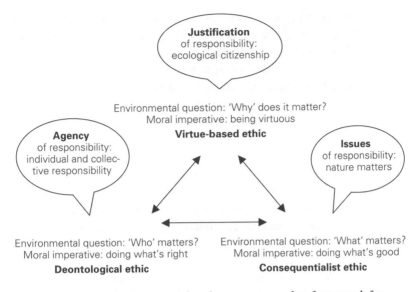

FIGURE 1 Environmental endeavours: towards a framework for environmental responsibility

pollution-causing activities), while a virtue-based approach might focus more on encouraging citizens to use less polluting fuel or companies to be more responsible for their emissions or political actors to deliver the objective of clean air.

While the three corners of the triangle in Figure 1 are founded upon ethical concerns related to readings in Part One, each corner might loosely be aligned with the particular emphases of contributors' concerns in Parts Two, Three and Four.

In Part Two the emphasis is on what issues matter: what is good (and what is harmful); what is of value? Such questions prompt a concern that is reflected in the readings regarding the direct perspective on nature and the duality between human and non-human worlds mediated through conceptual framing devices. Is responsibility served by the viewing of non-human nature as some pristine entity to be left alone or is it perhaps better served through a more hands-on managerial approach? Several contributors in this part suggest that what really matters for environmental responsibility are the implications of our distancing ourselves from nature, with communication (or 'conversing') with nature and about nature being a dominant theme.

Critical to our engagement with nature is the idea of continually developing value. So developing aesthetic values associated with the natural world, and capturing the value of interconnectedness, is important.

343

The readings in Part Two suggest how values may change, and new values emerge, through creative forms of framing. There is a need when framing the natural world to nurture new values that are a synthesis of, and an improvement upon, contrasting perspectives – between, say, science and arts, or between professional planners and radical activists. Issues such as climate change, energy, transport, pollution, poverty alleviation, biodiversity, animal rights and environmental justice are all concerns regarding what matters in environmental responsibility. They are all dependent on the perspectives taken on what matters and the context (for example, local, regional, national and/or global levels) in which these perspectives are taken. The natural or biophysical environment will be a part of this, but may not be the prime matter of concern for everyone. The important point is that we continually revise and improve upon our frames of reference.

This concern for perspectives is one shared among the contributors to Part Three. The emphasis here shifts towards perceptions among humans and the duality between individual and collective responsibility. These readings raise the impoverished notion of dualism; for example, regarding environmental issues as matters of either individual or collective responsibility. Focusing on human choices regarding safeguarding the commons (such as air, water and land), contributors express the importance of developing stakeholdings rather than protecting (individual or collective) stakes, and challenge the trend towards individualization. Ideas of meaningful social action, social learning and communities of practice in this part highlight the need for developing learning capacity among individuals and collectives in order to sustain environmental responsibility. While a deontological ethic emphasizes formal duties and rights (which can often lead to entrenched, static questions of whose duties and whose rights are involved), the readings in Part Three raise possibilities of using existing formalized expressions of duties and rights in less formal and more creative ways, and of negotiating and developing new duties and rights.

The Part Four readings engage more with the political realm in terms of governance and legitimate political participation in matters associated with environmental responsibility. The readings here signal important new debates on how responsibility relates to environmental justice and ecological citizenship. Institutional forms of governance and protest vary between countries of the global North and those of the global South, and can change and develop depending on the wider cultural and ecological circumstances. The importance of meaningful civic engagement with environmental issues in different policy domains as much as in the context of activism and protest is, however, a concern raised by many of the contributors. The Part Four readings reflect a virtue-based approach, questioning the existing institutional frameworks of justification for why it is that some issues appear privileged more than others and some ways of dealing with them are prioritized over others. Issues of justice arise in considering what and whose assumptions underpin these priorities. Environmental responsibility is a contested terrain open to competing definitions. The contributors in Part Four, like those in Parts Two and Three, emphasize the importance of change and encouraging the potential for change. In Part Four, though, the focus of change and creativity is institutional values and norms that permit or prohibit change; it seeks to allow ideas and 'facts' pertaining to environmental issues to be contested, and to allow contrasting perspectives to be expressed.

The air of doom and gloom often prevalent in discussion on environmental crises time and again prompts despair, fear and cynicism, which can cloud more creative forms of engagement in being more responsible. As our contributors make clear in their different ways, environmental responsibility requires appropriate creative space. Being environmentally responsible in a creative and inventive manner requires space for socio-ecological flourishing. So developing appropriate creative space might be seen as a driving force for synthesizing the three traditions underpinning environmental responsibility illustrated in Figure 1.

So what types of space might be associated with each tradition? First, in Part Two concern is given to ecological space. Though this is commonly measured in quantitative terms – for example, a measure of 'area' (hectares of land) in ecological footprint or 'weight' (tonnes of carbon dioxide) in carbon footprint – the readings in Part Two explore ecological space in more qualitative terms, focusing on the types of framing it involves. Scientific measurements provide one important type of framing, but other types of inventive framing might also be important in appreciating, re-evaluating and negotiating ecological space. Such space requires attention to ensuing changes in our obligations to the non-human natural world, which may in turn shape the development of new duties and rights. An important virtue here is environmental justice. Not justice in the familiar quantitative terms of providing the just distribution of environmental goods and bads, but rather in more qualitative terms, through appropriate framing devices that do justice to our ecological world. Such justice requires an appreciation and some understanding of the complexities of multiple interdependencies in the natural world, while keeping a simplicity of framing in order to communicate effectively with and about nature. The virtue of environmental justice in this sense warns against the extreme tendencies of, on the one hand, using oversimplistic models to understand the world (which often generates wilful ignorance of scientific information) and, on the other hand, of being too despairing over the complexity of our ecological world. Nurturing purposeful simplicity through, for example, systems thinking, combined with respect in being both inclusive and pragmatic, provide good guiding principles for framing our ecological space.

Second, environmental responsibility requires appropriate learning space, particularly space for interaction and learning among individual human agents of responsibility and between individuals and collectives. As explored particularly in the Part Three readings, such space is continually being negotiated through individual and collective action. The ideas of social learning and communities of practice raise the question of what this space ought to look like if it is to enable questioning and either the fostering of new principles and rules or the use of existing principles and rules in a creative manner for environmental responsibility. Appropriate interaction between our understandings and practices is required, taking heed of the change in values that may arise from the consequences of previous actions. New understandings and practices can arise through this kind of learning. Here, a dominant virtue might be identified as practical wisdom, a virtue that warns against, on the one hand, self-righteousness and, on the other hand, apathy. Practical wisdom thrives in a space where questions are continually being asked of the right approach to environmental responsibility, and innovative experimentation is encouraged to improve responsible practice.

A third type of space is political space. This represents the spheres – social (civil society) and individual (private lives) – in which ethical and political concerns can be contested. Ideas of ecological citizenship, presented particularly in the Part Four readings, provide some signposting towards a more virtuous engagement with political space. Here humility might be seen as a particularly important virtue. Humility prompts the possibility of other virtues appropriate for different circumstances in different institutional settings at different times, providing political space for exploring new values and new principles that might be necessary in emergent socio-political circumstances. Humility also warns against complacency and arrogance on the one hand and cynicism on the other, which too often prevent meaningful ecological citizenship. There are many other virtues associated with environmental responsibility, however, and some are more relevant than others, depending on the circumstances. In campaigning for environmental justice in authoritarian societies, for example, courage is perhaps seen as an equally important virtue. But virtues of environmental responsibility do not stand still. Like values and principles, they may change and develop in the course of our engagement with changing environmental issues.

Each part of this anthology thus provides a unique space that itself allows concerns of value, principle and virtue to be expressed, albeit with different emphases. But the collection is more than just the sum of its parts. Two quotations were used to open the introduction to this anthology. First, reference was made by Wangari Maathai to our 'special responsibility to the ecosystem of this planet' in order to sustain a flourishing of human and non-human worlds. She implicitly called on a virtue of hope and care in voicing concerns meaningfully rather than through tokenism or opportunism. Second, Sir Geoffrey Vickers prompted us to think more carefully about the precise ways in which we 'regulate our responsiveness so as to preserve the stability of the manifold systems on which we depend, and ... make a collective world in which we individually can live'. These two concerns represent responsibility as a developmental attribute, a continually creative endeavour: first, caring for an environment comprising the natural world of life and life support, of which humans are an integral part; and second, ensuring accountability for any harm or wrong done to the environment. Together they provide the creative space required for continuing a dialogue; the essence of environmental responsibility.

Sources

Part one

Chapter 1 'A Fable for Tomorrow' and 'And No Birds Sing', from *Silent Spring* by Rachel Carson. Copyright © 1962 by Rachel L. Carson, renewed 1990 by Roger Christie. Reprinted by permission of Houghton Mifflin Company. All rights reserved. In the UK and Commonwealth, reproduced by permission of Pollinger Limited and The Estate of Rachel Carson.

Chapter 2 Aldo Leopold, 'The Land Ethic', in *Sand County Almanac – and Sketches Here and There*, Oxford University Press, 1968. By permission of Oxford University Press, Inc.

Chapter 3 Luke Martell, 'On Values and Obligations to the Environment', in *Ecology and Society*, Cambridge, Polity Press, 1994, pp. 86–94, 205–7, 213–15. Reproduced with the permission of Polity Press.

Chapter 4 Martin Reynolds, 'Environmental Ethics for Environmental Responsibility', in *Environment, Development and Sustainability in the Twenty-first Century*, Open University and Oxford University Press, 2009. By permission of Oxford University Press.

Chapter 5 Daniel Holbrook, 'Consequentialist Side of Environmental Ethics', in *Environmental Values*, 6, 1997, pp. 87–96. Reproduced with the permission of The White Horse Press.

Chapter 6 Robert Elliot, 'Deontological Ethics', in Dale Jamieson, *A Companion to Environmental Philosophy*. Copyright © 2003 Blackwell Publishing. Reproduced with the permission of Blackwell Publishing Ltd.

Chapter 7 Dobson, Andrew, and Derek Bell (eds), *Environmental Citizenship*, 4,000-word excerpt from pp. 49–73. Copyright © 2005 Massachusetts Institute of Technology, by permission of The MIT Press.

Part two

Chapter 8 Steve Talbott, 'In the Belly of the Beast'. First published in *NetFuture* #27 (10 January 2002), available at netfuture.org/2002/Jan 1002_127.html. Reprinted with permission of the author.

Chapter 9 Andrew Light, 'Contemporary Environmental Ethics from Meta-ethics to Public Philosophy', in *Metaphilosophy*, 33(4), 2002, 426–49. Copyright © 2002 Blackwell Publishing. Reproduced with the permission of Blackwell Publishing Ltd.

Chapter 10 E. Higgs, 'The Two-Culture Problem: Ecological Restoration and the Integration of Knowledge', in *Restoration Ecology*, 13(1), 2005, 159–64. Copyright © 2005 Blackwell Publishing. Reproduced with the permission of Blackwell Publishing Ltd.

Chapter 11 Ronald Moore, 'The Framing Paradox', in *Ethics, Place and Environment*, 9(3), 249–67, 2006. Reprinted by permission of Taylor & Francis Ltd, www.tandf.co.uk/journals.

Chapter 12a   From *The Web of Life* by Fritjof Capra, copyright © 1996 by Fritjof Capra. Used by permission of Doubleday, a division of Random House, Inc., and, in the UK, reprinted by permission of HarperCollins Publishers Ltd.

Chapter 12b   From *The Hidden Connections: Integrating the Biological, Cognitive, and Social Dimension of Life into a Science of Sustainability* by Fritjof Capra, copyright © 2002 by Fritjof Capra. Used by permission of Doubleday, a division of Random House, Inc., and, in the UK, reprinted by permission of HarperCollins Publishers Ltd.

Chapter 12c   Reprinted by permission, Ulrich Werner, 'Can We Secure Future-responsive Management Through Systems Thinking and Design?', *Interfaces*, 24(4), 1994, 26–37. Copyright 1994, the Institute for Operations Research and the Management Sciences (INFORMS), 7240 Parkway Drive, Suite 300, Hanover, MD 21076, USA.

Chapter 13   Robyn Eckersley, 'Environmental Pragmatism', pp. 49–69 in *Democracy and the Claims of Nature*, Ben A. Minteer and Bob Pepperman Taylor (eds), Rowman & Littlefield Publishers, 2002. Used by permission of Rowman & Littlefield Publishers, Inc.

Part three

Chapter 14   S. Visvanathan, 'Knowledge, Justice and Democracy', in *Science and Citizens: Globalization and the Challenge of Engagement*, Melissa Leach, Ian Scoones and Brian Wynne (eds), Zed Books, 2005.

Chapter 15   Geoffrey Vickers, 'Autonomous Yet Responsible', from Geoffrey Vickers, *Responsibility – Its Sources and Limits*, Intersystems Publications, California, 1980, pp. 3–11. Copyright © Sir Geoffrey Vickers' Archives, 2001.

Chapter 16   Michael F. Maniates, 'Individualization: Plant a Tree, Buy a Bike, Save the World?', *Global Environmental Politics*, 1(3) (August 2001), 31–52. Copyright © 2001 the Massachusetts Institute of Technology. Reprinted with permission.

Chapter 17   M. P. Golding, 'Obligations to Future Generations', *THE MONIST*, 56(1) (January 1972). Copyright © 1972 *THE MONIST: An International Quarterly Journal of General Philosophical Inquiry*, Peru, Illinois, USA 61354. Reprinted by permission.

Chapter 18   Excerpts from 'The Tragedy of the Common' by Garret Hardin, *Science*, 162: 1243–8 (1968). Reprinted with permission from AAAS.

Chapter 19   Excerpts from 'The Struggle to Govern the Commons' by Dietz et al., *Science*, 302: 1907–12 (2003). Reprinted with permission from AAAS.

Chapter 20   J. Poritt and C. Fauset, 'The Big Debate: Reform or Revolution?' in *New Internationalist*, December 2007, Issue 407, pp. 14–16. Reproduced with permission of *New Internationalist*.

Chapter 22   Robin Grove-White, 'Uncertainty, Environmental Policy and Social Learning', *Environmental Education Research*, 11(1), 2005, February, pp. 21–4. Reprinted by permission of Taylor & Francis Ltd, www.tandf.co.uk/journals.

Sources

Index

Index

353

Index